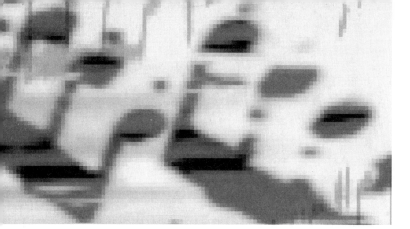

The Desktop Musician

David M. Rubin

Osborne **McGraw-Hill**

Berkeley   New York   St. Louis   San Francisco   Auckland   Bogotá   Hamburg   London   Madrid   Mexico City
Milan   Montreal   New Delhi   Panama City   Paris   São Paulo   Singapore   Sydney   Tokyo   Toronto

Publisher
Lawrence Levitsky

Acquisitions Editor
Joanne Cuthbertson

Special Contributor
Herb Schildt

Project Editor
Bob Myren

Copy Editor
Kathryn Hashimoto

Computer Designer
Jani Beckwith

Illustrator
Marla Shelasky

Quality Control Specialist
Joe Scuderi

Osborne **McGraw-Hill**
2600 Tenth Street
Berkeley, California 94710
U.S.A.

For information on translations or book distributors outside of the U.S.A., please write to Osborne **McGraw-Hill** at the above address.

The Desktop Musician

567890 DOC 9987

ISBN 0-07-881209-7

Series Design: Seventeeth Street Studios

About the Author...

David M. Rubin owns a computer-music studio where he composes for film, video, and multimedia. He is the author of **The Audible Macintosh** and co-author of **The Audible PC**. He has a master's degree in music theory and composition, and his articles have appeared in a number of music and computer-related magazines.

I dedicate this book with love to my wife Katherine and my son Aaron

CONTENTS

ACKNOWLEDGMENTS, *xv*

INTRODUCTION, *xvii*

1   The Computer-Music Connection   1

Music and Technology, 2

Leveling the Playing Field, 4

Opportunities, 5

    Composing, 5

    Working with Live Musicians, 7

    Other Uses, 10

Conclusion, 10

2   The Nature of Sound and Music   13

What Is Sound? 14

    Frequency and Pitch, 16

    Amplitude and Loudness, 17

    Timbre, 18

    The Envelope, Please, 21

Terms of Endearment, 22

    Notes and Staves, 22

    Clefs, 23

    Intervals, 23

    Scales, 24

    Sharps and Flats, 24

    Duration, 25

    Measures and Meters, 26

The Development of Electronic Music, 27

    The 20s, 29

    The 30s and 40s, 30

    The 50s, 30

    The 60s, 31

    The 70s and 80s, 32

3 All About MIDI 35

The Birth of MIDI, 36

What's It All About, MIDI? 37

What Does MIDI Do? 38

The Message and the Medium, 39

Getting the Message, 41

Channeling Your Creativity, 49

A La Mode, 50

Getting Compatible, 51

Standard MIDI Files, 51

General MIDI, 53

Conclusion, 57

4 Setting Up Your MIDI System 59

Computers, 60

MIDI Interfaces, 63

IBM PC Interfaces, 64

Macintosh Interfaces, 69

The Interface Alternative, 72

Sound Sources: The Many Flavors of MIDI, 74

Synthesizers, 75

Samplers, 77

Hybrid Synthesis, 80

Sound Modules, 81

Polyphony, 82

Multiple Sounds, 83

Low-Cost Sound Modules: A Foot in the Door, 84

Higher-Priced Sound Modules: Two Feet in the Door, 86

Sound Cards, 86

Drum Machines, 88

MIDI Keyboard Controllers, 90

Important Features, 91

Alternative Controllers, 92

Wind Controllers, 95

Guitar Controllers, 97

String Controllers, 99

Percussion Controllers, 101

Vocal Controllers, 104

Pedal Controllers, 106

Mind Controllers, 106

Other Controllers, 107

Tape Recorders and Timecode, 108

Expanding Your System, 112

Mixing It Up, 114

Desktop Speakers, 115

    Drivers, 116

    Amplifier Output, 117

    Frequency Response, 117

    Looking Around, 118

5   Working with Sequencers   **123**

What Is a Sequencer? 125

    In Control, 125

    Making Tracks, 126

    Behind the Counter, 127

    On the Beat, 129

    Recording Events, 130

    Step on It, 131

    In the Loop, 131

Editing, 132

    The Event List, 133

    The Piano-Roll Display, 134

    The Notation Window, 136

    Other Windows, 137

    Quantizing, 138

    Getting Organized, 140

6   Comparing Sequencers   **143**

Performer, 146

    Controls, 147

    Tracks, 148

    Event List, 148

    Graphic Editing, 149

    Notation, 150

    Other Windows, 150

    More Editing, 152

Master Tracks Pro, 155

    Controls, 155

    Tracks, 156

    Event List, 157

    Graphic Editing, 157

    Other Windows, 159

    More Editing, 160

Vision, 161

    Controls, 162

    Tracks, 163

      Event List, 164

      Graphic Editing, 164

      Notation, 165

      Other Windows, 166

      More Editing, 166

      EZ Vision/Musicshop, 167

Cubase, 170

      Controls, 171

      Tracks, 171

      Event List, 173

      Graphic Editing, 174

      Notation, 174

      Other Windows, 175

      More Editing, 177

      Cubase Lite, 179

Cakewalk Professional, 179

      Controls, 179

      Tracks, 180

      Event List, 181

      Graphic Editing, 182

      Notation, 182

      Other Windows, 184

      More Editing, 185

      Cakewalk Home Studio, 186

Metro, 186

      Controls, 187

      Tracks, 187

      Event List, 189

      Graphic Editing, 189

      Other Windows, 191

      More Editing, 191

SeqMax, 193

      Controls, 193

      Tracks, 193

      Event List, 195

      Graphic Editing, 195

      Notation, 196

      Other Windows, 197

      More Editing, 197

      SeqMax Presto! 199

Studio for Windows, 199

      Controls, 199

      Tracks, 200

Event List, 200

Notation, 201

Other Windows, 202

More Editing, 203

MIDI Kit/Recording Session, 203

Ballade, 203

Controls, 204

Tracks, 204

Notation, 204

Graphic Editing, 207

Other Windows, 207

More Editing, 209

Musicator Win, 209

Controls, 210

Tracks, 210

Graphical Editing, 211

Notation, 212

Other Windows, 213

More Editing, 215

7 Orchestrating with Electronic Instruments   217

Loudness, Pitch, and Timbre, 219

Pitch Versus Loudness, 219

Choosing Timbres, 220

Doubling Up, 220

Mixing Timbres, 221

On the Attack, 221

Variety, 223

Polyphonic Colors, 223

Adjusting the Volume, 224

Voicing Your Thoughts, 224

Home on the Range, 226

Think Like a Player, 226

Strings, 228

Wind Instruments, 230

Panning for Gold, 232

Lost in Space, 234

Last Word, 236

8 Spontaneous MIDI   239

Music Mouse, 241

Jam Factory, 243

UpBeat, 246

Band-in-a-Box, 249

MiBAC Jazz, 253

The Jammer, 256

Power Chords Pro, 258

FreeStyle, 261

Final Thought, 265

9   The Paper Connection: From Music to Manuscript   267

Input, 270

Output, 271

Staves, 272

Notes and Rests, 274

Rhythms and Beams, 275

Clefs, Keys, and Meters, 277

Chord Symbols, 278

Text, 279

Finale, 280

Finale Allegro, 284

Mosaic, 284

Encore, 287

MusicTime, 290

ConcertWare, 291

Other Options, 294

10   Working with Digital Audio   297

An Introduction to Digital Audio, 300

Analog Recording, 300

Digital Recording, 301

Resolution, 302

Sampling Rate, 303

At the Movies, 305

Numbers into Sound, 309

Getting Started, 310

Built-in Recording, 312

Setting Recording Levels, 313

Working with Silence, 314

Changing the Volume, 316

Changing Direction, 318

Changing the Specs, 320

Equalization, 321

Reverb, 321

Cleaning Up, 323
Other Views, 324
Destructive/Non-Destructive Edits, 325
A Closer Look at Several Audio Editors, 325
Sound Designer II, 326
Wave for Windows, 329
SoundEdit 16, 332
Sound Forge, 335

11   Combining Digital Audio with MIDI   341

The Three Approaches, 343
Adding Audio to MIDI, 343
Adding MIDI to Audio, 354
MIDI, Audio, and Multimedia, 358
Last Thought, 361

12   Using Your Computer to Learn About Music   363

Learn the Basics, 366

Just for Kids, 367

Sing a Song of Sixpence, 369

Improve Your Singing, 370

Learn to Play Piano, 372

Learn from the Pros, 374

A Well-Rounded Introduction, 376

Learn About Composers, 379

Learn About Classical Styles, 380

Learn About the Orchestra, 382

Learn About Musical Instruments, 384

A Close Analysis, 386

More Analysis, 389

Music History, 391

Modern Music, 393

All That Jazz, 394

60s Rock, 395

Conclusion, 397

A   Glossary   399

B   Companies to Contact   413

Index   423

Acknowledgments

The writing of this book has been a long, arduous journey, and one that would certainly not have been possible without the generous assistance of a great many people.

In particular, I'd like to thank the following companies (and representatives) for sending me their products for review: Altech Lansing Consumer Products (Andrew Bergstein), Big Noise Software (Richard Johnson), Coda Music Technology (Tom Johnsojn and Susie Bongaarts), Compton's NewMedia (Christina Germscheid), Digidesign (Marsha Vdovin), Dr. T's Music Software (Al Hospers and David Lavallee), Dynaware USA (Toshi Ide), Howling Dog Systems (Eric Bell), Jump! Software (Mukunda Penugonde), Labtec Enterprises (David Dietz), Macromedia (Mary Leong), Mark of the Unicorn (Jim Cooper), MiBAC Music Software (John Ellinger), Microsoft Corporation (Tracy Van Hoof), Midisoft Corporation (Chuck Robb), Musicator A/S (Ted Fong), Opcode Systems (Paul de Benedictis), Opcode Interactive (Stephen Thomas), OSC (Josh Rosen and Todd Souvignier), Passport Designs (Denis Lebrecque and Pamela Papas), PG Music (Gerald Fallis), Software Toolworks (Tracy Egan), Sonic Foundry (Monty Schmidt), Soundtrek (David Castles), Steinberg/Jones (Craig Lewis), Time Warner Interactive (Drew Tappon), Turtle Beach Systems (Stacey Pierson), Twelve Tone Systems (Christopher Rice), and Voyager Company (Nancy Perlman).

I'd also like to thank the following companies for providing me with literature and/or photographs of their products: Advanced Gravis, International Jensen, Apple Computer, Akai Professional, Alesis Corporation, Creative Labs, E-mu systems, Music Industries Corporation, JLCooper Electronics, KAT, Key Electronics, Korg USA, Kurzweil Music Systems, Midiman, Midivox Marketing, Monster Cable Products, Music Quest, Roland Corporation US, WaveAccess, Voyetra Technologies, Yamaha Corporation of America, and Zeta Music Systems.

Writing a book is very much a team effort and I would be remiss if I didn't express my sincere appreciation to the many people at Osborne/McGraw-Hill who made this project a reality.

Opcode Systems, OSC, Passport Designs, PG Music, Soundtrek, Steinberg/Jones, and Twelve Tone Systems.

Writing a book is very much a team effort and I would be remiss if I didn't express my sincere appreciation to the many people at Osborne/McGraw-Hill who made this project a reality.

Thanks to Jeff Pepper for starting me off on this extravaganza. And special thanks to Joanne Cuthbertson whose tenacity and unflagging optimism kept this project alive and on track when the going got rough.

Thanks as well to Herb Schildt whose insights and contributions made this book a lot more interesting. And thanks to Bob Myren and Kelly Vogel of the editorial staff, for enduring my complaints with good humor and for keeping things from falling apart. Also thanks to Marla Shelasky for her great illustrations, Kathy Hashimoto for her careful editing, and Linda Medoff for proofreading.

Finally, I'd like to thank my wife Katherine and my son Aaron for their support during the many months that it took to write this book. It was difficult being so busy for so long, and I couldn't have done it without their help and understanding.

Introduction

The word "music" embraces such a broad range of experiences that everyone seems to have a different idea about its meaning. To some people, music means dots, lines, and squiggles on a piece of paper. To others music can only mean the sounds that those markings help to produce. Some people think of music as an activity involving composition and innovation. Others think in terms of developing performance skills and techniques. Still others view music purely as a listening experience or perhaps as a subject for analysis and study.

In most cases, however, music involves some combination of these meanings and the more involved you are in the music-making process, the broader your particular definition will become. That's where computers enter the picture. Now that we're fully immersed in the "age of electronics," we have new tools at our disposal that are ideally suited to exploring music in all of its kaleidoscopic identities.

Affordable personal computers—with powers undreamed of twenty years ago— are now routinely available from department stores and mail-order houses all over the world. It seems that we've finally reached the point where computers are about as common as electric can openers. But the computer, unlike the can opener, is not just a one-trick pony—it can do many things at once, and it often does them quite well. In recent years this has become especially true in the field of music.

However, this exciting new confluence of art and technology is not necessarily self-explanatory. By analogy, a stick lying on the ground is just a stick. But if you pick it up and use it to direct a room full of musicians, it suddenly becomes a conductor's baton. The metamorphosis from stick to baton doesn't just happen by itself. It takes some background knowledge and a bit of skill. By the same token your computer may start out as a plastic box that sits around chewing on numbers all day. But you can transform it into a powerful tool for music production. You just have to learn how to do it. And that's why I wrote this book.

The Desktop Musician takes a double-barreled approach in promoting the leap from common computer to desktop music studio. First it explores the necessary hardware and software components that you'll need for your desktop studio. Then it examines in detail many of the products that are currently available, so you'll have a better idea of what to expect as you explore your many options.

Is This Book for You?

The Desktop Musician was written with a variety of readers in mind. People are drawn to music for a great many reasons, and as much as possible I've tried to address these different areas of interest. Furthermore, not everyone is starting at the same place as they make the computer-music connection. For example, some people know a lot about computers, but relatively little about music. Others are experienced musicians but relative newcomers to the world of computers. Some people are amateurs in the truest sense— pursuing music as a pastime for the sheer love of the art. Others are dedicated professionals seeking new avenues to expand their capabilities and improve their output. Whichever category fits you (and even if you fall into the cracks), you should find something worthwhile in this book to help you along your path.

In summary:

- This book is for computer users who want to learn more about music—especially electronic music.

- This book is for musicians who want to learn about computers and how to set them up for music production.

- This book is for desktop musicians at all levels who want to explore the many tools and resources that are currently available to them.

- And this book is for everyone who wants to investigate the fascinating world that is now open to us through the computer-music connection.

What's Inside?

The Desktop Musician begins with a brief overview of music, its relationship with technology, and some of the opportunities born of that relationship. Then it sets the groundwork for the rest of the book with an explanation of sound and the basic sound-related concepts that you'll need to know. This is followed by a review of musical concepts and terminology. After that, it takes a quick look back at the history of electronic instruments, and how we got to our current state of affairs.

Next, *The Desktop Musician* explores MIDI—the pivotal tool of electronic musicians. It explains what MIDI is, how it works, and what it can do for you. Then you'll learn about synthesizers, how to set up your own desktop music system, and how to choose from the myriad hardware options that are currently available.

To record, play, and edit electronic music, you'll need to know about applications called sequencers. So, *The Desktop Musician* explores the subject with a close look at what sequencers are, how they work, and what you can expect in a typical program. This is followed by an in-depth look at the most popular sequencer programs for the Macintosh and the PC.

For those interested in the orchestral possibilities of electronic instruments, there's a chapter devoted to orchestrating with your desktop music system. It teaches some of the tricks and techniques that professionals use to produce great-sounding scores. There's even a chapter that explores interactive computer-music programs and programs that encourage creativity. Another chapter examines how music manuscript software works and what to look for in a good notation program.

The Desktop Musician also covers the topic of digital audio, with an overview of how it works and what you need to know to use it effectively. After explaining important terms and concepts, the book then examines digital-audio recording and editing programs and the amazing things that you can do with them. If you're interested in combining digital audio with MIDI, there's also a chapter that takes a look at some pro-level programs that give you the best of both worlds.

Finally, *The Desktop Musician* takes a look at music education software for all ages and all levels. If you or your children want to learn more about music, this chapter will interest you. It includes descriptions of programs that can teach you to play the piano, analyze the music of famous composers, learn more about music history, improve your musicianship, and brush up on music fundamentals.

The CD-ROM

Because music is a "doing" kind of thing, *The Desktop Musician* comes with a CD-ROM that's packed with great software for you to try out. On this disc, you'll find demo versions of some of the most powerful and popular music software on the market. These are exciting programs ranging from professional-level sequencers and notation programs to entry-level applications and music education titles.

Throughout the book you'll find CD-ROM icons next to products that are mentioned in the text. The icons mean that those products also appear on the CD. This lets you read about a product in the book and then try it out for yourself. There's even an assortment of professionally recorded MIDI files for you to play with and edit to your heart's content.

Have fun with the CD-ROM. It's a terrific way to learn about music software without the pressure of a serious financial commitment in advance.

Last Thought

The Desktop Musician covers a lot of territory. In part, that's because each person who enters the world of computer-based music does so with a different set of skills. As much as possible, I've tried to accommodate the needs of this varied group of users who seek to combine the power of computers with electronic instruments. I hope that you enjoy your explorations. And I especially hope that you find this book to be a valuable tool along the way.

CHAPTER 1

The Computer-Music Connection

'M a one-man band. No, I don't carry a guitar and walk around with a bass drum on my back, a harmonica around my neck, and cymbals on my knees. I have a setup that's much better than that. And it's sitting on my desk. It consists of a computer, a few electronic devices, and a set of speakers.

I'm one of a growing number of musicians who create music by combining the power of the personal computer with electronic music technology. This new approach to composing has already had a profound effect on the world of music, and it promises great things for the future.

Now anyone can be a one-man (or one-woman) band and you don't even have to strap anything to your body to do it. You just have to understand how these new tools work so you can transform your ideas into musical sounds. In other words, you have to get acquainted with the current music technology.

Music and Technology

Music has always been the art form of technology. Born of the primal need for self-expression, music consistently draws on the prevailing resources to give flight to thoughts and feelings. When a prehistoric hunter, upon hearing the twang of his bow, first decided to use that sound creatively he was using the available technology to make music. When tribal members discovered that pounding on hollowed-out logs had some interesting rhythmic potential, they too were using the current technology. And when someone found that you can make pleasing sounds by blowing into a section of bamboo, yet another kind of music was born of technology.

The close relationship between music and technology is of more than passing interest. It's at the very center of musical expression. The twanging of the prehistoric bow gave rise ultimately to the captivating cadenzas of pianist Vladimir Horowitz. The pounded logs led thousands of years later to Buddy Rich's dizzying drum solos. And the whistling of a bamboo shoot led eventually to the spiraling saxophone riffs of Charlie Parker.

It's important to realize that in every case music has been a reflection of the available technology, and this has created a dynamic situation where improved technology is continually pressed into service for the greater good of musical expression. Thus the hunting bow eventually became the harp, then the harpsichord, and finally the piano. And as the tools of the trade evolved, so did the music—from the mediaeval tunes of the Irish harpists, to the intricate harpsichord textures of Domenico Scarlatti, and finally to the thunderous piano works of Franz Liszt.

What we refer to as "instruments" are actually nothing more than specialized tools or machines. And the limitations of the instruments become the limitations of the music. Of course, limitations *per se* are not always a bad thing. (Who would criticize a Beethoven string quartet for having too few instruments?) But they do define the nature of the final result.

As woodworking tools and techniques improved, for instance, simple instruments made from turtle shells, sticks, and strings evolved into the exquisitely ornamental lutes of the Renaissance. And the music followed suit. As metallurgy skills developed we got the forerunners of trumpets, horns, and tubas, and new ensembles and sounds were born.

So it's not very surprising that when electricity arrived on the scene, its power was also harnessed in the name of music. Electricity begat the vacuum tube, which was superseded by the transistor. The transistor then led to the modern-day microprocessor chip and the personal computer.

The first popular instruments to use electricity—the electric guitar, the electric organ, and the electric piano—quickly changed the sound of popular music by introducing new colors to the sonic palette. When affordable synthesizers arrived a few years later, the sonic palette was broadened by a quantum leap.

Musicians now have a cornucopia of musical sounds with which to express themselves. And there has never been a time in history with such a rich aural landscape for listeners to enjoy. This is a great time to be exploring the world of music, and computers are an important part of the experience.

Leveling the Playing Field

For hundreds of years, composers have relied on the patronage system to support them and their craft. A wealthy patron (usually a king, or prince, or some other person of high standing) would put up the money to support a composer and an appropriate number of musicians for a period of time. In return, the composer created works for the pleasure of the patron and those who attended his social events.

Franz Joseph Haydn, for example, spent many of his most productive years (during the 18th century) at the Esterházy estate in Hungary where he was free to refine his creative talents. Unfortunately, the average guy on the street didn't get invited to Prince Esterházy's affairs so he never got to savor much of Haydn's music. That doesn't mean that the patronage system wasn't any good. After all, most composers didn't, and still don't, have the financial resources to produce a concert on their own. It's just that the system naturally limited access to the music.

The situation is a lot better now. Thanks to technology, the average person can listen to so many different types of music that it boggles the mind. And he or she can listen to music 24 hours a day, any day of the week. Nonetheless, some vestiges of the past still remain. In a funny way the patronage system still exists—only now, its function has been taken over by the recording industry. Executives in plush offices atop monolithic towers make daily decisions about which musicians or groups will be offered contracts. Without a contract there's no CD, and without a CD no one will hear your music, right? Well, not necessarily.

The personal computer is having a tremendous impact on how music is being created. And electronic music-making technology has finally filtered down to the average person. There was a time when the only way to make a high-quality recording was to go to a recording studio. There, surrounded by millions-of-dollars-worth of tape transports, mile-long mixing consoles, processing units, microphones, cables, sound-absorbing panels, and isolation booths, you captured your performance on tape. And this was only the first step in a long and costly editing and production process.

Now with a personal computer, some electronic instruments, and the right software, you can record CD-quality audio right at home. Of course, I'm not saying that recording studios are obsolete. Far from it. They're absolutely essential for many kinds of projects. The important point is that the recording industry is no longer the sole purveyor of high-quality music.

The personal computer has gone a long way to level the musical playing field. It lets you compose, notate, edit, record, and play back your music as often as you want. It makes lightning-fast calculations, lets you view your

By most yardsticks, I am the quintessential desktop musician. I use my desktop studio to compose and produce music, both for commercial projects and for myself. However, it was not always this way. I was trained as a classical musician, studying theory and composition. In other words, I was taught to write for live players.

So you might be wondering why I got started with electronic instruments in the first place. The answer is actually quite simple: I was frustrated because I couldn't get my pieces played! I wanted to write for large ensembles. However, it's difficult and very expensive to assemble and rehearse an orchestra or jazz band (let alone record them). In fact, I knew many excellent composers who had shelves of music that they had written, but had never heard performed because of lack of resources.

To solve this problem, I turned to synthesizers as a way of producing my own music. Using a synthesizer, some software, and a computer, I can compose a piece of music and then hear it performed as often as I like. And I can modify it and add to it over time.

Throughout this book, you will learn about the ways that you can use your computer to create, arrange, learn about, and most importantly, play music. As you'll see, whether you're a trained, professional musician or simply a curious amateur, your desktop studio can take you wherever you want to go in the musical world.

compositions in a variety of ways, and helps you record your work so that others can enjoy it. It even lets you synchronize your music to film and video.

Opportunities

Some musicians bemoan the fact that computers and synthesizers are taking jobs away from drummers, violinists, trombone players, and others. But these same people fail to notice the burgeoning marketplace for electronic music that personal computers have created. By gaining access to the tools of music making, desktop musicians can now explore a number of musical opportunities that never existed before.

Composing

The most obvious opportunities lie in the area of composition. Through the use of specialized software, desktop musicians can use their computers to compose music in any style imaginable (Figure 1-1). There are even programs that turn your computer into an interactive participant in the creative process—either as a player or as a composer.

Most people don't realize how much of what they hear on television, in the movies, and on the radio is produced with computer-based music systems. Although it's not always obvious, everything from cartoons to documentaries and industrial films are using electronic music. And don't forget commercials, radio promos, and educational videos. The list goes on and new venues appear every day.

Multimedia

One of these venues—multimedia—is strictly a product of the computer age. Multimedia presentations often incorporate generous amounts of music, and what more logical way to create it than with a computer system? The term multimedia is one of those words that actually becomes more cloudy the more it's used. But this diversity just adds more categories of music that desktop musicians can fill.

Games

Games—especially those on CD-ROM—have now become an important area of interest for desktop musicians (Figure 1-2). In part, that's because computer-based music systems are so flexible. It's much easier to adapt to the changing conditions in a program when you're working with an ensemble of "virtual" instruments, rather than a recording of live musicians.

FIGURE 1-1

Mark of the Unicorn's Performer is one of many programs that let you compose music with your computer

Electronic instruments can make sounds that no orchestral or band instrument could possibly produce, so your available palette of sounds is often greater. That's especially good for "spacey" or atmospheric background music. Furthermore, because games are software-based, they need their music in the form of computer files. So it's logical for computers to be involved in the music-making process from the start.

Business and Education

Of course, there are other kinds of multimedia besides games. The business community has begun to recognize multimedia as a valuable tool. As a result, music is appearing more often in business presentations for such things as sales meetings, trade shows, and advertisements. And finally, educational software often uses music to enhance the learning experience for children and young adults.

Working with Live Musicians

Some desktop musicians work regularly with nonelectronic music. But they have found their computer-music systems to be important tools nonetheless.

Trial Runs

For example, a number of composers—especially those in the advertising field--use their desktop systems to produce preliminary arrangements of soundtracks. These "mock ups" give them a good idea of how pieces will sound before they're performed by live musicians. The composer can try out different arrangements and see how they work against the picture. Then he or she can present the music to the advertising executive for final approval. Once everyone is happy with the electronic version, large amounts of money can be spent to hire musicians, recording engineers, and studio time.

Desktop music systems can therefore avert possible disasters by giving everyone involved in a project the chance to review the music before proceeding further.

Into Print

Another opportunity for desktop musicians lies in the area of music manuscript production (Figure 1-3). People who work exclusively with live musicians still need to have printed music for the conductor and the players to read. Notation programs have now become so sophisticated that computer-generated scores and instrumental parts are starting to replace

FIGURE 1-3

Encore from Passport Designs is one of several music manuscript programs

traditional hand-printed music—even in the entertainment industry, where time is at a premium.

Anyone with a computer, a mid- to high-end notation program, and a good printer can produce publisher-quality scores. And with only a few keystrokes, you can do things like correct mistakes, transpose parts, or reformat a page—tasks that are laborious by hand.

Digital Recording

Keep in mind that electronic music and live recording are no longer mutually exclusive categories. There are now several programs that can turn your computer (with the proper hardware) into a sophisticated digital recorder (Figure 1-4). Your computer monitor provides on-screen controls while you capture live performances as soundfiles on your hard disk. You can then use the same programs to edit and enhance the recordings in ways that are far beyond the capabilities of standard tape recorders.

Furthermore, there are powerful professional-level programs that let you integrate electronic music with live performances. They let you do things like add a singer to an electronic score, or overlay narration and sound effects onto a musical soundtrack.

FIGURE 1-4

OSC's Deck II turns your computer into a digital recorder

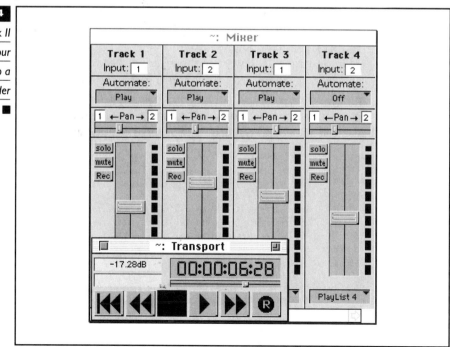

Other Uses

Computer-based music systems are showing up in a surprising number of places. For instance, many colleges recognize the importance of electronic music and now boast computer-music labs so students can explore this new technology.

Recording studios routinely use computers for all kinds of tasks from preparing invoices to operating tape decks and audio mixers. In fact, it is now unusual to find a full-service studio that doesn't provide a computer and an assortment of software for working with electronic music.

Computers are also appearing on stage more and more often. Many rock bands now tour with a computer and a stack of synthesizers and other electronic gear. The computers function as another member of the band supplying background tracks as the featured performers strut their stuff. In some cases, the computer even controls the lighting and other special effects.

Conclusion

Music technology is like any technology: it's how you use it that counts. And to use it effectively you must first understand it. That's why this book exists. In the following chapters, we'll explore the different tools that are available to desktop musicians and examine up-close the software that lets you transform your thoughts into music.

In only the past few years the marriage between music and technology has spawned so many exciting offspring that one can only wonder what lies ahead. The world is riding the crest of a new musical renaissance, and computers and electronic instruments are leading the way. So if you have creative ideas and the drive to express them, now is a great time to start.

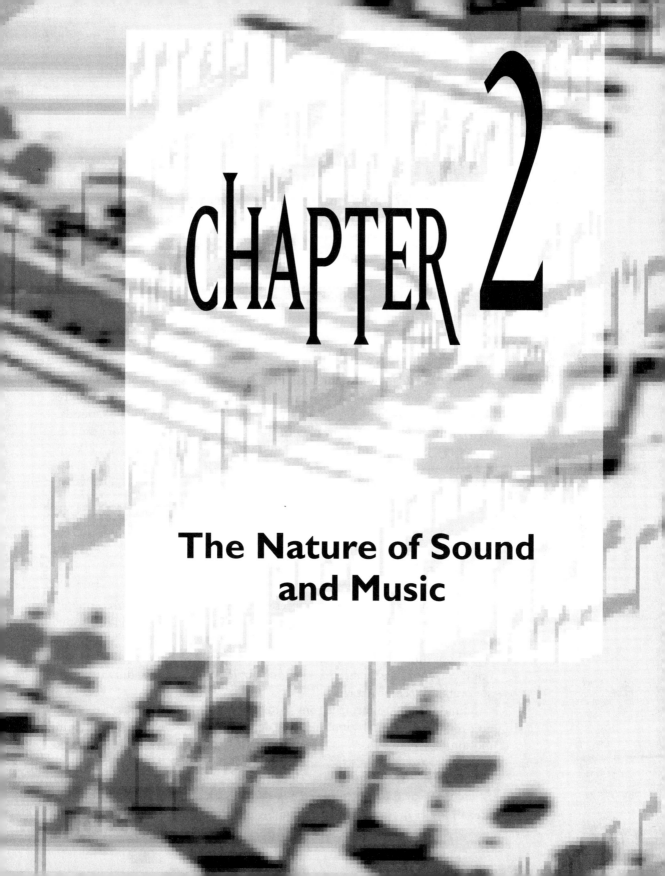

cHAPTER 2

The Nature of Sound and Music

THE world is awash in sounds: high sounds, low sounds, bright sounds, dark sounds, pleasant sounds, obnoxious sounds. From the moment we're born (and even before), we're exposed to an unending cavalcade of sounds. As a result, most of us take the phenomenon of sound completely for granted. Music is a special kind of sound. And the process of becoming a desktop musician involves creating and controlling sounds in a number of ways. To be effective at this task, it's important to have a basic understanding of what sound is all about.

What Is Sound?

Many people have seen sound represented on paper or on their computer screens as a wavy line from left to right (Figure 2-1). This image has led some people to conclude that sound consists of invisible wavy beams of some kind that shoot through the air from place to place. Sound does consist of waves, but if you could see them, they wouldn't actually look like the drawings you see on the screen or paper.

Sound waves are formed from patterns of high and low pressure in the air around us. When a sound-making device, such as a tuning fork, is set in motion, it vibrates (*oscillates*) forward and backward. As the tuning fork flexes forward, it causes the air molecules in front of it to bunch together. This creates a region of higher-than-normal pressure. As the tuning fork flexes backward, it leaves a region with fewer-than-normal molecules—an area of lower pressure. When the tuning fork again flexes into the forward

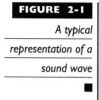

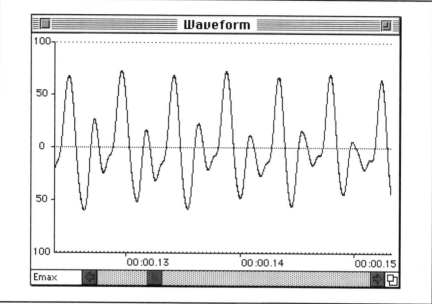

position, it creates another area of compression. This process continues over and over again, many times per second (Figure 2-2).

The resulting series of pressure patterns is called a *pressure wave* or *sound wave*. When the sound wave reaches our ears, it sets our ear drums in motion in a way that parallels the pressure fluctuations. Our brain then interprets these vibrations as a particular sound.

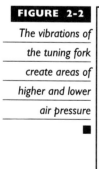

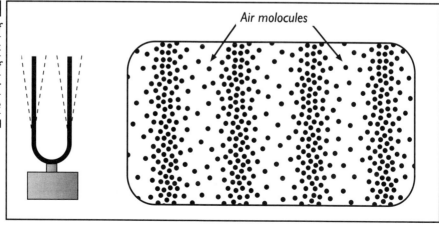

Air molocules

As the sound wave moves away from the source (spreading in all directions), it loses more and more energy, and the changes in pressure become smaller. In other words, the sound gets fainter the farther it gets from the source, until it eventually dies away completely. If no changes occur in the surrounding air pressure, then we perceive the condition as silence.

Sound therefore consists of four elements:

- A *vibrating object:* Examples are a tuning fork, a guitar or violin string, a drum head or cymbal, a reed, a column of air, or a speaker cone

- A *transmission medium:* Usually the air around us, but it can be other things, such as water or wood

- *An ear:* To capture the vibrations

- *A brain:* To interpret the vibrations

The wavy line depicted in Figure 2-1 is actually just the graph of a sound wave. It shows the amount of pressure along the vertical axis and the passage of time along the horizontal axis. Through the center of the graph, a horizontal line indicates the normal ambient air pressure. Values above this line form *crests,* which represent areas of compression in the sound wave. Values below the horizontal line form *troughs,* which represent areas of lower-than-normal pressure. These changes in pressure over time produce a graphic depiction of sound called a *waveform.*

Frequency and Pitch

Most musical sounds produce waveforms that consist of repeating patterns; they're called *periodic* waveforms. Each individual pattern represents a single vibration of the sound source, called a *cycle* or *period* (Figure 2-3). The term *frequency* refers to the number of cycles that occur each second.

Rather than describing frequency in terms of cycles per second, however, we use the term *hertz,* named after the nineteenth-century scientist Heinrich Rudolf Hertz. One cycle per second equals one hertz (abbreviated Hz). One thousand cycles per second equal one kilohertz (kHz). People with good hearing can hear frequencies that range from about 20Hz to approximately 20kHz.

tip   *The term hertz is relatively recent. In older books, frequency was described in cycles-per-second, or cps. For example, in older usage the frequency 2,000Hz would have been printed as 2,000cps.*

FIGURE 2-3

A simple periodic
waveform

∎

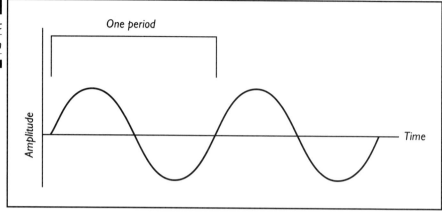

Frequency is specified in hertz. A hertz is one cycle per second.

The term frequency, then, refers to a specific number of vibrations per second. The term *pitch,* on the other hand, is a more general term that refers to how high or low a sound is perceived within a musical context. Sounds that consist of faster vibrations (more cycles per second) are said to be "high" in pitch. Sounds with slower vibrations are said to be "low" in pitch. You'll also hear the terms *treble* and *bass* applied in a general way to high and low pitches, respectively.

Amplitude and Loudness

The amplitude of a sound indicates its strength. A sound's strength is measured in decibels.

The amount of pressure that a waveform exhibits at a given point in time is referred to as its *amplitude.* As with frequency, amplitude is a specific measurement. It indicates the intensity with which a sound wave vibrates. Although the term *loudness* is related to amplitude, it's a more subjective term. That's because our perception of a sound's strength is influenced by such things as whether the sound has a high or low frequency. Our ears tend to favor certain frequencies over others, so two sounds with the same amplitude might appear to have different loudness levels. For example, high-pitched sounds typically sound louder than low-pitched sounds of equal amplitude.

The unit of measurement that indicates a sound's strength is called the *decibel* (dB), named after Alexander Graham Bell. The decibel, however, does not simply denote a specific amplitude for a single sound. Instead, it uses a logarithmic scale to indicate the ratio between a sound's amplitude (sound pressure level) and a standard reference value. The level at which sounds are first perceived—the *threshold of hearing*—is assigned a value of 0dB. Other sounds are then expressed in relation to this reference.

The normal listening range extends from 0dB to beyond 120dB—a level commonly referred to as the *threshold of pain*. Two identical sounds played one after the other must have a difference of about 2 or 3dB before most listeners will perceive a change in loudness. And it takes an increase of 10dB to make a sound seem twice as loud.

note   *Decibels are used to measure other phenomena besides sound pressure level. The most common among these are various types of electrical characteristics, such as power (dBm, dBW) and voltage (dBV). So, it's important to know what is being referred to when you see the term decibel.*

Timbre

When you hear the same note played on a trombone and on a violin, you know immediately which is which. In fact, in a blindfold test, most people would have no trouble at all distinguishing a sustained note on an oboe, a saxophone, a flute, a trumpet, or a cello. Even when the loudness and pitch of the waveforms are identical, each instrument has a distinctive and identifiable tone color or timbre (pronounced "tambur"). *Timbre* refers to the quality of a sound that makes it unique from other sounds at the same pitch and loudness.

Timbre is the quality that distinguishes one sound from another. The tuning fork mentioned earlier produces the simplest kind of waveform, called a *sine wave* (Figure 2-3). Sine waves appear as smoothly undulating lines that reflect the regular alternations of a single frequency. As you might expect, a simple sine wave is considerably lacking in character. Musical instruments, on the other hand, produce rich sounds that are highly complex. Their waveforms consist of a blend of different frequencies.

A vibrating string, for example, vibrates as a whole, producing a frequency referred to as the *fundamental*. The fundamental in most cases establishes the musical note that is being played. But as the string is vibrating as a single unit, it is also vibrating simultaneously in smaller segments that are one-half, one-third, one-fourth, one-fifth, and so on, of the string length (Figure 2-4). These smaller segments produce frequencies, called *harmonics* or *partials,* that are whole-number multiples of the fundamental. A vibrating column of air works the same way.

The fundamental is referred to as the first harmonic. The second harmonic is twice the frequency of the fundamental. The third harmonic is three times

FIGURE 2-4

A string vibrates in several segments at once

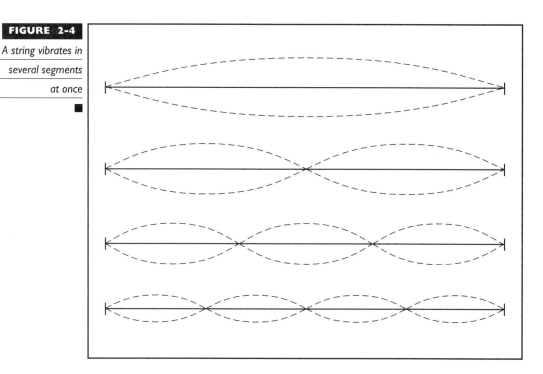

The fundamental is called the first harmonic. It establishes the musical note. Each subsequent harmonic is a whole-number multiple of the fundamental.

the frequency of the fundamental, and so on. (The harmonics that appear above the fundamental are also known as *overtones.*) This pattern of harmonics—beginning with the fundamental and continuing upward—is called the *natural harmonic series*. In theory, the harmonic series can extend upward to infinity, although partials that are far above the fundamental are seldom very strong.

Different musical instruments tend to favor different members of the harmonic series, and some partials may be missing completely. In fact, the particular combination of different harmonics and their relative strengths give musical instruments their characteristic tone color. Timbre is therefore the result of the unique harmonic content that each instrument produces.

When you look at the waveform of a musical tone, it doesn't usually look like a sine wave. Instead, it has numerous wrinkles and extra peaks and valleys. That's because the fundamental, which starts out as a simple waveform, is altered by the addition of the higher frequencies. If you take all of the instantaneous amplitude readings of a sine wave and add to them all of the corresponding amplitude readings of a sine wave at a higher frequency, you end up with a new waveform that represents the combination of the two frequencies (Figure 2-5). Adding more frequencies produces an even more complex waveform.

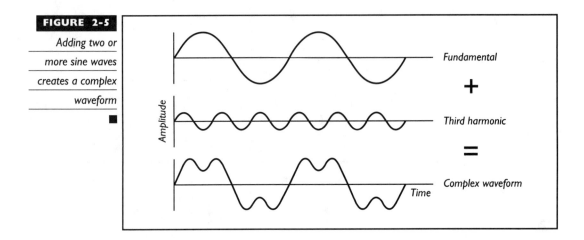

FIGURE 2-5

Adding two or more sine waves creates a complex waveform ∎

This explains how complex waveforms get their irregular shapes. It also shows that you can analyze a complex waveform in terms of the various component sine waves that belong to it. This process, known as *Fourier*

In My Experience

When working with electronic music, you must often create the sounds that you want. Sometimes, finding the right sound can be difficult. Inspiration for new sounds often comes in odd ways and from unlikely sources. In fact, I often use the sounds of things around me as the basis for musical sounds that I use. For example, one day I needed a new percussion sound for a piece of music that I had been working on. After several unsuccessful attempts, I decided to take a walk to clear my mind. In the distance, I noticed the sound of an air hammer being used to repair a road; this gave me an

idea for the percussion sound that I had been looking for. I combined the sound of the air blast from a compressor with a cymbal. The result was just what I needed.

Sometimes you will find that a sound you have created sounds great by itself but it isn't quite right when played with the rest of the parts, and vice versa. For example, a trumpet sound may work fine as part of an ensemble, but it may sound tinny and weak for a solo part. As an electronic musician, you will probably spend nearly as much time selecting and fine-tuning sounds as you will actually creating the music.

Remember, sounds are the palette of the electronic musician. In fact, one advantage of working electronically is that you have full control over the sounds that make up your music. This control has not always been available to musicians and composers. For example, when Beethoven wrote music, a flute always sounded like a flute—even if the flute's sound was not quite perfect for what he wanted. However, when you are working with a synthesized "flute," you can tailor the sound to be precisely what your piece of music requires.

analysis, was named after the French mathematician Jean Baptiste Joseph Fourier, who discovered it in the early nineteenth century.

The Envelope, Please

One reason why musical tones sound so rich and interesting to us is that they possess a certain dynamic quality. Musical notes are seldom produced from simple blasts of unchanging sound. Instead, they change both in harmonic content and amplitude as they evolve over time. Changes in the harmonic spectrum are sometimes rather subtle. But the changes to the overall amplitude level are quite apparent. They contribute considerably to our perception of what kind of instrument is being played and what the nature of the performance is. In fact, the amplitude of a musical sound typically passes through a number of different stages before it disappears.

Take, for example, the sound of a piano. When the piano hammer first strikes the string, a sudden transfer of energy occurs as the string is set into motion. This results in a burst of sound as the amplitude rises quickly to its maximum level. The sudden rise from zero to maximum amplitude is called the *attack,* and the time that it takes to occur is referred to as the *attack time.*

A sound's envelope is the combination of the attack, decay, sustain, and release.

After the initial burst of energy, the sound settles down to a somewhat lower level. This slight drop in amplitude is called the *decay.* As long as the pianist holds the key down, the sound will continue at a more or less steady amplitude. This stage is called the *sustain.* Finally, when the key is released, the dampers mute the string and the sound quickly dies away. This is known as the *release.*

note   *The attack is the initial burst of sound. The decay is the small drop in intensity that follows the attack. The sustain is the part of a note that continues after the decay. The release is the final sound of the note ending.*

The changes in amplitude that occur during the course of a sound are known as the sound's *envelope.* An envelope can be very simple or it can have many more stages than described here. The piano example illustrates the most common type of envelope, known as an ADSR (attack, decay, sustain, release) envelope (Figure 2-6). Synthesizers (and computers) can create the different stages in an envelope with a function called an *envelope generator.* It enables synthesizers to replicate the acoustic properties of a great many instruments both real and imagined.

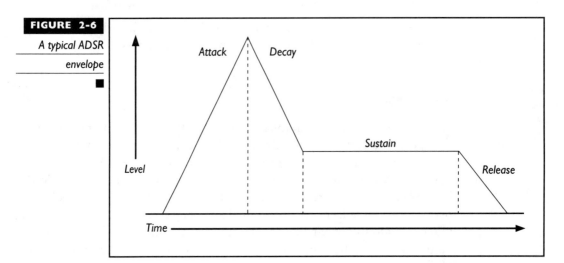

FIGURE 2-6

A typical ADSR

envelope

Terms of Endearment

Just because desktop musicians spend their time working with microprocessors, floppy disks, and oscillators doesn't mean they don't need to know any musical terminology. In fact, most music programs use common musical terms to describe various functions and how they work.

In Chapter 12 I'll describe several programs that can teach you about music. If you can't read music or you're a little rusty in the musicianship department you might look there for some help. Otherwise, I strongly advise you to spend a little time studying music theory. It will help you better understand the fundamental concepts that form the basis of most music software.

For now, however, let's take a very quick run through some of the musical terms that you'll likely encounter as you explore the field of computer-based music. If you're not familiar with a piano keyboard, take a few minutes to acquaint yourself with its layout. It can help you visualize many of the concepts. Those of you who already read and write music can skip ahead. The rest of you should fasten your seat belts. You're about to enter the world of musical terminology.

Notes and Staves

Anyone who has seen written music knows that it consists of parallel lines with dots and symbols placed on them. The dots, called *notes,* may have stems, and some of the stems may have little flags attached to them. The color of the note heads (black or white) and the presence or absence of stems and flags indicates the duration of the notes.

The five horizontal lines upon which notes are written is called a staff.

Notes and other symbols are superimposed on a group of five horizontal lines (and the four spaces between them) called a *staff*. The staff's lines and spaces are labeled alphabetically in succession from A to G. The next line or space after G is labeled A, and the sequence starts again. The pitch and letter name of any given note are determined by its vertical placement on the staff: the higher the position on the staff, the higher the pitch. To extend the range of notes beyond the staff, extra lines called *ledger lines* are added for the notes that need them (Figure 2-7).

Clefs

The funny looking symbol at the beginning of each staff is called a clef. A *clef* provides a reference that indicates how the lines and spaces on the staff will be named. Actually, several kinds of clefs exist, but the two most common are the treble clef and the bass clef. To provide an extended range for reading music, the two clefs are often combined to form a *grand staff*, which consists of the two staffs parallel and connected by a brace (Figure 2-8).

Intervals

A note whose frequency is twice that of another note is said to be an octave higher than the lower note.

The difference in pitch between two notes is called an *interval*. If you play a note with a given fundamental frequency and then play another note whose fundamental frequency is exactly twice that of the first, you will have played an interval called an *octave*. The two notes that created the octave will have the same letter name. This means that any two notes with the same letter name will always be one or more octaves apart, unless the two notes have exactly the same pitch. In that case, the interval is called a *unison*. Other intervals include seconds, thirds, fourths, fifths, and so on. You can identify any interval by counting up the lines and spaces from one note to the other, including the first note (for example, A to C equals a third, A to E equals a fifth, and so on).

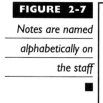

FIGURE 2-7

Notes are named alphabetically on the staff

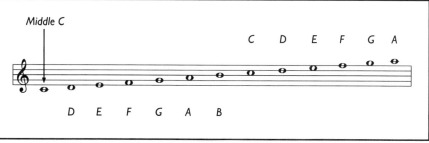

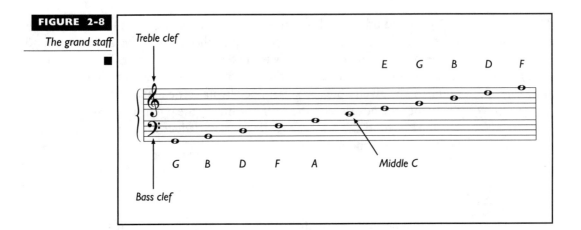

FIGURE 2-8

The grand staff

Treble clef

E G B D F

G B D F A   Middle C

Bass clef

Scales

A *scale* is any series of notes upon which a composition is based. If you play only the white notes on a piano in succession from any C to the next C an octave higher, you will have played a *major scale* (do, re, mi, fa, so, la, ti, do). If you do the same thing starting on A and ending on A, you will have played a *natural minor scale*. These are only two of the many scales that are in current use. Of course, you could play the same two scales starting on other keys, but you would then have to use some of the black keys to maintain the same intervals between successive steps in the scale. (In fact, it's really the pattern of intervals that determines the type of scale you're using, not the notes *per se*.)

tip   *The major and minor scales consist of eight notes. For example, the C major scale is comprised of the notes C, D, E, F, G, A, B, and C (the second C is one octave higher than the first). The major and minor scales are called diatonic scales.*

Sharps and Flats

For a given note, a sharp is one half-step higher and a flat is one half-step lower.

The black keys on a piano allow you to raise or lower an adjacent note by a half step. If you want to play a note that is a half-step higher than D, for instance, you simply substitute the black key to the right of D. This note is called D-sharp. The same key can be used to lower the neighboring E by a half step. It is then called E-flat. Sharps and flats that appear next to notes on the staff are called *accidentals*. Notes that produce the same pitch but are named differently—such as D-sharp and E-flat—are called *enharmonic equivalents* (Figure 2-9).

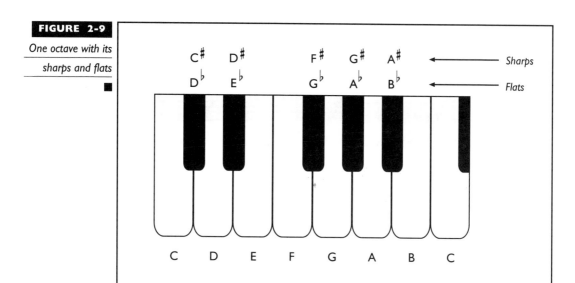

FIGURE 2-9

One octave with its sharps and flats

Rather than place an accidental in front of every note that needs it, the most often used sharps or flats for a particular scale are grouped together in a pattern called the *key signature*. Appearing just to the right of the clef, the key signature indicates which notes are to be routinely raised or lowered by a half step. In so doing, it also indicates which key the piece is in.

The chromatic scale consists of all twelve notes within an octave.

Our system of tuning, called the *equal temperament system,* divides every octave into 12 equal steps. These are represented on a piano by all of the black and white keys within an octave. The resulting 12 notes when played in succession form a *chromatic scale.* Any combination of three or more notes that sound together is called a *chord.*

Duration

Every musical note has two important parameters: pitch and duration. Unlike pitch, which is determined by a note's placement on the staff, duration is determined by the appearance of the note itself. The longest note value in common usage today is the *whole note,* which consists of a white note head with no stem. Adding a stem to the note head creates a half note. Making that note head black turns it into a quarter note. Logically enough, four quarter notes equal one whole note or two half notes. Adding a flag to the stem of a quarter note turns it into an eighth note. Adding another flag makes it a sixteenth note. Another flag yields a thirty-second note, and so on (Figure 2-10).

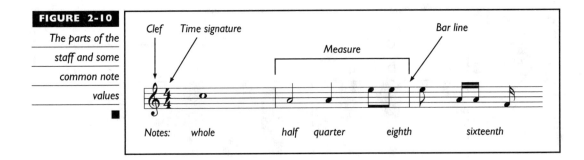

FIGURE 2-10

The parts of the

staff and some

common note

values

Notes with flags are often grouped together with the flags replaced by beams, which make them easier to read. The same durations that apply to notes also apply to rests. A rest is simply a period of silence.

It's important to understand that none of these note values represent a specific duration. Whole notes, half notes, and quarter notes are only meaningful in relation to one another. The actual duration of a note is determined by the *tempo*, the speed at which the music is performed.

A rest is a period of silence.

Measures and Meters

Underlying nearly all music is an ongoing pulse consisting of recurring strong and weak accents or beats. To organize this metrical pulse, music divides the beats into groups called *measures*. These measures are separated on the staff by thin vertical lines called *bar lines*. In fact, another term for a measure is a *bar*.

Each measure contains a combination of note durations that equals a specified total value. This value is first established at the beginning of the staff (it can be changed at any time) with a two-digit number called the *time signature*. The time signature (which is not a fraction) indicates how many beats there are in each measure—with the upper number—and which note value represents each beat—with the lower number. This establishes the *meter*. The different combinations of notes and rests within the context of the meter is what is meant by the term *rhythm*.

In addition to pitch and rhythm, music notation also includes many other performance indications. The tempo of the piece, for example, is expressed with descriptive words (often in Italian) above the staff. For example, here are several of the more common Italian tempo marks:

The time signature indicates how many beats are in each measure and which note represents one beat.

Tempo Mark	Meaning
Largo	Very slow, solemn
Lento	Slow
Adagio	Slow (but less than *Lento*)
Andante	Moderately slow
Moderato	Moderate
Allegretto	Moderately fast
Allegro	Fast
Vivace	Fast and lively
Presto	Very fast
Prestissimo	As fast as possible

As you might guess, the interpretation of the tempo marks is left to the conductor or individual musician. This, of course, leads to variations. For a more precise indication, many composers include a metronome marking. It consists of a small note followed by an equal sign and a number. A quarter note followed by 120, for example, would indicate that the tempo equals 120 quarter-note beats per minute.

Obviously, music theory involves a great deal more than what has been covered here. This whirlwind tour of terminology is only intended to touch on some of the common terms that musicians use. If you're not familiar with the rudiments of music, I strongly urge you to explore the subject further.

The Development of Electronic Music

Depending on your definition, electronic music-making machines of one sort or another have been around for quite awhile. But by most accounts, the evolutionary path that led to the modern synthesizer began about a hundred years ago. In the late 1890s, Thaddeus Cahill began work on a new keyboard instrument that could generate sounds electrically. He called it the Telharmonium, and over the next several years he continued to refine it until its formal introduction in 1906.

The Telharmonium was definitely not a portable instrument. Using a massive array of telephone receivers and rotary dynamos running on alternating current, it weighed several tons and transmitted its music over telephone wires. The European composer Ferruccio Busoni wrote enthusiastically of the device, and Cahill's work sparked a great deal of interest in

Of Interest

A Brief History of Music

Music has been around as long as humans have walked the earth. And throughout the centuries, the pursuit of musical expression has given rise to a number of important compositional styles. Three of these are called *monophonic, polyphonic,* and *homophonic.*

The beginning of the monophonic period predates history. It ended about 1300 A.D. Monophonic music consists of only a melody without accompanying harmony or counterpoint. For example, a single person singing is monophonic. A group of monks singing in unison (such as Gregorian chant) is also monophonic.

Polyphonic music began to appear several hundred years before monophonic music fell into disuse. It flourished during the Renaissance period (sixteenth century) and reached its pinnacle in the works of the great baroque composers of the seventeenth and early eighteenth centuries. Polyphonic music consists of two or more melodies that interact (more or less equally) with each other. Polyphony is also called *counterpoint.* Composers such as Bach and Handel made heavy use of polyphony in their compositions. In fact, the great keyboard, choral, and instrumental works of these composers and their contemporaries come to mind when we think of polyphonic music today.

A third style of music gained in popularity during the eighteenth century and rose to prominence in the nineteenth century, called homophonic music. Homophonic music consists of a melody line supported by a harmonic accompaniment. Thus, instead of two or more interacting melodies, as is the case with polyphonic music, homophonic music typically features a single melody played on top of chords. Most of the symphonies and sonatas of the nineteenth century employ homophonic writing. As do most of the popular songs that you hear on the radio every day.

In the modern age, new styles of music have appeared, including twelve-tone music, also known as *serial* music. This style of "atonal" composition attempts to free music from its reliance on a specific key. While meeting with mixed success on the concert stage, examples of atonal music are commonly heard in film and TV scores. Today, the composer is free to draw upon all of the major styles of composition as well as new innovations. The defining aspects of the next musical epoch are currently being written.

ways to produce musical sounds from electricity. In the following year, Lee De Forest patented the "Audion" vacuum tube, and the world stepped decisively into the Electronic Age. The next decade brought further advances in electronics that provided inventors with amplifiers, filter circuits, wave-form generators, and loudspeakers.

The 20s

By the 1920s, a number of electronic instruments were attracting widespread attention. The Theremin, introduced in the early 1920s by Leon Theremin, was perhaps the most widely known. One performed on it by waving one hand over and around a box with a metal loop attached to it. The proximity of the hand to the loop controlled the volume level. To control the pitch, the other hand was waved along a vertical antenna attached to the top of the box. The closer the hand got to the antenna, the higher the resulting pitch. This produced a series of eerily evocative sounds that swooped from pitch to pitch.

The haunting sound of the Theremin soon found its way into a number of movie soundtracks and also gained some popularity as a concert instrument. Theremin himself continued to invent other less famous instruments, including a keyboard instrument, an electronic cello, a type of drum machine called the Rhythmicon, and a device called the Terpsitone, which used sounds triggered by dancers.

A few years after the introduction of the Theremin, a French musician and scientist named Maurice Martenot invented an instrument named the Ondes Martenot. This was a keyboard instrument that used an unusual slide-wire glissando generator. The right hand played the keys and operated the glissando control. To glide from one note to the next, the wire was pulled over the key range to be affected. The left hand controlled a number of levers and buttons to shape the sound. The unique tone color and sweeping glissandi of the Ondes Martenot made it a popular instrument with French composers, including Milhaud, Honegger, Messiaen, and Varèse.

At around this same time, the German Friedrick Trautwein introduced the Trautonium. It was an unusual device with a unique metal band at the front of the instrument that allowed the player to change the pitch continuously, depending on where the tape was pressed—much like the fingerboard on a violin. By varying the finger pressure, the player could control the volume and the rate of decay. The instrument's design also allowed unusual scales. Both Hindemith and Richard Strauss were among the composers who wrote for it. A more advanced version of the instrument, called the Mixtur Trautonium, was created by Oskar Sala, a former student of Trautwein. It was in wide use for a number of years and was especially popular for creating movie soundtracks.

The 30s and 40s

In 1934, Laurens Hammond patented the enormously popular electronic organ that bears his name. It created its sounds by generating electrical oscillations from small motor-driven rotary generators. The resulting alternating current produced frequencies that corresponded to the notes of the chromatic scale. The richness of the Hammond organ's harmonic content attracted a number of composers, including Karlheinz Stockhausen.

During the thirties and forties, a few experimental composers began creating music by manipulating phonograph records. By slowing them down, speeding them up, playing them backwards, and scratching the surfaces to make short fragments repeat, these avant-garde composers started to explore new kinds of musical content. Not until the invention of the tape recorder in the 1940s, however, did this approach to music-making reach fruition.

Around 1948, two French composers, Pierre Schaeffer and Pierre Henry, along with several of their associates in Paris began producing tape "collages." Drawing on the work of their predecessors, these tape compositions consisted of recorded sounds (often modified) from a variety of sources, such as noises, percussion, vocal sounds, musical fragments, and sound effects. These were looped, spliced, juxtaposed, and processed in various ways. Schaeffer named the works *musique concrète,* because they depended largely on "real" or concrete sounds (environmental sounds) as opposed to the more abstract sounds used in traditional music.

The Paris group enjoyed a substantial degree of success during the ensuing years, and they're largely responsible for establishing tape manipulation as an accepted form of electronic composition. In the United States, two composers at Columbia University, Otto Luening and Vladimir Ussachevsky, continued to explore the musical possibilities of the tape medium. Together with another composer, Milton Babbitt, they later organized the Columbia-Princeton Electronic Music Center, where a number of professional composers studied.

The 50s

The first true synthesizer made its debut in 1955. It was designed by Harry Olson and Herbert Belar at the RCA laboratories in Princeton, New Jersey. The formidable RCA Electronic Music Synthesizer, as it was called, was noteworthy for a number of reasons. Not only did it provide an unprecedented level of control over the parameters of sound production, but it was capable of reproducing a series of sounds. By punching numbers on a paper input roll, a composer could specify a sequence of pitches, along with such parameters as timbre, duration, articulation, and other qualities. The RCA synthesizer was a massive device, taking up an entire wall, and it wasn't exactly user-friendly. Milton Babbitt, who took a special interest in the instrument, dedicated a great deal of time to it. It was said that he was one of the few composers who understood the device well enough to compose at it without the help of an engineer.

The 60s

Around 1960, the introduction of a new circuit called the voltage-controlled oscillator (VCO) ushered in the age of the modern analog synthesizer. A new breed of electronic instrument began to appear that was smaller, lighter, less expensive, and easier to use. The two names that dominated the field during the sixties were Moog (rhymes with vogue) and Buchla.

Robert Moog introduced the first commercially available synthesizer around the middle of the decade. The Moog synthesizer used a piano-style keyboard that sent different voltages from each key. The voltage-controlled oscillators responded by producing the appropriate pitches. The different sounds were created by setting an array of knobs and by plugging a variety of cables into jacks. These cables were known as *patch cords*, and the sound that resulted from a particular configuration of patch cords and knob settings came to be known as a *patch*. Even though today's digital synthesizers don't use patch cords to create their sounds, the term has stayed with us. Now it simply means a particular sound, timbre, or preset on a synthesizer.

 n o t e *One of the most popular synthesizers produced by Robert Moog was the Minimoog. The Minimoog was a simplified version of Moog's larger, studio-based synthesizers.*

In 1968, a Columbia recording by Walter Carlos created quite a stir in the music industry. The collection of transcriptions entitled *Switched-on Bach* was performed on an early Moog synthesizer. These imaginative and highly popular electronic orchestrations of baroque music triggered an avalanche of interest in synthesizers and brought electronic music to the doorstep of the general public.

By 1969, Donald Buchla had introduced his Buchla Electronic Music System, a modular synthesizer based on principles similar to the Moog instrument. Unlike the Moog, however, the Buchla did not use a traditional keyboard. Instead, it incorporated a series of touch-sensitive plates, which some composers preferred. The most important works realized on the Buchla synthesizer were those of Morton Subotnick, including his famous *Silver Apples of the Moon.*

The 70s and 80s

During the seventies, synthesizer technology continued its process of refinement. Patch cords began to disappear, and synthesizers from such venerable names as Oberheim, Sequential Circuits, and E-mu Systems became a regular part of the recording industry. Rock musicians, from local bands to the Beatles, began to explore the new sonic possibilities brought on by these intriguing instruments, and the sound of popular music was changed forever.

By the 1980s, a new generation of digital synthesizers began to appear. And by the middle of the decade, personal computers were so ubiquitous that it was only natural to combine synthesizers with the power of computers to create affordable desktop music workstations. This was all made possible by the introduction of a new standard called the Musical Instrument Digital Interface (MIDI), which we'll examine in detail in the next chapter.

CHAPTER 3

All About MIDI

M

IDI (pronounced "middy") is an acronym for Musical Instrument Digital Interface. As you might deduce from the name, it has something to do with sending and receiving data between musical instruments. But MIDI is not just another obscure technological side trip. MIDI is at the very heart of the entire music industry. By enabling computers to communicate with electronic instruments, MIDI has spread forth a feast of opportunity to desktop musicians everywhere.

MIDI is an acronym for Musical Instrument Digital Interface.

Through the magic of MIDI, anyone can transform a personal computer and a few pieces of hardware into a powerful music workstation. With MIDI, you can perform, edit, arrange, orchestrate, produce, notate, and record your music without even leaving the room. And MIDI enables you to create music in a wide variety of styles, from down-home-simple tunes to cyberpunk techno-extravaganzas. Whether composing music is a creative outlet or a professional necessity, you will find that a working knowledge of MIDI is essential if you want to make great-sounding music from the desktop. But what exactly is MIDI and how did it come about in the first place?

The Birth of MIDI

It all began around two decades ago, as the electronic music juggernaut swept through the entertainment industry. Musicians, in an effort to develop new musical timbres, began playing notes simultaneously on different synthesizers set for different sounds. This process, known as *layering,* produced musical passages that were richer and "fatter" than any single instrument could provide.

Unfortunately, there was no easy way to layer notes with these early synthesizers, because they all used different methods for creating and triggering their sounds. You could play two keyboards together—one with each hand—but this had obvious limitations. In the studio it was common to overdub passages with different instruments, but this was cumbersome at best and of no value for live performance.

What musicians really needed was a simple way to connect different brands of synthesizers so that anyone could play two or more instruments from a single keyboard. In 1981, at a meeting of the Audio Engineering Society, Dave Smith of Sequential Circuits addressed the incompatibility problem by proposing what he called the Universal Synthesizer Interface. This proposal was refined and expanded during the following years as other manufacturers took notice. Finally, in 1983, several major manufacturers of American and Japanese electronic instruments introduced the newly entitled MIDI 1.0 Detailed Specification. And the world of music has never been quite the same.

What's It All About, MIDI?

The MIDI Specification establishes a set of standards that ensure proper hardware compatibility among different brands of electronic instruments. It also provides a standardized protocol for transmitting and receiving data between MIDI-compatible devices. In other words, MIDI makes it possible to create a kind of local area network (LAN) for musical instruments.

MIDI is a serial interface that transmits at 31,250 bits per second. It uses specially designed serial cables with identical five-pin DIN plugs at both ends (Figure 3-1). These are the same types of plugs that are commonly used with European hi-fi equipment, although MIDI only uses three of the five pins. Under normal conditions, standard MIDI cables should not exceed 50 feet in length, to avoid the possibility of data loss.

---

 note   *The transmission of digital information occurs in one of two ways: serial or parallel. A parallel port transmits data in 8-bit chunks (called bytes). A serial port (which is used by MIDI interfaces) transmits data one bit at a time. The rate at which a serial port transmits data is measured in bits per second, abbreviated as bps.*

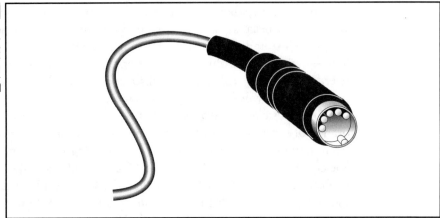

Because MIDI data can only travel in one direction at a time on each cable, MIDI instruments usually provide at least two connections: In and Out. The MIDI In port receives data from other devices, while the MIDI Out port transmits data that is created by the instrument itself. Most MIDI devices also include a third connection labeled Thru. The MIDI Thru port retransmits an exact copy of the data received at the MIDI In port (Figure 3-2). As you'll see in Chapter 4, this provides an easy way to expand your system by chaining together instruments.

What Does MIDI Do?

In spite of what you may have seen at rock concerts or in recording studios, MIDI systems are not always mind-boggling stacks of arcane-looking hardware connected by dense bundles of forbidding cables. In fact, you can create a simple MIDI system by connecting just two synthesizers with a single MIDI cable. This setup lets you play notes on one keyboard, called the *master,* and have the corresponding notes respond on the other instrument, the *slave.*

If you set the master synth to make a piano sound and you set the slave synth to make a string sound, you'll hear a piano and a string sound every time you press a key on the master keyboard (Figure 3-3). If you add a second MIDI cable running in the opposite direction (master In to slave Out), then either instrument can function as the master or the slave (but not both at the same time). Furthermore, if you add a third instrument to the recipe, you can create a piano, string, and trumpet sound. (You'll need an audio mixer to combine these individual sounds into a single stereo signal—more on this in Chapter 4.)

FIGURE 3-2

The MIDI Thru

port retransmits an

exact copy of the

data received at

the MIDI In port

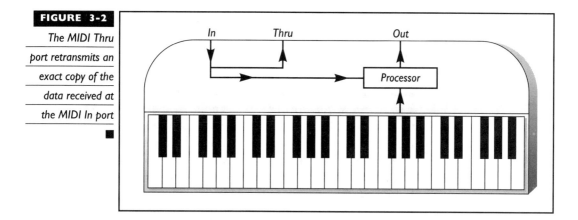

FIGURE 3-2

The MIDI Thru port retransmits an exact copy of the data received at the MIDI In port

This simple example of layering barely scratches the surface of what MIDI can do, especially when it's combined with the power of the personal computer. Before exploring MIDI's greater potential, however, let's take a closer look at how MIDI devices communicate and what they say to each other.

The Message and the Medium

Right from the start, it's important to understand that MIDI cables do not carry audio signals. This is a common source of confusion. You cannot, for instance, make a Yamaha DX7 sound like a Roland D-50 by simply connecting the two devices with MIDI cables. Each instrument can only make the sounds that it is capable of making on its own. Nor does MIDI add new features to an instrument that it doesn't already have.

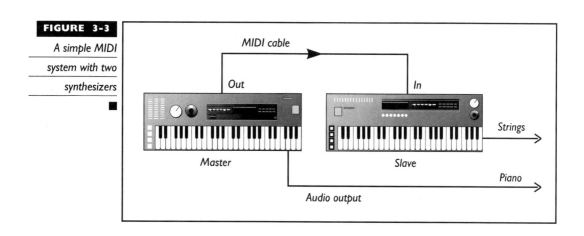

FIGURE 3-3

A simple MIDI system with two synthesizers

What MIDI does is allow you to send performance data from one device to another. That way, you can operate instruments remotely in a live setting or as part of a computer-controlled system. In fact, MIDI serves many of the same functions for electronic instruments as written music has served for traditional acoustic instruments for hundreds of years.

When a composer writes down a piece of music and hands it to a performer, he or she is, in essence, transmitting the performance data for that musical work. The sheet of paper with its notation provides the necessary instructions to re-create the music. You can hold the paper up to your ear until the cows come home and you won't hear any music. That's because music notation is not actually music, it's simply a set of instructions for playing music. The manuscript tells the performer which notes to play, how long to hold them, how loud to make them, and various other important bits of information. MIDI works in much the same way. It sends performance data from one electronic device to another. This is done through a series of messages that tell the receiving device what is happening with the transmitting device.

MIDI lets you control synthesizers and sound cards by sending them data. It does not generate its own sounds.

Furthermore, written music doesn't really indicate how the intended instrument should sound. A violin part, for instance, doesn't specify whether it should be played on a Stradivarius or a Guarnerius violin. A piano part never indicates that it is only for a Steinway or a Baldwin. The same is true for MIDI. It makes no difference whether the receiving MIDI instrument is a Korg 01/W or a Roland JV-90. The performance data is still the same. (There's an exception to this rule called System Exclusive data, which I'll discuss a little later.)

And finally, written music can often be played on more than one type of instrument. A melody written for a trumpet might also be playable on a clarinet or saxophone, for example. Again, the same holds true for MIDI. The sounds you hear coming from your MIDI system depend solely on how you set your synthesizers. This is one of the truly great things about composing with MIDI. You can quickly change from one orchestration to another—often in midstream—with just the twist of a knob or the click of a button. Don't like that viola part in measure 12? Try it as an English horn, or alto flute, or tubular bells, or electric guitar. By separating the performance from the sound, MIDI encourages experimentation and provides a veritable orchestra for the desktop composer.

Keep in mind that your results depend on the quality of your components. Uninformed statements such as "MIDI doesn't sound good" are meaningless, because MIDI doesn't have a sound. The ultimate quality of a MIDI system's output is entirely the result of the quality of the instruments involved. Cheap components often produce poor sound quality. More sophisticated—and therefore more expensive—instruments typically provide more satisfying results. It's one aspect of musical instruments that hasn't changed much in the past hundred years.

Getting the Message

When you play music on a MIDI instrument, it instantly sends a series of messages from its MIDI Out port to any MIDI instruments that are connected to it. If set appropriately, those instruments will respond by playing the same notes (although not necessarily the same sounds) at the same time as the master. MIDI devices all contain microprocessors that interpret the incoming MIDI messages and enable the slave instruments to respond to such actions as keystrokes, pedal actions, switch settings, lever movements, and other performance gestures. There are several types of MIDI messages. Some of the more common ones are discussed in the following sections.

Note On

Every time you press a key on a MIDI keyboard, a message is sent indicating that a note has been played. As described in the MIDI Specification, the Note On message identifies the note within a range of 128 possible notes, numbered from 0 to 127. Middle C on a piano corresponds to MIDI note number 60. The highest note on a piano corresponds to MIDI note number 108, while the lowest note is represented by MIDI note number 21. Clearly, MIDI's range of possible note values extends well above and below the traditional piano keyboard range. Because MIDI's capabilities now run the gamut from sound effects placement to stage lighting and tape-deck control, this extended range provides added flexibility for musical and non-musical applications alike.

note   *A MIDI device can control another MIDI device by sending it performance messages. A Note On message, for example, indicates that a note has been played.*

Some MIDI instruments allow you to divide their keyboards into zones, which you can assign to different sounds. This arrangement, called a *keyboard split,* is especially handy for live performances, but it is often used in other situations as well. With a keyboard split, you can assign the notes above middle C to play a piano sound, while the notes below middle C play an acoustic bass sound. This lets you play the bass with your left hand while your right hand plays the piano part. Some MIDI keyboards allow for multiple split points. They're often used with ensembles of related instrument sounds. You might, for example, assign the zones on a keyboard to the different instruments in a string ensemble. Then, as you play from left to right, the sounds can change from bass to cello to viola to violin. Or—with a woodwind ensemble—from bassoon to clarinet to oboe to flute (Figure 3-4). Keyboard splits are also useful for creating custom rhythm section layouts.

Velocity

Velocity is not actually a separate message but rather a part of the Note On message. It indicates how hard the note is struck within a range of 128 possible values. In most cases, Velocity is used to control the loudness of a note. Then, as with a piano, the harder you play a key, the louder the sound. But, depending on how it's assigned, the Velocity parameter offers much more potential than just the control of loudness. Velocity might, for example, control how bright a sound gets, depending on how hard the key is played.

Although most synthesizers support Velocity sensing, a few do not. With these instruments, every Note On message includes a default Velocity value, typically 64. MIDI instruments that don't have their own keyboards can still respond to Velocity data from a master keyboard. They are said to be *Velocity-sensitive*.

Some synthesizers can switch between two entirely different sounds, depending on whether the Velocity value is above or below a specified threshold. This use of Velocity data is usually referred to as a *Velocity switch*. It's quite effective for controlling certain instrument sounds in real time. You might, for example, set up a Velocity switch for a trumpet sound that changes from a soft attack when played gently to a hard attack when played with

FIGURE 3-4

Keyboard splits let you play different instruments from a single keyboard

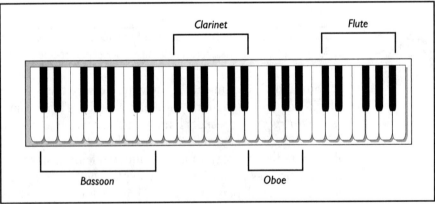

Clarinet   Flute

Bassoon   Oboe

more force. Or, you could have an electric bass that switches from a normal plucking sound to a slap bass sound.

Velocity switches have many useful applications that can add an element of spontaneity to a performance. You might, for instance, add a bell chime to a string sound when the keys are played softly. Or you could add the sound of thunder to a cymbal crash if the right key is struck hard enough. It's important to keep in mind, however, that not all MIDI instruments have these capabilities. So check before you buy if this seems like an important feature.

Note Off

Logically enough, the Note Off message indicates that a key has been released. It signals the receiving device to turn off the corresponding note. Many people don't realize that Note Off messages also include Velocity data (with 128 possible values). *Release Velocity* is often used to control how quickly a sound dies away. Low values represent a gradual release, and higher values cause the sound to die away more rapidly. As with any MIDI parameter, however, the effect that Release Velocity has on a sound depends on what you assign it to do. As mentioned earlier, not all MIDI instruments implement Note On Velocity, and far fewer keyboards include Release Velocity sensing. Again, these devices add a default Velocity value (usually 64) with each Note Off message.

Of Interest

As you know, piano keyboards are velocity-sensitive. Because the piano is the instrument most associated with the keyboard, it is easy to overlook the fact that many other commonly used keyboards are not velocity-sensitive. Two of the most frequently encountered nonvelocity-sensitive keyboards are the harpsichord and the organ. With these instruments, how hard (fast) you press the keys has no effect on the volume of the tone produced or upon its timbre. Although extremely pleasing music has been written for the organ and harpsichord, it is the velocity sensitivity of the piano that has helped make it the dominant keyboard instrument today. Indeed, it is this attribute that gives a piano its expressiveness.

Aftertouch

Aftertouch is the common term for Pressure data. It indicates how hard a key is pressed (over a range of 128 values) after it is played and before it is released. Aftertouch is often used to add vibrato to sustained notes, but it can also change a sound in a variety of other ways, depending on how it's assigned. It might, for example, cause a sound to swell in volume or become brighter as you change the amount of pressure on the key.

The great value of Aftertouch is the way that it allows you to exert expressive control over the notes that you play—without removing your hands from the keyboard. Aftertouch-sensitive keyboards work by sending out a stream of continually varying messages that correspond to the amount of pressure that you apply to the keys. Aftertouch messages are referred to as *continuous controller* data, because they're sent in a continuous stream that corresponds to a variable action (in this case the amount of pressure) made by the keyboard player.

Actually, there are two types of Aftertouch: *Channel Pressure* and *Polyphonic Key Pressure*. With instruments that support Channel Pressure—by far the most common type—only a single series of messages represents the entire keyboard at any one time. When several notes are played simultaneously, the key with the greatest pressure establishes the Aftertouch values.

Polyphonic Key Pressure, on the other hand, is much less common. With this type of Aftertouch, a separate series of values is transmitted for each individual key that is held. The different notes in a chord, for example, can send out entirely different values. As you might imagine, this often results in a great flood of MIDI data that can consume much of the MIDI bandwidth. And it adds considerably to the complexity and expense of the instrument.

Why would you want Polyphonic Key Pressure? Let's say you're using a keyboard split to perform a piece in which the right hand plays a melody on violin, while the left hand provides a countermelody on piano. With Polyphonic Key Pressure, you can add vibrato to the violin part without also adding it to the piano part.

Pitch Bend

Pitch Bend is usually triggered from a wheel or lever. This message lets you temporarily slide pitches up or down to "scoop" or "bend" notes the way you can with instruments such as trombones, saxophones, and guitars. This feature is especially useful when playing in blues, rock, and jazz styles. With Pitch Bend, the term *continuous controller* refers both to the Pitch Bend control itself and to the type of data that it sends. As with Aftertouch, Pitch

Bend information is sent as a stream of messages. In this case, they reflect the changing positions of the controller.

note *A Pitch Bend control lets you increase or decrease the frequency of a note in a gradual, gliding manner.*

The most common type of Pitch Bend control is a spring-loaded wheel that is oriented at a right angle to the plane of the keyboard (Figure 3-5). A center detent position represents a Pitch Bend value of zero (no deviation). As you move the wheel from the center position, the controller sends a stream of messages that cause the pitch to rise. Releasing the wheel allows it to snap back to the zero position. Moving the wheel in the opposite direction causes the pitch to drop.

To avoid introducing a stairstep quality to a note as its pitch changes, Pitch Bend data provides 16,384 subdivisions from the lowest to the highest position of the controller. These values, however, only represent a relative amount of pitch deviation. Each individual synthesizer will respond to Pitch Bend differently, depending on how it is set. You can, for example, set the maximum range to represent a one-octave change in pitch. This can produce some rather dramatic bending effects. On the other hand, you can set the bending range to cover only a semitone (half step). This will provide you with more precise control over the pitch, because the Pitch Bend values are scaled according to the interval that the maximum value produces.

FIGURE 3-5

The Pitch Bend

wheel

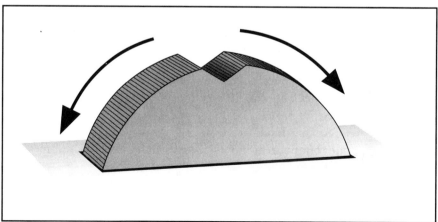

Program Change

Program Change tells a synthesizer to switch from one internal sound—called a *preset, patch,* or *voice*—to another. This is a great feature, because it lets you change instrument sounds on a remote device without actually operating its front panel controls.

All synthesizers organize their sounds according to an internal numbering scheme. MIDI provides 128 values for selecting those sounds. Unfortunately, synthesizers are all quite different in the number of presets that they offer. They also vary widely in the types and arrangements of those sounds.

Some synthesizers hold fewer than 128 presets in memory, but most hold far more. Furthermore, some instruments organize sounds sequentially by number, while others group sounds into banks with letter and number designations. This can lead to much confusion when it comes time to send a Program Change message. Program number 23 on one synthesizer might be a flute sound, while on another synthesizer it might be a tuba or electric piano or conga drum. Before using Program Change messages, therefore, it's important to study the numerical arrangement of the patches in each of your MIDI instruments. That way, you can anticipate the effects of any given Program Change number.

This lack of uniformity in the way sounds are numbered led to an addition to the MIDI Specification called General MIDI. It specifies a particular group of sounds that must be organized and numbered in a particular way. Most MIDI instruments are not General MIDI–compatible, although a growing number are. We'll take a closer look at General MIDI and its importance later in this chapter.

System Exclusive

MIDI was originally developed as a universal protocol for all electronic instruments. But the designers of the MIDI Specification also recognized that different brands of instruments have different internal parameters for creating their sounds. To provide a means of accessing these parameters, MIDI includes a special kind of message that is specific to each make and model of MIDI device.

System Exclusive (SysEx) messages always include an ID number that identifies the brand of instrument for which the message is intended. In

A System Exclusive (SysEx) message always includes data that identifies a specific brand of instrument.

Japan, the ID numbers are assigned by the Japan MIDI Standards Committee (JMSC). In the rest of the world, ID numbers are obtained from the MIDI Manufacturers Association (MMA)

Although a Program Change message allows you to call up a particular preset by number, a SysEx message actually lets you edit a sound by changing its internal settings. Over the years this has become an important tool for developing new synthesizer patches. If you hook up two synthesizers of the same model, they can exchange information concerning the internal sound-producing architecture of the units. The master can serve as a remote front-panel control for the slave, and either device can send patch information to the other.

When a MIDI system includes a computer, its monitor can provide a "virtual" front panel that makes editing patches a whole lot easier than most hardware front panels with their multifunction buttons and tiny LCD displays (Figure 3-6). With SysEx, you can send patch data from a MIDI instrument to your computer for editing and storage and then retrieve it at a later time as needed.

SysEx messages can do many more things than the examples given here. They provide a valuable means of expanding MIDI's capabilities beyond the

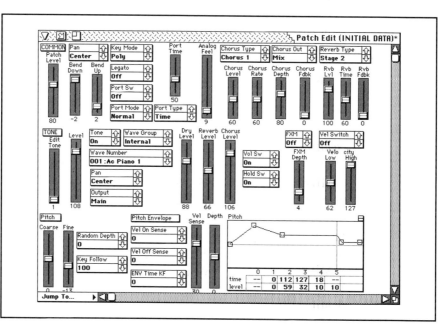

FIGURE 3-6

Unisyn from Mark of the Unicorn is one of several programs that provide a fast and efficient way to edit synthesizer patches

scope of the usual MIDI messages—in performance and nonperformance settings alike. Keep in mind, however, that SysEx functions and capabilities vary widely among different brands of synthesizers.

Other Controllers

Aside from Pitch Bend and Aftertouch, MIDI accommodates many other ways of controlling sounds. Most MIDI instruments include an array of wheels, levers, switches, and pedals that provide real-time, expressive control over a performance. Each type of controller is assigned a number that identifies it when its messages are sent to a receiving instrument. Following are several kinds of controllers that you will likely encounter.

MODULATION (#1)   Like Pitch Bend, Modulation is usually triggered from a wheel or lever, although it's not spring-loaded. Most MIDI keyboards include this control next to the Pitch Bend wheel. The Modulation wheel (also called Mod wheel) is commonly used to add a controlled amount of *vibrato* (frequency modulation) or *tremolo* (amplitude modulation) to a sound. It can also be used to control loudness, brightness, or other elements of expression, depending on how it's assigned.

FOOT CONTROLLER (#4)   This controller, like the Mod wheel, can perform a variety of functions. But the Foot controller, unlike the Mod wheel, lets you keep both hands on the keys.

VOLUME (#7)   Unlike Velocity, Volume messages control the overall loudness level of a sound. Usually MIDI Volume messages are sent from a knob or fader (slider). With a computer in your MIDI system, you can use Volume messages to do an automated MIDI mixdown or control the balance of instruments using on-screen graphic faders. In addition to Volume, MIDI includes messages for Balance (#8) and Pan (#10).

SUSTAIN PEDAL (#64)   This controller works just like the sustain pedal on a piano. It allows notes to continue sounding after you release the keys. The other piano-like pedals are Sostenuto (#66) and Soft Pedal (#67).

In My Experience

My first synthesizer was a Yamaha DX7. When I bought it, the DX7 was so popular, there was a long waiting list to purchase one. The DX7 was significant because it was one of the first commercially available synthesizers to implement MIDI. And it used a new, groundbreaking method of digital synthesis called FM synthesis, which enabled the DX7 to sound better than most other synthesizers at the time. And MIDI made it possible to control the instrument using a computer. Without a doubt, the DX7 helped usher in the MIDI revolution.

While the DX7 was the best of its kind at the time, it is outdated by today's standards. For example, it could only produce one sound at a time, it only transmitted on MIDI channel 1, and its sounds were often difficult to edit. Although the DX7 provided me with a tabletop orchestra, I still had to record one sound at a time, one track at a time, using a multitrack studio recorder. While this process worked, it was slow, inefficient, and often frustrating. So I sought a better way to compose, and what I found was computer-controlled MIDI. Now, I can simultaneously play several parts in real time by having the computer control my synthesizers. The tedious chore of tape-recording one sound at a time has been eliminated.

Today, you can do on your desktop using your PC what only a few years ago took me a lot of time, effort, and equipment. Now, millions of sound cards and synthesizers are hooked up to PCs all over the world, and some of these provide capabilities that rival those once found only in the best recording studios. In fact, today, few people would consider buying a synthesizer that couldn't play several different sounds at once or provide a link to their computer. The MIDI revolution is complete.

Channeling Your Creativity

These days, most MIDI instruments can play more than one sound at a time. That is, they function like several separate instruments in a single box (or on a single expansion card). And MIDI systems may include several different MIDI devices. To ensure that the appropriate performance data reaches only the intended devices (or virtual instruments), MIDI provides 16 channels (numbered 1–16) to subdivide and organize the information. Without these channels, you would hear a cacophonous mess, as all of the instruments in the system tried to respond to all of the incoming messages at the same time.

Unlike audio signals, which travel through individual cables, MIDI channels all flow through the same cable. The channel designation is embedded in the MIDI messages. Each device responds only to the messages that it's set to receive and ignores all the others. It's a lot like a cable television system that carries dozens of channels simultaneously over a single cable. You determine which channel to watch by setting the tuner on the TV. If your family has several television sets attached to the cable, you can have each set receive a different station.

Channels provide MIDI with the versatility it needs to function as part of a complex and powerful music system. By using channels to organize your MIDI data, you can create elaborate multi-instrument orchestrations, while keeping the MIDI system itself relatively simple.

A La Mode

In addition to channels, MIDI specifies several *modes* that determine how a synthesizer will respond to the note information that it receives. *Channel Mode messages*, as they're called, prepare the receiving instrument based on two criteria: (1) whether the receiving device will respond to all incoming channels (Omni On) or only to a single channel (Omni Off), and (2) whether the receiving device will play polyphonically (Poly) or monophonically (Mono).

Combining these two categories yields four modes: Omni On/Poly, Omni On/Mono, Omni Off/Poly, and Omni Off/Mono.

- *Omni On/Poly:* This mode is especially useful for setting up or troubleshooting a system, because the receiving instrument will respond to all incoming channels and will play as many incoming notes as it receives (within its own limitations). In other words, you don't have to worry about matching the channel of the sending device with that of the receiving device to verify that data is flowing between them. This mode is also useful in some setups for combining sounds from different instruments.

- *Omni On/Mono:* This is unquestionably the least useful and least popular of the four modes. In this mode, the receiving device responds to all channels but only plays one note at a time. Even if the slave instrument can play more than one note at a time and the sending instrument is transmitting more than one note at a time, the receiving instrument only responds monophonically.

- *Omni Off/Poly:* This is the most widely used of the modes. With this configuration, the slave instrument responds polyphonically to any incoming notes (within its limits) but only on a single specified channel. It's therefore important to verify that the master and slave are set to the same channel or they won't communicate. Omni Off/Poly mode lets you create musical arrangements with several different instrument sounds. By assigning the different instruments to separate MIDI channels you can ensure that each slave will respond to the necessary notes while ignoring those notes intended for other devices.

■ *Omni Off/Mono:* In this mode, the receiving instrument responds monophonically on one or more specified channels. Because individual notes are assigned to separate channels, you can apply expression controls such as Pitch Bend and Aftertouch to a single note within a group without affecting the other notes. This mode is often used with synthesizers that can generate more than one patch at a time (see Chapter 4).

Getting Compatible

The birth of MIDI in 1983 ushered in an era of universal interconnectivity for electronic musical instruments. But MIDI's new age of hardware compatibility hit a snag when synthesizers became joined at the hip with personal computers. Sequencer programs—the primary applications for creating and editing MIDI music—did not provide the same level of universality for software that MIDI offered for hardware.

In most cases, music files created on one computer platform were unreadable by another. And worse yet, you couldn't even exchange files between different sequencers on the same computer. This deplorable situation was soon resolved with the introduction of the Standard MIDI File (SMF) format.

Standard MIDI Files

The need for a universal file format became apparent a few years after MIDI's inception. In 1988, spurred on by the efforts of Opcode Systems, the MIDI Manufacturers Association officially adopted the Standard MIDI File as an addition to the MIDI Specification. Now, virtually all MIDI composing, editing, and notation programs import and export this generic file format in addition to their own proprietary file formats.

We'll examine sequencer programs in great detail in Chapters 5 and 6, but for now it's enough to know that sequencers are to MIDI performance data as multitrack tape decks are to audio signals. That is, they allow you to create musical works by combining different tracks, all of which play back together. MIDI sequencer tracks include MIDI messages such as Note On, Note Off, Pitch Bend, Volume, and so on, along with other musical elements, such as tempo and meter.

Standard MIDI Files actually come in three formats, although only two are commonly used:

- *Format 0* files consist of a single multichannel track that includes all of the MIDI messages, tempo data, and other relevant information. When you save a sequencer file as a Format 0 SMF, the sequencer program bundles together all of the separate tracks into one. This simplifies the file, but makes it more difficult to edit.

- *Format 1* is the most widely used and practical format. It's especially useful for serious musicians who want to exchange MIDI data with other musicians. In Format 1 files, several separate tracks play back at once. The first track contains the tempo data, which applies concurrently to all of the other tracks. Because this format preserves the tracks as they were originally recorded, less information is likely to be lost in the translation from proprietary to SMF format. It also facilitates viewing and editing the MIDI data.

- *Format 2* files are more theoretical than practical at this point, because virtually no one supports them. They consist of a number of independent tracks, each of which includes its own meter and tempo data. In a way, a Format 2 file is like a collection of Format 0 sequences combined into a single file. Perhaps in the future this file format will gain some popularity.

Regardless of which file format you use, Standard MIDI Files all include the same types of data. As you might expect, this consists mainly of the usual MIDI performance messages and can include (depending on your sequencer software) SysEx data as well.

But Standard MIDI Files can also include a special kind of non-MIDI information called meta-events. Meta-events include end-of-track designations, track names, tempo and time signature changes, text events, lyrics, and instrument names. Although these meta-events (and others) are defined in the SMF specification, they aren't universally supported by all MIDI software. A little experimentation will show which information is lost when importing and exporting Standard MIDI Files with your sequencer. This doesn't render the SMF sequences useless, but it may mean re-entering such things as track names each time you import a file.

Although SMF implementation varies widely among different brands and types of MIDI software, the SMF format is still a valuable and often essential tool for working with MIDI. With Standard MIDI Files, you can transfer a file back and forth between two sequencers. This lets you take advantage of the unique editing features of each program. Or you can collaborate with a composer in another city by uploading and downloading SMF sequences from a bulletin board system—even if you're using different computers and different software. And, of course, you can always save your files to disk and share them with other musicians even if they use different sequencer software than you do.

tip   *Even though you can share MIDI files when working with different computers and sequencers, this is not the ideal situation. If you will be co-composing on a regular basis with another musician, it is still easier and faster if you can each use the same software and equipment. That way, the music will always sound the same for both of you, and you won't have to worry about unexpected incompatibilities.*

General MIDI

Through the combination of MIDI hardware and the Standard MIDI File format, it is now possible to compose music on a Yamaha keyboard using Passport software, for example, and then play the music back on a Roland synthesizer using an Opcode sequencer. Unfortunately, there's still one little problem. Although the software will most likely re-create the performance perfectly, the music itself will sound completely wrong! That's because, as mentioned earlier, MIDI instruments are entirely different in the types and numbers of sounds that they offer. Furthermore, they also differ in the ways that they organize and implement those sounds.

Trying to include Program Change messages in a performance becomes an exercise in frustration. It's unlikely that different brands of instruments will have the same presets in the same numerical locations. So you may find that the lovely woodwind trio that you composed in your studio will end up as a trio for banjo, trumpet, and snare drum on someone else's system.

Of Interest

You might be wondering why different synthesizers or sound cards produce different qualities of sound. There are actually several reasons. First, synthesizers use various synthesis methods to generate their sounds (these are discussed in Chapter 4).

Second, apart from the synthesis method used, an instrument's design characteristics, its internal architecture, and the quality of its components each contribute to its unique "sound." Of course, how a synthesizer sounds is an important factor in whether musicians will purchase and play it. This means that competition for the "best sounding" instrument is often quite fierce. And there is always enough advertising hype flying around to fuel many a debate. Classic keyboard synthesizers such as the Minimoog, the Prophet-5, the Yamaha DX7, and the Roland D-50 became well known for their unique and identifiable sounds.

Finally, individual preset sounds, such as trumpet, flute, guitar, and so on, can be created using a number of different programming and editing techniques. And each of these yields a distinctly different result. Ultimately, because the perfect trumpet sound is subjective, no one method of emulation will satisfy all players. Although it may seem confusing at times, in the final analysis, all of this sonic variety makes the world of electronic music much richer.

This lack of predictability in sound output represents an important missing link in the hardware/software compatibility chain. It's a particular problem for third-party developers and multimedia producers. They can't add real-time MIDI soundtracks to presentations and feel confident that the final results will sound as planned on other setups. Fortunately, there is now a solution to this problem, and it's called General MIDI.

General MIDI (GM) is actually a subset and an addition to the original MIDI Specification. It describes a number of characteristics that a MIDI instrument must possess to qualify as a GM-compatible device. For example, a General MIDI instrument must provide at least 24-note polyphony. It must respond to all 16 MIDI channels, with channel 10 reserved for percussion parts. And it must designate middle C as MIDI note number 60. GM-compatible instruments must also respond to a specific list of MIDI messages including Pitch Bend, Aftertouch, Velocity, Modulation, Panning, Master Volume, and others.

The most significant component of the General MIDI standard, however, is the Instrument Patch Map. It's a list of 128 sounds along with their assigned program numbers (Figure 3-7). The sounds are grouped into 16 broad categories, each containing 8 related entries. The Instrument Patch

Map offers an excellent sonic palette that is suitable for a wide range of applications. The sounds include a good selection of orchestral instruments, keyboards, vocal ensembles, synthesizer timbres, ethnic instruments, sound effects, and more.

Drum parts are reserved for MIDI channel 10. The individual sounds and their placement across the keyboard are specified in a chart called the Percussion Key Map (Figure 3-8). These two maps provide an important template of sounds that introduce a much-needed level of predictability into the reproduction of MIDI music files.

FIGURE 3-7

The General MIDI

Instrument Patch

Map

• **Piano**	• **Bass**	• **Reed**	• **Synth Effects**
1. Acoustic Grand Piano	33. Acoustic Bass	65. Soprano Sax	97. FX 1 (rain)
2. Bright Acoustic Piano	34. Electric Bass (finger)	66. Alto Sax	98. FX 2 (soundtrack)
3. Electric Grand Piano	35. Electric Bass (pick)	67. Tenor Sax	99. FX 3 (crystal)
4. Honky-tonk Piano	36. Fretless Bass	68. Baritone Sax	100. FX 4 (atmosphere)
5. Electric Piano 1	37. Slap Bass 1	69. Oboe	101. FX 5 (brightness)
6. Electric Piano 2	38. Slap Bass 2	70. English Horn	102. FX 6 (goblins)
7. Harpsichord	39. Synth Bass 1	71. Bassoon	103. FX 7 (echoes)
8. Clavi	40. Synth Bass 2	72. Clarinet	104. FX 8 (sci-fi)
• **Chrom Perc**	• **Strings**	• **Pipe**	• **Ethnic**
9. Celesta	41. Violin	73. Piccolo	105. Sitar
10. Glockenspiel	42. Viola	74. Flute	106. Banjo
11. Music Box	43. Cello	75. Recorder	107. Shamisen
12. Vibraphone	44. Contrabass	76. Pan Flute	108. Koto
13. Marimba	45. Tremolo Strings	77. Blown Bottle	109. Kalimba
14. Xylophone	46. Pizzicato Strings	78. Shakuhachi	110. Bag pipe
15. Tubular Bells	47. Orchestral Harp	79. Whistle	111. Fiddle
16. Dulcimer	48. Timpani	80. Ocarina	112. Shanai
• **Organ**	• **Ensemble**	• **Synth Lead**	• **Percussive**
17. Drawbar Organ	49. String Ensemble 1	81. Lead 1 (square)	113. Tinkle Bell
18. Percussive Organ	50. String Ensemble 2	82. Lead 2 (sawtooth)	114. Agogo
19. Rock Organ	51. SynthStrings 1	83. Lead 3 (calliope)	115. Steel Drums
20. Church Organ	52. SynthStrings 2	84. Lead 4 (chiff)	116. Woodblock
21. Reed Organ	53. Choir Aahs	85. Lead 5 (charang)	117. Taiko Drum
22. Accordion	54. Voice Oohs	86. Lead 6 (voice)	118. Melodic Tom
23. Harmonica	55. Synth Voice	87. Lead 7 (fifths)	119. Synth Drum
24. Tango Accordion	56. Orchestra Hit	88. Lead 8 (bass + lead)	120. Reverse Cymbal
• **Guitar**	• **Brass**	• **Synth Pad**	• **Sound Effects**
25. Acoustic Guitar (nylon)	57. Trumpet	89. Pad 1 (new age)	121. Guitar Fret Noise
26. Acoustic Guitar (steel)	58. Trombone	90. Pad 2 (warm)	122. Breath Noise
27. Electric Guitar (jazz)	59. Tuba	91. Pad 3 (polysynth)	123. Seashore
28. Electric Guitar (clean)	60. Muted Trumpet	92. Pad 4 (choir)	124. Bird Tweet
29. Electric Guitar (muted)	61. French Horn	93. Pad 5 (bowed)	125. Telephone Ring
30. Overdriven Guitar	62. Brass Section	94. Pad 6 (metallic)	126. Helicopter
31. Distortion Guitar	63. SynthBrass 1	95. Pad 7 (halo)	127. Applause
32. Guitar harmonics	64. SynthBrass 2	96. Pad 8 (sweep)	128. Gunshot

Key #	Drum Sound	Key #	Drum Sound	Key #	Drum Sound
35	Acoustic Bass Drum	51	Ride Cymbal 1	67	High Agogo
36	Bass Drum 1	52	Chinese Cymbal	68	Low Agogo
37	Side Stick	53	Ride Bell	69	Cabasa
38	Acoustic Snare	54	Tambourine	70	Maracas
39	Hand Clap	55	Splash Cymbal	71	Short Whistle
40	Electric Snare	56	Cowbell	72	Long Whistle
41	Low Floor Tom	57	Crash Cymbal 2	73	Short Guiro
42	Closed Hi Hat	58	Vibraslap	74	Long Guiro
43	High Floor Tom	59	Ride Cymbal 2	75	Claves
44	Pedal Hi-Hat	60	Hi Bongo	76	Hi Wood Block
45	Low Tom	61	Low Bongo	77	Low Wood Block
46	Open Hi-Hat	62	Mute Hi Conga	78	Mute Cuica
47	Low-Mid Tom	63	Open Hi Conga	79	Open Cuica
48	Hi Mid Tom	64	Low Conga	80	Mute Triangle
49	Crash Cymbal 1	65	High Timbale	81	Open Triangle
50	High Tom	66	Low Timbale		

It's important to realize that General MIDI does not specify how the individual sounds are created, nor does it indicate any standards for sound quality. It merely requires that a certain collection of sounds be present in a certain order. Individual manufacturers are free to use any synthesis method that they prefer. Additionally, GM-compatible instruments need not limit their sounds to the GM list. Many manufacturers have chosen to add a GM subset to an instrument's internal library.

General MIDI is not intended to restrict the development of new sounds or synthesis methods. Nor will it homogenize the MIDI marketplace, as some had initially feared. It is designed simply to promote a class of "consumer-level" MIDI instruments with a preconfigured setup for reliable playback with minimal aggravation. General MIDI makes it possible to create MIDI files that are compatible with a wide range of devices rather than being limited to a few specific instruments.

Because each brand of sound module produces its sounds through its own unique method of synthesis, GM instruments will not all sound the same when playing identical MIDI Files. Furthermore, manufacturers have some latitude in interpreting the required instrument sounds. An English horn, for example, can sound quite different on different General MIDI instruments. Nonetheless, the overall orchestration and the basic sound of a MIDI performance should not deliver any shocking surprises if a Standard MIDI File, composed for General MIDI, generates a performance on different

brands of GM-compatible instruments. For many people, this provides the necessary common ground that will further enhance MIDI's usefulness.

Although the concept of General MIDI was initially met with some indifference, the reality of General MIDI has proven itself valuable and is gaining considerably in popularity. You should be seeing the General MIDI logo (Figure 3-9) on a growing number of MIDI instruments for pros and amateurs alike.

Conclusion

MIDI may have begun life as a means of hooking together synthesizers, but its talents really began to bloom when personal computers entered the scene. With the right software, musicians can now compose, arrange, record, play back, edit, organize, and print their own music. MIDI's capabilities have surpassed the expectations of even its most avid promoters. Computer-based MIDI systems can now control stage lighting, operate tape decks, configure mixing panels, synchronize music and sound effects to video, and much more. After all these years, MIDI has become a mature and robust technology, ideally suited to bring high-quality sound to the desktop. In the next chapter, we'll take a nuts-and-bolts look at how to set up a MIDI system and what you'll need to get going.

CHAPTER 4

Setting Up Your MIDI System

O N E of the best things about MIDI is the great flexibility that it offers for setting up a music system. You can do quite respectable work with little more than a computer, one or two pieces of MIDI equipment, and a stereo system. Or you can enter the ranks of the pros with elaborate rackmount setups and high-end digital recording systems. Either way, MIDI always provides the option of expanding (or scaling back) your desktop studio as your budgetary situation changes.

Regardless of how simple or complex you make your computer-based MIDI system, it will still consist of at least three essential components: a computer, a MIDI interface, and some kind of MIDI instrument. Even though two or more of these components may be combined (a sound card might include a MIDI interface, for example), the individual functions remain the same. Most people will also want a stereo system or a set of amplified speakers, so they can listen without headphones. Of course, you'll also need MIDI cables and audio cables. And as your system expands, you may need a mixer. But first, let's look at the core components that constitute a basic setup, and then we'll examine some of the available options for enhancing your studio.

Computers

If you don't already have a computer, selecting one for a desktop MIDI system can be a daunting task. The computer is, after all, not only the brains of the entire setup, but it also provides the user interface that lets you run the whole shebang. Comparing dissimilar processors and trying to make sense of cryptic computer terminology can give anyone a headache. The good news is, if you're choosing from the most recent batch of offerings, you can't really go too far wrong. The fiercely competitive computer marketplace has significantly narrowed the differences between computer platforms, while the ever-expanding market for music software now offers a wide range of sophisticated titles to choose from.

MAC

Because of its built-in sound capabilities and its emphasis on graphics, the Macintosh quickly established itself during the 1980s as the music computer of choice. The Mac had powerful sequencer and notation programs back when the IBM was still viewed primarily as a business machine. Without the compatibility problems that often plagued IBM clones, and with the enthusiastic support of the artistic community, the Macintosh was anointed the premier music computer for serious musicians. To this day, the Mac is found in more professional recording studios than any other type of computer, and it continues to lead the way in the number of sophisticated professional-level sequencers on the market. Furthermore, the Mac's intuitive graphical user interface (GUI) makes it ideal for beginners as well.

PC

But an IBM PC running Microsoft Windows ain't exactly chopped liver. With the recent introduction of the Multimedia PC (MPC) standard, PC music applications have gotten a much needed shot in the arm. Windows 3.1 has brought a consistent graphic interface to the PC, and audio applications have now become all the rage. Literally millions of sound cards are installed in PCs all over the world, and the numbers are growing apace. Because most of these sound cards have at least some MIDI capabilities, these numbers translate into a huge installed base of potential desktop musicians. Indeed, MIDI itself is an important part of the MPC Specification.

Responding to the growing marketplace, many software developers have introduced new MIDI programs, and many companies have ported titles over to Windows that were originally only available for the Mac. All of this has substantially reduced the gap between Macs and PCs.

As the prices for new Macs decline, the relative cost issue between platforms becomes less significant. And with the introduction of the Power-PC–based computers, the two platforms are beginning to share a great deal of common ground.

Of Interest

Choosing a Computer for Your Desktop Studio

Given the variety and large number of choices available, you might have trouble deciding which computer to buy for your desktop studio. Here are several tips to help you decide:

1. First find the software that you want, and then buy the computer that will run it. Many people work the other way around, which often leads to frustration when they find that their creative efforts are hampered because the right kind of program isn't available.

2. Consider non-musical applications. The Macintosh is very strong in the areas of desktop publishing, graphics, and multimedia development. The PC has traditionally been stronger in the area of business software. (This book focuses on the Mac and PC platforms because that's where most of the action is in the music software marketplace.)

3. Buy the computer that your friends and/or coworkers use. This is especially important for beginners. Learning to use a computer can be exasperating, and having a friend to help you through the rough spots is invaluable. Also, try to find people who use the same software that you want to use. Have them demonstrate its features and capabilities.

   Ask the people you know if they're satisfied with their computers and software. These users can help you decide on how fast a computer model you'll need, how much RAM you'll have to install, and what other peripherals are important. If you don't have friends or coworkers who can help with your decision, then join a local user's group. Many of these organizations have special interest groups dedicated to music and related subjects.

4. Consider your future plans and possible expansion needs. Most MIDI sequencers actually don't require a huge amount of processing speed to run properly. Many of the new entry-level computer models will work just fine. But if you decide to enlarge your system, you may need additional expansion slots. And if you move into the area of hard-disk recording, you'll certainly need something beyond an entry-level system. In general, it's best to buy the most advanced model you can afford. It'll work faster, provide faster screen redraws, work well with high-end programs, and handle future hardware and software demands.

5. Don't skimp on the monitor. Although most music software works fine on a monochrome monitor, the trend in music programs is for better implementation of color. Either way, it's best to shop for a monitor with a clear, sharp, stable image. Music editing—whether MIDI or digital audio—often involves precise selections and on-screen movements, as well as small blocks of text and numbers. A good monitor will save you many a bleary-eyed night and will make your composing and editing experience more rewarding.

MIDI Interfaces

Once you have a computer, the next thing you'll need for your desktop music system is a MIDI interface. Although the term "MIDI interface" seems a little redundant, it actually makes sense. The job of the MIDI interface is to translate MIDI data into and out of a form that the computer can under-stand—a kind of interface for the interface (Figure 4-1).

In reality, this task is not all that difficult for most computers. MIDI information simply consists of bits and bytes, the kind of stuff that computers eat for breakfast every day. So it might surprise you that there are so many options to consider when you're looking for a MIDI interface. Compatibility, number of ports, and additional features all have to be taken into account to arrive at a good cost/benefit ratio for your particular needs.

While shopping for a MIDI interface, watch for several features. One important consideration is the number of MIDI inputs and outputs. Inex-pensive, entry-level interfaces usually have only one input and one output. For a simple system with only one or two instruments, this may be enough. Better interfaces usually offer two or more MIDI Outs. They let you plug each MIDI device directly into the interface. As you'll see a little later, this lets you configure your system more efficiently.

The very best interfaces provide *multiport* capability, which provides not only two or more outputs, but each output is controlled by a separate processor. The ports may be designated by numbers or letters, and each can carry a discrete set of 16 MIDI channels—kind of like having several separate interfaces rolled into one. The ability to access more than 16 channels at a time is a very useful feature for mid- to large-size systems and for those composers who work with complex musical arrangements. For most people, 32 channels (16 × 2) will probably be more than enough. But several interfaces provide 64 channels and more for large-scale setups.

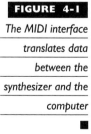

FIGURE 4-1

The MIDI interface translates data between the synthesizer and the computer

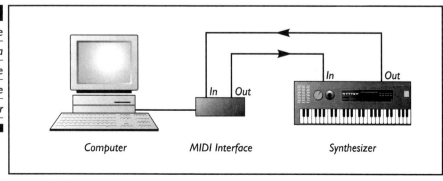

Computer   *MIDI Interface*   *Synthesizer*

A multiport MIDI interface provides two or more sets of MIDI channels.

The more expensive interfaces also provide a number of MIDI handling and processing features, including *merging* (combining incoming MIDI data from two or more sources), *muting* (temporarily filtering out one or more types of data), *routing* (controlling the flow of MIDI data), and *rechannelizing* (assigning new channel numbers to incoming MIDI data).

Another important feature found only on high-end interfaces is the ability to read and write *timecode*, especially SMPTE timecode. Timecode lets you operate your computer's recording and playback activities in sync with an external device. This is particularly important for those who regularly work with audio or video tape recorders. (I'll discuss timecode in more detail in the "Tape Recorders and Timecode" section of this chapter.)

IBM PC Interfaces

PC interfaces typically come in the form of an expansion card that plugs into a computer slot. In most cases, the card interacts with the outside world through an external box that attaches to the card with a cable. The box supplies the necessary MIDI In and Out ports and may include other circuitry, jacks, and switches.

Instead of an external box, some less-expensive interfaces only provide a set of adapter cables with MIDI In and Out jacks at the ends. They attach to the card in the same way but obviously offer fewer features. And for laptop users and those without available slots, several interfaces plug directly into a computer's parallel or serial port. Many of these are rather minimal in design, but a few boast a significant list of features.

MIDI interfaces for the PC have been around since the earliest days of MIDI. In 1984, Roland Corporation introduced the first commercially available interface for IBM-compatible computers—the MPU-401 (MIDI Processing Unit). The original MPU-401 consisted of a solidly built external metal box that attached to Roland's MIF-IPC expansion card.

The MPU-401 was noteworthy for its ability to operate in two modes, called Intelligent and Dumb (Dumb mode is also known as *UART* mode, for *universal asynchronous receive/transmit*). In Intelligent mode, the MPU's internal processor handled many of the important tasks that MIDI demanded, thereby freeing up the computer to attend to other things. Because the early PCs were considerably less powerful than today's machines, Intelligent mode helped keep things moving along more efficiently and reduced problems caused by insufficient processing capability. In Dumb mode, the MPU acted as a simple MIDI I/O (Input/Output) that passed along data for the computer to process.

The Roland MPU-401 was the first commercially available MIDI interface for the PC and became the de facto industry standard.

Because Roland made the MPU-401 technology available to other hardware companies, the unit quickly established itself as the archetypal MIDI interface for the PC. To remain competitive, software developers had to support the popular Roland standard, and to this day, the Roland MPU-401 is a kind of de facto standard for PC music applications. With the PC's history of hardware/software compatibility problems, this was an important unifying force. But the standard is weakening now, as new demands are placed on MIDI-equipped computers. Furthermore, Microsoft's Windows has gone a long way to resolve the problems that had existed between applications and incompatible device drivers.

With today's more powerful PCs, the MPU Intelligent mode is rapidly becoming obsolete. In fact, it may become a liability in some cases, because it gets in the way of the computer's processing and interferes with the implementation of more advanced MIDI capabilities. In response to newly developing trends in MIDI hardware and software, many interface manufacturers have introduced hybrid devices that offer MPU-401 compatibility along with a number of advanced features. Other companies have abandoned MPU compatibility altogether. To be on the safe side, check with the manufacturer to verify that a particular interface will work with your software and hardware. If you're using Windows, this should not be much of a problem.

Following are several examples from each of the categories of PC MIDI interfaces.

Entry-Level PC Interfaces

PC

If you're on a tight budget and your system needs are modest, a One-In/One-Out or One-In/Two-Out 16-channel interface should suffice. Fortunately there are several to choose from, with most prices ranging from around $100 to about $140 (see Table 4-1 and Figure 4-2).

Mid- and Pro-Level PC Interfaces

PC

Mid- and pro-level interfaces cost more—sometimes a lot more—than the entry-level units described earlier. For the jump in price to a mid-level interface, you get the advantage of true multiport operation (for more than 16 MIDI channels). Pro-level interfaces also boast timecode capabilities and sophisticated MIDI-handling options. Most prices range from as low as about $130 to around $500 (see Table 4-2 and Figure 4-3).

Company	Model	Type	Ins/Outs	401-Compatible	Multiport	Comments
Key Electronics	MS-101	serial port	1/1	no	no	
Midiman	MM-401	1/3-size card	1/1	yes	no	Short color-coded cables
	Portman PC/P	parallel port	1/1	no	no	
	Portman PC/S	serial port	1/1	no	no	
Music Quest	PC MIDI Card	card	1/1	yes	no	
	MIDI Engine Note/1	parallel port	1/1	no	no	
	MIDI Engine Note/1+	parallel port	1/2	no	no	Printer pass-thru port; LEDs
Roland	MPU-IPC	card/box	1/1	yes	no	Modern version of original MPU-401
Voyetra	VP-11	parallel port	1/1	no	no	

TABLE 4-1   Entry-Level PC Interfaces ■

FIGURE 4-2

Midiman MM-401,
Midiman Portman
PC/S and
Portman PC/P

■

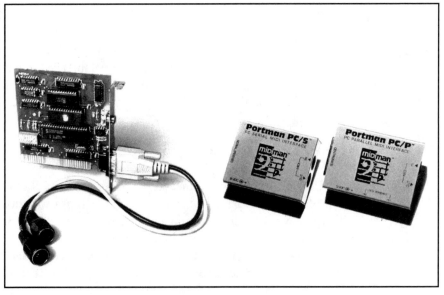

Company	Model	Type	Ins/Outs	401-Compatible	Multiport	Comments
Key Electronics	MS-124	serial port	1/4	no	64-channel	
	MP-128N	parallel port	1/4	no	64-channel	
	MP-128X	serial port	1/8	no	128-channel	
	MP-128S	serial port	2/8	no	128-channel	Timecode capability
Mark of the Unicorn	MIDI Time Piece II	card/box	8/8	no	128-channel	LCD display, timecode capability, advanced features, LEDs
	MIDI Express PC	card/box	6/6	no	96-channel	LEDs, advanced features
Music Quest	MQX-32M	card	2/2	yes	32-channel	Timecode capability
	MIDIEngine 2Port/SE	parallel port	2/2	no	32-channel	Timecode capability
Roland	Super MPU	card/box	2/2	yes	32-channel	Timecode capability, advanced features
Voyetra	V-22	card	2/2	no	32-channel	
	V-22m	card	2/2	yes	32-channel	
	V-24s	card/box	2/4	no	64-channel	LEDs, timecode capability
	V-24sm	card/box	2/4	yes	64-channel	LEDs, timecode capability

TABLE 4-2   *Mid- and Pro-Level PC Interfaces* ■

The IRQ and I/O Dilemma

Most of the time, installing a MIDI interface card in a PC is not terribly difficult—especially if you don't have any other cards already installed. Still, it's not that uncommon for internal conflicts among hardware devices to cause problems. If your MIDI software hangs up when you try to use it, or you keep getting messages such as "MIDI Interface Not Found," your first thought should be to check the interrupt request line (or IRQ, as it's more commonly known).

IRQs are hardware lines over which *interrupts* (requests for service) are sent. They provide the different pieces of hardware in your PC with a system

From top to bottom: Key Electronics MS-124, Mark of the Unicorn MIDI Time Piece II, Mark of the Unicorn MIDI Express PC, Roland Super MPU ■

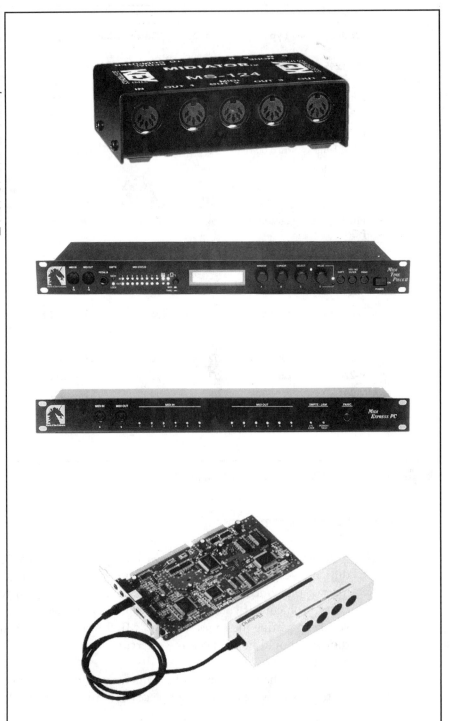

of priorities for taking care of business. The interrupt request is like an urgent phone call to the CPU, demanding immediate attention. The message tells the CPU to drop what it's doing and attend to another task. The timing-intensive commands that are a part of operating a MIDI interface must take precedence over other less critical operations, or the MIDI hardware just can't work. If you have two different pieces of hardware set to the same IRQ number, you may get the equivalent of a data train wreck.

An interrupt is a special signal that requests immediate attention.

Most MIDI interfaces have user-selectable IRQs. Typically you set them by flipping tiny switches (called DIP switches) mounted on the expansion card or interface housing. In some cases, you might have to move an equally tiny "jumper" from one set of pins to another. In any case, you must be certain that your software will work with the new setting.

A better solution, if possible, is to change the IRQ of the competing card or device. The MPU-401 and most 401-compatible interfaces (as well as many others) come from the factory set to IRQ2. This usually works fine. If it doesn't, you'll have to track down the source of the conflict. Some MIDI interfaces come with helpful setup and diagnostic software—an excellent feature that lets you make your settings on-screen.

Another possible source of conflict may lie with the I/O (Input/Output) addresses. The computer equivalent of street addresses, they tell the CPU where to send and receive information for each of its hardware components. Some devices need more than one address to accommodate different functions. A common default setting for MIDI interfaces is 330—as expressed in hexadecimal numbers. For your MIDI interface to work properly, both the IRQ and the I/O address numbers must be set correctly. This may involve a little trial and error, so take notes as you go along.

Macintosh Interfaces

Compared to PCs, shopping for and installing a Macintosh interface is a piece of cake. Because all Macs have built-in serial ports—labeled Modem and Printer—they provide a standardized means for connecting a MIDI interface. Inexpensive Macintosh interfaces usually connect to either port, providing access to MIDI's 16 channels. Mid- to high-end interfaces connect to both of the ports. With this configuration, you can access 16 channels on the modem port and 16 more channels on the printer port, for a total of 32 MIDI channels—as long as the software supports this dual-port arrangement.

Because these units monopolize both of your serial ports, they always include a bypass (serial-port thru) switch, which allows you to switch between the modem and/or printer and the MIDI interface, without plugging and unplugging cables. You simply connect the interface to the computer and connect the peripherals to the interface.

In the past, there was some inconsistency in the clock speeds that different brands of Mac interfaces used when transferring MIDI data. In recent years, however, things have pretty much settled, and 1MHz is now generally viewed as the de facto standard. Nonetheless, most (but not all) Macintosh sequencers still let you match the software to the interface speed, in case you are using one of the older devices. If you buy a new interface, you shouldn't have any problems with any of the current software titles.

Following the maxim that if two are good, eight are much better, several Macintosh interfaces have recently been introduced that offer advanced multiport capabilities. Under some circumstances, these devices can offer hundreds of MIDI channels, as well as MIDI merging and other advanced features. They also provide sophisticated timecode reading and writing capabilities.

These professional-level interfaces typically come in the form of one- or two-space rackmount units that connect, as usual, to the modem and printer ports. The front panels provide LED indicators, buttons, and sometimes alphanumeric displays. Dedicated software lets you route the MIDI channels along software "cables" to the various outputs. Before you buy one of these interfaces, though, make sure that your software can take advantage of their advanced features.

Following are several examples from each of the categories of Macintosh MIDI interfaces.

Entry-Level Mac Interfaces

MAC

The entry-level interfaces for the Macintosh are about as simple as things get. They use a single cable that connects a small external box to one of the Mac's serial ports (modem or printer). The box provides a single MIDI In port, one to three MIDI Out ports, 16-channel capability, and sometimes a few extra features. With prices ranging between $40 and $100, this is an inexpensive way to get started with MIDI (see Table 4-3 and Figure 4-4).

Mid- and Pro-Level Mac Interfaces

MAC

As with the PC interfaces, the mid-level Macintosh interfaces usually (though not always) cost more than comparable entry-level units. For the extra money, you get additional inputs, outputs, and true multiport capa-

Company	Model	Computer Ports Used	Ins/Outs	Multiport	Timecode Support	Comments
Apple	Apple MIDI Interface	1	1/1	no	no	
JLCooper	MacNexus	1	1/3	no	no	1/4 rackspace
Midiman	MiniMacman	1	1/1	no	no	LEDs
	MacMan	1	1/3	no	no	LEDs, serial-port thru switch
Music Quest	MIDI Strip	1	1/3	no	no	One-piece molded cable with jacks
Opcode	MIDI Translator II	1	1/3	no	no	LEDs, serial-port thru

TABLE 4-3   *Entry-Level Mac Interfaces* ■

FIGURE 4-4

JLCooper MacNexus, Midiman MiniMacman, Midiman Macman ■

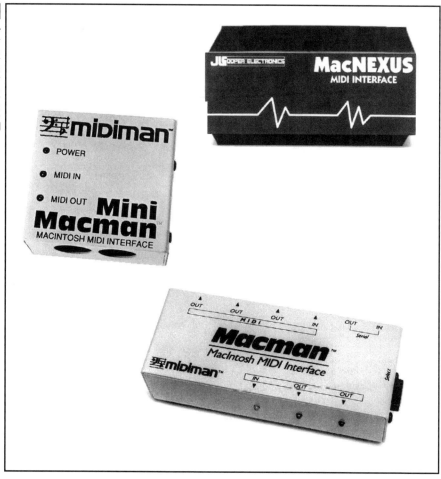

bility. The pro-level interfaces expand your studio options even more, with large numbers of inputs and outputs, the ability to manipulate MIDI data, and especially, the ability to read and write SMPTE timecode. Prices range from around $100 to well over $1,000 (see Table 4-4 and Figure 4-5).

The Interface Alternative

Although at the heart of every computer-based MIDI system is a MIDI interface, it's not always necessary to purchase a separate stand-alone unit for making music with MIDI. A number of PC sound cards come combined with a dedicated MIDI interface. Right out of the box, they let you plug in MIDI keyboards and make music. Other sound cards make you purchase an additional cable or adapter to access their MIDI capabilities.

In either case, it's not likely that the interface you get will be MPU-401–compatible. There are a few exceptions: **Roland's SCC-1** (Figure 4-6), for example, provides the equivalent of a synthesizer on a card combined with an MPU-compatible interface. In most cases, however, the interface that you get with a sound card is minimal in both the number of inputs and outputs

Company	Model	Computer Ports Used	Ins/Outs	Multiport	Timecode Support	Comments
JLCooper	SyncLink	2	2/2	32-channel	yes	1/2 rackspace, LEDs
Mark of the Unicorn	MIDI Time Piece II	2	8/8	128-channel	yes	LCD display, LEDs, rackmount, advanced features
	MIDI Express	2	4/6	96-channel	yes	LEDs, rackmount, advanced features
Opcode	Translator Pro	2	2/6	32-channel	no	LEDs
	Studio 3	2	2/6	32-channel	yes	LEDs, rackmount
	Studio 4	2	8/8	128-channel	yes	LEDs, rackmount, advanced features
	Studio 5LX	2	15/15	240-channel	yes	LED display, 2-rackspace, advanced features

TABLE 4-4 *Mid- and Pro-Level Mac Interfaces* ∎

FIGURE 4-5

JLCooper SyncLink,
Mark of the
Unicorn MIDI Time
Piece II, Mark of
the Unicorn MIDI
Express, Opcode
Studio 4, Opcode
Studio 5LX

■

FIGURE 4-6

Roland's SCC-1

synthesizer card

includes an

MPU-401–

compatible MIDI

interface

■

and in the number of useful features. Additionally, it may lack the broader level of compatibility that most stand-alone interfaces provide.

There are also several MIDI instruments—especially General MIDI sound modules (we'll look at these a little later in the "Sound Modules" section)—that come with a built-in MIDI interface. These instruments are available for both the Macintosh and the PC. They integrate the interface into the unit in such a way that you just plug the instrument directly into an available serial port to make it work. For the most part, these are inexpensive, entry-level (or "consumer-level") instruments. Again, the main drawback with these onboard interfaces is the lack of features and especially the lack of flexibility and potential for expansion from multiport capabilities.

As with everything else that has to do with computers, you always end up needing more than what you start out with. So, as a general principle, choose your MIDI interface for its versatility and future potential. Dedicated interfaces may be fine for a first tentative step into the world of MIDI, but if you're serious about your music, you may eventually find them limiting.

∫ound Sources: The Many Flavors of MIDI

Once you have a computer and a MIDI interface, it's time to add the final part to the basic computer/MIDI triumvirate: the sound source. Whereas it would be completely impractical to describe the myriad devices that populate the vast reaches of the MIDI universe, I'll take a more down-to-earth approach and examine the different categories that MIDI instruments fall into. Once you understand the differences and similarities in MIDI instruments, you'll be in a better position to select one based on your needs and personal preferences.

In the broadest sense, MIDI instruments fall roughly into two, sometimes nebulous, categories: synthesizers and samplers.

Synthesizers

In general, the term *synthesizer* refers to any musical instrument that creates its sounds electronically (as opposed to electrically or acoustically). More specifically, however, synthesizers create their sounds using sound-generating components called *oscillators*. Through the use of oscillators, a synthesizer can "synthesize" new sounds from scratch, making it a powerful and creative musical tool. Early analog synthesizers used *voltage-controlled oscillators* (VCOs) to create waveforms that were altered with filters.

An oscillator is the part of a synthesizer that generates a tone.

Most of today's synthesizers are digital (Figure 4-7). In place of the hardware oscillators and filters of the earlier synths, today's synthesizers use microprocessors and digital signal processing (DSP) to simulate the effects of oscillators. In other words, they create their individual waveforms from a series of numbers. The digital data is then converted into an audio signal—by a *digital-to-analog converter* (DAC)—and sent out to an amplifier.

The process of synthesizing sounds can be approached in a variety of ways, and synthesizers are often characterized by the synthesis method they use. Following are a few that you'll likely encounter.

FIGURE 4-7

Yamaha's unique VL-1 is the first commercially available synthesizer to use physical modeling technology for creating its sounds

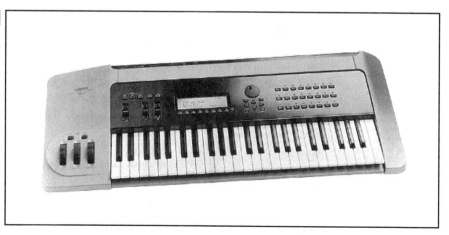

SUBTRACTIVE SYNTHESIS   This was first used by analog synthesizers. It involves creating complex, harmonically rich waveforms and then modifying them by filtering out specific harmonics until the desired tone color is achieved.

ADDITIVE SYNTHESIS   This process uses the reverse approach from subtractive synthesis. Additive synthesis combines simple sine waves to form complex sounds. Because each sine wave has a different frequency and amplitude—both of which are variable—you can create harmonically complex sounds that change over time.

FREQUENCY MODULATION (FM) SYNTHESIS   Invented by Dr. John Chowning at Stanford University and made famous by Yamaha's enormously popular DX7 synthesizer, this method of synthesis is still being used in millions of PC sound cards around the world. FM synthesis works by using simple digitally generated waveforms, called *modulators,* to control other simple waveforms, called *carriers.* Modulators and carriers are called *operators.* The six operators in the DX7 are available in 32 different preset configurations called *algorithms.* The carriers determine the pitch of a sound, while the modulators affect the harmonic content. The six operators in the DX7 allow it to produce a wide range of musical timbres with both quality and subtlety. The FM synthesis chips on most sound cards, however, must make do with fewer operators and algorithms, and as a result they sound considerably less satisfactory.

FM synthesis is currently being used in millions of PC sound cards for generating musical sounds.

These are only a few of the synthesis methods that are possible—I'll describe a few more later in the "Hybrid Synthesis" section—and you can be sure that new methods will appear as electronic instruments evolve. The main thing to keep in mind is that one method of synthesis isn't necessarily any better than another. What counts is how it sounds to you and how easy you find it to use. Some people relate to one approach for sound creation better than others. And everyone has a sense of what kinds of sounds they like. Everything boils down to preferences and priorities—what sounds the best and works the best within the available budget.

In general, synthesizers excel at producing unusual musical sounds, other-worldly sounds, and especially sounds that evolve or change over time. Because they build sounds from the ground up, synthesizers provide an unparalleled opportunity to shape and control musical timbres for those who are willing to learn the inner workings of their instrument.

However, synthesizers do have one drawback. Because they create their sounds electronically, they often sound rather "synthetic." This may not be a big problem for pop musicians or those who write atmospheric music, but if you're trying to capture the perfect oboe or string section or choir sound, you'll probably be frustrated with a synthesizer. Those in search of true-sounding acoustic timbres would do well to consider an alternative: samplers.

Of Interest

Analog Synthesizers

In the early days of synthesizers, tones were produced using voltage-controlled oscillators. This approach is called *analog synthesis*. The early Moog synthesizers, for example, were analog. Analog synthesizers produced a distinctive, "synthetic" sound, which was quite popular in the 1960s and 70s. Some musicians, such as Keith Emerson, relied heavily upon analog synthesizers.

Analog synthesizers have now been almost entirely replaced by digital instruments, in large part because of the greater reliability of digital devices. For example, it was virtually impossible to keep an analog synthesizer in tune! Because they used voltage-controlled oscillators, even the slightest variation in voltage caused a pitch change. Voltage fluctuations can be caused by a variety of sources—such as heat—and are nearly impossible to completely eliminate.

Furthermore, the various filters that were used to create a specific timbre were also subject to "drift" (as it was called) and difficult to set precisely. Nonetheless, the fact that sound characteristics and timbres could be easily modified during performance made the analog synthesizer an excellent solo instrument.

Samplers

Unlike synthesizers, samplers do not simply create their sounds out of thin air. Samplers make short digital recordings—called *samples*—of actual sounds, store them, and allow you to play them from a keyboard (or other controller). Because of this, samplers are especially adept at reproducing the harmonically complex timbres of acoustic instruments. In fact, samplers can reproduce virtually any sound, from breaking glass to a 40-piece orchestra (Figure 4-8).

You might say that samplers are to musicians as scanners are to graphic artists. That is, they use pre-existing source material and digitize it so that it can then be edited and applied to a number of situations.

A sampler makes short digital recordings and lets you use them (after editing) as the basis for musical sounds.

If, for example, you record a clarinet playing middle C and assign it to middle C on your keyboard, every time you play middle C you'll hear the clarinet play at that pitch. As you play up the scale, the clarinet's pitch will follow. That's because the sampler increases the playback speed of the recording as you play up the keyboard to the right and decreases it as you play to the left from the original key.

In theory, it seems that you should be able to reproduce an instrument's entire range from a single sample. Unfortunately, it doesn't work that way.

FIGURE 4-8

The Kurzweil

K2000 is a

popular pro-level

sampler

"Stretching" samples up or down by too much makes them sound funny. As the samples increase in pitch, they take on a kind of chipmunk quality. Notes that decrease too much in pitch start to sound like a record player that's losing power. As a result, most samples cover a limited keyboard range, typically several semitones, above and below the original pitch.

To more faithfully reproduce an instrument's sound, therefore, samplers must use several samples taken at strategic places throughout the instrument's range. These *multisamples* are then mapped accordingly across the keyboard.

Multisampling accomplishes two important tasks. First, it reduces the amount of pitch change that any single sample must endure. And second, it allows the sampler to capture the unique timbres that are inherent in the different registers of acoustic instruments. The high notes on a clarinet, for instance, sound entirely different in tone color than the low notes. In fact, clarinetists even have names for these registers: chalumeau (dark and hollow), middle register (neutral sounding), clarion (clear and bright). The same is true for many other instruments.

A number of characteristics determine the sound quality of a sampler, but the two most important are its resolution and its sampling rate. *Resolution—*expressed in bits—refers to the number of increments that are available to describe the amplitude of a waveform at any given point in time. The greater the number of bits, the finer the gradations and the better the sound. An 8-bit sampler would give you the sound quality of an inexpensive sound card or the built-in sounds from an early Macintosh; 12 bits provides much better sound quality. But these days, all professional and semi-pro samplers use at least 16-bit resolution—the same as compact disc players.

The other important parameter, *sampling rate* (sometimes called *sampling frequency*), refers to the number of times per second that the digital circuitry examines the incoming sound waves and assigns them values. As with resolution, the higher the number, the more accurate the recording and the better the sound. Pro-level samplers and compact discs use a sampling rate of 44.1kHz. Some samplers offer even higher sampling rates, although you can often get quite respectable results from rates as low as 30kHz. (Chapter 10 explores digital recording in more detail, along with a further discussion of resolution and sampling rates.)

Fond Memory

One problem that all samplers must confront is how best to manage their available memory. Large amounts of onboard memory can add substantially to the cost of a sampler, but too little memory can be limiting. The greater the resolution and the sampling rate, the more memory is needed per second of sound. Furthermore, the number of multisamples and whether they're monophonic or stereo also determine memory usage. When shopping for a sampler, be sure to take into account the amount of available memory and whether or not it's expandable.

To conserve valuable memory, samplers often employ a technique called looping. *Looping* involves taking a short snippet of sound and repeating it over and over again—in as seamless a manner as possible—to give the impression of a much longer sustained sound. This creates the illusion of a long sound without the memory requirements that such a sound would demand.

Sample Players

Because many people are not interested in capturing and editing their own samples, there's a class of instruments called *sample players*; these are essentially the same as samplers, except they don't provide any recording capabilities. The samples are usually stored in ROM and/or downloadable from a storage medium, such as a compact disc or floppy disk.

Samplers (and sample players) are good choices for those interested in working with orchestral sounds and other difficult-to-synthesize sounds, such as vocals, sound effects, and ensembles. Because samplers can record virtually anything, they're extremely versatile, allowing you to capture and play back whatever you like—from a barking dog to a vintage analog synthesizer or a Bösendorfer concert grand piano.

Hybrid Synthesis

With the growing popularity of synthesizers and samplers, it was inevitable that manufacturers would try to capitalize on the unique advantages that each kind of instrument offered. Several "synthesis" methods arose from these efforts.

WAVETABLE SYNTHESIS   This is a generic term for sample-based synthesis. Most wavetable synthesizers are actually just sample players that allow you to modify their sounds (stored in ROM) to a greater or lesser degree. Wavetable synthesis has now become the most common type of synthesis for modern MIDI instruments. It's sometimes referred to as PCM (pulse code modulation) synthesis.

RS-PCM   This stands for Resynthesized Pulse Code Modulation. With this method of synthesis (introduced by Roland), a sampled sound is analyzed and then re-created from the data through additive synthesis.

LINEAR/ARITHMETIC (L/A) SYNTHESIS   This approach to synthesis was introduced by Roland in the late 1980s and reached considerable popularity in the Roland D-50 synthesizer and subsequent models. The basic concept involves taking a short sample—usually the attack portion of a sound—and combining it with a synthesized waveform. The attack portion of a sound is often the most difficult part to create with a synthesizer, yet it's also one of the most critical elements for capturing the quality of a sound. L/A synthesis therefore provides a more realistic quality to the sound with much less demand for memory. And the resultant waveform can then be modified and controlled through filters, amplifiers, and signal processors.

ADVANCED INTEGRATED SYNTHESIS   This method of synthesis was first introduced with Korg's popular M1 and was later used in several other models. It uses sampled attacks and other waveforms (sometimes only a single-cycle looped waveform) combined with subtractive synthesis. The waveforms can be modified with multi-effects processors, filters, and other components.

VAST   This was first introduced by Kurzweil in the early 1990s on its K2000 sampler. VAST stands for Variable Architecture Synthesis Technology, and it's essentially a form of sample-based DSP synthesis that combines sampled sounds with an open-ended synthesis architecture. The sheer power and flexibility of this system has garnered the admiration of many dedicated users.

Z-PLANE SYNTHESIS   This unique form of synthesis was introduced by E-mu Systems in its Morpheus sound module. It involves—through the use of sophisticated filters—the real-time, continuous, "morphing" of one wave-form by another, using a third waveform as the path between the two. This allows you to combine sounds in unusual ways. You might, for instance, run the sound of a flute through the body of a violin. This unusual approach to synthesis offers some interesting potential.

PHYSICAL MODELING SYNTHESIS   First introduced commercially by Yamaha in its VL-1 (Virtual Lead) synthesizer (see Figure 4-7), this processor-inten-sive approach to synthesis may be the wave of the future. In fact, it really belongs in a category by itself, because it doesn't involve sample playback at all. Physical modeling synthesis creates its sounds in real time by applying complicated mathematical formulas that describe how acoustic instruments work. These formulas, or instrument models, are based upon the various physical characteristics that cause instruments to generate the highly com-plex sounds that they do.

These are a few more examples of the many types of synthesis that have appeared during the past several years. Others are sure to follow. It's clear, however, that sampling technology has made a serious impact on the world of electronic instruments and will continue to do so.

Sound Modules

When most people think of a synthesizer, they think of an electronic *keyboard* instrument. And for good reason. Since the early days of analog synthesizers, electronic instruments have nearly always come with a piano-style keyboard attached to them. But now that MIDI has arrived, things have changed. MIDI has made it easy to hook together lots of instruments, and the wisdom of having a dedicated keyboard for each of your synths and samplers is questionable. Keyboards are, after all, mechanical devices, and they add considerably to the cost and complexity of an instrument. Furthermore, keyboards are big, so they add to the size and weight of an instrument as well.

If you're setting up a small system with only one or two MIDI instru-ments, then a keyboard synthesizer (or sampler) makes sense. It lets you record and play back music with your computer, and it makes a conven-ient package. If you add a second instrument to the system, the keyboard can act as the master and send MIDI messages to the slave. But if you expand your system by adding more instruments you'll soon have a room full of keyboards. This is not only redundant, it takes up a lot of space and makes it hard to reach everything.

A sound module is a synthesizer without an attached keyboard.

That's why a rapidly growing number of MIDI musicians are putting together their systems with *sound modules*. Sound modules are essentially the same as synthesizers or samplers, without an attached keyboard. In other words, they're the sound-producing part of the instrument repackaged in a compact case (Figure 4-9). Most keyboard instruments are available in a sound module version as well.

Some sound modules are designed to sit neatly on the desktop, while others are designed to mount in an equipment rack. Some desktop modules can be adapted to fit in a rack as well. In any case, sound modules need to be hooked up to a master keyboard or other controller if you want to play them.

Building a MIDI system with sound modules makes a lot of sense. It saves money and space and provides a great deal of flexibility for changing things around. It also lets you choose a keyboard based on its own merits, rather than forcing you to use a mediocre keyboard just because it's attached to a great synth.

Polyphony

Whether you're looking for a synthesizer, a sampler, a sound module, or a sound card, you need to be aware of an instrument's available polyphony. The term *polyphony* refers to the number of simultaneous notes that an instrument can play. Bassoons and trumpets are *monophonic,* because they can only play one note at a time. Pianos, harps, and guitars are *polyphonic,* because they can play several notes at once.

Most MIDI instruments provide at least 16-note polyphony. In other words, they can play as many as 16 notes at once in a chordal or contrapuntal setting. The General MIDI standard requires at least 24-note polyphony, and 32-note polyphony is now becoming commonplace. A few sound modules even go beyond this limit.

FIGURE 4-9

The E-mu Systems Morpheus is a popular rackmount sound module

As a general rule, the more polyphony, the better. Why do you need so much polyphony? Consider a situation where you play a sweeping arpeggio up the keyboard. With limited polyphony, you may quickly run out of notes before the first notes stop sounding. Or suppose you play an eight-note chord that fades slowly and you play another eight-note chord on top of it. Again you may run out of notes. Once computers enter the picture, you can have the equivalent of several players all performing at once. So the available polyphony is especially important.

Keep in mind, however, that when manufacturers refer to polyphony, they're actually talking about *maximum polyphony*. This can be a bit misleading, because an instrument's polyphony is closely tied to the number of oscillators that it has available. If you have a synthesizer with 24-note polyphony and you're playing a patch that only uses one oscillator per note, then you can have the full 24 notes sounding at once. But many sounds require more than one oscillator. If you choose to play a rather complex sound and it requires three oscillators per note, you'll end up with only 8-note polyphony.

tip   *What happens to notes beyond the limit of polyphony? Different instruments handle this problem in different ways. Some will just ignore the new notes. Others adopt a note-stealing scheme. For example, the first note played may be replaced by the newest note. Therefore, if notes begin to drop out when you add a new part, you have probably reached your polyphonic limit. That's why it's important to be aware of how much polyphony an instrument provides.*

Multiple Sounds

Early analog synthesizers could only play one sound—or timbre—at a time. Modern MIDI instruments, on the other hand, are almost always *multitimbral* (pronounced "multy-tambrul"), which means that they can produce two or more instrument sounds simultaneously. It's an especially important characteristic, because it enables you to reproduce instrumental ensembles from a single MIDI instrument.

In essence, having a multitimbral sound module is like having several MIDI instruments rolled into one. Each instrument part is assigned a different MIDI channel and plays independently of the other parts. From a single multitimbral MIDI device, you can create the performance of a jazz ensemble (sax, guitar, piano, bass, drums) or a woodwind ensemble (flute, clarinet, oboe, bassoon) or any other combination of instruments or sounds (Figure 4-10).

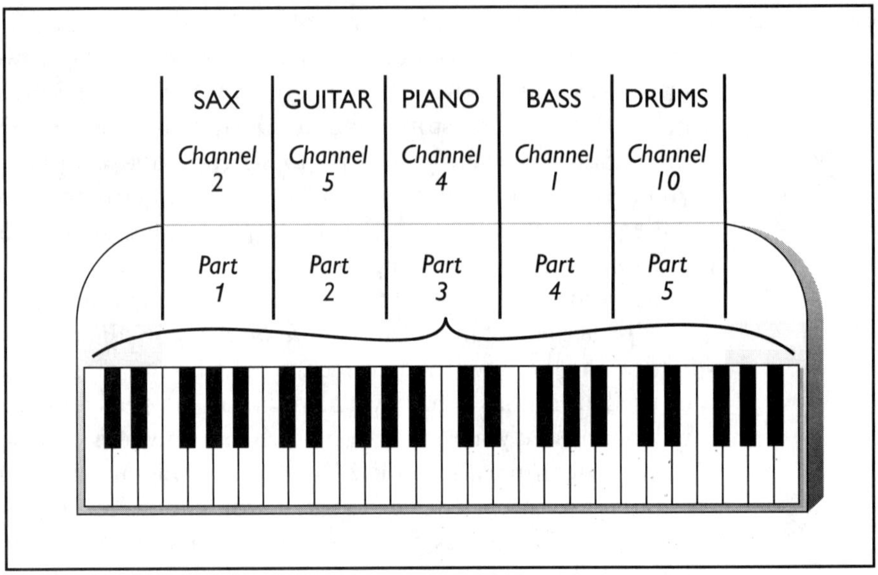

FIGURE 4-10

A multitimbral
sound module can
re-create several
different
instrument parts at
once
■

SAX	GUITAR	PIANO	BASS	DRUMS
Channel 2	Channel 5	Channel 4	Channel 1	Channel 10
Part 1	Part 2	Part 3	Part 4	Part 5

Multitimbral MIDI instruments are described in terms of the number of different instrument parts that they can play at once. Eight-part multitimbral capability is common, but because MIDI has 16 channels, many instruments now provide 16-part multitimbral capability. A few sound modules even go beyond that.

Early instruments made you choose a specific configuration for distributing the notes. For example, you might have two notes per part, or a combination of four, two, or one note per part. Most of today's MIDI instruments use *dynamic voice allocation* (in this context, "voice" refers to a note of polyphony, e.g., 16-voice polyphony). With dynamic voice allocation, the different instrument parts draw on the available polyphony as the need arises. This is a required feature for General MIDI instruments.

tip *An instrument's maximum polyphony stays the same regardless of how many sounds it makes. In other words, a sound module or synth with 16-note polyphony and 8-part multitimbral capability must distribute its 16 notes among the eight different instrument sounds.*

Low-Cost Sound Modules: A Foot in the Door

If you've had some experience working with MIDI, then you probably have some idea of what to look for in a new instrument. Shopping for MIDI instruments is just a matter of finding the right device with the right

FIGURE 4-11

Roland SC-50,

Yamaha TG300

combination of features at the right price. And of course, it must also sound good to you. But if you're a complete neophyte to the world of MIDI, it's hard to know what you'll need and which features are important. One way to approach this dilemma is to check out the latest batch of General MIDI sound modules.

General MIDI compatibility ensures that you'll have a good multipurpose assortment of sounds, an adequate degree of polyphony, sufficient multitimbral capability, and a good overall level of MIDI implementation. Not surprisingly, just about every major MIDI instrument manufacturer has jumped on the General MIDI bandwagon, so you have lots of models to choose from. Many include a built-in MIDI interface, so you can use them with or without a stand-alone MIDI interface. They mostly fall in the $400 to $800 (retail price) range (see Table 4-5 and Figure 4-11).

Company	Model	Multitimbral Capability	Polyphony	Presets	Comments
E-mu	SoundEngine	16-part	32-note	384	Mac interface, printer-port thru switch
Korg	05R/W	16-part	32-note	236	1/2 rackspace, 8 drum sets, Mac/PC interface
Roland	SC-50	16-part	28-note	226	9 drum sets, Mac/PC interface
Yamaha	TG300	16-part	32-note	456	9 drum sets, Mac/PC interface

TABLE 4-5   *Low-Cost Sound Modules*   ■

Higher-Priced Sound Modules: Two Feet in the Door

If you're willing to spend substantially more for your sound module, the same companies also offer more powerful and more sophisticated instruments (although not necessarily GM-compatible). Table 4-6 shows a few that cost between about $1,000 and $1,800 (see Figure 4-12).

The MIDI sound modules mentioned here are only a few of the many instruments currently on the market. Prices range from just a few hundred dollars to many thousands of dollars. And as you might expect, the old adage "You get what you pay for" generally holds true. The bottom line, however, is always sound quality. The most awesome feature list in the universe doesn't amount to a hill of beans if the instrument doesn't sound the way you want it to. So before deciding on a synthesizer, sampler, or sound module, be sure to give it a thorough listening test.

$ound Cards

PC

Any discussion of MIDI instruments would not be complete without mentioning sound cards. Thanks to the recent tidal wave of interest in multimedia, millions of PC users are adding sound cards to their computers. A baseline card that adheres to the original MPC Specification includes some digital audio and MIDI capabilities.

Unfortunately, the typical PC sound card is a jack-of-all-trades and master of none. The digital audio capabilities are rudimentary at best, and the quality of the MIDI instrument sounds leaves much to be desired. That's

Company	Model	Multitimbral Capability	Polyphony	Presets	Comments
E-mu	UltraProteus	16-part	32-note	384	Non–GM-compatible, ROM card slot, dual stereo effects
Korg	X3R	16-part	32-note	336	8 drum sets, internal sequencer, disk drive, PCM card slot, 2 rackspace
Roland	SC-88	32-part	64-note	654	22 drum sets, Mac/PC interface, large display
Yamaha	TG500	16-part	64-note	384	90 digital effects, 4 card slots

TABLE 4-6 Higher-Priced Sound Modules ■

FIGURE 4-12

E-mu

UltraProteus,

Roland SC-88,

Yamaha TG500

because early cards, such as the **Sound Blaster** from Creative Labs, were primarily aimed at game players and were later adopted by multimedia developers because of the large installed base.

These first-generation cards used Yamaha's inexpensive OPL-2 FM-synthesizer chipset with 11-note polyphony. Because it had only two operators, the OPL-2 could not approach the sound quality that most people now expect from synthesizers. Later improvements in sound-card technology also brought improved MIDI performance from the more advanced OPL-3 chip. With its 20-note polyphony and 20-part multitimbral capability, the four-operator OPL-3 was a step in the right direction. But even this improved synthesis chip did not bring the MIDI sound quality that serious musicians demanded.

Fortunately, things have changed. In addition to greatly improved digital audio capabilities, a new generation of sound cards is offering high-quality wavetable synthesis for MIDI playback (synthesis chips from such well known sampler manufacturers as E-mu, Ensoniq, and Kurzweil are now appearing on a number of cards). Products such as the new **MultiSound**

Monterey from Turtle Beach Systems, the **UltraSound** from Advanced Gravis, and Roland's popular **SCC-1** and **RAP-10** cards are bringing General MIDI–compatibility and more realistic instrument sounds to the desktop. Those users who already have a Sound Blaster 16 card can add the **Wave Blaster** daughterboard. It provides high-quality, General MIDI sample-play-back, along with a number of other features.

If you're in the market for a sound card and you plan to include it as part of your desktop studio, be sure to find out what type of synthesis the MIDI section uses. There are still many Sound Blaster–compatible cards that use the old-style FM chips. And these will certainly limit your creative potential.

MAC

PC

Professional Macintosh and PC musicians who need a top-notch MIDI instrument inside their computers should consider Digidesign's **SampleCell II**. This powerful 16-bit RAM-based sample player offers 32-note polyphony and eight analog outputs. It comes with two CD-ROMs filled with sounds and the SampleCell Editor application. This software provides a mixer-like window, which makes it easy to set up and mix instruments. Although it's a bit pricey, this card can provide MIDI-controlled studio-quality output directly from your computer.

Drum Machines

Drum machines are specialized sound modules that are designed to produce drum sounds and rhythm section parts. As with other sound modules, they may use synthesized or sampled sounds. But the sounds in drum machines are oriented specifically toward emulating various types of drum sets. A typical drum machine (Figure 4-13) will provide a good complement of percussion sounds, including various snare drums, kick drums, and tom-toms. You'll also find at least one hi-hat cymbal (open and closed), ride cymbal, crash cymbal, hand clap, tambourine, and cowbell. Additionally, most drum machines provide an array of Latin sounds, including congas, bongos, timbales, claves, shakers, etc.

A drum machine is a percussion-oriented synthesizer that records and plays back rhythm patterns.

Because they're optimized for creating rhythm section parts, drum machines have several unique features. To begin with, they all have specialized onboard sequencers. Drum machine sequencers allow you to work in a small section, usually one to four measures long. The sequencer loops this short segment over and over as you pile on the different percussion parts. For instance, you might begin with the kick drum in a two-measure segment. As the two measures continually repeat, you play the kick drum part. Then while listening to the kick, you can add the snare drum. Then add the hi-hat or toms, and so on. The process continues until you have a complete

two-measure "pattern." After you create various patterns, you can string them together into longer sequences or "songs." Both songs and patterns can be stored in memory and recalled for future use.

To enter the notes into a pattern, drum machines provide several (usually about 12 to 16) oversized buttons or pads. Each pad is assigned a particular percussion sound. By tapping on the different pads, you can trigger the corresponding sounds. Good quality drum machines have Velocity-sensitive pads. They cause the drum sounds to respond in a more realistic way (usually getting louder or softer), by sensing how hard you tap the pads. Even drum machines that don't have Velocity-sensitive pads can usually respond to Velocity data when it's received from an external controller or computer.

The pads on a drum machine are a lot like the keys on a keyboard. Each represents a specific MIDI note number. This means that you can also trigger the drum sounds from an external piano-style keyboard by playing the appropriate notes. Most drum machines will let you remap the note numbers to provide a more convenient arrangement of keys.

Drum machines are handy, but not essential, components in a desktop system. Most of the pro-level sequencers now offer drum-machine–style recording capabilities that let you construct rhythm tracks using the same approach as dedicated drum-machine sequencers. Furthermore, virtually all synthesizers and sound modules include at least one—and usually several— drum sets as part of their collection of presets. In fact, all General MIDI instruments must have an onboard drum set available that can play on MIDI channel 10 (see Chapter 3).

tip *Many people find a drum machine to be a useful composing tool. If you have a computer, you can use the drum machine to produce the rhythm track and then transfer it to your software sequencer. After that, the drum machine can function as a drum-specific sound module under the control of the computer.*

MIDI Keyboard Controllers

If you're a keyboard player and you're shopping for a new synthesizer, it seems logical to look for one with an attached keyboard. Combining the keyboard with the sound source is, after all, the most popular approach to instrument design. Pianos, organs, and harpsichords have come that way for hundreds of years. But the advent of MIDI has now moved us decisively into the era of modularity. One look at the burgeoning marketplace for MIDI sound modules, and it's clear that people want the freedom to pick and choose their components individually.

Of course, keyboard synthesizers do offer some advantages. They can be useful for stage shows and certain kinds of live performances. And if you only own a single instrument, keyboard synthesizers make a convenient, well integrated device for playing and recording your music.

But they have disadvantages as well. Although most MIDI instruments will respond to MIDI's full range of 128 notes, some keyboard synthesizers come with as few as 49 or 61 keys. And the keyboards themselves are often less than ideal in terms of overall responsiveness and feel. But the biggest disadvantage is that as you acquire new instruments, your studio space will quickly be consumed by stacks of large, awkward keyboards.

A keyboard controller is a keyboard that generates MIDI messages, but does not produce any sounds of its own.

That's why a growing number of desktop musicians are designing their studios around a single master keyboard controller (Figure 4-14). *Keyboard controllers* send out MIDI messages, but they don't make any sounds of their own. They rely on sound modules, sound cards, or synthesizers to produce the actual sounds. A keyboard controller confers several important benefits. First, it lets you select the keyboard according to your specific needs and preferences. Second it lets you operate your studio from a single centralized position. And third, it saves you money and space. Furthermore, keyboard controllers by their very nature make it easy to add or subtract instruments from your MIDI setup and to control the instruments more efficiently.

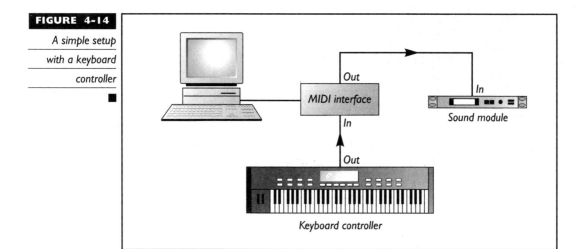

FIGURE 4-14

A simple setup
with a keyboard
controller

Keyboard controller

Important Features

Before buying a keyboard controller, you have a number of characteristics to evaluate; the keyboard range is one. Although there are keyboard controllers with as few as 25 keys, this is clearly too limiting for serious work. Pro- and semi-pro controllers always offer either 76 or 88 keys. Some inexpensive keyboards—designed for use with multimedia setups and/or sound cards—offer a 49-key range. This saves space on the desktop and cuts costs, but many users may find the range too restrictive.

Controllers with 76 keys are a good compromise for those who can't afford a full-size keyboard. They work well for most composing tasks and are suitable for playing most styles of music. If you plan to perform piano music, for instance, and your tastes run toward the early baroque period, a 76-key controller should work fine. On the other hand, if your repertoire includes much music from the late romantic period and the twentieth century, you'll want to move up to a full-size 88-note keyboard.

Because 88-note keyboards represent the top of the keyboard-controller line, they often include high-end features that make them especially appealing to serious musicians. For example, pro-level keyboards usually have weighted keys to more closely simulate the feel and responsiveness of acoustic pianos. Most synthesizers and inexpensive controllers, by comparison, use unweighted, plastic keys that feel much like those on an electric organ. Weighted keys are sometimes made of wood, and some companies even go so far as to incorporate a piano-like mechanism in the keyboard to approximate the resistance and touch of a piano. In a blindfold test, however, few people would confuse a quality grand piano with a MIDI keyboard controller. But if you're used to playing pianos, you'll probably adapt more easily to a keyboard with weighted keys. Nonetheless, many people prefer the lighter, faster, organ-like feel of unweighted keys. So, as always, your decision should be based on personal preference.

The list of additional features for a keyboard controller is largely a matter of its MIDI implementation. Bottom-of-the-line controllers send only Note On and Note Off messages. They sometimes lack Pitch Bend and Modulation wheels and seldom provide an alphanumeric display or additional front-panel controls.

At the other extreme, pro-level keyboards always include Velocity and Aftertouch sensitivity, Pitch Bend and Modulation wheels, assignable sliders for sending MIDI data (on different channels), a front-panel display, and numerous buttons for sending MIDI messages to your different instruments. They also provide sophisticated functions that let you adjust such things as Velocity responsiveness and keyboard splits. And you can expect to find several jacks for various kinds of footpedals.

Many kinds of keyboard controllers are currently available (Table 4-7). Prices range from as little as a few hundred dollars to as much as several thousand dollars. See Figure 4-15.

Alternative Controllers

Since the earliest days of electronic instruments, the piano-style keyboard has reigned supreme as the most popular type of input device for making music. It's easy to see why. A piano or organ keyboard is really nothing more than a row of buttons. And the simplicity of the one-button/one-note concept is hard to argue with. But not everyone is proficient with keyboard instruments, and this has disenfranchised many otherwise creative musicians who wound up on the outside looking in on the MIDI party.

Although alternative controllers have been around since MIDI's infancy, during the past years they have achieved a level of reliability and sophistication that makes them worth consideration. For guitarists, woodwind players, violinists, percussionists, or almost any kind of non-keyboard player, there are now several ways to join the MIDI bandwagon.

Company	Model	Keys	Velocity	Aftertouch	Pitch Bend	Modulation	Comments
Akai	MX1000	76-weighted	yes	yes	yes	yes	4 sliders, LCD display, advanced features
Fatar	Studio 49	49-unweighted	yes	no	no	no	1 MIDI out
	Studio 61	61-unweighted	yes	no	no	no	
	Studio 90 Plus	88-weighted	yes	no	yes	yes	
	Studio 2001	88-weighted	yes	yes	yes	yes	4 sliders, LCD display, advanced features
	CMS 61	61-unweighted	yes	no	yes	yes	Provides shelf for computer keyboard and mouse
Roland	PC-150	49-unweighted	no	no	no	no	Battery powered
	PC-200mkII	49-unweighted	yes	no	yes	yes	Data entry slider, front-panel buttons
	A-30	76-weighted	yes	no	yes	yes	Data entry slider, front-panel buttons, AC/DC
	A-80	88-weighted	yes	yes	yes	yes	4 sliders, LCD display, advanced features
Yamaha	CBX-K3	49-unweighted	yes	no	yes	yes	Especially designed for GM sound modules
	KX-88	88-weighted	yes	yes	yes	yes	4 sliders, LCD display, advanced features

TABLE 4-7 *MIDI Keyboard Controllers* ■

FIGURE 4-15

Akai MX1000,

Fatar Studio 2001,

Roland A-30,

Roland A-80,

Yamaha KX-88

Wind Controllers

If your primary instrument is the saxophone (or similar wind instrument), some excellent MIDI controllers offer uniquely sax-like expressiveness. The **Akai EWI3000** (Figure 4-16) uses a recorder-like fingering similar to that of a saxophone. The instrument has a special breath sensor, a lip sensor, and various touch sensors for controlling pitch shift, pulse width, vibrato, and glide.

A wind controller allows sax and woodwind players to control a synthesizer.

In addition to brass-like tonguing effects, the mouthpiece lets you change the pitch depending on how hard you bite. By varying the amount of bite pressure, you can produce a vibrato effect. Furthermore, depending on how hard you blow, you can also change the pitch, tone, and/or volume. With your right thumb you control two "plates" that let you bend notes up or down. And your left thumb can produce a glide effect by touching a Glide Plate. Or shift the note range over eight octaves with the Octave Shift Roller.

The EWI3000 is specifically designed to function with the **EWI3000m**, an analog synthesis sound module optimized for wind performance. The EWI3000m comes in a desktop design with a 16-character, backlit LCD display and 100 internal sounds. It's primarily a monophonic instrument, but it can mix two sounds together in Dual mode. Because the back panel provides a MIDI Out port, you can use the EWI3000 to control other MIDI sound modules or to enter data into a sequencer. A MIDI In port allows you to use it with other external controllers.

Looking like a space-age clarinet, the **Yamaha WX11** (Figure 4-17) takes a slightly different approach to wind-controlled synthesis. Its light-action keys use a standard Boehm fingering configuration, which will feel immediately comfortable to most players. The sax-like mouthpiece incorporates

---

FIGURE 4-16

The Akai EWI3000

FIGURE 4-17

The Yamaha

WX11

■

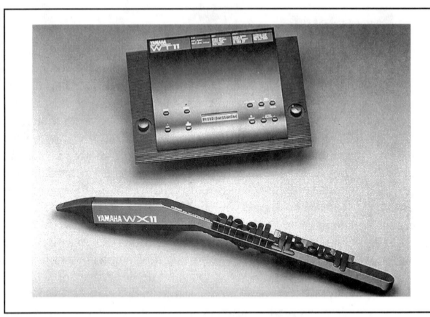

what Yamaha calls a "reed." The single, non-vibrating reed doesn't produce any sound on its own. It's simply there to provide a means of adding expressiveness to your music in a natural way.

By applying lip pressure to the reed, you can introduce vibrato and pitch changes to your playing. How hard you blow into the mouthpiece can affect parameters such as volume and timbre. Breath pressure can even substitute for lip pressure in sending vibrato information.

The WX11 has a range of over seven octaves and offers a number of unique features. The Key Hold feature, for example, lets you sustain a single note while you play phrases on top of it. And the two Trill keys can be used with any note to allow a variety of fingerings.

The other half of the Yamaha Wind MIDI system is the **WT11**. This desktop sound module uses FM synthesis (4 operators, 8 algorithms) and provides 8-note polyphony with ten onboard digital effects, including reverbs, delays, distortion, and echo. Its front panel includes a 16-character, backlit LCD display. The WT11 has tuning, lip pressure, and breath pressure utilities that optimize it for use with the WX11. It includes 96 performance combinations that specify sounds, effects, and vibrato settings, and you can add up to 32 more of your own.

In addition to its MIDI In and Out jacks, the WT11 provides a MIDI Thru jack that lets you drive any external MIDI sound module. You can even bypass the WT11 entirely by using an optional MIDI/power pack.

Guitar Controllers

Guitar controllers, in one form or another, have been around for a number of years. But not all efforts have been entirely successful. That's because guitars—unlike keyboards and wind instruments—are especially problematic when it comes to sending note information. With only six strings to handle several octaves of notes, the guitar's polyphonic capabilities, and idiomatic playing techniques that guitarists use, it takes a lot of sophisticated processing to produce reliable results. Recent refinements in hardware and software capabilities, however, have made guitar synthesizers truly viable as serious MIDI controllers.

A guitar controller allows a guitar player to control a synthesizer.

During the past decade, Roland has introduced several models of guitar synthesizer/driver combinations. Its most recent addition, the **GR-09** (Figure 4-18), should interest a great many guitarists. Its precise handling of data combined with its processing speed allow it to manage a range of guitaristic techniques, including hammer-ons, pull-offs, chokes, and bottlenecking.

To use the GR-09 Guitar Synthesizer, you must first install the **GK-2A** Synthesizer Driver. The GK-2A mounts easily—without tools—on any electric or acoustic steel-string guitar, regardless of body type. It provides a thin hexaphonic pickup that sits under the strings near the guitar's bridge. The GK-2A itself attaches to the pickup by a thin cable and provides the necessary connections to the synthesizer. A three-position switch lets you select the GR-09 output, the guitar's direct sound, or a mix of the two. A rotary knob lets you remotely set the volume of the synthesizer.

FIGURE 4-18

The Roland GR-09

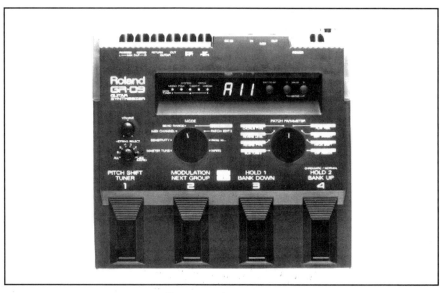

The GR-09 sound module, which is designed to sit on the floor, includes a three-digit LED display and four footswitches to access sounds and control various performance functions. The unit provides 28-note maximum polyphony and 180 PCM-waveform instrument sounds that are optimized for guitar-synthesizer applications. These include acoustic sounds, such as piano, strings, and brass, as well as synthesized textures. An optional expansion board lets you add another 180 sounds.

With the GR-09, you can assign a different MIDI channel to each string on the guitar or sub-group sounds as needed. This lets you play, for example, a flute part on the first string, piano on strings two through four, and a bass sound on the last two strings. You can also layer sounds, and each string can have its own transposition.

To round out the list of features, the GR-09 includes 56 built-in effects—31 types of reverb/delay and 25 types of chorus/flanger. The rear-panel MIDI Out port lets you send MIDI data to another sound module or to a sequencer.

If you're a keyboard player who's frustrated because you can't get up and dance around the way guitarists do, then help is on the way. Roland offers the **AX-1** (Figure 4-19)—a uniquely designed keyboard controller that attempts to bridge the gap between guitar and keyboard. The fire-engine-red AX-1 is similar to Roland's A-30 keyboard controller, except that it only has 45 unweighted, Velocity-sensitive keys. As with the A-30, the AX-1 provides a selectable Velocity curve (high/medium/low), an Octave Up/Down function that extends the keyboard range, and a Transpose function. It also provides an adjustable split point to give you two keyboard zones, and a set of front-panel buttons for direct access to General MIDI patches.

FIGURE 4-19

The Roland AX-1

■

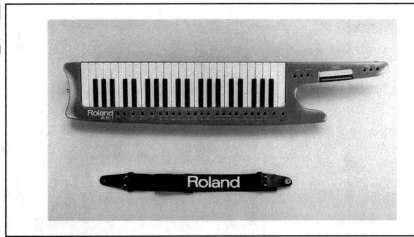

The most salient difference between the two keyboards (aside from color) is the AX-1's unique shape. The left side of the keyboard housing extends into a guitar-like neck, so you can hold the light-weight controller with a strap and play it like a guitar. The right hand plays the keys while the left hand operates a special built-in Expression Bar. The Expression Bar serves the same function as the Pitch Bend/Modulation lever on the A-30, but it works a little differently. Finger position left to right affects Pitch Bend, while downward pressure on the bar adds Modulation.

All in all, the AX-1 is an interesting hybrid controller. Keyboard players will appreciate the freedom that it affords—especially during live performances—and guitarists will enjoy the quirky design that packages a keyboard in a somewhat guitar-like form.

String Controllers

Guitars aren't the only stringed instruments that are being used as MIDI controllers. Orchestral stringed instruments, such as violins, violas, and cellos have also passed through the threshold of electronics and entered the world of MIDI. The leader in this field is Zeta Music Systems. It markets a complete line of MIDI-capable instruments as part of its **Quartet Series**. Aside from looking like works of modern art, these well-crafted, solid-body instruments come standard in high-gloss black or white lacquer and incorporate a number of innovative design features that enhance playing. The models include a four- and five-string Jazz Violin, a four-string Jazz Viola, and a four-string Cello.

String controllers allow violinists and other string players to control a synthesizer.

Zeta also markets several **RetroPaks**, which let you convert a standard acoustic instrument into a four- or five-string violin, four-string viola, or cello. The RetroPaks consist of a bridge/pickup assembly, an aluminum tailpiece with fine tuners for each string, a low-noise preamplifier, and a cable with locking connectors. The preamp comes housed in a small aluminum chassis that you can clip to your belt. The unit provides individual volume controls for each string and a multi-pin audio output jack for use with MIDI systems.

To use any of the Quartet Series instruments or any retrofitted acoustic instrument with MIDI, you'll also need the **Zeta MIDI System**. It's a two-part hardware setup, consisting of a rackmount interface and a dedicated footswitch assembly. The Zeta interface receives incoming audio signals from the multi-pin cable and rapidly analyzes the signals for pitch and amplitude information. The data is processed and sent to any multitimbral sound module or synthesizer. Because the Zeta MIDI System is fully polyphonic, it supports double and triple stops.

With the Zeta MIDI System, you can assign a different MIDI channel to each string, so each string can produce a different instrument sound. You can also adjust the Pitch Bend range of the violin (or viola or cello) in semitones to match the settings on your sound module. That helps the Zeta interface track correctly for glissandos and vibrato.

A Transpose function lets you change the pitch (in semitones) of any string over a six octave range. The Sensitivity function lets you set the amplitude threshold level that determines when a MIDI Note On message is sent (to accommodate different bowing styles). And a Dynamics Scale lets you set how much your sound module will respond to changes in playing loudness. The interface can also send Program Change messages as well as various types of performance data, such as Aftertouch, Volume, and Velocity.

The MFS-40 footswitch unit provides a two-digit LED display and five footswitches, which let you control such things as Sustain, Hold, preset selection, and MIDI Bypass.

In My Experience

If you feel a little overwhelmed when designing, assembling, or configuring your desktop studio, remember that electronic music has always been "fraught with peril." For example, the first time I used a synthesizer in a composition was in the mid-1970s. The piece was called "Tango for Flute, Bassoon, and Two Synthesizers." The synthesizers were the old, analog style, making them difficult to keep in tune. Further complicating things was the rather cumbersome and intricate method by which sounds were created. To create a sound, patch cords were used to connect a matrix of inputs to another matrix of outputs. By the time you were done creating a sound, the front panel looked like a plate of spaghetti.

The old analog synthesizers modified and shaped sounds by using a number of components with exotic sounding names, such as "ring modulators" and "low frequency oscillators." To create a specific effect, you might have to patch together several different components. This process was exciting but often arcane. For example, incorrectly patching the synthesizer was a common problem. And sometimes a combination of connections produced an unintended result. (One positive side effect of patching errors, however, was that occasionally an interesting new sound was discovered.) Generally, obtaining the specific sound that I wanted was a process of experimentation and trial-and-error.

While front-panel patch cords are now a thing of the past, you are still able to create your own sounds using MIDI synthesizers. The difference is that now the chaotic jumble of patch cords has been replaced by software. This not only makes things more orderly, but also makes it easier for you to change "patches" as you experiment.

Percussion Controllers

Drummers have come a long way since the days of pounding on hollow logs. The typical modern drum kit is a surprisingly complex set of devices that offers a great deal of potential for creating subtle and varied sounds. With improved synthesis and sampling techniques and faster data processing speeds, many drum qualities can now be successfully exploited. Drummers can now join the ranks of MIDI musicians by using their instruments to play melodies, chords, sound effects, electronic timbres, and, especially, powerful layered percussion sounds. And drummers can now use sequencers to record their live performances as well.

A percussion controller uses a drum pad or drum trigger to control a synthesizer.

The three leaders in the field are Yamaha, Roland, and a small company called KAT, which specializes in percussion controllers. Although each company's individual products may vary, they all must incorporate three basic components to form a complete system: one or more triggering devices, a trigger-to-MIDI converter, and a sound module. These may come as separate components or as all-in-one stand-alone units.

There are two types of drum triggers. One type consists of a small device (such as the Yamaha DT10 or KAT KDT 1) that attaches to an acoustic drum and converts each drum hit into an electronic pulse. These are useful for adding MIDI sounds to acoustic drum parts. And you can use acoustic triggers on a wide range of percussion devices, including non-traditional instruments.

An increasingly popular approach, however, involves special drum "pads" with built-in triggers. These pads are typically round rubber-coated discs, which clamp on to drum stands, so you can arrange them in a familiar pattern (Figure 4-20). They serve as triggers for snare drums, tom-toms, and cymbals. Some models, such as Roland's PD-7, Yamaha's EP75, and KAT's flatKAT, can produce two different trigger outputs, depending on whether you hit the main pad area or the rim. You can assign these triggers to different sounds, for example, snare drum and rim shot or normal cymbal and "choked" cymbal. But you can also assign them to completely unrelated sounds such as timbale and horn stab.

Hi-hats pose additional problems, because they sound differently when they're open than when they're closed. Roland markets a special pedal, the FD-7, that helps you capture the real tonal variations of a hi-hat, depending on how much you depress the pedal. Other companies use a footswitch in conjunction with a drum pad to produce the open and closed sounds. Special kick-drum trigger/pads, such as Roland's KD-7, Yamaha's KP75, and KAT's kicKAT, work in conjunction with traditional kick pedals.

Once you have your drum pads set up, you'll need a trigger converter to turn the drum hits into sounds. The converter takes the incoming signals and

FIGURE 4-20

Roland's Compact Drum System is shown here with eight PD-7 drum pads and the TD-7 Percussion Sound Module

■

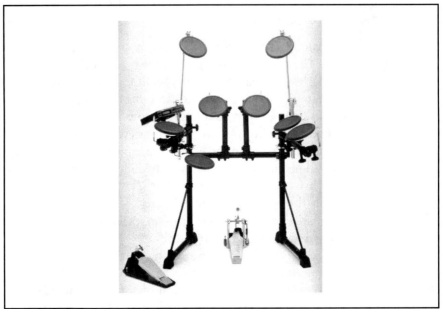

converts them into MIDI messages. Most trigger converters also include onboard sounds designed to work especially well with electronic drum sets.

Roland's **TD-7 Percussion Sound Module** provides up to 512 sounds—from standard drum sounds and percussion to specialized sounds and bass. It also provides onboard effects that include reverb, delay, chorus, and flanger. The TD-7 offers 14-note polyphony and allows you to store up to 32 Kits of different sounds. The front panel provides a 16-character/2-line LCD display, while the rear panel provides nine trigger inputs as well as MIDI In and Out ports.

Yamaha's **TMX Drum Trigger Module** shares a number of features with the Roland unit. It too uses 16-bit waveforms for its 245 sounds. It provides 16-note polyphony with storage for 32 performance setups (25 from the factory). The rear panel provides 12 trigger inputs and MIDI In and Out ports. The front panel includes a 16-character/2-line LCD display and a Zap button, which lets you quickly access certain voice parameters.

Not all drum pads come as separate components. A number of popular drum controllers come as a collection of small pads mounted in a single unit. One of the most powerful of these is KAT's **drumKAT 3.5**. It combines ten pads, nine trigger inputs, two MIDI Ins, four MIDI Outs with 32-channel capability, and a host of sophisticated features. The more affordable **drumKAT EZ** (Figure 4-21) looks the same as the 3.5, but it offers fewer features (such as six trigger inputs, one MIDI In, two MIDI Outs, 16

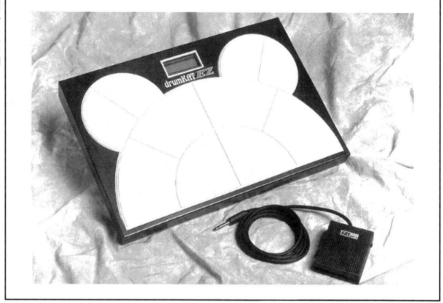

channels, and a smaller display). You can also get the same pad configuration in the entry-level **dk10**, which offers basic drum-pad capabilities.

Roland's **PAD-80 Octapad II** (Figure 4-22) features eight pads to which you can assign MIDI channels, note numbers, Program Change numbers, and other parameters. Each pad on the PAD-80 can control up to three MIDI notes with individual Velocities. In Mix Mode, you can trigger three notes simultaneously to create chord progressions or layered drum sounds. The Velocity-Mix Mode lets you set a different Velocity threshold for each note, so the sound becomes thicker the harder you hit the pad. The Velocity-Switch Mode lets can change from one sound to another, depending on how hard you play. To expand the system, you can add up to six external pads, for a total of 14 pads. The top panel provides three displays: a two-digit LED display for patch numbers, a 16-character/2-line LCD display for messages, and five LEDs to indicate Velocity. The rear panel provides MIDI In, Out, and Thru ports.

The **SPD-11**, also from Roland, looks much like the PAD-80, except that this unit includes its own sound source with 255 instrument sounds and 14-note polyphony. The SPD-11 also offers 25 onboard effects, including reverb, delay, chorus, and flange. The top panel provides eight pads, a three-digit LED display, and a dozen buttons for accessing and editing the built-in sounds. The rear panel supplies four additional trigger inputs and MIDI In and Out ports.

FIGURE 4-22

Roland's PAD-80

Octapad

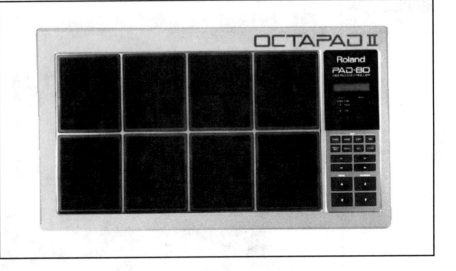

If you're a vibraphone or marimba player, you can now ply your trade with MIDI. KAT now offers a one-piece, three-octave mallet controller called the **malletKAT PRO**. Its surface looks much like a modern-day marimba, but instead of the tone bars there are a series of 39 neoprene pads (two of these are function pads). If you wish, you can add two more octaves, for a total of five octaves. The malletKAT has the ability to dampen notes and lets you sustain one note as you solo with another. It also allows you to split or double notes and provides a foot-function feature as well. You can store 128 setups (including MIDI channel, octave, minimum/maximum Velocity, Program Change, Volume, etc.). The malletKAT PRO includes three footswitch inputs and an LCD display.

Vocal Controllers

Whenever the topic of MIDI controllers comes up, someone always asks if there is a device that converts singing into MIDI data. Think of the possibilities. You just sing into a microphone and your performance is captured with a sequencer and transformed into printed music with a notation program. Or you sing into a microphone and your voice becomes a cello, or flute, or saxophone.

A vocal controller allows your voice to control a synthesizer.

In fact, there have been several such devices, called pitch-to-MIDI converters, over the years, but few have proven very successful. That's because the process of converting vocal music into MIDI data is enormously complex and fraught with pitfalls. For one thing, MIDI expects each note to be at exactly the right pitch—that's how it identifies the note number. If your singing is a tad out of tune (as nearly everyone's is), the converter must send an appropriate amount of Pitch Bend data along with each note number. Add volume changes to the formula, and you're suddenly dealing with huge amounts of data.

The other option is for the converter to guess which note you are intending to sing. If you're close in pitch to the note, this works fine, but if you swoop from note to note, as singers often do, the results can be highly unpredictable. Singing into a microphone may also produce unpredictable jumps in register, as the converter tries to decide—from the often complex timbres that voices produce—which octave you're in. You can also expect a slight lag after you sing a note before you hear a connected sound module respond. This makes converting rapid passages impractical.

All in all, pitch-to-MIDI converters are most effective when used with instruments that produce clear, stable tones without significant intonation problems. Pianos, clarinets, trumpets, and harps, for example, usually work better than the human voice. But this still leaves the question of how to convert the human voice into MIDI music.

One company, SynchroVoice, has come up with an innovative solution called the **MidiVox**, which works far better than previous pitch-to-MIDI converters. In fact, SynchroVoice doesn't even refer to its device as a pitch-to-MIDI converter, because the MidiVox doesn't convert audio signals to MIDI; instead, it reads and tracks vocal-chord movements and uses the information to generate MIDI messages.

The basic setup consists of a special polyurethane neck band, called a *biosensor,* and a single-space rackmount interface. Inside the neck band are four gold-plated sensors connected by a lightweight cable. To use the MidiVox, you wrap the band around your neck so the sensors are positioned correctly on either side of your Adam's apple. A six-foot cable then connects you to the rackmount unit. On the rear panel of the interface are two parallel MIDI Out ports.

Through the biosensor, the MidiVox determines the frequency and volume of your singing and converts this information into MIDI Note On, Pitch

Bend, and Volume messages. The unit provides two vocal range settings, designated Male and Female/Child. It also provides two volume-tracking modes, Variable and Fixed. In Variable mode, the unit responds to changes in your singing level by sending out Volume messages. In Fixed mode, all notes receive the same MIDI Volume setting of 64.

There are also two pitch-tracking modes as well: Continuous and Chromatic. Continuous mode sends Pitch Bend data along with the Note On messages. As you swoop and bend notes, the MidiVox sticks with you. In Chromatic mode (the hardest to control), the interface chooses the closest note to the pitch that you produce. In either mode, the MidiVox responds to the very first vibrational cycle of your vocal chords and instantly sends a Note On message. This combination of near-instantaneous response and isolation from extraneous audio interference enables the MidiVox to significantly outperform pitch-to-MIDI converters.

MidiVox holds great potential for both performers and students. It is already being used by universities for voice research, pitch training, music education, and other applications. And professional musicians are exploring its potential as well. At the very least, singers now have a way to join the MIDI club.

Pedal Controllers

If you're an accomplished organist and you want to expand your synthesizer's capabilities, you might consider adding a MIDI pedalboard. Fatar's **MP-1** (Figure 4-23) is a one-octave unit that offers a number of creative possibilities. With the MP-1, you can add bass lines with your feet as you play chords and melodies on your keyboard. Even non-organists can benefit

Pedal controllers let your feet control MIDI events.

from this controller. You can use it to play sustained notes, send Program Change messages, trigger percussion sounds, or send commands to a variety of MIDI devices.

The non–Velocity-sensitive MP-1 lets you transpose its range into any of eight octaves, and you can also select any MIDI channel for transmitting.

Mind Controllers

PC

Have you ever wanted to create music by just thinking about it? Well, WaveAccess might help you do it. The company offers a hardware/software combination that works with Microsoft Windows to turn "biowaves" into music. The user dons a head or arm band and connects it to the external **WaveRider** box, which in turn plugs into your computer's serial port. The

FIGURE 4-23

*The Fatar MP-1
MIDI pedalboard*

■

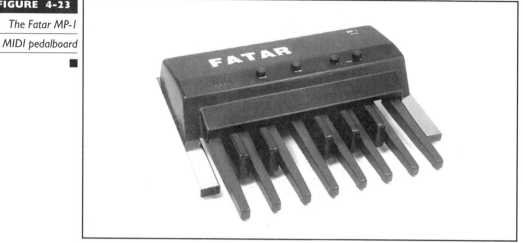

The mind controller is at the frontier of human/ synthesizer interfaces.

device collects a combination of data from your brain, heart, and muscles and also provides a measurement of skin resistance (galvanic skin response). All of these signals are acquired and processed in real time and displayed on the computer's monitor in several different formats.

The **WaveWare** software lets you map the data to any user-selectable notes, scales, keys, and Continuous Controller messages. By hooking up a sound card or MIDI sound module to the WaveRider, you can transform your mind's and body's biological signals into music. Of course, you're not likely to compose the next great American symphony by just "feeling" it. You might, however, come up with an interesting combination of sounds.

This product will certainly interest devotees of biofeedback, relaxation therapy, and avant-garde performance art, among others. As WaveAccess states, "By connecting their bodies and minds to their computers users can compose and perform musical works as well as gain insight into their creative states of consciousness." Welcome to musical cyberspace.

Other Controllers

The MIDI controllers covered in this chapter are by no means the only ones available. Innovative engineers are always developing new ways to manipulate MIDI data. We have controllers that use electrodes attached to a dancer's body to transform movements into MIDI messages. And sticks that you wave in the air, "harps" that use infrared light beams to send MIDI messages, and gloves that sense positions and proximity. The list will continue to grow and change, as new approaches come and go. Also, many retrofit kits are available that let an increasing number of acoustic-instrument musicians join the MIDI crowd. There are already MIDI organs, pianos, and accordions, and more are sure to follow, as players are drawn to MIDI's siren song.

Tape Recorders and Timecode

Most desktop musicians create their compositions by simply recording multiple performances—with multiple instrument sounds—into a sequencer. Once the piece is edited, the sequencer plays back the entire composition in real time. If you want to save your work in a convenient format, you can record it onto tape with a stereo tape recorder. This is analogous to the way recording studios have operated for years. Recording studios use multitrack tape decks to record a number of separate tracks that all play back together. The music on any given track never gets out of alignment with the other tracks, because all of the tracks are on the same physical piece of tape. Likewise, a sequencer's tracks always play back together, because the computer is running the whole show and makes sure that everything is working from a single reference.

What happens when you need to run a sequencer in tandem with a tape deck? That's when the problem of synchronization arises. But why use a tape deck in the first place? For one thing, if you write large, complex musical works and you don't have enough synths or sound modules (or external effects units) to cover all the parts, you can build your compositions a few tracks at a time by transferring them from the sequencer to a multitrack tape (Figure 4-24). In this way, you can also combine singing and performances on acoustic instruments with MIDI tracks. Furthermore, if you plan to do film or video scoring you'll need to synchronize your sequencer with a videotape deck.

The need to synchronize playback from and recording to a variety of different devices has given rise to a number of synchronization schemes. MIDI actually includes a built-in timing reference based on MIDI Clock messages. These real-time, music-based messages divide each quarter note into 24 pulses, to provide a common reference for keeping MIDI devices such as drum machines and sequencers in sync.

The device designated as the master derives its timing reference internally, while the slave unit—set to External Sync—derives its clock pulses from the master. But MIDI Clocks don't provide an absolute timing reference. That's because the elapsed time between clock pulses depends on the music's tempo. The various tempos used in a piece of music form a *tempo map* that's locked

in for that piece and can't be changed without losing the synchronization. Furthermore, MIDI Clocks aren't designed for use on tape. You can, however, convert the MIDI Clock pulses into a recordable sync tone called FSK (frequency-shift keying).

FSK sync tones use two alternating frequencies to provide the necessary timing pulses with the rate of alternation indicating the music's tempo. Once it's recorded on tape and played back through a converter, FSK supplies a master timing reference that a sequencer can follow. You just set your sequencer to Tape Sync or External Sync mode and start the tape rolling.

Unfortunately, FSK suffers from the same limitations—including low resolution and tempo-based format—as MIDI Clocks. Although FSK has enjoyed some popularity during the past years (many MIDI interfaces still support it), it has been far overshadowed by a much more accurate, more sophisticated, and more universal timecode format called SMPTE timecode. SMPTE (pronounced "simpty") stands for the Society of Motion Picture and Television Engineers, which adopted the timecode standard over twenty years ago for use in film and video applications.

SMPTE timecode works by stamping an elapsed-time designation on each frame of videotape. Unlike film, you can't see the frames on a videotape just by looking at it. But the frames are there nonetheless. SMPTE timecode identifies each frame in terms of hours, minutes, seconds, and frames (e.g., 04:57:23:19). Because most videotape operates at or very near 30 frames per second (fps), and because SMPTE timecode is accurate to within a small fraction of a frame, it enables devices to stay very tightly synchronized with one another. You can also use SMPTE timecode equally well with audiotape, even though it doesn't use frames. In the case of audiotape, the frames are simply treated as subdivisions of the seconds.

SMPTE is an acronym for the Society of Motion Picture and Television Engineers.

Here's how you work with SMPTE timecode and a multitrack recorder:

1. "Stripe" the tape with timecode. This means to prepare the tape by recording the timecode onto an empty track—preferably one of the

edge tracks—for the entire length of the tape. You can do this with any of the pro-level MIDI interfaces that have SMPTE timecode read/write capabilities built in.

2. Use an audio cable to connect the output from the timecode track to the Tape Sync input on the MIDI interface (Figure 4-25).

3. Open your sequencer program and set it to Receive External Sync mode. Click on the sequencer's Play or Record button and then start the tape rolling. The sequencer (acting as the slave) will wait until it receives the timecode signal and then instantly lock up to the tape and run in parallel. Most pro-level sequencers will also display the incoming timecode, which will appear as a series of double-digit numbers separated by colons (Figure 4-26). Additionally, the sequencers will translate the incoming timecode into measures and beats so you can work with more familiar musical concepts.

The role of the MIDI interface, therefore, is twofold. First, it generates the timecode so you can prepare the tape for playback. And second, it reads the incoming SMPTE timecode from the tape and converts it into MIDI timecode—a form of timecode, corresponding to SMPTE, that computer sequencers and MIDI devices can understand.

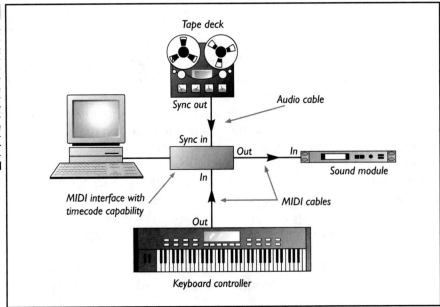

Tape deck

Sync out

Audio cable

Sync in

Out In

Sound module

In

MIDI interface with
timecode capability

MIDI cables

Out

Keyboard controller

FIGURE 4-26

This SMPTE

timecode display

from Mark of the

Unicorn's

Performer is large

enough to read

from across the

studio

■

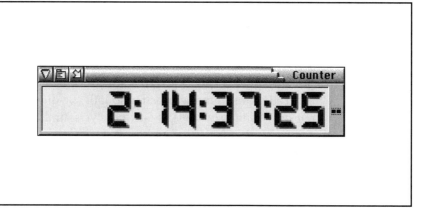

The procedure for working with videotape is essentially the same as for audiotape. In most cases, when a work print of a video is made, it will include a timecode signal on one of the audio tracks and a corresponding visual display (a timecode "window") superimposed on the picture. This *window dub* lets you see the SMPTE numbers fly by as the picture plays. With the SMPTE numbers on-screen, you can easily identify the start and stop times where music and sound effects need to be placed. The audio timecode—also known as *Longitudinal Time Code* (LTC)—is fed from the audio output of the video player to the MIDI interface, as described earlier. With the sequencer following the tape master, any music that you write will remain synchronized with the picture, no matter where or how often you start and stop.

Of Interest

SMPTE Frame Rates

SMPTE timecode can use any of several different frame rates. The original frame rate for black-and-white broadcasting was 30fps. When color television entered the scene the original frame rate had to be adjusted slightly to 29.97fps. A variant of this, called *drop-frame,* skips occasional numbers to maintain timing consistency. Film uses a 24fps rate and European television uses a 25fps rate.

Virtually all audio-only and black-and-white video applications use 30fps, so most of the time you can get along nicely with just that one rate. But if you plan to work with other studios or if you're interested in broadcast-related projects, you may need to use other frame rates. Not all SMPTE-capable devices read and write all formats.

Expanding Your System

A daisy chain is when several devices are connected in a series so that the output of one device feeds the input of the next device, and so on down the line.

It's a simple fact of human nature. We always seem to need more than what we have on hand. And when it comes to MIDI equipment, this axiom is especially true. It's hard not to want just one more sound module. Maybe you need more sounds, or better sounds, or different sounds. Especially if your only sound source is an inexpensive sound card, sooner or later you'll want to break out and expand your musical palette. Fortunately, the people who brought you MIDI anticipated this condition and included in the MIDI Specification a quick and easy means to add instruments to your system: the MIDI Thru port. You just connect the MIDI Thru port of one instrument to the In port of another, and connect that instrument's Thru port to the In port of another, and so on (Figure 4-27). In this way, you can *daisy chain* two or more sound modules or other MIDI devices. And all you need to add is another MIDI cable for each new device.

But the MIDI Thru port is an optional part of the MIDI Specification, and some MIDI devices (especially non-musical ones) don't have one. Furthermore, as your system grows to include four or five or more sound modules, daisy chaining becomes less desirable. Some people worry about "MIDI lag"—a cumulative delay that arises after the MIDI signal is transferred through several devices. In fact, MIDI lag (except in extremely large systems) is nowhere near the problem that most people fear, and its effects are

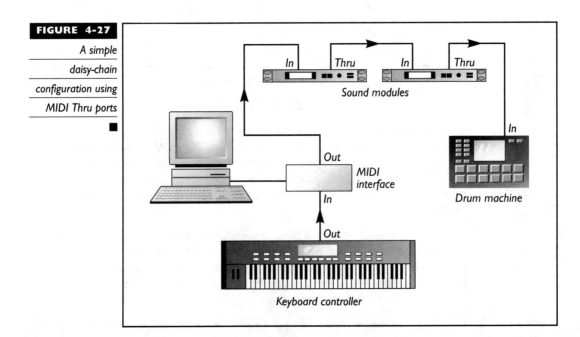

FIGURE 4-27

A simple daisy-chain configuration using MIDI Thru ports

Sound modules

Drum machine

In
Thru
In
Thru

Out
MIDI interface
In

In

Out

Keyboard controller

generally unnoticeable. What most people think is MIDI lag is more likely the result of a slow attack characteristic of a particular sound.

Even so, there's a better way to expand your system that is both theoretically and practically more satisfying. By using a MIDI interface with multiple Outs, you can arrange your devices in a configuration like a star network (Figure 4-28). That way, the MIDI messages are sent simultaneously to all instruments in the system.

A MIDI Thru box splits the output from one device into two or more ports.

If you don't have a multiple-port interface, you can buy a *MIDI Thru box* (Figure 4-29). You just connect the Out from the interface to the In on the Thru box and the data is passed along to several additional ports. There are also more elaborate devices called *MIDI patchbays*, which provide several Ins and Outs for routing the data, so you can reconfigure your system in a variety of ways.

There are several advantages to using a multiple-port configuration. First, it's much easier to add, subtract, or rearrange your sound modules when they're not daisy chained. It's also easier to troubleshoot problems by turning units off and on or removing them from the system. And finally, a multiple-port setup will put to rest any worries about MIDI lag. Furthermore, if your MIDI interface has true multiport/multichannel capabilities, you can break MIDI's 16-channel barrier and expand your sound-handling capabilities as well.

FIGURE 4-28

With a multiport MIDI interface, you can configure your system more efficiently

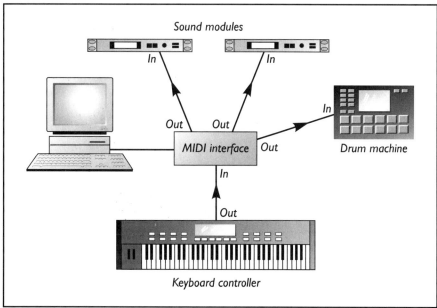

Sound modules

In   In

Out   Out

MIDI interface   Out

In

Drum machine

In

Out

Keyboard controller

FIGURE 4-29

*ForeFront
Technology's FT5
MIDI Thru box
functions as a
single 1-In/8-Out
unit or as two
1-In/4-Out units*

■

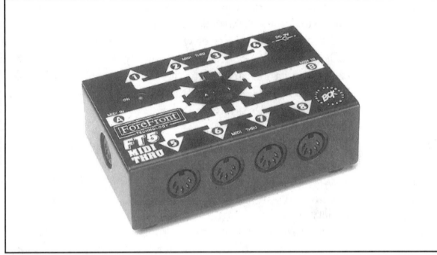

Mixing It Up

In order to hear music from your MIDI system, you'll need to amplify the audio signals from the instruments and send the signals to a set of speakers. If your desktop studio only has a single sound module or synthesizer, then the procedure is simple. Just take the stereo output from the sound module and plug it into your stereo system or into a set of amplified speakers. But once you start adding more instruments, you run into a problem. Suddenly you're faced with several sets of outputs and only one input on your amplifier. It's time to buy a mixer.

A mixer combines two or more audio signals into a single stereo output.
In the simplest terms, a *mixer* is a device that accepts audio signals from several different sources and combines them into a single stereo output. There are mixers that handle as few as four channels of audio and others that handle many dozens of channels. Some mixers sit nicely on the desktop (Figure 4-30), others are rackmountable, and others—like those in recording studios—take up the better part of a room.

For a small MIDI studio, a rackmount *line mixer* may be enough: it will provide a set of knobs and/or faders to control the different audio signals as they're being mixed. Typical controls on a small mixer include knobs or faders to control individual volume levels, knobs to adjust pan position (left/right balance), knobs to let you add effects (such as reverb) from external devices, and sometimes, knobs to add equalization (bass/treble boost or cut) to a signal.

The number of channels that you'll need depends on the number of outputs provided by your synths and sound modules (some provide more

than two), whether your system includes a tape deck, and if you'll be adding audio from other sources, such as singers and acoustic instruments.

Many sequencers now include on-screen faders that let you send MIDI Volume messages to your instruments (Figure 4-31). With these, you simply set your hardware faders to a good all-around setting. Then you do the actual mixing from the computer by changing the volume of each instrument sound. The great thing about MIDI faders is that (in many programs) you can automate their movements and save the settings to disk.

Desktop Speakers

At the end of the audio chain, the speakers transform electrical impulses into actual sounds. As the physical interface between music-machine and human

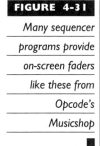

FIGURE 4-31

Many sequencer

programs provide

on-screen faders

like these from

Opcode's

Musicshop

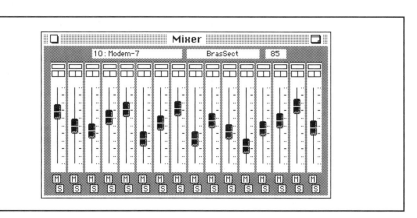

hearing, their function is therefore very important. With the music marketplace now heavily populated with 16-bit sound cards, samplers, and sound modules, new demands are being placed on speakers.

Many people just use a home stereo to serve as an audio playback system. This works fine if you can do it. But sometimes the stereo is in another room, or it doesn't have any extra inputs, or other people need to use it while you're working. Furthermore, many people just don't have the space to keep a stereo system near their computer. Fortunately there's a solution to this problem—desktop speakers.

Desktop speakers come in a wide variety of shapes and sizes, but they all share three important characteristics. First, desktop speakers must be magnetically shielded to prevent stray magnetism from distorting the images and colors on your screen. In most cases, you'll have to place the speakers near your computer monitor to produce the proper stereo image for close-range listening. Magnetic shielding makes this possible and also reduces the risk of data loss to nearby floppies—although you still shouldn't place a disk directly on any speaker. Second, desktop speakers include built-in amplifiers to boost the line-level output from sound cards, MIDI sound modules, and mixers. Integrating the amplifier with the speaker helps reduce desktop clutter and makes setup and operation easy. Finally, these speakers are compact, to conserve valuable desktop real estate; and they're easy to move around.

Drivers

Aside from the obvious cosmetic differences, speakers vary considerably in their internal designs. The individual sound-producing components in each speaker enclosure are called *drivers*. The simplest speaker design employs a single driver to reproduce the entire sound spectrum. Other designs use specialized drivers that are optimized to reproduce specific frequency ranges.

An individual speaker component is called a driver.

A *two-way* system uses a driver called a *tweeter* for the high frequencies and a separate driver called a *woofer* for the low frequencies. *Three-way* speakers add another driver between these two called a *midrange*.

In theory, using specialized drivers to divide up the frequency range should produce better results. High-end systems typically use two or more drivers in each speaker. But the number of separate drivers per se is not a guarantee of superior sound quality. That's because speaker design and quality vary so much from one manufacturer to the next. In fact, some of the best sounding desktop speakers use the fewest number of drivers. Therefore, driver configuration alone is not necessarily the definitive gauge of audio fidelity.

Because desktop speakers are small, they often have difficulty reproducing very low frequencies. To overcome this limitation, some manufacturers offer systems that include (in addition to the stereo speakers) a third speaker called a subwoofer. The *subwoofer*—optimized for frequencies below about 100Hz—can sit on the floor beneath the desk to provide the low frequencies lacking from the stereo "satellite" speakers above. Very low frequencies are primarily nondirectional in nature, which means it's often hard to tell precisely where they're coming from. A single subwoofer unit placed on the floor can do a good job of providing the low bass response, while the satellite units above handle the higher (and more directional) frequencies and provide the sense of stereo separation.

Amplifier Output

The integrated amplifiers in desktop speaker systems are designed to handle the line-level signals coming from sound cards, MIDI modules, and other similar hardware. But the amount of power that the amplifiers deliver to the drivers varies considerably from one model to the next.

The speakers mentioned in this chapter have power output ratings that range from as few as 10 watts to as many as 35 watts per channel. In general, the more power a speaker system has, the greater the volume it's capable of producing without distortion. But speaker construction and driver efficiency vary quite a bit from product to product. *Efficiency* refers to the ease with which a driver responds to an amplifier's signal. An efficient driver requires less power to produce a given volume than an inefficient driver. This is not necessarily related to sound quality, but it's important to keep in mind. Because some drivers need less power than others, the rated output of a speaker's amplifier does not tell the whole story about that speaker's potential loudness. That's why output power is best viewed as an approximate guide to potential volume.

Frequency Response

The range of frequencies that a speaker can reproduce (within a set of specified tolerances) is referred to as its *frequency response*. Here, again, is another possible source of confusion. Although people hear frequencies ranging from approximately 20Hz to 20kHz, small speaker systems seldom match that range entirely. Most people will not mind a somewhat narrower frequency response if distortion is kept low. But if too much bass is missing, music will sound thin and lack substance. And if too much high-end is missing, music will lack clarity and crispness.

As a general guide, therefore, the wider the frequency response, the better. Even though two brands of speakers might cover the same audio range, however, they will usually emphasize or de-emphasize different frequencies within that range. That's why two different speakers can have the same frequency response and yet sound totally different (and produce different amounts of distortion as well). It's therefore best to consider frequency response as a general rather than a definitive indicator of sound quality.

tip *When you begin scrutinizing printed specifications it quickly becomes clear that they often tell you more than you want to know about some things and much less than you need to know about others. Therefore, the best policy when shopping for speakers is to listen before buying. And don't forget the other important features, such as the number of inputs and the type and number of front-panel controls. Depending on your specific needs, these factors might weigh heavily in favor of one model over another.*

Looking Around

The sudden explosion of interest in multimedia has brought with it a new interest in audio. As a result, desktop speakers have begun popping up left and right. Unfortunately, most of the hundreds of models that are currently available are not suitable for serious work with music. If your primary computing activities consist of playing Flight Simulator and listening to system beeps, a $20 set of speakers may suffice. But music demands higher standards for audio quality. Table 4-8 shows a few top-of-the-line models from some well-known companies. These speaker systems range in price from about $150 to around $400 (retail). They won't sound as good as a set of pro-level studio monitors, but they keep your setup compact and they'll work well with your computer.

note *All specifications were supplied by the manufacturers themselves.*

See Figure 4-32.

Company	Model	Watts per Channel	Drivers	Inputs	Frequency Response	Comments
Advent	Powered Partners 570	35	1-inch tweeter, 5-inch woofer	1	40Hz–25kHz	Wedge-shaped, aluminum alloy enclosures, AC/DC
Altech Lansing	ACS 300.1	18	0.5-inch tweeter, 4-inch woofer, subwoofer	2	35Hz–20kHz	Unique clamshell design allows for different positions; DSP control simulates stereo
Apple	AppleDesign Powered Speakers	N/A	Single 2.5-inch	2	N/A	Active EQ and noise reduction circuitry
Labtec	CS-1400	15	2-inch tweeter, 3-inch woofer	1	60Hz–20kHz	
Monster Cable	MacSpeaker/ Persona PC	10	Ribbon tweeter, 2-inch midrange, 3-inch woofer	1	75Hz–18kHz	Sonic imaging control simulates stereo
Roland	MA-20	15	Two-way coaxial design, 5-inch woofer	3	N/A	Can mix inputs with front-panel controls
Yamaha	YST-M10	10	Single 3.5-inch	1	80Hz–20kHz	Spruce wood cones; "presence" control

TABLE 4-8   *Self-Powered Desktop Speakers* ■

FIGURE 4-32

Clockwise from top left: Advent Powered Partners 570, Altech Lansing ACS 300.1, Monster Cable MacSpeaker/Persona PC, Yamaha YST-M10

■

CHAPTER 5

Working with Sequencers

A s I mentioned in Chapter 2 the great RCA synthesizer of 1955 marked a milestone in the evolution of electronic composition. Its ability to generate rich musical timbres, however, was only part of its legacy. Just as important was the fact that you could program it to generate a series of tones along with settings for timbre, duration, and other parameters. The RCA synthesizer used a paper input roll to store its data and in so doing employed a method of reproducing music that resembled the method used by the player pianos of the nineteenth century.

Of course paper rolls do not directly produce musical sounds the way a phonograph record does. Instead they provide the necessary performance data that enables an instrument to create the sounds. When MIDI came along decades later paper rolls, cards, and other similar storage methods had already been replaced by floppy disks and hard drives. And the initially primitive programs that grew out of the early electronic studios quickly gained in sophistication. Now anyone with a personal computer can manipulate musical elements in ways that were undreamed of as recently as 20 years ago. With a nod to the past, however, we still think of composing electronic music as programming a series or *sequence* of events. And the hardware or software that you do it all with is therefore called a *sequencer*.

A sequencer allows musical events to be recorded, edited, and played.

There have been stand-alone hardware MIDI sequencers for many years, but they can't begin to compare with the power and versatility that you get from a computer-based sequencer. Because of its graphical user interface, the Macintosh quickly established itself as the platform most preferred by professional musicians. Hampered by the unfriendly DOS environment, the PC lagged behind in the evolutionary process. Now, however, with the introduction of Microsoft's Windows, the PC is rapidly closing the gap, and currently several powerful, pro-level programs are available in versions for both platforms.

What Is a Sequencer?

A sequencer is a lot like a multitrack tape deck. It lets you record and play back performance data the way a tape deck records and plays back audio signals. And like a tape deck, today's sequencers let you create compositions of enormous complexity involving a great many instrumental sounds.

But a sequencer's capabilities go far beyond those of a tape recorder. With a good sequencer you can edit your work down to a gnat's eyelash. You can change instruments, transpose sections up or down, insert or delete a single note or a large segment of music, nudge a note forward or backward by a few milliseconds, and straighten out the rhythm from a sloppy performance. Fixing most common mistakes is a breeze. And you can even enter passages that would otherwise be impossible to perform in real time.

You might think of a sequencer as a sophisticated word processor for music. And the frequent use of commands like Cut, Copy, and Paste tend to bolster the analogy. Just as a word processor lets you view and modify your work before it goes to its final output stage—the printer—a sequencer lets you do the same before your music goes to its final output stage—the sound module. That's why you can do things with a sequencer that a tape recorder could never do, such as change the tempo of a piece without changing its pitch or copy a passage over and over without degrading its audio quality.

In Control

All sequencers provide you with some variation of the familiar tape recorder metaphor. So one of the first things you see when you start a sequencer program is a set of transport-like buttons. They let you shuttle from place to place in a sequence and provide the same Play, Record, Stop, Fast-Forward, and Rewind functions as on a tape deck (Figure 5-1). Since there is no tape to shuttle back and forth, these controls all act instantaneously. When you push the Rewind button, for example, you're immediately relocated to the beginning of the sequence. Many sequencers also let you enter a measure and beat location, which they'll shuttle to in a fraction of a second.

The Record button on a sequencer lets you capture your MIDI performance in real time. Most mid- to pro-level sequencers provide several recording modes including Replace, Overdub, and Punch In/Out. Replace mode is

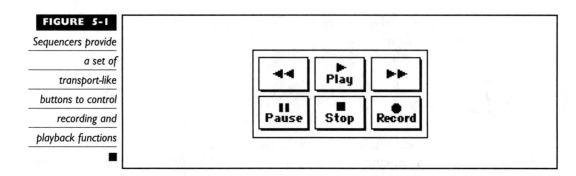

FIGURE 5-1

Sequencers provide a set of transport-like buttons to control recording and playback functions

---

Overdub mode lets you record a new passage of music over an existing passage without erasing the earlier material.

the most common. It replaces any existing material with new performance data as you enter it. With Replace mode you can repeat a performance over and over while only retaining the most recent "take."

By contrast, Overdub mode does not replace existing data. With each pass through a section of music the new material is added to the old. This makes it possible to build up a line of music with successive performances.

Punch In/Out mode lets you specify a section in the middle of a piece where you want the sequencer to automatically enter and then leave Record mode. This lets you insert a few notes or several measures of new material (in real time) without disturbing the surrounding music.

Making Tracks

Each performance that you record with a sequencer is assigned to one or more *tracks*. These "virtual" tracks are analogous to the physical tracks on a multitrack recorder. When you click the Play button all of the tracks in the sequence play back together.

Sequencer tracks are where you store musical performance data for the different parts of your composition.

It's important that you not confuse tracks with channels. Tracks hold the individual performances that together form a sequence. They can contain anything from a single note to thousands of notes and other types of messages. Channels are the numerical designations that determine which instruments will receive which MIDI messages.

In most cases you'll want to assign one channel for each track. The track numbers and channel numbers, however, need not agree. You might, for example, decide to assign track 1 to produce a flute sound on channel 2. Track 2 might produce an oboe sound on channel 5 and track 3 might produce a guitar sound on channel 11. Some entry-level sequencers limit you to this one-track/one-channel arrangement. They consequently provide only 16 tracks—one for each MIDI channel.

More advanced sequencers are not so limiting. They may provide 100 or more tracks (depending on how much RAM you have). These sequencers also let you assign two or more MIDI channels to each track. You might, for example, have a trumpet sound on channel 4, a violin on channel 6, and a piano on channel 9. All three sounds could then be assigned to track 7. When that track plays back, all three instrument sounds will respond to the same performance data. This is a quick and simple way to layer sounds, and it encourages textural experimentation.

Most sequencers also let you do the reverse. They let you assign several tracks to a single MIDI channel. You might, for example, have the right-hand piano part on track 1 (channel 8) and the left-hand part on track 2 (channel 8). That way you get the same instrument sound from both tracks but you can edit each part separately.

tip   *Assigning several tracks to one MIDI channel is especially popular with drum parts. You can place the hi-hat on one track, the snare drum on another, the toms on another, and the kick drum on yet another. This "exploded" drum part lets you shift the instruments in relation to one another to adjust the "feel." Or you can apply global editing commands to only a single instrument or group of instruments.*

It's easy to see that a sequence can quickly build up a number of tracks, so to help you stay organized most sequencers provide some kind of Tracks window (Figure 5-2). Although the appearance and name varies from program to program, the Tracks window always serves the same basic function. It shows the track names in a column along with the assigned channels and often includes some indication of which measures contain MIDI data. To let you hear different combinations of tracks most sequencers also provide a Mute and a Solo button for each track.

Behind the Counter

Somewhere close to the transport controls, all sequencers provide some kind of counter display. The counter shows you the current location within a sequence in terms of elapsed measures, beats, and subdivisions of a beat known as ticks, clocks, parts, or *pulses* (Figure 5-3). The number of subdivisions determines the sequencer's *resolution*. An entry-level program may provide a resolution of less than 100 ppqn (pulses per quarter note), while pro-level sequencers commonly provide resolutions well above 400 ppqn.

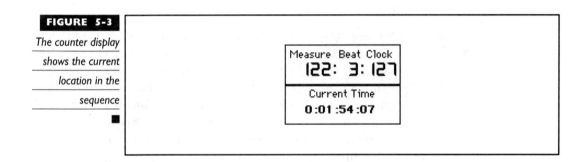

FIGURE 5-2

A typical Tracks window

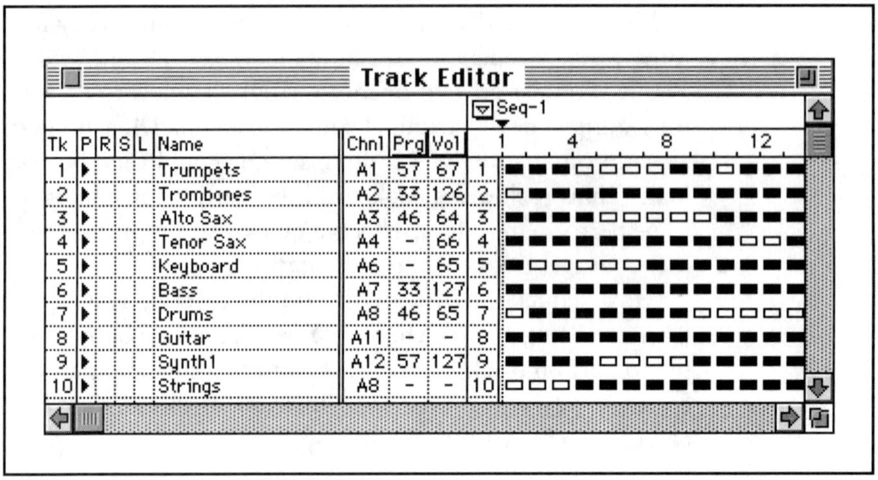

Track Editor

Tk	P	R	S	L	Name	Chnl	Prg	Vol				
1	▶				Trumpets	A1	57	67	1			
2	▶				Trombones	A2	33	126	2			
3	▶				Alto Sax	A3	46	64	3			
4	▶				Tenor Sax	A4	–	66	4			
5	▶				Keyboard	A6	–	65	5			
6	▶				Bass	A7	33	127	6			
7	▶				Drums	A8	46	65	7			
8	▶				Guitar	A11	–	–	8			
9	▶				Synth1	A12	57	127	9			
10	▶				Strings	A8	–	–	10			

A sequencer's resolution determines the smallest time interval that it can distinguish.

Resolution is an important consideration when shopping for a sequencer. It determines how precisely the sequencer will capture the subtle rhythmic nuances of each performance. If you write jazz or classical music or you'll be using your sequencer for film scoring, a high resolution (over 400 ppqn) is a desirable feature.

Aside from capturing your performances more accurately, high-resolution sequencers also enable you to make extremely precise adjustments while editing the rhythmic placement of notes. For most people a resolution of 240 ppqn or higher should work fine. Lower resolutions will suffice for those whose editing demands are minimal. Some sequencers actually allow you to choose one of several resolutions to optimize processing performance.

In addition to the usual measure, beat, and subdivision display, many counters show elapsed time as well. Pro-level sequencers also include a SMPTE timecode readout for those who work with film and video.

FIGURE 5-3

The counter display shows the current location in the sequence

Measure Beat Clock
122: 3: 127

Current Time
0:01:54:07

On the Beat

One essential feature that all sequencers offer is a metronome. It helps you keep the beat as you record and provides a uniform reference for all the tracks in a sequence. Most sequencers will generate a metronome pulse that plays back through your computer's speaker. Ideally, the sound—which may be a tick or a beep—should not have a specific pitch. Pitched beeps can drive you crazy if they're not in the same key as your performance. Furthermore, metronome beeps that come from the tiny speaker in your computer can easily get buried as the music gets louder. In many cases, you can route the metronome's audio signal from your computer (or from some PC MIDI interfaces) to your mixer to amplify the sound as needed.

Most sequencers now offer a good alternative. They let you assign a MIDI note number (and channel) to act as the metronome beat. This lets you choose an appropriate unpitched sound—like a rim shot or wood block—or a pitched sound that won't clash with your performance (Figure 5-4). The metronome pulse coming from your synthesizer is then amplified along with the other MIDI sounds.

Most sequencers offer several ways to use the metronome feature. For starters, you can set a *count-off* before the downbeat to establish the tempo

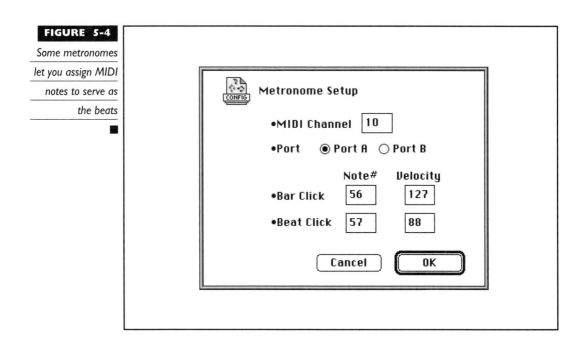

FIGURE 5-4

Some metronomes let you assign MIDI notes to serve as the beats

and to give you time to prepare. The best programs let you set any length for the count-off while others always use a default value—typically one or two measures. You usually set the metronome tempo with an on-screen slider that shows the current setting. Sometimes the tempo slider is part of a separate Conductor window.

Following the count-off you can have the metronome sound during recording and playback, only during recording, or not at all. The most sophisticated sequencers even let you play freely and add the bar lines later by tapping on your keyboard in time with the music.

tip   *If you've never played with a metronome before, it will most likely feel awkward at first. Don't worry, you'll soon become accustomed to it. In fact, after you get used to working with a metronome, you'll probably find that you don't notice that it's there. However, if you find that playing along with a metronome beat is just too unmusical, try recording a basic rhythm pattern from a drum machine. That may provide a slightly more musical reference to play against.*

Recording Events

Recording with a sequencer is actually quite simple. First be sure that your MIDI equipment is properly hooked up and that the MIDI channels are assigned to the proper instrument sounds. Then make sure that the "Thru" function in your sequencer is set correctly so you can hear your music as you play it. In most cases the procedure for real-time recording is as follows:

1. Set the tempo and the metronome count-off.

2. In the Tracks window, record-enable the track where you want your performance to appear. Also remember to assign the MIDI channel that you want the track to play back on.

3. Click the Record button in the transport controls.

4. After listening to the count-off begin your performance.

5. When you're through, click the Stop button and then the Rewind button.

6. Disable the track's record function.

7. Click the Play button to hear your performance.

Once you've recorded the first track you can listen to it while recording another track. Simply repeat steps 2 through 7. You can then listen to those two tracks as you record another track and so on. If you're having difficulty with a particular passage you can always set the tempo lower during recording and raise it during playback. You can also keep different versions of a performance on different tracks. Then you can select the best parts of each and by cutting, copying, and pasting them together create a single perfect performance. If an otherwise good performance is marred by a section with mistakes in it you can use the Punch In/Out recording mode to lay in a better performance just where it's needed.

Step on It

Real-time recording is generally the fastest, easiest, and most musical way to create MIDI music. There are times, however, when a piece of music is just too hard to play, even by slowing down the tempo. Or in some cases a piece may actually be physically impossible to play. That's why most sequencers provide a second recording method called *step-time* recording. In step-time recording you enter notes one at a time without regard to tempo. The usual procedure involves first selecting a rhythmic value (whole note, half note, etc.) and then playing the desired key on your MIDI keyboard to assign the pitch. The better sequencers will let you enter chords as well as single notes.

The note and rest durations are typically displayed on a menu or palette that makes it easy to switch from one value to the next (Figure 5-5). In spite of this, step-time recording is often rather tedious. Furthermore, since all durations are precisely accurate and the note placement is always rhythmically perfect the music comes out sounding rigid and mechanical. Some sequencers include a "humanize" function that lets you add small amounts of randomness to a passage, but it's hard to capture the true feel of a real-time performance.

---

t i p *Sometimes, interesting musical effects can be generated by playing a series of notes very rapidly (that is, playing the notes faster than is humanly possible). For example, an arpeggiated chord produces an interesting effect when played extremely fast. Step-time recording is a good way to experiment with such techniques.*

In the Loop

Some sequencers also include a third method of recording called *loop recording*. This is sometimes referred to as drum-machine–style recording because it uses the same approach as drum machines use. In loop recording

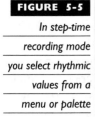

FIGURE 5-5

In step-time recording mode you select rhythmic values from a menu or palette

A loop is a section of music that plays repeatedly.

you specify a number of measures or beats that you want to cycle over and over again. Then using the overdub recording mode you perform in real time as the section repeats. You can add new notes with each pass while listening to the previously recorded notes and in so doing you build up the track by layering new performances on top of old. This technique is most often used for creating rhythm parts but it has other useful applications as well.

Editing

Recording and playing back MIDI music is actually only one part of what a sequencer does. The real power that sequencers bring to desktop music making comes from the editing capabilities that they offer. Unlike a simple tape recorder, once you have your basic tracks in place you can modify your music in myriad ways, making adjustments that range from infinitesimal to global. And to accomplish this in the most effective way possible sequencers allow you to view your MIDI data in a number of formats. In addition to the Tracks window mentioned earlier, there are several other windows that sequencers often include.

Composing with a sequencer is not the same as composing with paper and pencil. When working on paper, you can easily see the entire score laid out before you. From this vantage point, it's readily apparent how each part relates to the others while you compose. You can easily add notes to the flute part, for example, and then skip to the violin part and then to the trombone part as needed. The relationship between the parts is always in full view.

Getting from part to part using a sequencer is a little more cumbersome. Your approach to composing,

therefore, has to be adjusted to the nature of the desktop medium and, additionally, to the type of music that you're writing. For instance, when I'm writing in a classical style, I will most often start with the melody line. From this cornerstone, I then add harmonies and counter melodies to fill out the orchestral texture. Popular and commercial styles, on the other hand, are generally built upon a rhythm section. You need to first record the rhythm part as a foundation and then build the rest of the piece upon it. Many styles of jazz rely heavily on chord progressions. So, in this case, I might record

an accompaniment part first and then add solo parts on top of the harmonies.

Even though each style of music uses a different approach they all begin with a single track (or tracks) upon which the other parts are built. As you will see, most often the first track becomes the reference point for the entire piece. Remember, when working electronically, you can always go back and change anything about any of the previous parts. And, unlike working with paper and pencil, you also have the advantage of being able to hear how all the parts fit together as you go along.

The Event List

Most sequencers can show you any track's performance data in a chronological, alphanumeric display called an *event list*. The Event List window (Figure 5-6) includes every Note On message in the track along with other relevant information including the pitch, velocity, and duration of each note. Event List windows can also show other types of data including Pitch Bend, Modulation, Volume changes, pedal messages, tempo changes, patch changes, and more. Sometimes these are identified with a small icon that indicates the type of data that is represented on that line.

An event list contains the chronological record of the performance data contained in a track.

Having so many types of data displayed in a single area makes the Event List window an important tool for locating and correcting problems. It also provides the greatest amount of information in the smallest space of any of the editing windows. If you want to correct a wrong note on the third beat

FIGURE 5-6

A typical Event List

window

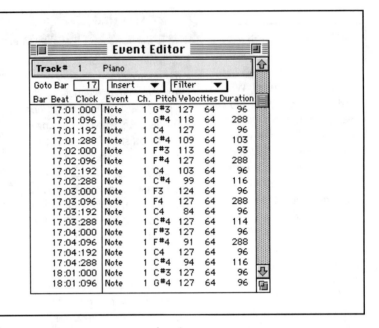

of measure 27, for example, you simply scroll down to the appropriate line, highlight the desired parameter, type in the right information, and you're on your way.

Event lists do, however, have some disadvantages. If the track is filled with lots of notes and other information—especially if the events don't fall close to the beats—it can be difficult to locate the note that you're looking for. Furthermore, a chronological list is not always the best way to view music. Counterpoint can be especially frustrating to decipher since notes from the different melody lines will be intermingled in the list. That's why most sequencers now include a more graphical display of MIDI data.

The Piano-Roll Display

Event lists provide lots of useful information but they don't do a very good job of conveying a sense of what's happening musically in a piece. So most sequencers provide a type of graphical editing window known generically as a *piano-roll display*. That's because its appearance is reminiscent of the old player-piano rolls (Figure 5-7).

Piano-roll displays indicate the musical pitches vertically along the left side of the window, while the measures (elapsed time) are indicated along a horizontal scale. Against the resulting grid, the notes appear as lines or bars of varying length. The length of each bar indicates the note's duration while

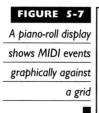

FIGURE 5-7

A piano-roll display shows MIDI events graphically against a grid

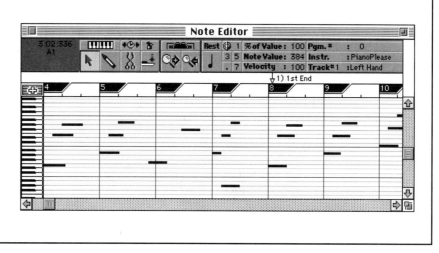

the position of the bar—higher or lower—indicates its pitch. This provides a view of the music that in some ways resembles traditional notation. As the notes go up in pitch they appear higher on the grid and the bar lines clearly show each note's position in the measure.

In fact, piano-roll displays have many advantages over standard notation when it comes to editing MIDI data. For instance, standard notation might show a quarter note on the second beat of the measure, but a piano-roll display would also show that it was played slightly behind the beat. You can then select the note by clicking on it and move it so that it's dead on the beat if you want. Or you might move it farther away from the beat to give it a more laid-back feel. In either case you can make extremely fine adjustments of just a few ticks one way or the other and view the changes in the graphic display.

In some programs you can also drag notes from one pitch to another to correct wrong notes or to change harmonies. By selecting a note or group of notes you can quickly delete them or copy and paste them to another location. Most sequencers also provide a tool that lets you insert a new note anywhere you want.

To view other types of data like Pitch Bend, Volume change, Modulation, and Velocity some piano-roll windows include a display area that shows these messages graphically. This additional display usually appears below the main grid area and shows the specified MIDI data in the form of a bar or line graph. With this display you can select and edit many types of continuous controller data the way you can with Note On and Note Off messages. You can also apply global editing commands to any selected region of the data.

The Notation Window

The piano-roll display provides a great tool for viewing and editing MIDI data and, with a little practice, anyone can become quite adept at using it. Still, many people feel more comfortable working with traditional music notation. In fact, during the past couple of years there has been a significant trend by music software developers to include notation windows in their sequencers (Figure 5-8). The competition from the marketplace has now produced a number of sequencers that offer notation capabilities that rival dedicated music manuscript programs. Much of this attention to improved notation capabilities is certainly an attempt by developers to attract new customers. But notation windows do offer several advantages over other types of displays.

Although traditional notation doesn't provide much information about the subtleties of a performance, it does give you an excellent view of what is happening musically in a piece. For instance, locating a wrong note in a seven-note chord is not always easy in a piano-roll display, which presents you with a stack of little black bars that all look alike. With notation, on the

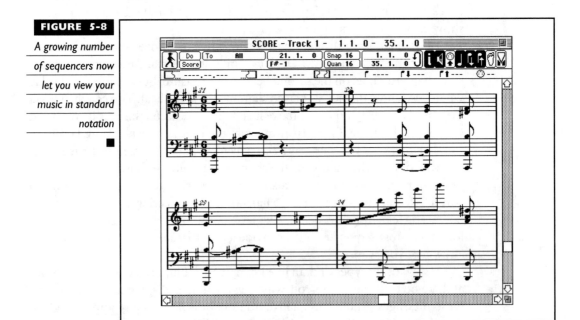

FIGURE 5-8

A growing number of sequencers now let you view your music in standard notation

other hand, it's a snap to pick out the G-sharp in a C major chord. Then all you have to do is select the errant note, enter the correct pitch and you're through. This sense of musical context is especially helpful when you're working with melodies. And counterpoint often becomes clearer when it's viewed in standard notation.

Notation windows do have disadvantages however. For one thing, some programs don't make very efficient use of on-screen real estate. To maintain legibility, standard notation must have space around the notes. This may make it hard to view a large number of measures at once. If you zoom out too far the notation quickly degenerates into a jumble of overlapping note heads, flags, and accidentals.

Furthermore, it's often difficult for the software to interpret your MIDI performances into notation. You may find yourself staring at a thirty-second note tied to a sixteenth note tied to an eighth note tied to a quarter note just because you were a little slow hitting one note of a chord. Most sequencers provide ways to clean these problems up, but it takes a little extra effort to produce usable notation. Once you have your music in notation format, however, you can print out the results. This is very useful if you're preparing music for later performance on acoustic instruments.

Other Windows

In addition to the editing windows that I've already mentioned, sequencers may employ a variety of other types of displays as well. For instance, rather than include an extra display area within a piano-roll window some sequencers provide additional windows dedicated to different types of data including Pitch Bend, Modulation, Tempo, Velocity, etc.

Most sequencers also provide some kind of Faders window. These on-screen controls are usually applied to Volume changes but the more advanced software also lets you assign them to control all kinds of other MIDI messages. In some of the pro-level sequencers the Faders window has been expanded to include an array of customizable knobs, switches, and sliders that you can configure any way you want to create individualized control panels.

A few sequencers also provide a special window for producing drum patterns. They let you drag little symbols—representing the different percussion notes—onto a grid that shows elapsed time (Figure 5-9). You may appreciate this approach to developing drum patterns, especially if you have experience working with drum machines.

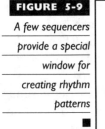

FIGURE 5-9

A few sequencers provide a special window for creating rhythm patterns

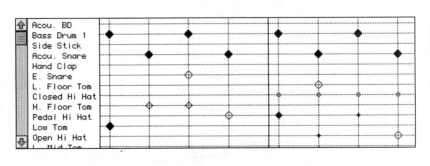

Quantizing

One of the great things that a sequencer can do is to clean up sloppy rhythms in a performance. This process of correcting the rhythmic placement of notes is called *quantizing*. When you quantize a number of notes the sequencer shifts their positions in time to align them with the nearest beat or division of a beat. Here's how it works. First you specify a level of quantization such as quarter note, eighth note, sixteenth note, etc. The sequencer then moves all of the selected Note On events to coincide with the nearest specified division (Figure 5-10).

Quantizing is the process by which the timing of a note is shifted to align it with the nearest chosen metrical subdivision, such as a quarter note or eighth note.

If you quantize to the nearest quarter note, for example, and you play a note slightly behind the beat, the note will be shifted forward so that it's precisely on the quarter note beat. A note played slightly ahead of the same beat will be shifted back until it's sitting exactly on that beat as well. Any notes that are already on the beat will be left alone. If a note is too far away from the beat it will be shifted to another quarter-note beat that is closer. This can occasionally produce some surprising results so it's best to start with a small quantization level such as sixteenth notes. This will keep the notes from moving too far.

In most cases you'll only quantize the beginning of the notes while leaving the duration the same. Some sequencers let you quantize both the beginning and the duration of the notes. You can quantize a chord and have all of its notes occur at exactly the same time. Or you can quantize a string of eighth notes and have them play back in perfect rhythm.

FIGURE 5-10

A group of notes
shown before and
after they are
quantized

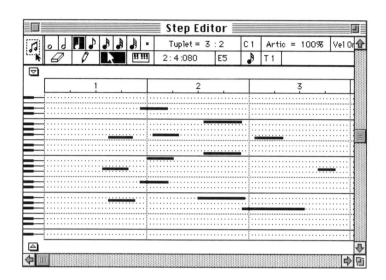

Before

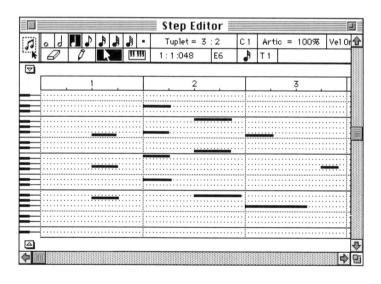

After

Of Interest

Problems with Quantizing

Since quantizing brings your performance into perfect timing, it sounds like a terrific idea. But, unfortunately, it's a double-edged sword. Quantization can make your music so rhythmically perfect that it sounds completely unnatural. Music depends on the small variations in performance to give it life. For most styles of composition, overly quantized music tends to sound robotic and dull. This is the same problem that occurs when too much of a piece is entered with step-time recording.

For this reason, professional-level sequencers often provide a number of options to help combat the mechanical sound that quantizing typically produces. Some sequencers provide a "humanize" function that adds small programmable amounts of randomness to the rhythmic placement of notes. Other programs let you specify a variable amount of quantizing "strength." You might, for instance, specify a strength of 50 percent. That will cause notes to move only half way from where they are to the nearest beat. The rhythmic placement of the notes will therefore be improved but not made perfect. Another option—sensitivity—lets you determine how close or far away a note must be before it is affected by quantization. Most programs make you quantize after you've entered the notes. A few sequencers also let you quantize on input the way drum machines do.

The bottom line is that quantizing is most effective when it's used with discretion. Grabbing everything in a sequence and quantizing it will probably make the music worse than if it had been left alone. Your best bet is to choose the areas that really need quantizing and leave some imperfections throughout the rest of the piece. That way you can have the best of both worlds.

Getting Organized

Sequencers take different approaches to organizing their data. These approaches fall roughly into two camps: linear- and pattern-oriented. Linear-oriented sequencers encourage you to build up your compositions by combining tracks into complete through-composed works. With a linear sequencer you think first in terms of the tracks and then how they'll combine to form the whole.

Although with a pattern-oriented sequencer you still work with tracks, the overall design of the program encourages you to create smaller sections—often called subsequences or parts—and chain them together to form the completed work—also called a song or arrangement.

Both systems work equally well but they do assume a certain mind-set on the part of the user. If you write mainly classical-style music or music for films you might prefer the linear approach. If, on the other hand, you write in mainly jazz or pop styles you'll appreciate the pattern-oriented approach. It lends itself especially well to structures like Verse A, Chorus, Verse B, Bridge, Verse C, Chorus, etc.—where each section is a subsequence and the sections combine to form the complete piece.

The truth is, however, that the distinction between these two approaches is rapidly becoming blurred beyond recognition. The natural cross-pollination that exists in the field of music software has caused sequencers to adopt many of the characteristics of their competitors. This has also had an effect on the overall structure of the programs. Most pattern-oriented sequencers, for example, will let you create subsequences of any length. So if you want to use a through-composed style of writing simply work within a subsequence and don't combine it with anything. On the other hand, many linear-oriented sequencers now let you chain together different sequences to form larger pieces. In that way they can function much like a pattern-oriented program.

Although the issue of compositional approach has become less crucial during the past few years it still influences the general look and feel of a program so it's worth considering when you go shopping for a sequencer. In the next chapter we'll take a close look at several popular sequencer programs to see what makes them tick and to help you find the right software for your desktop studio.

CHAPTER 6

Comparing Sequencers

O F all the different types of software that desktop musicians use, none are as vital to the creative process as a good sequencer. If you're serious about making music with your computer you can expect to spend many hours looking at and working with your sequencer. You'll get to know all of the little nooks and crannies that form the architecture of the software and you'll either be amazed and pleased by them or you'll be hindered and frustrated by them. That's why it's a good idea to choose a sequencer first and then buy the computer that will run it.

Of course in the real world this isn't always possible or practical. So the next best thing is to explore the many programs that are out there and find the one that most comfortably fits your composing needs and your budget. Fortunately, there are many excellent sequencers available for both the Mac and the PC and they come with a wide range of price tags. In fact, the overall level of software sophistication has now reached the point that even some of the entry-level programs are surprisingly powerful.

When you go shopping for a sequencer there are a number of characteristics that you should be aware of. Here are several to consider:

THE FEATURE SET Since all sequencers are not created equal, it's important to have a clear idea of your needs. The lack of only one or two crucial features can make a sequencer aggravating to use. On the other hand, some programs are so laden with arcane functions that they just get in your way. If you're new to this whole business of MIDI music-making then an entry-level program might be a good place to start. They're inexpensive and readily accessible. But if you aspire to professional-level composing and music production you're better off starting with one of the high-end programs. They're not necessarily harder to use and they provide sophisticated editing features that you'll probably need eventually.

THE PRICE As a general rule, you get what you pay for. Pro-level sequencers often cost as much as $500 or more. But they offer a very high level of sophistication as well as many essential features for pro-level work. Entry-level programs typically cost less than $200. They provide a basic feature set without a lot of bells and whistles. If your needs are modest look at these. Also keep in mind that a number of companies let you upgrade from an entry-level program to a pro-level one if your needs expand. It's worth asking about.

LOOK AND FEEL Both Macintosh- and Windows-based sequencers depend heavily on graphics. The quality of the graphics, the text areas, and the overall layout of the editing screens varies quite a bit from one program to the next. Although some people may dismiss this as mere cosmetics, most people will appreciate having an attractive (and uncluttered) user interface. After all, you may be staring at the screen for hours at a time and it doesn't hurt to have something pleasant to look at. Also, most sequencers are adding better support for color. If you have a color monitor this might be worth taking into account. When used effectively, color can definitely add functionality to a program.

COMPOSING APPROACH Every sequencer offers its own unique approach to creating music. Some programs, for instance, are based almost entirely on standard notation. Others implement notation as a side feature or not at all. Some programs offer a number of different ways to tackle a given problem while others are more limited. If you write in a verse-chorus-verse style of music, consider a program that lets you chain together sections to form a whole sequence (see Chapter 5).

SPECS For an absolute beginner with minimal needs, specs may be largely unimportant. But for more advanced users, comparing specs can pay off in the long run. The number of tracks, for example, can make a big difference if you write complex arrangements. Entry-level sequencers sometimes offer as few as 16 tracks while high-end programs can offer over a hundred. Resolution is another important consideration with numbers ranging from less than 100 ppqn to more than 900 ppqn (see Chapter 5). And don't forget support for SMPTE timecode if you work with film or video.

In My Experience

Because I use sequencers professionally, I often find myself in the position of evaluating their relative merits. Over the years, I have developed a fairly standard review procedure. You may find it useful too.

After installing the sequencer and confirming that everything is working OK, I take a quick look through the menu headings, open all the windows, examine the main options, and try to get a general feel for the architecture of the program. Next, I take the program out for a "test drive." To do this, I usually import a MIDI file that I already have. It's interesting to see how the music appears in the different windows and how the information is presented. I also compare the display capabilities of the new sequencer with the one I'm currently using. It's revealing to see what type of data the new sequencer does and doesn't display.

To get a sense of how intuitive the program is to use, I try manipulating several of the various musical parameters. For example, if the program has a piano-roll display, can you stretch notes? Can you select noncontiguous notes? Can you drag a group of notes or only one note at a time? These are all things that give you a sense of the sequencer's flexibility and versatility. Also, they quickly let you know whether the dynamics of the user interface match your composing style.

Even though I have reviewed many sequencers over the years, after my initial tour of the system is complete, I always sit down and read the manual to learn the deeper aspects of the program. The manual often alerts me to unique features and capabilities that I might have otherwise overlooked. It also tells me the design limits of the sequencer.

To help make choosing a sequencer easier, the rest of this chapter is devoted to a comparative description of the most popular sequencers currently available for the PC and the Macintosh. In these reviews I present the main structural components of the different sequencers in more or less the same order. That should make it easier to relate the elements of one program to their counterparts in other programs.

The best way to proceed is as follows: first skim through the descriptions, noting those that seem the most appropriate to your needs. Then, go back and compare the features of the ones you picked. After narrowing your list, make your final determination by actually trying out each remaining candidate, if possible.

Performer

MAC

Mark of the Unicorn's **Performer** has been around almost as long as the Macintosh itself. In the early days of MIDI it quickly gained a loyal following and it continues today as one of the most popular pro-level sequencers for the Mac. Performer boasts an extensive list of sophisticated editing features and numerous editing environments, yet its logical and intuitive design make it relatively easy to learn, in spite of its complexity. The excellent documentation helps as well.

With Version 5, Performer has added a number of new features and a jazzy new look that includes 3-D graphics and full support for color. Long-time Performer users will be pleased that the overall structure of the program is the same.

The new version of Performer runs in conjunction with FreeMIDI, a system extension that in many ways resembles OMS (Open Music System) from Opcode Systems. With FreeMIDI you create a setup document by arranging icons in a window. The icons—representing your MIDI devices and serial ports—are connected with on-screen cables to provide a graphic representation of your MIDI system. This information is then shared with any program that uses FreeMIDI and allows the programs to refer to MIDI devices by name.

Controls

When you open Performer the first thing you see is the Consolidated Controls panel. It includes a Metronome window on the left, a set of transport controls in the middle, and a counter display on the right (Figure 6-1).

The Metronome window shows the current tempo and meter. A Tempo Slider lets you change the tempo in real time by dragging its triangle indicator. You can also vary the tempo remotely from an external MIDI source using the Pitch Bend or Modulation wheel.

The Counter display—with its mock LED numerals—shows the current playback/recording time in bars, beats, and "ticks" (pulses). Performer has a resolution of 480 ppqn. Beneath the main display an auxiliary display shows elapsed time or SMPTE timecode.

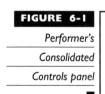

FIGURE 6-1

Performer's

Consolidated

Controls panel

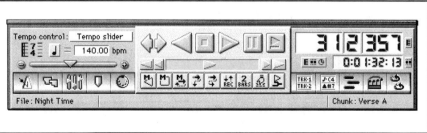

Tracks

In Performer the process of composing begins with the Tracks window (Figure 6-2). You can have an unlimited number of tracks depending on your available RAM. Each track appears as a horizontal row that you can move up or down in the list and record- or play-enable as needed. Performer lets you choose which types of information will appear in each track including such things as device names, track names, patch names and/or numbers, and comments. You can also include a small level meter for each track that shows MIDI activity during playback—a nice touch.

On the right, the Tracks Overview lets you see where the music in the different tracks starts and stops. The colored segments in the grid contain music or other MIDI data. Dark-colored segments indicate dense data, light-colored segments indicate less data. You can drag segments to move them and cut, copy, and paste between tracks.

The Solo button above the Track list lets you isolate a track or tracks during playback. The Solo button also provides a unique "partial-solo" mode. In this mode the non-soloed tracks have their volumes (velocities) brought down by a selectable amount instead of being muted completely. This lets you emphasize certain tracks while still hearing the others—very handy.

Event List

Once you've recorded one or more tracks, Performer lets you view and edit the MIDI data in a number of ways. The Event List (Figure 6-3) shows all of a track's MIDI data in chronological order.

FIGURE 6-2

Performer's Tracks window

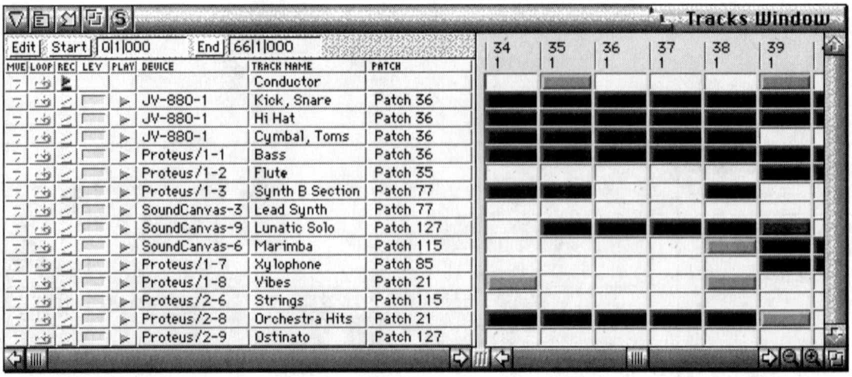

FIGURE 6-3

Performer's Event

List window

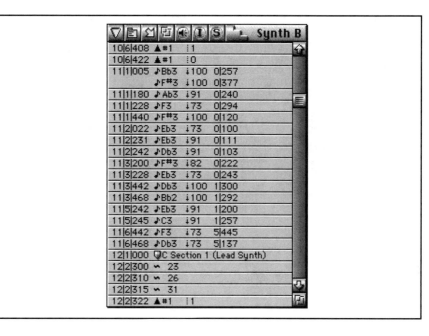

You can select events by clicking on them one at a time or by dragging through them. Performer even lets you select non-adjacent events. This is an important editing capability. A View Filter lets you limit the types of data that are included in the list, so you can focus your attention on certain kinds of events.

The button with the small speaker on it activates Audible mode, which lets you hear each note as it's selected. This helps you find your way around in the track and may point out a wrong note or two.

Graphic Editing

The Graphic Editing window (Figure 6-4) displays notes in a familiar piano-roll format. You can select a note by clicking on it or you can select several notes by dragging a selection box over them. As in the Event List you can also select non-adjacent notes.

Clicking any key on the vertical keyboard selects all of the notes in the track at that pitch. This is especially useful for editing drum parts since each key represents a different instrument sound. Once a note is selected you can drag it up, down, left, or right. A group of selected notes will move together as a unit.

Beneath the Note Grid a second display called the Continuous Data Grid shows the various types of MIDI data that affect the notes above. Tiny icons represent different kinds of MIDI data, which can include such things as Velocity, Volume, Pitch Bend, Modulation, and other controllers.

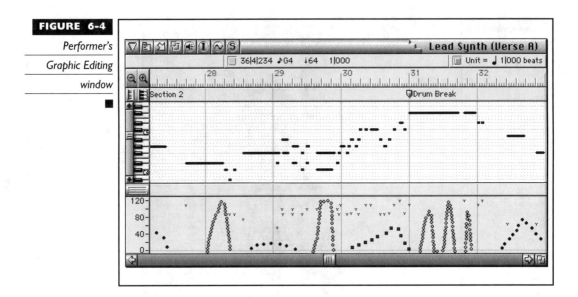

FIGURE 6-4

Performer's

Graphic Editing

window

Notation

Performer's QuickScribe Notation window (Figure 6-5) can display (and print) the music from one or more tracks using standard musical notation. Its intuitive design makes it an effective tool for both composing and editing. You can enter notes easily by choosing a note value from the tool palette (in the upper-left corner) and then clicking on the staff where you want the note to appear. You can also enter notes using the Mac's keyboard or you can step-record notes and chords from your MIDI controller. Selecting notes for editing is much the same here as in the Graphic display. Once a note is selected it can be dragged up or down in pitch and moved to another beat or measure.

When you open a MIDI file in the QuickScribe window Performer visually "quantizes" the music to provide a cleaner more normal appearance to the notation. The music itself, however, is not changed so it plays back with the same feel as the original performance. This gives you the best of both worlds—legible notation with accurate playback.

The notation window also lets you enter text for titles, tempo markings, instructions, and other things.

Other Windows

In addition to its main editing windows, Performer provides other windows that let you control and assemble your music. Chief among these is the Song window (Figure 6-6). Although Performer began life as a strictly linear,

FIGURE 6-5

Performer's

Notation window

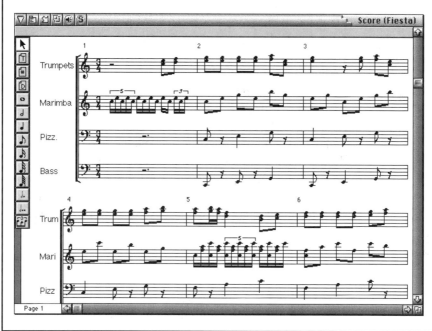

track-oriented sequencer, it has borrowed some ideas from other programs to accommodate songwriters and those who prefer a more pattern-oriented approach to writing.

The Song window lets you build a larger piece by combining sequences (and even other "songs") into a larger work. The sequences are then referred to as Chunks and you combine Chunks by simply dragging and dropping them into the Song window where they'll play seamlessly from one to the next. You can even stack Chunks to make them play simultaneously. The usual Cut, Copy, and Paste commands are available as in other windows.

FIGURE 6-6

Performer's Song

window

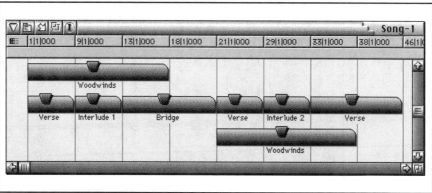

After you record and edit your music Performer lets you control the playback with on-screen faders. Although most sequencers now provide some kind of fader window, Performer goes one step further by allowing you to create your own custom control panel (Figure 6-7). It can include various kinds of sliders (large or small, vertical or horizontal) and an assortment of knobs, buttons, pop-up menus, and value boxes. You can use these controls for just about any musical purpose that involves sending and receiving MIDI data.

To help you troubleshoot problems in your MIDI system, Performer thoughtfully includes a MIDI Monitor window (Figure 6-8). It provides a display for each device in your setup. Small boxes that represent the different MIDI channels light up to indicate the presence of incoming MIDI data on those channels. This is a very useful feature and one that all sequencers should adopt.

More Editing

Once a region of notes is selected, Performer offers you a wide variety of sophisticated editing capabilities. And it's typical of Performer to provide an assortment of options within each editing function to let you fine-tune your work. The Transpose function, for example, does more than just move a bunch of notes up or down. In Performer you can change notes by interval or diatonically. And you can transpose a passage from major to minor or from any key and scale into any other key or scale.

Editing of velocities, tempos, and durations is similarly flexible. You can limit values to a specific range, add or subtract a fixed amount, or change values by a percentage. A Humanize function lets you apply a random factor to any of the same types of data.

FIGURE 6-7

Performer lets you create custom control panels

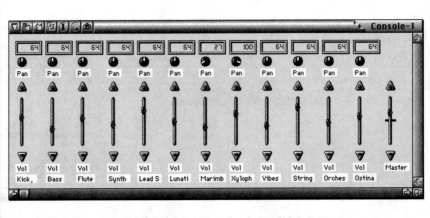

FIGURE 6-8

Performer's MIDI
Monitor window

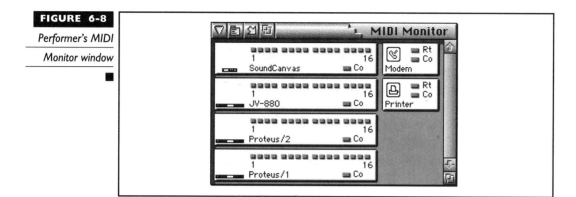

Performer's quantizing capabilities are even more elaborate. Standard quantizing options include settings for sensitivity, strength, swing, and amount of randomness. A Smart Quantize function prepares tracks for importation into a notation program. Deflam aligns the notes in a chord so their attacks sound together. And the recently introduced Groove Quantize function brings to Performer a feature that some other sequencers—most notably Cubase—have had for some time.

In musical terms a *groove* is a particular rhythmic feel that results from a combination of variables including note timings, durations, velocities, and other things. Performer lets you treat these variables as a template that you can apply to any rhythm track to give it a more life-like feel. A unique graphic slider interface (Figure 6-9) lets you control how much timing, velocity, and duration effect is applied to the track. You can create your own grooves or use one of the 50 professional grooves supplied with Performer. You can even import grooves created in Cubase.

FIGURE 6-9

Performer's Groove

Quantize dialog box

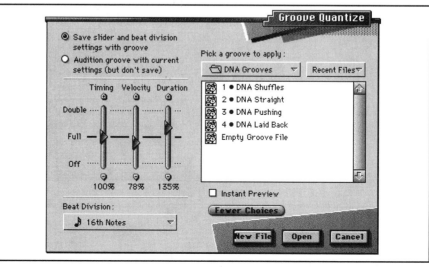

MAC

Unisyn

Although Performer doesn't include patch editing capabilities, Mark of the Unicorn does market **Unisyn**—a separate editor/librarian program that integrates especially well with Performer. In fact, Unisyn runs in real time with Performer and lets you play a sequence while you edit your patches. Unisyn also shares its patch lists with Performer so your studio configuration is always kept up to date.

Unisyn provides comprehensive cataloging and database functions that include the application of user-definable *keywords* to identify patch characteristics. Unisyn's Find command (Figure 6-10) then lets you search for patches by combining keywords with qualifiers (And, Or, and Not) to arrive at likely choices. If you're the experimental type you can even create new patches using Unisyn's Random Patch Generator or you can use the Blend and Mingle feature to combine characteristics from two patches into a hybrid patch.

Unisyn's real power, however, lies in its intuitive editing screens. The program supports over a hundred different MIDI devices with on-screen control panels called templates or *profiles* (Figure 6-11). Unisyn's profiles—which include sliders, pop-up menus, and envelope graphs with grab bars—are consistently well-organized and clearly drawn. They make patch editing a whole lot easier than most MIDI devices do with their tiny front-panel displays and confusing hierarchical menus.

FIGURE 6-10

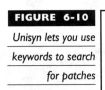

Unisyn lets you use keywords to search for patches ■

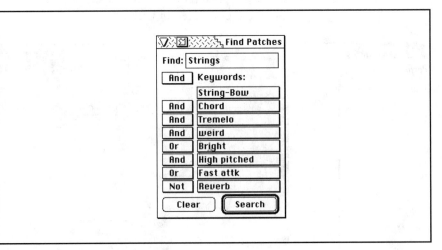

FIGURE 6-11

Unisyn's Patch Edit

window

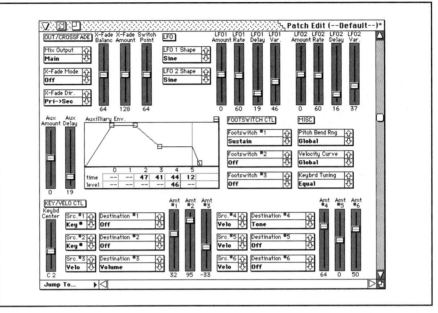

Master Tracks Pro

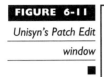

PC

MAC

CD-ROM

Since 1987 **Master Tracks Pro** from Passport Designs has sustained a well-deserved reputation for being one of the most straightforward and intuitive pro-level sequencers. The Macintosh version (Master Tracks Pro 5) and the Windows version (Master Tracks Pro for Windows) are essentially the same program with only a few minor differences. The Windows version, for example, has more of a 3-D look in its toolbars and buttons and also uses color in a few of its details. The monochrome Mac version is plainer but more legible and has a few extra features. Overall the two programs maintain the same look and feel.

Controls

The Transport window (Figure 6-12) provides six buttons to operate the sequencer. On the right side of the window a second set of buttons activates such things as the auto-return function, the metronome click, and the count-off (one measure only). One of the buttons also lets you select any of

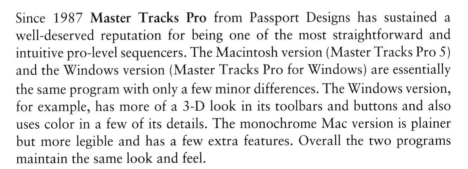

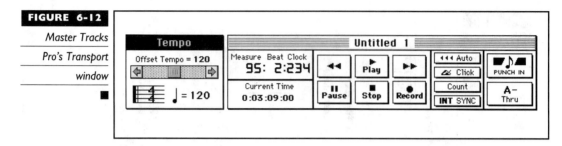

FIGURE 6-12

Master Tracks

Pro's Transport

window

■

four record modes: Punch In, Overdub, Looped Record, and Looped Over-dub (drum-machine–style recording).

The left side of the Transport window includes the Counter display. It shows the current position in elapsed time as well as measures, beats, and clocks (pulses)—Master Tracks Pro has a resolution of 240 ppqn. The neighboring Tempo window lets you change the tempo by dragging a slider from left to right.

Tracks

The Track Editor window in Master Tracks Pro (Figure 6-13) is a model of clarity and user-friendliness. You can have up to 64 tracks in a sequence and these are numbered in the first column on the left. The adjoining columns let you play-enable, record-enable, solo, loop, and name each track. The Program column lets you specify patches by number. Or if you prefer, you can use one of the Device List dialog boxes to select a patch by name. The program comes with lists of presets for several popular instruments (you can create your own too). Just click on a name and it appears in the Track window—very nice.

Next to the program name or number each track has a volume control. Although you can record their movements, these faders are not as versatile

FIGURE 6-13

Master Tracks

Pro's Track Editor

window

■

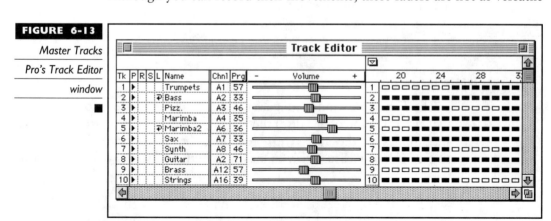

as the assignable knobs and sliders that come with Performer, Cubase, and some other pro-level sequencers. They're strictly for adjusting the volume of each track.

On the right side of the Track Editor window, you're given an overview of the sequence that shows where the music occurs in each track. Recorded tracks appear as horizontal rows of little boxes. Each box represents a measure—the black boxes indicate the presence of MIDI data, the white ones indicate the absence of data. You can select boxes in the usual ways and cut, copy, paste, and clear the data to move sections of music within a sequence.

Event List

The Event List window in Master Tracks Pro (Figure 6-14) is much like the one in Performer. On the left side of each line a small icon indicates the type of data represented. You can select individual events for editing or drag through several to select a region, but you can't select nonadjacent events.

Graphic Editing

At the heart of Master Tracks Pro, the Step Editor window (Figure 6-15) provides an easy-to-use piano-roll display. As with the Event List, you can click any note to select it or you can drag across a group of notes to select a region. Once selected, notes can be dragged up or down and left or right.

FIGURE 6-14

Master Tracks Pro's Event List window

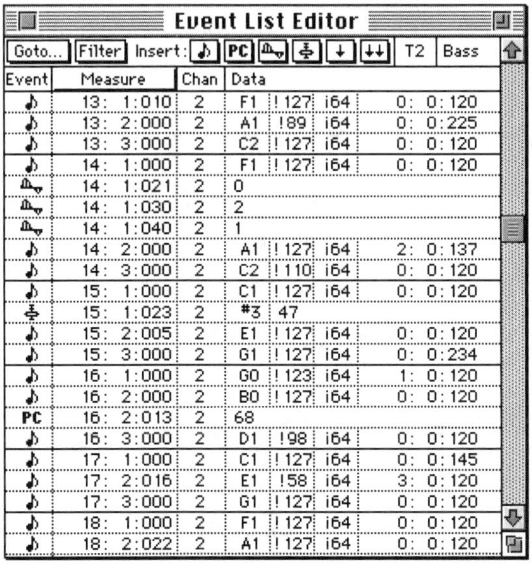

Event	Measure	Chan	Data					
♪	13: 1:010	2	F1	!127	i64	0:	0:120
♪	13: 2:000	2	A1	!89	i64	0:	0:225
♪	13: 3:000	2	C2	!127	i64	0:	0:120
♪	14: 1:000	2	F1	!127	i64	0:	0:120
♫	14: 1:021	2	0				
♫	14: 1:030	2	2				
♫	14: 1:040	2	1				
♪	14: 2:000	2	A1	!127	i64	2:	0:137
♪	14: 3:000	2	C2	!110	i64	0:	0:120
♪	15: 1:000	2	C1	!127	i64	0:	0:120
♣	15: 1:023	2	#3	47			
♪	15: 2:005	2	E1	!127	i64	0:	0:120
♪	15: 3:000	2	G1	!127	i64	0:	0:234
♪	16: 1:000	2	G0	!123	i64	1:	0:120
♪	16: 2:000	2	B0	!127	i64	0:	0:120
PC	16: 2:013	2	68				
♪	16: 3:000	2	D1	!98	i64	0:	0:120
♪	17: 1:000	2	C1	!127	i64	0:	0:145
♪	17: 2:016	2	E1	!58	i64	3:	0:120
♪	17: 3:000	2	G1	!127	i64	0:	0:120
♪	18: 1:000	2	F1	!127	i64	0:	0:120
♪	18: 2:022	2	A1	!127	i64	0:	0:120

Event List Editor

Goto... | Filter | Insert: ♪ | PC | ♫ | ♣ | ↓ | ↓↓ | T2 | Bass

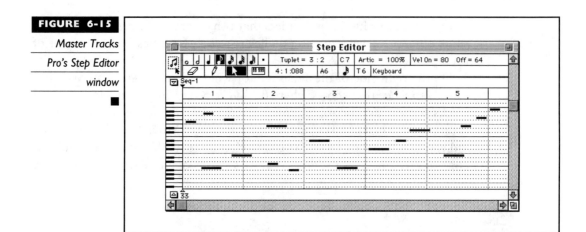

FIGURE 6-15

Master Tracks Pro's Step Editor window

Double-clicking a note opens a pop-up window showing the note's parameters. You can change any of these by typing in a new value.

Clicking any key on the vertical keyboard selects all notes at that pitch. By dragging up or down on the keyboard you can move the selected notes to a new pitch. You can also select all notes within a measure by clicking in the measure ruler above the grid.

Master Tracks Pro does not include a continuous data display as part of its Step Editor window. Instead it provides separate dedicated windows for the different types of data. In the Macintosh version, you can, however, view note velocities along with the notes in the piano-roll display. When you choose the Show Velocity command, a small stem appears at the head of each note (Figure 6-16). The stem indicates the velocity value of the note to which it's attached—the longer the stem the higher the value. You can easily

FIGURE 6-16

The Show Velocity command indicates each note's velocity with a small stem

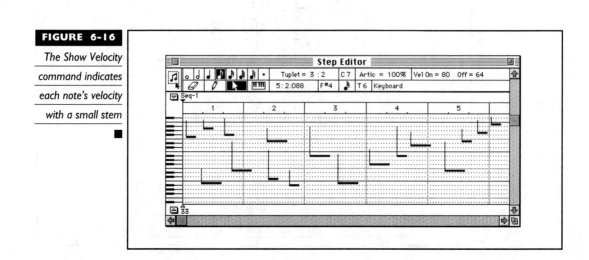

edit the velocity of any note by dragging the velocity stem up or down. This is very convenient for making quick changes to notes that are too loud or too soft.

With the Pencil tool you can enter notes into the Step Editor by selecting a note value from the small palette in the upper-left corner of the window. Then you simply deposit the note or notes wherever you want in the note grid. For a more efficient method, however, you can step-record notes by selecting the values with the mouse and entering the pitches from your MIDI keyboard.

Other Windows

To view and edit various kinds of non-note MIDI data such as Pitch Bend, Modulation, Aftertouch, and Tempo, Master Tracks provides a number of MIDI Data windows. These all look more or less the same except that the vertical scale along the left side of each window is appropriate for the type of data shown. The Pitch Bend window, for example, shows both positive and negative values (Figure 6-17).

In the Macintosh version there's an additional feature that makes it easier to correlate the MIDI data to the note events. The Ghost Notes feature superimposes a view of the notes from the Step Editor window onto the MIDI Data window (Figure 6-18). The notes—appearing as grayed-out copies of the originals—show precisely how the continuous controller data relates to the note events. This helps a lot when editing the data.

FIGURE 6-17

Master Tracks Pro's Pitch Bend window shows both positive and negative values

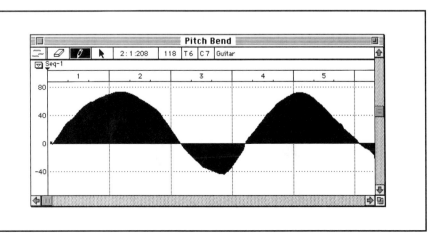

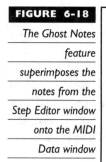

FIGURE 6-18

The Ghost Notes

feature

superimposes the

notes from the

Step Editor window

onto the MIDI

Data window

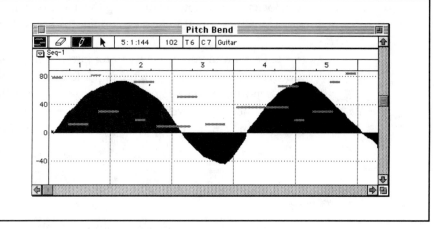

More Editing

As with other pro-level sequencers, Master Tracks Pro provides a wealth of editing commands. You can change duration and velocity by a specified amount or by percentage. You can also change velocity by specifying a range of values. Quantizing options include strength, swing, and the ability to slide notes left or right. As in Performer, there are also Humanize, Fit Time, and Scale Time options.

For even more precise application of editing commands Master Tracks Pro provides a powerful tool called the Change Filter. Under normal circumstances, when you apply an edit command to a selected region of data, all of the data is affected by the command. With the Change Filter dialog box (Figure 6-19), however, you can restrict most editing functions to musical events that fall within certain criteria.

You might for example choose to apply an editing command only to notes that fall between C4 and G5 with durations longer than 40 pulses and velocity values between 70 and 120. You might even further restrict the command to notes that fall only on the first and third beats of each measure. The Change Filter clearly adds some sophisticated editing possibilities to Master Tracks Pro and it can save you time as well.

Finally, if you like to play your sequences live for an audience you'll appreciate the Song Playlist feature. It lets you open as many as 16 sequences and play them back in any order. The Song Playlist window lets you build a list of sequences and specify how long to pause between each piece. You can also have each piece wait until you trigger it from your computer or MIDI keyboard.

FIGURE 6-19

Master Tracks
Pro's Change Filter
dialog box

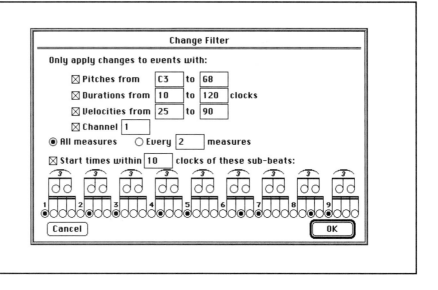

Master Tracks Pro may not be as powerful or as sophisticated as some other high-end programs like Performer, Vision, and Cubase, but its learning curve is lower and it does provide a comfortable, yet professional, working environment for serious composing and editing.

Vision

MAC

CD-ROM

Opcode Systems was one of the first companies to introduce sequencing to the Macintosh and **Vision** represents the fruits of a long and productive evolutionary path. Vision is a powerful though often complex program that boasts an impressive list of features. In fact, Vision has made a name for itself as an innovative product that sometimes introduces new features years before the competition does. With the introduction of Version 2.0, Vision has undergone a significant renovation with a new look and feel and, of course, several new features.

Before using Vision you must install a system extension called OMS (formerly Opcode MIDI System but now referred to as Open Music System). With OMS (which is similar to FreeMIDI) you create a document that includes information about the instruments in your MIDI setup, whether they're receivers and/or controllers, which channels they're assigned to, and which MIDI ports they use (Figure 6-20). This information—shared with all

FIGURE 6-20

*With OMS you
create a setup
document that
describes your
system*
■

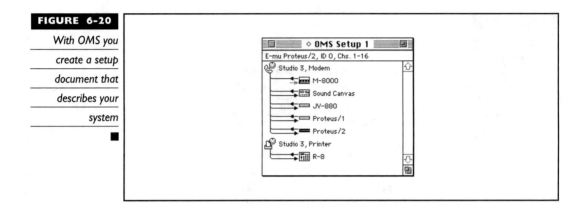

other OMS-compatible software—lets you refer to your MIDI devices by
name while working within Vision.

Controls

Vision's Control Bar (Figure 6-21) provides an array of buttons and
displays that let you record and play back your sequences.

On the left side of the Control Bar there are five button/displays that each
produce a pop-up menu. The Record mode button at the top offers four
different methods for recording: Replace, Overdub, Step Replace, and Step
Overdub. The remaining buttons let you set the current sequence, the current
track, the Thru instrument, and the current instrument sound.

To the right of the transport controls, a Counter display provides a
readout in SMPTE numbers as well as measures, beats, and units (pulses)—
Vision has a resolution of 480 ppqn. Beneath the Counter there's a Tempo
display and a small thermometer-style Memory display that shows how
much memory Vision has left. Clicking on the display opens a pop-up
window that gives you a detailed look at your memory situation and an
option to defragment your RAM if possible.

FIGURE 6-21

Vision's Control Bar
■

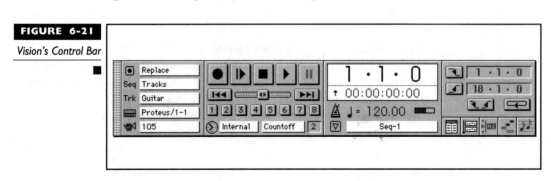

Tracks

Vision's newly designed Track window (Figure 6-22) offers the kind of information that you'd expect in a track window along with a few surprises. On the left side there are columns that let you play-enable, record-enable, mute, and solo any of Vision's 99 tracks. You can also grab any track and drag it vertically to a new position to rearrange the order of the tracks in the window.

The right side of the Track window provides a Track Overview display that shows where the music in each track starts and stops. This is much like other track overviews except that Vision adds a twist. Instead of using little boxes to indicate the presence or absence of MIDI data, Vision provides a miniature piano-roll display for each track. If you have a color monitor the tracks appear in different colors to help you better see what you're doing.

The miniature piano rolls are an excellent way to jog your memory about the kind of music that exists at various places in the tracks. They also make it easier to select sections for further editing—a great idea. Vision even lets you view the piano rolls in three ways: as phrases (rectangles of MIDI events separated by silence), blocks (user-defined, equal-sized rectangles), or tracks (one continuous rectangle for the entire track).

As in other track overview windows you can select any track or part of a track and cut, copy, and paste to rearrange the sequence. Unlike most overviews, however, Vision lets you include entire sequences in the display along with the track data. These secondary sequences—when they're imported into another sequence—are called *subsequences*. Each appears as a single unit in the overview display represented by a rectangle enclosing the name of the subsequence.

FIGURE 6-22

Vision's Track window

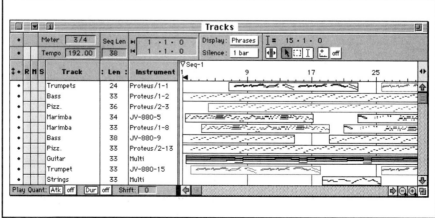

Combining subsequences with individual tracks lets you build complex musical arrangements and adds to the versatility of the program. It also lets you easily construct sequences by chaining together subsequences. Vision's Track Overview window then functions much like the Chunks window in Performer allowing you to develop your music in sections.

Event List

Vision's List window actually comes in three variations. The normal list—called the Performance track (Figure 6-23)—is much like the event list windows in other programs. It also shows where subsequences occur.

The other two variations of the List window include the Meter track—which shows meter changes, markers, and key signatures—and the Tempo track, which only shows tempo changes.

You select and edit events in the List window much as you do in other programs. Aside from individual and contiguous events, Vision also lets you select nonadjacent events.

Graphic Editing

Vision's Graphic window (Figure 6-24) uses the familiar piano-roll format for displaying notes. Instead of a vertical keyboard for representing pitches,

---

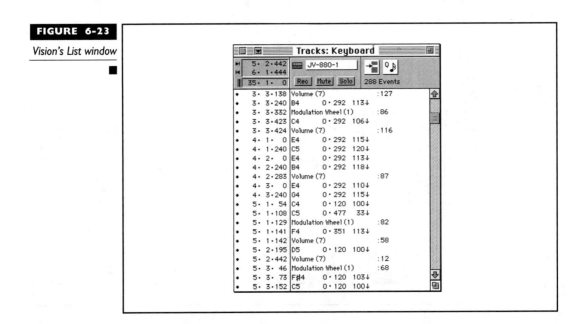

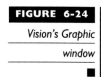

FIGURE 6-24

Vision's Graphic

window

■

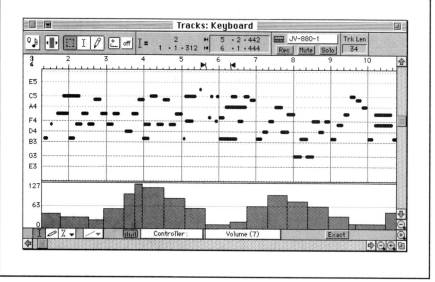

Vision identifies notes by name. You can select notes in all of the usual ways and drag them up or down and left or right. You can also stretch them and shrink them to change their durations. Very short notes appear as Xs.

Unlike most sequencers, however, Vision lets you display more than one track at a time. If you're using a color monitor you can even assign a different color to each track. This is a powerful feature that lets you see how the notes in the different tracks relate to one another. It's also fun to watch your music scroll by as the flute enters in blue, the trumpet in red, the sax in green, and the electric bass in brown.

Below the piano-roll display, another area called the Strip Chart gives a graphic display (for a single track) of non-note MIDI data such as Velocity, Pitch Bend, Aftertouch, Modulation, Volume, or others. Each event is represented by a rectangle—the height determines the value, the width determines the duration.

Notation

Vision's Notation window (Figure 6-25) looks quite a bit like its Graphic window except that the piano-roll display is replaced by standard music notation. Each track is represented by either one or two staves (depending on note range) and you can view more than one track at a time or have more than one Notation window open simultaneously.

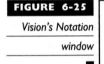

FIGURE 6-25

Vision's Notation

window

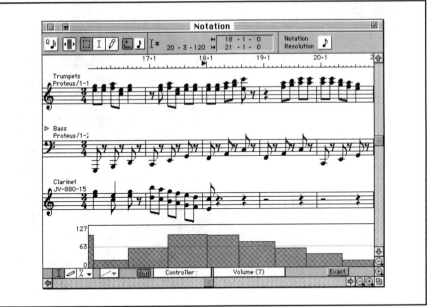

You can select any note by clicking on its note head or you can select several notes by dragging across a region. Once selected you can move a note up and down to change its pitch or move it left and right to change its location. To compensate for the discrepancy between the actual performance and the notation, Vision provides a Notation Resolution pop-up menu that lets you select a visual quantization level without changing the way the music sounds.

Other Windows

Vision's Faders window (Figure 6-26) is not as graphically sophisticated nor as versatile as its counterparts in Performer and Cubase. It does, however, support up to 32 faders and you can send any kind of MIDI controller data (except Pitch Bend or Aftertouch) or perform a Velocity fade on any track. You can also assign a fader to control tempo.

You can change the fader positions with the mouse or initiate changes from an external MIDI controller. And Fader movements can be recorded and then edited in either the List window or the Strip Chart.

More Editing

As you might expect, Vision offers a full range of editing options. You can transpose notes up or down by interval, diatonically, or from one

FIGURE 6-26

Vision's Faders

window

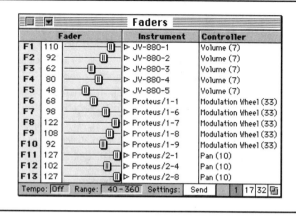

Faders			
Fader		**Instrument**	**Controller**
F1 110		▷ JV-880-1	Volume (7)
F2 92		▷ JV-880-2	Volume (7)
F3 62		▷ JV-880-3	Volume (7)
F4 80		▷ JV-880-4	Volume (7)
F5 48		▷ JV-880-5	Volume (7)
F6 68		▷ Proteus/1-1	Modulation Wheel (33)
F7 98		▷ Proteus/1-6	Modulation Wheel (33)
F8 122		▷ Proteus/1-7	Modulation Wheel (33)
F9 108		▷ Proteus/1-8	Modulation Wheel (33)
F10 92		▷ Proteus/1-9	Modulation Wheel (33)
F11 127		▷ Proteus/2-1	Pan (10)
F12 102		▷ Proteus/2-4	Pan (10)
F13 127		▷ Proteus/2-8	Pan (10)

Tempo: Off   Range: 40 - 360   Settings: Send   1 17 32

scale to another. Pop-up menus offer a wide range of scales and modes to choose from. You can even use the Constrain to Scale option to ensure that all incoming notes conform to the specified scale—even if you hit a "wrong" note.

To edit note velocities and durations, another pop-up menu offers several options, including set to a specified value, scale by percentage, add a specified amount, and restrict values to set limits. You can also edit tempos in a number of ways that include a Scale Time option. And a Reclock command lets you align beats to measures after a performance without a metronome.

Vision's quantizing options are up to par for a high-end sequencer. You can set parameters for sensitivity, strength, shift, swing, and smear (humanize). There's also a quantize-on-input option to quantize during recording.

The Groove Quantize function in Vision is not as elegant or as versatile as its counterpart in Performer. It does, however, offer a good degree of flexibility. The program comes with a Vision Grooves file that contains special sequences in different styles to act as sources for the Groove Quantize function. You can choose these from a pop-up menu and edit them to create new grooves.

For the experimental types among you Vision provides a Generated Sequence feature. It can create a new sequence based on a performance that you have recorded. By blending four elements—notes, attacks, durations, and order—it generates one or more sequences that may or may not be useful.

EZ Vision/Musicshop

MAC

CD-ROM

Opcode may have built its reputation on its high-end software, but it hasn't forgotten the beginners among the Macintosh-using population. Its entry-level sequencer—**EZ Vision**—is an excellent way to get started with MIDI. It costs less than a hundred dollars and provides a good assortment of features including full support for color. EZ Vision even lets you view

MAC

Galaxy Plus Editors

Although Vision is not designed to provide patch editing capabilities, Opcode markets a powerful universal editor/librarian called **Galaxy Plus Editors**. Galaxy's librarian functions support over 135 MIDI devices and the program provides editing templates for more than 50 popular MIDI instruments. When Galaxy is combined with Vision (it requires OMS) it can update patch data from the editor to the sequencer. In that way, changes made to patch names in Galaxy are immediately reflected in Vision. And Vision can call up instrument sounds by name directly from Galaxy.

In general, Galaxy provides the same kinds of features as Unisyn. To locate certain types of sounds, Galaxy provides a sophisticated Find command that uses keywords and categories to identify patches by their characteristics (Figure 6-27). Qualifying words—And, Or, and Not—help you narrow the search.

The editing templates in Galaxy (Figure 6-28) typically fill the screen with pop-up fields and envelope drawings. Clicking on the miniature envelopes expands them for editing with grab handles or numerical fields. In this way Galaxy manages to cram a lot of information onto a single screen. To create new banks of sounds from old, Galaxy also provides Patch Factory—a random patch generator—that may produce some usable results.

several tracks at once in its piano-roll display. And each track can appear in a different color just like in Vision.

Of course, EZ Vision is considerably scaled down compared to its older sibling. For example, you're limited to 16 tracks, there's no List Editor, no

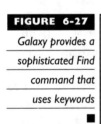

FIGURE 6-27

Galaxy provides a
sophisticated Find
command that
uses keywords

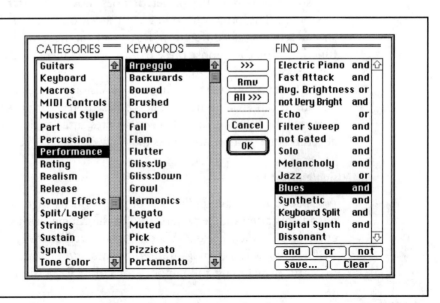

FIGURE 6-28

Galaxy's editing templates fit a lot of information onto the screen

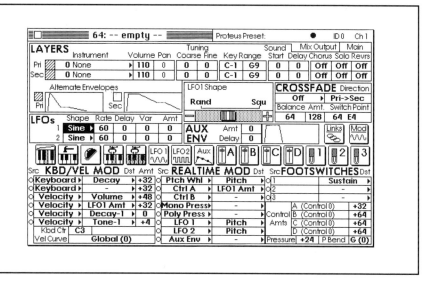

Track Overview, and none of the sophisticated editing options found in Vision. Quantizing options are similarly basic.

Nonetheless EZ Vision's piano-roll display (Figure 6-29) is well designed and easy to use. A Strip Chart like the one in Vision appears below the notes and lets you view and edit (with the same pop-up menus) the same kinds of MIDI data.

For those interested in pattern-based composing, EZ Vision provides an Arrangement window (Figure 6-30). In this display, sequences appear as blocks of varying sizes that you can stretch, shrink, and move around to create larger compositions. EZ Vision also provides a Mixer window that

FIGURE 6-29

EZ Vision's Edit window

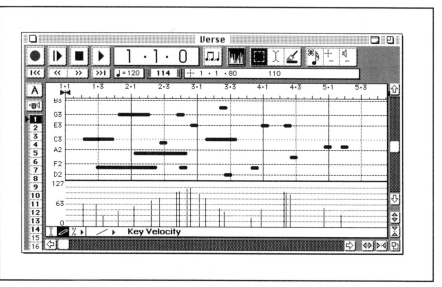

FIGURE 6-30

EZ Vision's

Arrangement

window
■

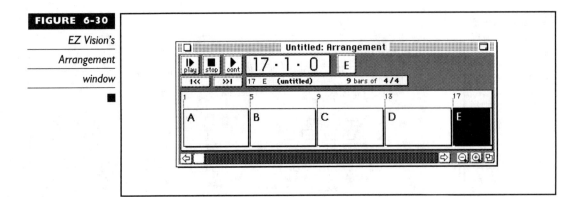

lets you solo, mute, and adjust the volume and pan position of each track.

If you prefer working with standard music notation, you'll be happy to know that Opcode has released a version of EZ Vision that includes notation. It's called **Musicshop** and it has all of the features in EZ Vision plus an Edit window (Figure 6-31) that lets you view, edit, and enter notes on musical staves. Musicshop even includes the same Strip Chart and support of color as EZ Vision. You can also use either program with Galaxy for added versatility.

Cubase

Originally released by Steinberg for the Atari several years ago, **Cubase** quickly established itself as one of the most powerful sequencers for that platform. Now it's also available for the Macintosh and Windows platforms

FIGURE 6-31

Musicshop lets you

view and edit

music in standard

notation
■

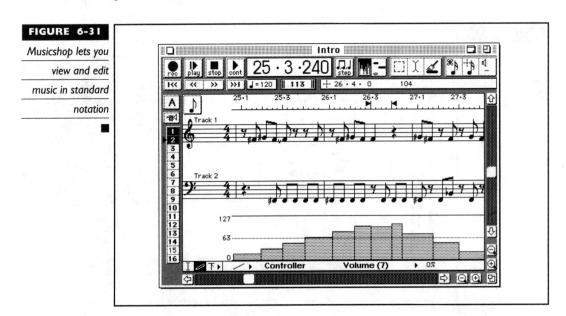

PC

MAC

CD-ROM

where it has cemented its reputation as a versatile, though complex, pro-level sequencer. If you like fiddling around with your music in myriad different ways, Cubase should interest you. It has more ways of viewing and manipulating music than just about any other program on the market. This level of versatility, however, comes at a price. If you've been working with another sequencer, Cubase may take a little getting used to. The program uses a number of unfamiliar terms and is sometimes less intuitive than some of its competitors. Once you get to know it, however, you'll be surprised by the tools that Cubase offers.

Controls

The Transport Bar in Cubase (Figure 6-32) supplies the usual controls for running the sequencer including a set of tape-style buttons. The Locator displays let you set the left and right boundaries for looping and punch-in/out operations.

The right side of the Transport Bar provides a small counter display that shows SMPTE time along with measures, beats, and ticks (pulses). Cubase has a recording resolution of 384 ppqn. You can, however, select a lower resolution (192 or 96 ppqn) for playback. This may help with such things as screen updates if your computer's processor has a hard time keeping up with things.

The right side of the Transport Bar also provides an adjustable tempo display. The In and Out indicators on the far right show the presence of MIDI activity.

Tracks

What you would normally refer to as the Tracks window in other programs is called the Arrange window in Cubase (Figure 6-33). It shares a number of features with other Tracks windows and adds a few twists of its own. Cubase lets you have up to 64 tracks in an Arrange window although

FIGURE 6-32

The Cubase

Transport Bar

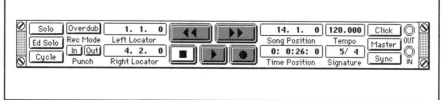

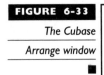

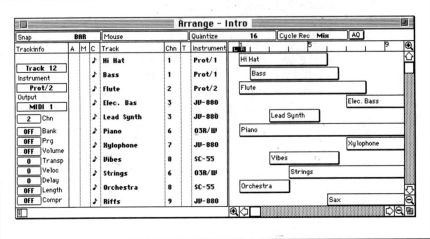

you can have several Arrange windows open at once. The tracks appear in a column on the left and you can mute a track or move it to another position in the list. A small icon below the Track List pops open an auxiliary display called the Inspector. It shows additional functions that relate to the currently selected track.

The right side of the Arrange window provides a graphic display showing where the music (and other MIDI data) lies within each track. This is where the program's unique approach to composing becomes apparent. When you record something in Cubase it doesn't go directly into a track (the way it does in Master Tracks Pro, for instance). Instead, the recorded material becomes a Part. Parts are the smallest elements of music that you work with in Cubase. A Part always resides in a track but it isn't locked to any particular track. You can drag a Part from one track to another, edit it in various ways, lengthen it, shorten it, cut it into pieces, or join it to another Part.

In the Arrange window, Parts appear as small rectangles. Their lengths indicate the durations of the recorded sections. Parts can appear with their names showing in the rectangle or with small bars that indicate where the MIDI data occurs.

Each track is comprised of one or more Parts. You can select any Part by clicking on it and you can select several Parts at once by dragging a selection box over them. The Arrange window lets you cut, copy, paste, delete, and move Parts as needed to create your arrangement.

Much of Cubase's versatility comes from the many ways that it lets you manipulate Parts. You can, for example, merge Parts by simply dragging one Part on top of another. If the Record mode is set to Replace, the data in the dragged Part will replace that in the other Part. If the Record mode is set to Overdub, the data in the two Parts will be combined. You can even drag a shorter Part into the middle of a longer Part. It will then only affect the data in the area covered. Overlapping one Part with another works the same way.

Cubase lets you do several other things with Parts. You can stretch or shrink a Part by dragging its end. You can listen to the contents of a Part with the Scrubbing tool. And you can create linked copies of Parts—called Ghost Parts—and assign them to other tracks and instruments. You can splice and dice to your heart's content, rename any Part, and mute individual Parts with the Mute tool.

But Cubase doesn't stop there. It lets you combine Parts into Groups. A Group consists of two or more Parts that play back as a unit. Each Group is handled separately as a discrete element and appears in a special Group track in the Arrange window. You can treat Groups much the way you treat Parts—moving them from one place to another in the arrangement. The Parts in a Group can play back simultaneously—such as the different horn parts in a brass section. Or they can play in succession like the parts of a song: intro/verse/chorus/verse/bridge, etc. If you prefer a pattern-based style of composition, this feature will come in handy.

Event List

In Cubase, the event list is called the List Edit window. It resembles most other event list displays, but, once again, offers something a little extra. The List Edit window actually consists of three sections (Figure 6-34). The first section is a standard chronological list of MIDI events.

Next to the list there's a graphical "event display." It represents each entry in the event list with a box. For notes, the length of the box corresponds to the length of the note. The boxes appear on a grid that shows elapsed time (in measures) horizontally along the top. The position of each box vertically corresponds to the event's position in the list. It takes a little practice to get used to this kind of display. A series of eighth notes, for instance, would appear as a diagonal line of boxes. As with the other windows in Cubase, you can select one or more events (including non-adjacent events) and cut, copy, and paste them. You can also lengthen and shorten the boxes and move them to other positions.

The third part of the List Edit window appears on the far right side. It displays Velocity and some other types of data (like Pitch Bend and Aftertouch) in the form of a bar graph. You can change the values for any event by simply dragging the corresponding bar to shorten or lengthen it.

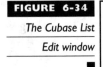

FIGURE 6-34

The Cubase List

Edit window

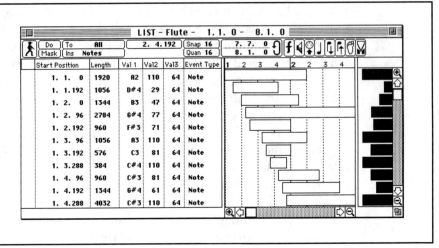

Graphic Editing

In Cubase the piano-roll display is called the Key Edit window (Figure 6-35). It works much like the graphical displays in other sequencers.

Below the main grid display there's another area called the Controller display. It shows continuous controller data and other non-note values such as Velocity, Program Change, Pitch Bend, and Aftertouch. This is similar to the Strip Chart in Vision.

There's one other feature that deserves mention. In the Functions Bar just below the Position box there's a small display that shows what chord is currently playing (during recording and playback). This is an excellent tool for analyzing your music and a feature that more sequencers should adopt.

Notation

Cubase lets you view and edit your music as standard notation in the Score Edit window (Figure 6-36). Selected Parts appear on separate staves and you can view up to 15 staves at once if your monitor is large enough. As in Cubase's other editing windows, you can select one or more notes and move, cut, copy, and paste them.

This is hardly a full-featured notation program, but it does offer the basic tools for working with music in standard notation. And the display quantize function helps to keep the notation legible when transcribed from other windows.

Two other versions of Cubase—**Cubase Audio** (see Chapter 11) and **Cubase Score**—provide more advanced score editing, printing, and page

FIGURE 6-35

The Cubase Key

Edit window

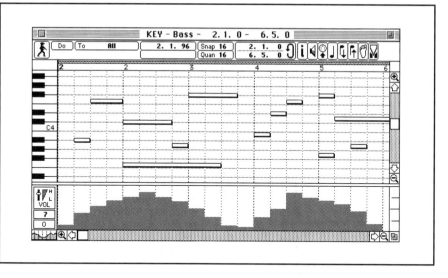

layout functions. These include such things as better handling of polyphony, beaming options, and custom markings. The program also provides a large palette of symbols. You can assign some of these a specific meaning for MIDI playback. This lets the score more accurately reflect the actual playback performance. You can also include text, chord symbols, and drum notation in your scores.

Other Windows

Unlike most sequencers that only provide a basic mixer display, Cubase offers a sophisticated MIDI Mixer window (Figure 6-37). As with Performer,

FIGURE 6-36

The Cubase Score

Edit window

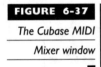

FIGURE 6-37

The Cubase MIDI

Mixer window

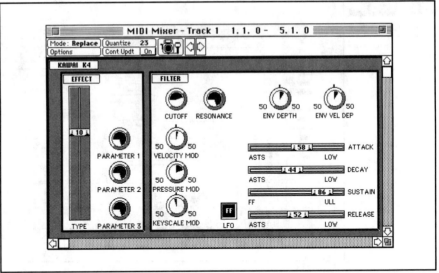

this window lets you create customized control panels that consist of any combination of faders (vertical and horizontal), knobs, switches, and numerical displays. You can assign these "objects" to control a wide variety of functions including the sending of System Exclusive data.

With the MIDI Mixer you can create not only mixing consoles, but a variety of switch boxes and "virtual" front panels for synthesizers and sound modules. Once you've assembled a control panel you can record the settings and movements of the objects for later playback.

For creating drum parts Cubase provides a dedicated Drum Edit window (Figure 6-38). This display is optimized for working with percussion sounds.

On the right side of the window there's a grid that shows measures along the top and provides a line for each drum sound. Creating a drum track is easy. As a 2-4 measure section loops you deposit notes onto the grid with the Drumstick tool. Four different diamond-shaped symbols indicate the assigned Velocity levels of the notes. By listening while you add or delete notes you can quickly develop a rhythm part that sounds good to you. It's also a fun way to experiment with different drum patterns. You can even open a Controller display like the one in the Key Edit window to add or edit non-note types of MIDI data.

One of Cubase's most unique features is its Interactive Phrase Synthesizer (IPS). Each IPS (there are actually two of them) lets you generate new music by interpreting your real-time input and applying various algorithms to it. The IPS doesn't create new sounds. It creates new phrases from your input and because it works in real time you can use it for live performances. With

FIGURE 6-38

The Cubase Drum

Edit window

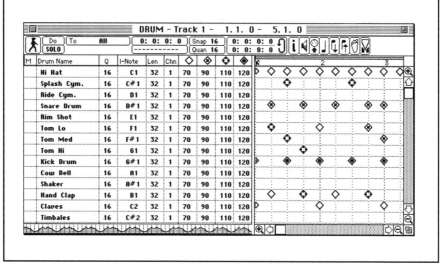

it you can create one-finger accompaniments, complicated arpeggios, and a great number of interesting effects. The Interactive Phrase Synthesizer, however, is not for the faint of heart. As you can see from looking at its window (Figure 6-39), you must first tackle a less-than-intuitive interface to use it. The manual devotes more than 30 pages to the IPS alone. For the experimental types among you this should hold your interest for some time.

More Editing

As with other high-end sequencers, Cubase provides a number of ways to modify MIDI events. For example, you can add or subtract an amount to Velocity and Duration values, scale the values by percentage, or simply change them to a specific amount. Most of these are accomplished through the Inspector display in the Arrange window. But Cubase also provides a means by which you can refine the effects of certain editing functions.

The Logical Edit window (Figure 6-40) allows you to change your music based on certain criteria. In this window you set up Conditions and Operations or specify Results that apply to the editing of events. In some ways this is similar to the Change Filter in Master Tracks Pro. But the Logical Edit window is more complex and consequently less intuitive. It offers great potential to those who think in mathematical terms. And it can save time when applied to many types of editing chores.

The quantizing functions in Cubase (amazingly there are six) are among the most powerful and sophisticated of any sequencer. Of course there's the standard type of quantize called Note On Quantize. This moves notes to the nearest specified quantize value in a measure.

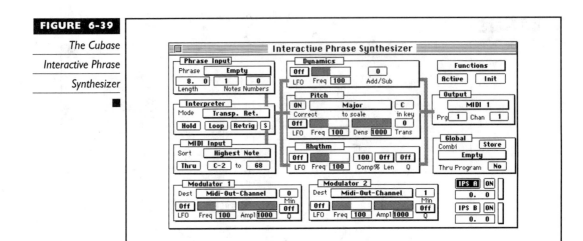

FIGURE 6-39

*The Cubase
Interactive Phrase
Synthesizer*

■

The Over Quantize function does the same but with a bit more intelligence. It detects chords and determines if you consistently play some of the chord notes ahead of or behind the beat. It then uses that information to move notes in such a way as to keep the chord together.

Iterative Quantize lets you move notes in small increments toward a selected Quantize value. You can specify a strength and a sensitivity so that certain notes won't be moved and others will be moved partway. This lets you apply quantizing in small steps.

Analytic Quantize is designed for complex passages—especially solos—where you may have straight eighth notes and triplets in a Part. The quantize value is not strictly adhered to but rather supplies an "impression" of how

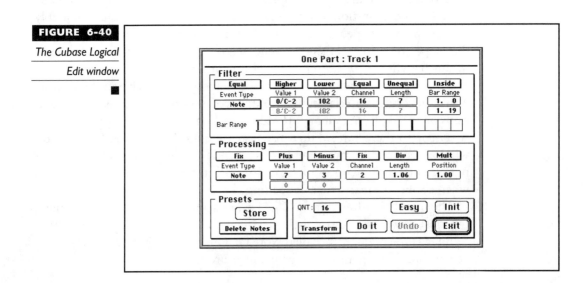

FIGURE 6-40

*The Cubase Logical
Edit window*

■

the rhythms should align. Cubase then analyzes the music, detects timing errors, and applies the appropriate quantization.

Match Quantize lets you match the feel of one Part with that of another. If you want the bass guitar part to follow the bass drum rhythm, Match Quantize makes it easy.

Finally there's Groove Quantize. This is similar to Match Quantize except that you are not matching another Part's rhythm. Groove Quantize uses Groove Maps that provide a particular "live" feel. The program comes with several professionally created Grooves and you can create your own with a dialog box that supplies tools and a small graphic display.

Cubase Lite

PC

MAC

As you can see, Cubase is a large and complex piece of software. For many users it may be a bit much. So Steinberg has released a scaled-down version of Cubase called **Cubase Lite**. It uses the same interface and overall architecture as its big brother but only provides 16 tracks for recording. There's no piano-roll display, event list, Drum Edit window, IPS, Logical Edit window, or MIDI Mixer and most editing functions have been significantly cut back. You can, however, view and edit your music in standard notation. And you can print it out when you're through. If you like Cubase's approach to composing but you're on a tight budget and don't need a lot of features, Cubase Lite might fit the bill.

Cakewalk Professional

PC

CD-ROM

Cakewalk from Twelve Tone Systems first made a name for itself as a solid meat-and-potatoes sequencer for the MS-DOS environment. Its newest incarnation, **Cakewalk Professional for Windows,** is a quantum leap beyond the original and fully plants the program in the ranks of the other graphics-oriented, pro-level sequencers.

Controls

When you open Cakewalk, the Control bar (Figure 6-41) appears at the top of the screen providing the usual complement of transport-like buttons. On the left, a counter shows the music's current position in SMPTE time as

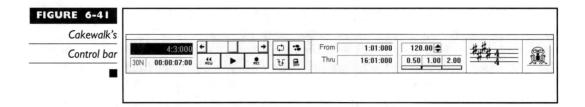

well as in measures, beats, and ticks (pulses). Cakewalk has a maximum resolution of 480 ppqn, but you can select any of 11 other "timebases" that range as low as 48 ppqn.

In the middle of the Control bar the From and Thru displays show the boundaries that affect looping and certain editing functions. And to the right of that there are Tempo, Meter, and Key Signature displays.

Cakewalk offers a unique feature in its Tempo Ratio buttons (below the Tempo display). They let you specify two offset ratios that temporarily change the tempo. By setting the buttons to 0.50 and 2.00, for example, you can have half-speed and double-speed playback at the click of a button—a nice feature.

On the far right, a large button with a screaming face (from the famous Edvard Munch painting) serves as a panic button. If you have a problem with a stuck note (a MIDI note that doesn't shut off properly and drones on) you can click this button. It stops playback, sends a Note Off message for every note on every MIDI channel, and resets all of the continuous controllers—very handy.

Tracks

Cakewalk's activities begin with its Track/Measure window (Figure 6-42). As with most track overview displays it consists of two sections. On the left the names and numbers of all the tracks appear. Cakewalk lets you have up to 256 tracks in a sequence and you can designate several offset parameters for each track including transposition, velocity, and timing.

The right side of the Track/Measure window provides a display that shows which measures in the various tracks contain MIDI events. Each track's measures are represented by a horizontal row of cells. If a cell contains a black dot it means that the measure contains one or more MIDI events. If a cell is empty it means that there are no events in that measure or in any later measures in that track. A cell with a dash means that the measure is empty, but there are later measures that do contain events. You can select one or more measures by clicking and dragging (although you can't select

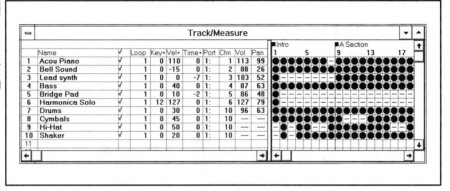

FIGURE 6-42

Cakewalk's

Track/Measure

window

non-adjacent measures) and cut, copy, and paste as usual. You can also drag measures from one track and drop them onto the measures in another track. A dialog box lets you determine whether the old material replaces or blends with the new material.

Event List

For the most part, Cakewalk's Event List window (Figure 6-43) follows the usual event-list format although with a few interesting extras.

It's more versatile than most other similar lists in its ability to display events from more than one track at a time. If you select tracks 2 and 5 in the Track/Measure window, for example, Cakewalk will intermingle the data from both tracks in the Event List display—the tracks are identified in the Track column on the left side of the window. You can also have several Event Lists open at once each showing any number of tracks. This makes the Event List considerably more versatile as an editing tool.

Cakewalk adds even more power to its Event List by letting you use it to insert Media Control Interface (MCI) and digital audio (WAVE) files into a track. MCI is part of the Multimedia Extensions in Windows 3.1. You can use MCI commands to control various kinds of hardware and software (such as CD-ROM drives, sound cards, and animation) during playback of your sequence. WAVE files consist of digital audio recordings that Windows 3.1 lets you play back from RAM. By treating MCI and WAVE files as events in the Event List, Cakewalk lets you trigger them from anywhere in a sequence. You can't edit these events from within Cakewalk and the program only triggers the events—it doesn't keep them synchronized with the sequence. Nonetheless this feature makes it possible to add such things as narration or sound effects to you music—a benefit to those working with multimedia.

FIGURE 6-43

*Cakewalk's Event
List window*

■

Trk	Hr:Mn:Sc:Fr	Meas:Beat:Tick	Chn	Kind		Values	
1	00:03:29:14	101:2:118	3	Note	G 4	127	6:058
1	00:03:30:08	101:3:236	3	Note	C 5	127	4:238
1	00:03:30:08	101:3:236	3	Note	E 5	127	4:238
1	00:03:32:26	103:1:000	2	Contrl	7	113	
1	00:03:32:26	103:1:000	3	Note	D 4	127	156
1	00:03:32:26	103:1:004	3	Note	G 3	127	156
1	00:03:33:05	103:1:135	2	Contrl	7	112	
1	00:03:33:08	103:1:180	3	Note	D 4	127	58
1	00:03:33:08	103:1:182	3	Note	G 3	127	58
1	00:03:33:14	103:2:030	2	Contrl	7	111	
1	00:03:33:19	103:2:118	3	Note	G 3	127	238
1	00:03:33:19	103:2:118	3	Note	D 4	127	238
1	00:03:33:23	103:2:166	2	Contrl	7	110	
1	00:03:34:01	103:3:061	2	Contrl	7	109	
1	00:03:34:05	103:3:118	3	Note	D 4	127	118
1	00:03:34:05	103:3:120	3	Note	G 3	127	118
1	00:03:34:10	103:3:197	2	Contrl	7	108	
1	00:03:34:13	103:4:000	3	Note	D 5	127	58
1	00:03:34:13	103:4:002	3	Note	A 4	127	58

Event List - Track 1: Acou Piano

Graphic Editing

Cakewalk provides a standard Piano-Roll display (Figure 6-44) for editing the notes in each track. The pencil tool makes it easy to insert and edit new notes. You can click on any note and drag it up or down and left or right. The Select tool lets you drag across several notes but it always selects all of the pitches within the time region that you drag through. This is not as useful as a tool that lets you draw a box around a few notes or a tool that lets you select non-adjacent notes by clicking on them.

If you click on an empty space in the note display you'll get a vertical line. Dragging this line left and right while holding the mouse button down lets you audition the notes out of tempo (a process known as *scrubbing*). This is very helpful for locating wrong notes or notes that need to be edited. Below the note display there's another area that shows Velocity levels in a bar graph format. To create drum tracks you can change the display to show percussion sounds along the left side.

Notation

Cakewalk's Staff display (Figure 6-45) lets you view and edit up to 24 tracks of your music in standard notation (with lyrics). Although it's not a full-featured notation program it does provide a good set of basic tools including the ability to print your results.

The Staff display is similar to the Piano-Roll display in many of its note-editing options. For example, you can select a note by clicking on it and drag the note head up or down and left or right. Clicking the right mouse

FIGURE 6-44

Cakewalk's
Piano-Roll display

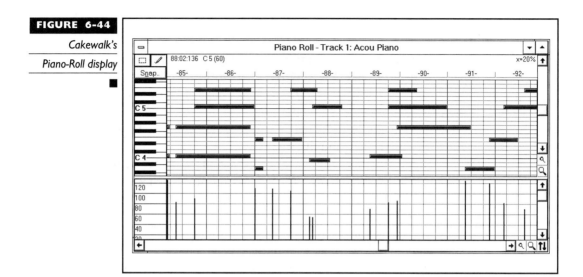

button opens a Note Parameter dialog box that lets you change things like pitch, velocity, duration, and MIDI channel for each note.

To keep the notation legible (without unnecessary rests and ties) Cakewalk provides three types of display quantization. These affect only the appearance of the music and not the actual playback. The Resolution option rounds off notes the way that standard quantization does. The Fill option rounds up durations to the next beat. And the Trim option cuts off notes that extend just slightly past the start of the next note.

FIGURE 6-45

Cakewalk's Staff
display

Other Windows

Cakewalk provides a graphical display for other kinds of MIDI data besides the Note and Velocity data shown in the Piano-Roll display. The Controllers window (Figure 6-46) looks much like the Velocity display in the Piano-Roll window except that it's dedicated to various types of continuous controller data. These include Volume, Pitch Bend, Modulation, Panning, Aftertouch, and others.

Although you can only view one type of data from one track at a time, Cakewalk lets you open several windows at once—each with a different type of data. Pop-up menus let you quickly change from one type of controller data and MIDI channel to another.

Cakewalk also provides a special window for viewing and editing tempos. The Tempo window looks a lot like the Controller window. In this display, however, the changing tempos are shown as a continuous line plotted along a grid. It's very similar to the Tempo display in Master Tracks Pro. The pencil tool lets you draw in new tempos and change old ones as needed.

Cakewalk's Faders window (Figure 6-47) provides 32 sliders and sets of knobs to generate MIDI controller events. Each fader applies to one track. The default settings have the sliders controlling Volume and the knobs directly above them controlling Pan position. You can easily change any of these assignments however with handy pop-up menus and dialog boxes. The Faders window in Cakewalk is not as sophisticated as its customizable counterparts in Performer and Cubase. Overall, however, the average user shouldn't find this feature too limiting.

Cakewalk also has a Play List window that lets you set up several sequences to play back jukebox-style. A Song Delay dialog box allows you to specify an amount of time to pause between selections.

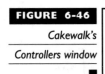

FIGURE 6-46

Cakewalk's

Controllers window

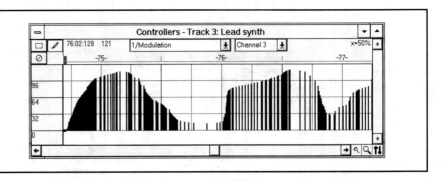

FIGURE 6-47

Cakewalk's Faders

window

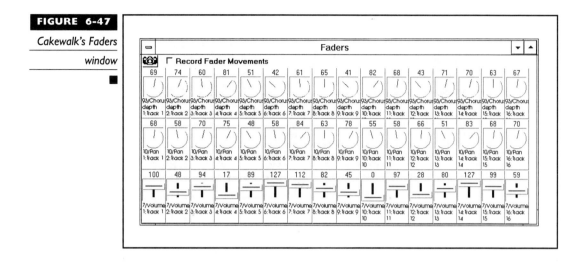

FIGURE 6-47

Cakewalk's Faders window

More Editing

Cakewalk offers most of the editing functions that you would expect in a pro-level sequencer. You can quantize (including groove quantize), transpose, change duration and velocity values, slide tracks forward and backward, and fit a selection to a specified time. These functions, however, are not always as advanced as their counterparts in other high-level programs like Performer, Vision, and Cubase. To expand its editing capabilities, therefore, Cakewalk provides a powerful Event Filter (Figure 6-48).

The Event Filter works much like the Change Filter in Master Tracks Pro or the Logical Edit window in Cubase. It allows you to apply a set of criteria

FIGURE 6-48

Cakewalk's Event

Filter

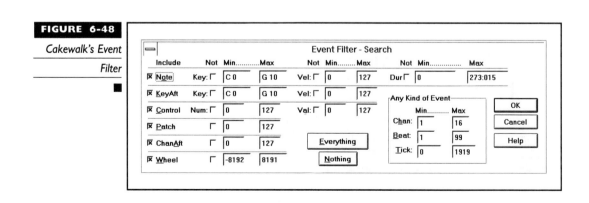

to an editing function to effect its final outcome. The Interpolate command, for instance, can open two Event Filters so you can apply search-and-replace operations to your music the way you can with a word processor. Other commands (such as Cut, Copy, and Quantize) open a single Event Filter so you can specify data ranges and event types that an edit will affect. The Event Filters ensure that Cakewalk will always provide a good level of power and versatility when it comes to selectively editing your MIDI data.

For the more adventurous among you Twelve Tone provides its own programming language called CAL (Cakewalk Application Language). You can use it to create your own programs that further expand Cakewalk's capabilities. Twelve Tone includes several examples to get you started.

Cakewalk Home Studio

PC

If you don't think you'll need all of the sophisticated recording and editing capabilities in Cakewalk Professional, you might consider **Cakewalk Home Studio**. It offers many of the same features as Cakewalk Professional but at about half the price.

Cakewalk Home Studio provides a fixed resolution of 120 ppqn along with most of the same editing windows as Cakewalk Pro including Track/Measure, Event List, Controllers, and Piano Roll. The Staff Notation window lets you view and print up to 16 staves. The Mixer window offers the same configuration as the Pro version but the sliders and knobs are pre-assigned to Volume, Pan, and Chorus.

Cakewalk Home Studio also lacks support for SMPTE timecode and MCI commands. And it doesn't include all of the editing commands found in the high-end version. It does, however, let you trigger WAVE files. If you're a Windows-based amateur musician or hobbyist this scaled-down version of Cakewalk is worth a look.

Metro

MAC

CD-ROM

OSC's **Metro** was originally released by Dr. T's Software as Beyond. When OSC acquired the software it beefed it up a bit and released it as a companion to its popular Deck II application for direct-to-disk recording. Although Metro and Deck II are designed to run in tandem (to combine sequencing with digital audio), Metro easily stands alone as a full-featured sequencer. If you're looking for high-end sequencing capabilities, with a well-designed user interface, and a reasonable price, Metro deserves consideration. It doesn't include a standard notation display, but it does include support for SMPTE, OMS, Galaxy, and Unisyn. It also offers a bunch of powerful editing functions, good color implementation, and several unique features that may interest you.

Controls

Metro's controls appear in its Transport window (Figure 6-49). It has the usual assortment of tape-style buttons along with a meter display, tempo display (with draggable indicator), and Counter display. The Counter shows your current location in SMPTE time as well as in measures, beats, and clocks (pulses). For recording and playback, Metro lets you select one of seven resolutions that range from as low as 24 ppqn to a maximum of 480 ppqn.

Metro provides two normal recording modes—Punch In (Replace) and Overdub. It also provides some unique loop-recording capabilities. You can decide if the recorded performances from each loop will end up on a single track (drum-machine style) or if the new material from each loop will be placed on separate tracks.

If you select the latter option, there are two other recording modes to choose from. In Song Building mode you can hear all of the recorded performances as the looped section repeats. It's especially useful for developing rhythm section parts with a drum-machine–style approach. As the music plays you can listen to and/or reject individual passes on-the-fly to try out different combinations.

In Multiple Take mode, Metro automatically mutes each previously recorded pass so you only hear the current performance. Multiple Take mode is particularly good for adding solo parts to a sequence. After you've recorded several takes you can choose the one that works the best.

Tracks

Metro's Tracks window (Figure 6-50) appears when you first open the program. It's simply a numbered list of the different tracks along with their names and associated patches.

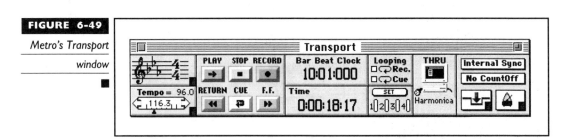

FIGURE 6-49

Metro's Transport window

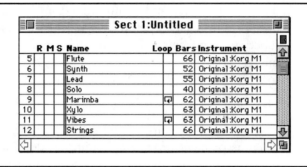

Metro refers to sequences as Sections and you can have up to 99 tracks in a Section. You can also take an entire Section and place it in a track in another Section. The added Section then becomes a SubSection. Since you can have up to 64 SubSections in each track, Metro provides a great deal of flexibility for constructing your music. This building-block approach to composing is somewhat reminiscent of the way that Cubase uses Parts to construct larger works.

Additionally, Metro lets you view and edit SubSections (it treats them as individual events) together with notes and other types of data in its event-list and piano-roll displays.

Metro takes a unique approach to viewing track data in its Track Overview window (Figure 6-51). Each track is represented by a horizontal band in which the presence of note data appears as a darkened area. Continuous controller data appears in a lighter color. You can select individual tracks (even nonadjacent tracks) or you can select a region across several tracks for editing. Double-clicking on the data in a track opens an appropriate edit window (at the correct location) according to the type of data that you click on.

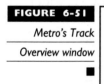
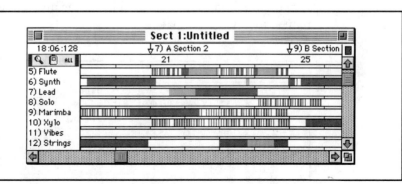

Event List

Metro's Event Editor window (Figure 6-52) is nicely designed and easy to read. A small check mark indicates the current position during playback. The large button at the top of the window lets you quickly switch from one track to another.

Changing an event's parameters is very easy. You just click on the value and drag the mouse up or down to change the numbers (or pitches). This works quite smoothly and makes editing fast and simple. SubSections can also appear in the Event Editor window. They're displayed as single events that you can move to other locations within the sequence.

Graphic Editing

Metro provides a standard piano-roll display in its Note Editor window (Figure 6-53). As you might expect, this piano-roll display offers some unique features. Metro lets you show up to eight tracks simultaneously in the Note Editor window. Each track appears in its own display aligned with the other displays.

As in most graphical displays, you can drag notes up or down and left or right. You can select notes individually (by clicking on them) or in groups (by dragging through a region), but you can't directly select non-adjacent notes. To audition notes you can click on them one at a time or you can use Metro's Scrubbing command. This lets you hear notes in context by slowly dragging the cursor back and forth over the range that you want to listen to.

One of Metro's most useful features is its ability to show both SubSections and notes in a single graphic display. This lets you combine fully developed

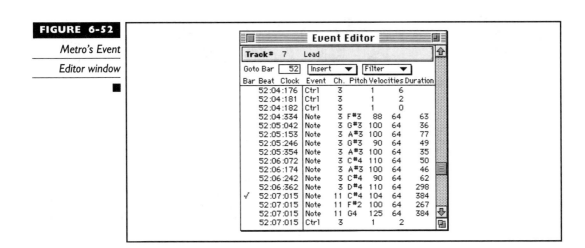

FIGURE 6-52

Metro's Event Editor window

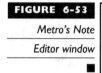

FIGURE 6-53

Metro's Note Editor window

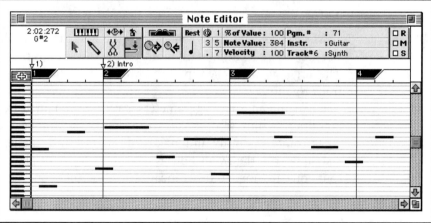

musical segments with individual instrumental parts. You can then move these different components around in relation to one another. This is a powerful tool for building musical arrangements. And it makes it easy to try out different musical combinations.

Metro's Note Editor window doesn't include a separate display for non-note data (like Vision's Strip Chart). It does, however, provide a couple of features that many people may prefer. Clicking the Velocity Stem button causes each note in the piano-roll grid to appear with a graphic display of Velocity values. In this display mode the head of each note sprouts a vertical line that represents that note's Velocity (Figure 6-54). To edit the Velocity you just click on this stem and drag it up or down to increase or lower the

FIGURE 6-54

Metro's Velocity Stem display mode

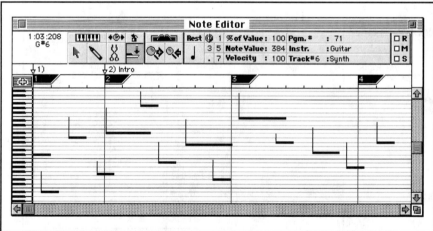

Velocity setting. This is very much like the corresponding feature in Master Tracks Pro and it works just as smoothly here.

Metro provides another ingenious display mode for viewing Pitch Bend. Clicking the Pitch Bend display button replaces the Velocity stems with notes that graphically depict pitch deviations. Notes that have Pitch Bend applied to them appear to droop or curve upward in relation to how the note's pitch has changed (Figure 6-55). This gives a good idea of both the direction and the approximate amount of the Pitch Bend. Unfortunately, you can't edit Pitch Bend values in this display. Metro does, however, provide a separate window for editing Pitch Bend and other continuous controller data.

Other Windows

To view and edit various kinds of non-note MIDI data, Metro includes its Continuous Data window (Figure 6-56). It looks and works much like its counterpart in Master Tracks Pro. The window consists of a graph-like grid with measures along the top and value markings along the left side. The display can show a variety of data types (from any track), including Aftertouch, Pitch Bend, Velocity, Program Change, Tempo, and various controllers.

You can also control Volume and other types of data in real time with Metro's Instruments window (Figure 6-57). It provides an array of faders (up to 254 are possible), knobs, and buttons. They let you mute, solo, and control the individual instruments in your MIDI setup.

More Editing

Metro offers a full assortment of well-implemented editing features and most include an excellent level of versatility. There are several options for

FIGURE 6-55

Metro's Pitch Bend display mode

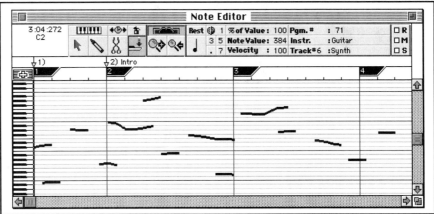

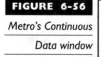

FIGURE 6-56

Metro's Continuous

Data window

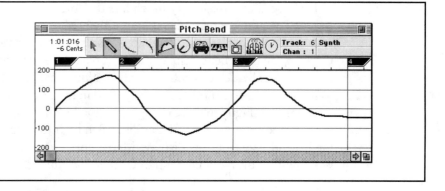

changing and scaling Velocity and duration values. The Transpose command lets you change notes chromatically or from one scale to another. A handy Harmonize feature can even create four-part harmonies from your melodies and the Quantize command includes the standard options along with a Groove Quantize function. Metro's time-scaling feature is truly unique. In the Note Editor window you can actually grab a bar line with the cursor and drag it to a new location to realign events. This is a powerful tool for editing music that does not strictly adhere to a steady tempo. Other recording features include the ability to enter Record mode on-the-fly during playback and the ability to step-enter notes directly into the Note Editor window.

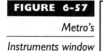

FIGURE 6-57

Metro's

Instruments window

Metro is not as well known as many of the other pro-level Macintosh sequencers. But its long list of interesting features, good use of color, clear design, and versatile architecture make it worth a closer look. This is especially true if you're interested in combining the digital audio capabilities of OSC's Deck II with the sequencing power of Metro.

∫eqMax

PC

CD-ROM

Big Noise Software's popular Cadenza sequencer has now been replaced by **SeqMax**, a full-featured composition program for Windows users. And to augment SeqMax's capabilities Big Noise now bundles the sequencer with a kitchen-sink assortment of auxiliary programs. This package is called the **MIDI MaxPak** and it offers lots of good tools for a reasonable price.

Controls

The Transport Bar (Figure 6-58) always appears at the top of the SeqMax window. Its five buttons provide the standard tape-recorder–style controls for running the sequencer. To the right of the buttons there's a small SMPTE timecode display. And to the right of that there's a much larger counter that shows the current position in measures, beats, and ticks (pulses)—SeqMax uses a resolution of 480 ppqn.

Tracks

SeqMax's Track Sheet window (Figure 6-59) appears just below the Transport Bar. Its familiar-looking format lists the 64 available tracks by number, track name, and instrument name.

FIGURE 6-58	
SeqMax's	
Transport Bar	

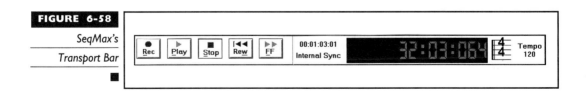

FIGURE 6-59

SeqMax's Track Sheet window

	Name	Instrument	+ Stat	Mode	Map	Port	Chan	Pitch	Bank	Prog	Vol	Pan	Events
1	Lead Voice	Choir Ahhs.	Play	Linear	--	1	2	0	0	52	111	0	44
2	Violin	Violin	Play	Linear	--	1	3	0	0	40	87	29	61
3	Classical Gtr	Nylon-str. Gt.	Play	Linear	--	1	1	0	0	24	77	-47	156
4	Intro Choir	Choir Ahhs.	Play	Linear	--	1	4	0	0	52	70	0	42
5	Intro Bass	Acoustic Bs.	Play	Linear	--	1	5	0	0	32	87	-17	67
6	Rock Keys	Synth Brass1	Play	Linear	--	1	6	0	0	62	82	40	417
7	Bass	Picked Bs.	Play	Linear	--	1	7	0	0	34	127	0	351
8	Guitar 1	Feedback Gt.	Play	Linear	--	1	8	0	8	30	75	-40	317
9	Lead	Halo Pad	Play	Linear	--	1	9	0	0	94	109	0	150
10	Drums	Drums Room Set	Play	Pattern	--	1	10	0	0	8	127	0	0

You can actually have several kinds of tracks in SeqMax. The type of track is specified in the Mode column:

■ A *Linear* track is a normal track that plays from beginning to end and then stops. A Loop track plays from beginning to end and then repeats until all of the other tracks have stopped.

■ A *Pattern* track consists of a series of smaller segments (called patterns) that you string together drum-machine style into a "song." These are well suited to creating rhythm section parts, but you can also use them for a variety of other types of music as well. You record patterns in a special display called the Pattern window. The patterns (up to 255 different ones per song) are then assembled in the Pattern Editor.

■ A *Setup* track plays before the first measure. It sends System Exclusive and/or controller messages to the MIDI instruments to configure the track for playback.

■ A *Link* track links together data from other tracks.

SeqMax's track-overview display appears in the Song Editor window (Figure 6-60). It's similar to the track-overview display in Master Tracks Pro. The track names are listed on the left and the individual measures are represented on the right by rows of little boxes. If a measure contains any MIDI data its box appears dark. Measures without MIDI events appear white. Muted tracks are grayed.

You select measures for editing by dragging the cursor over the desired area. This can include one or more measures on one or more tracks. You can also select non-adjacent tracks, but you must select adjacent measures within the tracks.

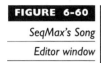

FIGURE 6-60

SeqMax's Song

Editor window

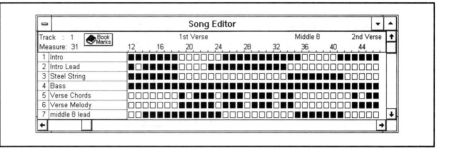

Event List

SeqMax's Event List Editor window (Figure 6-61) is simple and straightforward. Clicking on a new or existing event in the list opens a dialog box that is specialized for the type of data selected. The dialog boxes let you edit the entries by entering new values for the event parameters. The Note Edit dialog box, for example, provides fields for setting position, pitch, MIDI channel, Velocity, and duration. Several additional buttons let you quickly select standard note lengths.

As in Cakewalk, you can add an event to the Event List that will trigger an MCI command. You can use these to control external devices (like CD players or VCRs) or to play WAVE files for adding sound effects and narration to your music.

Graphic Editing

The Graphic Editor window (Figure 6-62) is SeqMax's most powerful editing tool. It consists of two parts: a standard piano-roll display for notes

FIGURE 6-61

SeqMax's Event

List Editor window

Position	Chan	Event	Name	Vel/Val	Rel Vel	Duration
78:02:422	3	Note	F6	61	53	0:254
78:03:177	3	Note	E6	66	41	0:307
78:03:432	3	Note	F6	73	65	0:278
78:04:182	3	Note	G6	71	55	0:154
78:04:456	3	Note	A6	58	33	1:249
79:02:211	3	Note	G6	64	33	0:470
79:03:201	3	Note	F6	65	44	0:259
79:03:456	3	Note	G6		21	2:446
80:02:465	3	Note	A6		25	0:317
80:03:225	3	Note	G6		27	0:259
80:03:441	3	Note	F6		23	0:307
80:04:182	3	Note	E6		46	0:326
81:01:000	3	Note	D6	71	27	1:292
81:01:000	1	Controller	7. Volume	114		
81:01:242	1	Controller	7. Volume	113		
81:02:004	1	Controller	7. Volume	112		
81:02:235	3	Note	E6	60	18	0:422
81:02:246	1	Controller	7. Volume	111		

Track 2 : Intro Lead

Event Edit Tools

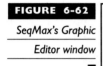

FIGURE 6-62

SeqMax's Graphic

Editor window

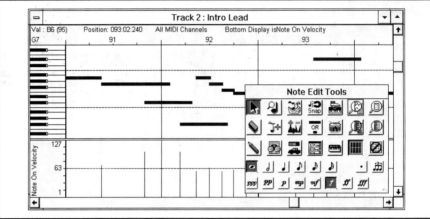

and a bar-graph–style display for Velocity and controller data. You can select an individual note by clicking on it. You're then free to drag the note anywhere in the piano-roll display changing its pitch, its position, or both simultaneously. Double-clicking on a note opens the same Note Edit dialog box that the Event List uses.

The Pencil tool lets you add new notes anywhere in the piano-roll grid just by clicking where you want the note to appear. You can also enter Step Record mode by clicking the Step Record icon. This opens a dialog box that lets you choose note durations and step amounts as you enter the pitches from your MIDI keyboard.

A handy Drum View icon changes the appearance of the piano-roll display by replacing the keyboard on the left with the key names (assigned drum sounds). This makes building and editing drum parts much easier.

Notation

SeqMax lets you view your music in standard notation in its Score window (Figure 6-63). This is not as sophisticated a notation display as is offered in some of the high-end sequencers mentioned earlier, but it does provide some basic tools for viewing and editing your music.

The Score window has its own palette of 32 icons, most of which consist of musical notes and symbols. You can add any kind of note to the score by selecting the appropriate icon and clicking in the score where you want it to appear. To move a new or existing note you just select it with the arrow cursor and drag it anywhere you want. You can also add expression marks

FIGURE 6-63

SeqMax's Score

window

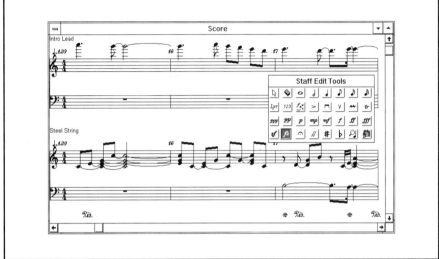

and other symbols, although these do not affect the actual playback of the MIDI data.

The Score window will display all unmuted tracks, although you'll probably need to do some scrolling to see everything. When you're through putting your score together SeqMax lets you print it.

Other Windows

The Track Mixer window (Figure 6-64) adds on-screen mixing capabilities to SeqMax. It provides a Volume fader and Pan position knob along with Solo and Mute buttons for each track in a sequence. Above each Pan control there are two other knobs that you can assign to other controllers such as Chorus and Reverb depth. For automated mixdown, you can record your fader and knob movements on all of the tracks.

More Editing

SeqMax's editing capabilities are not as elaborate as some of the high-end, pro-level sequencers. It does, however, provide a good set of basic tools for modifying your music. Aside from the usual Cut, Copy, and Paste commands you'll find such things as a basic Transpose command, a Harmonize function, a simple Quantize command (no groove quantize), and a Humanize feature.

FIGURE 6-64

SeqMax's Track

Mixer window

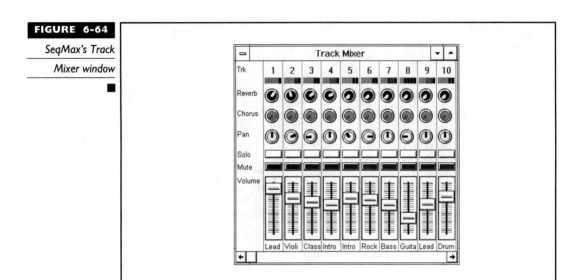

As part of the MIDI MaxPak, Big Noise has added several programs that expand the capabilities of SeqMax:

- **LibMax** is a universal librarian that supports over 35 synthesizers. It doesn't let you edit your sounds, but it does let you display patches by name and assemble them into banks. If you have a large number of sounds, this program can help you organize, store, and retrieve your patches.

- **MixMax** is an automated mixing panel. It resembles the Track Mixer window in SeqMax, but it's customizable and offers a number of advanced features. A toolbox of controls lets you combine such things as sliders, buttons, knobs, numeric displays, and text labels. You can have up to 200 controls in a layout and you can assign the controls to any kind of MIDI message. MixMax even provides graphic and event editing of controller data.

- **JukeMax** lets you assemble lists of sequences (up to 999 entries) that it will play back for live performances. It can also display lyrics, scrolling them in time with the sequencer.

- **TapeMax** lets you control external devices that respond to MIDI Machine Control messages. It provides eight user-defined auto-locate points that you can save and recall.

SeqMax Presto!

PC

CD-ROM

If you don't need all of the extras in the MIDI MaxPak, take a look at **SeqMax Presto!**—the entry-level version of SeqMax. It includes many of the same windows and editing commands, but it sells for considerably less than the MIDI MaxPak. If you're on a tight budget, this is a good general-purpose sequencer to consider.

Studio for Windows

PC

Midisoft's **Studio for Windows** is clearly aimed at amateurs, hobbyists, and beginners who are looking for a notation-based sequencer that can help them get started with MIDI. Studio for Windows offers no piano-roll display, nor does it provide support for SMPTE timecode. And you won't find graphical editing of Velocity and continuous controller data either. What you do get is a clear, well-written manual and a real-time notation program that provides the essentials in an easy-to-use package.

Controls

Studio's transport controls are contained in its Tape Deck View (Figure 6-65). The standard array of buttons are clearly labeled and provide the usual recording and playback functions.

When you click the Step button (last on the right) you enter Step mode. Clicking the Record button in Step mode opens a palette that lets you select note values. You then simply play the desired pitch from your MIDI keyboard.

You can further adjust settings for duration and Velocity with the Step Entry Parameters dialog box. It provides a slider that lets you choose the default length (shown as a percentage of full value) for step-entered notes. You can then choose Staccato, Normal, or Legato to enter notes that are shorter than, the same as, or longer than your default setting.

FIGURE 6-65

Midisoft Studio's Tape Deck View

Studio also offers a unique Step Play mode. It lets you play one note at a time—each time you click the Play button. This is helpful for locating wrong notes in complicated passages.

On the far right of the Tape Deck controls there's a Counter box. It shows your current position in measures, beats, and ticks (pulses). Studio has a resolution of 96 ppqn.

Tracks

Studio for Windows lacks a track-overview display, but it does provide a basic view of tracks and settings—which it calls the Studio Panel View (Figure 6-66). It contains the usual list of track numbers and names.

A Velocity Meter option produces small black bars next to the Velocity column when notes are playing. The flashing bars show the Velocity levels in each track during playback.

Event List

Although Studio is primarily a notation-based sequencer, it does offer an option for entering and editing MIDI events in an alphanumeric display. The MIDI List View (Figure 6-67) is very similar to other event list displays. You can increase the value of any parameter by clicking the right mouse button over the setting. The left mouse button lowers the setting.

FIGURE 6-66

Midisoft Studio's

Studio Panel View

window

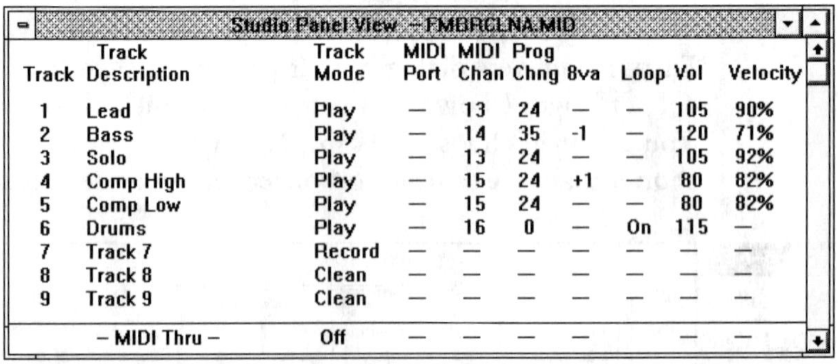

Studio Panel View – FMBRCLNA.MID

Track	Track Description	Track Mode	MIDI Port	MIDI Chan	Prog Chng	8va	Loop	Vol	Velocity
1	Lead	Play	—	13	24	—	—	105	90%
2	Bass	Play	—	14	35	-1	—	120	71%
3	Solo	Play	—	13	24	—	—	105	92%
4	Comp High	Play	—	15	24	+1	—	80	82%
5	Comp Low	Play	—	15	24	—	—	80	82%
6	Drums	Play	—	16	0	—	On	115	—
7	Track 7	Record	—	—	—	—	—	—	—
8	Track 8	Clean	—	—	—	—	—	—	—
9	Track 9	Clean	—	—	—	—	—	—	—
	– MIDI Thru –	Off	—	—	—	—	—	—	—

FIGURE 6-67

Midisoft Studio's

MIDI List View

window

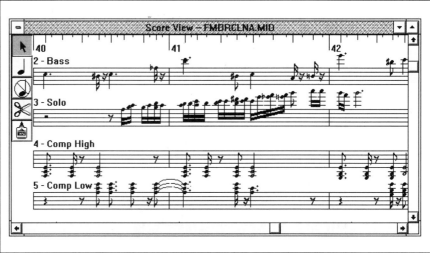

Type	Chan	Start Time	Duration/Data	Pitch	Vel On	Off
Note	[13]	1	4	53	0	1	17	B3	127	64
Note	[13]	2	1	11	0	0	45	G4	127	64
Note	[13]	2	1	79	0	2	43	B3	76	64
Note	[13]	2	1	82	0	0	55	G4	119	64
Note	[13]	2	2	50	0	0	59	F#4	127	64
Note	[13]	2	3	9	0	0	73	A4	113	64
Note	[13]	2	3	76	0	0	42	G4	125	64
PitchBend	[1]	2	3	80	8193					
PitchBend	[1]	2	3	82	8196					
PitchBend	[1]	2	3	84	8198					
Note	[13]	2	4	24	0	0	18	F#4	84	64
Note	[13]	2	4	40	0	0	25	G4	106	64
KeyAfTch	[1]	2	4	55	79		C4		64
Note	[13]	2	4	56	0	0	23	Gb4	119	64

Notation

The Score View display (Figure 6-68) is the heart of Studio for Windows. It shows the MIDI note data on each track in standard musical notation. On the left side of the window a small palette provides tools for selecting, inserting, deleting, cutting, and pasting notes.

FIGURE 6-68

Midisoft Studio's

Score View window

With the Selection tool you can select an individual note by clicking on it. You can then drag it left or right and up or down. You can also do both simultaneously and you can even drag notes from one staff to another. You can also select a group of notes for editing.

Clicking the Note Add tool opens a palette that offers you a selection of note durations and accidentals. You simply select a note and click on the staff where you want it to appear.

The notes that you add to the staff automatically appear in the proper key for that staff. To change a note chromatically you just add an accidental in front of the note. The Score View also provides an option that highlights each note as it occurs during playback. This makes it easy to spot wrong notes—a nice feature.

For transcribing a performance into notation Studio provides a dialog box that lets you adjust how the notation will appear. It provides scroll bars and buttons that let you set three parameters: Note Positions, Note Durations, and Rest Removal. These can help produce a legible manuscript even if the performance isn't perfect. When the appearance of your score is satisfactory you can print it. You won't get the high-quality output that a dedicated manuscript program can provide, but the printing is serviceable for many tasks.

Other Windows

Studio's mixer display appears in its Mixer View window (Figure 6-69). In this window each track is assigned a fader (for changing either Velocity or Volume data) along with a Record, Mute, and Solo button. There are also knobs for Pan, Reverb, and Chorus (these only work if your sound module responds to them) and each track has a VU-style meter that indicates Velocity values.

FIGURE 6-69

Midisoft Studio's

Mixer View window

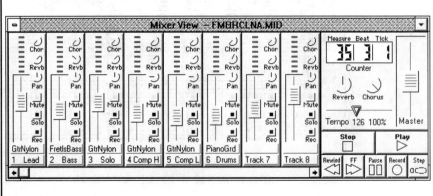

The right side of the window includes a Counter display, Master Reverb and Chorus knobs, a tempo slider, and a Master Volume control. The Mixer View also includes its own set of transport controls so you can use it like a multitrack tape recorder.

More Editing

Aside from the standard Cut, Copy, and Paste commands, Studio provides an assortment of basic editing functions. You can scale Velocity values by a specific number or by percent. Or you can have the values change from one setting to another. The Transpose options are more limited. You can transpose up or down by half step or by octave.

The Quantize command is similarly bare-bones. You can change the position and/or duration of notes and you can add a preset amount of randomness with the Humanize option. You can also affect the accuracy of the quantization with a scroll bar that lets you enter a percentage of "precision."

MIDI Kit / Recording Session

PC

Studio for Windows is well suited for beginners. But if all you've got is a sound card and you want to get started fooling around with MIDI, you might consider Midisoft's **MIDI Kit**. It includes a set of MIDI cables and a MIDI interface that attaches to the joystick port on most PC sound cards. It also comes with **Recording Session**, a scaled-down version of Midisoft's Studio for Windows. Recording Session has most of the main features from Studio, although it comes with a rather abbreviated owner's manual. As with Studio, Recording Session includes a large assortment of professionally recorded sequences of famous pieces. So you can get started playing right off the bat.

Ballade

PC

MAC

Dynaware's **Ballade** makes a serious attempt at bringing the process of sequencing down to the level of the MIDI neophyte. It simplifies recording and editing procedures by limiting the number of windows and editing options. And it strives for an intuitive approach to music making that will appeal to a range of users. The result is an interesting mixed bag of features combined with a unique notation-based interface.

Controls

Ballade's recording and playback activities revolve around its two primary displays: its automated Mixer window and its Score Editor window. Each of these has a different floating palette with small transport-like controls (Figure 6-70). The controls for the Mixer window include the usual tape-deck–style buttons. The Score Editor replaces the Fast Forward, Rewind, and Pause buttons with Step Record, Solo, and Music Follower (automatic scrolling) buttons.

Ballade can import, record, and play back sequences with resolutions that range from as low as 48 ppqn to as high as 960 ppqn. This is surprising for an entry-level sequencer, as is Ballad's support for SMPTE timecode—a feature typically found only on high-end programs.

Tracks

Ballade will work with any MIDI instrument, but to maintain its entry-level appeal it is especially adapted for General MIDI sound modules and, in particular, for Roland GS instruments. (GS refers to Roland's expanded version of General MIDI, which it uses in a number of its synths and sound modules—see Chapter 4.) To that end it supplies only 16 tracks—one for each MIDI channel.

The tracks, program numbers, and names appear in a display called the Track Sheet palette (Figure 6-71). There is no overview of measures in Ballade. There is only this list, which also shows each track's MIDI channel and corresponding MIDI device.

Notation

The Score Editor window (Figure 6-72) provides a musical staff that shows one track at a time. Above the staff there are three horizontal bands

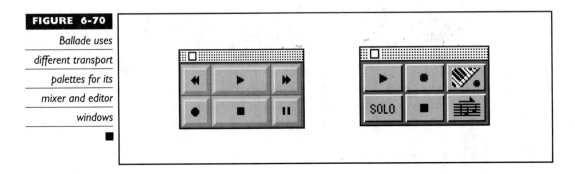

FIGURE 6-70

Ballade uses different transport palettes for its mixer and editor windows

FIGURE 6-71

Ballade's Track

Sheet palette

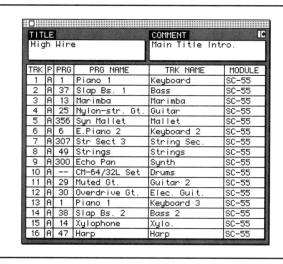

TRK	P	PRG	PRG NAME	TRK NAME	MODULE
1	A	1	Piano 1	Keyboard	SC-55
2	A	37	Slap Bs. 1	Bass	SC-55
3	A	13	Marimba	Marimba	SC-55
4	A	25	Nylon-str. Gt.	Guitar	SC-55
5	A	356	Syn Mallet	Mallet	SC-55
6	A	6	E.Piano 2	Keyboard 2	SC-55
7	A	307	Str Sect 3	String Sec.	SC-55
8	A	49	Strings	Strings	SC-55
9	A	300	Echo Pan	Synth	SC-55
10	A	--	CM-64/32L Set	Drums	SC-55
11	A	29	Muted Gt.	Guitar 2	SC-55
12	A	30	Overdrive Gt.	Elec. Guit.	SC-55
13	A	1	Piano 1	Keyboard 3	SC-55
14	A	38	Slap Bs. 2	Bass 2	SC-55
15	A	14	Xylophone	Xylo.	SC-55
16	A	47	Harp	Harp	SC-55

that graphically display data affecting the sequence as a whole. Markers, tempo changes, and master volume changes appear in these horizontal bands above the appropriate measures in the staff.

Below the staff several track-specific controls appear in a similarly graphic manner. They include Program Changes, Pan position messages, Sustain Pedal events, Volume control messages, Modulation data, and Pitch Bend data.

FIGURE 6-72

Ballade's Score

Editor window

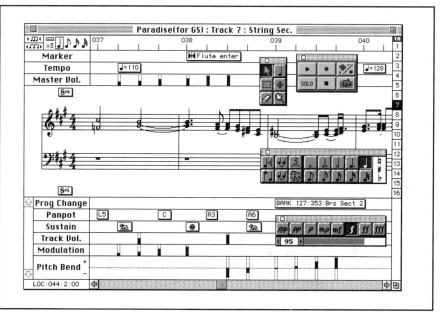

In the upper-left corner of the window there are buttons that let you adjust the width of the measures in the score. In the lower-left corner there's a small counter that shows the current position in the sequence.

Recording in the Score Editor is easy. You just select a track and click the Record button in the Transport palette. You can have a two-measure count-off if you want. When you're through, you simply click the Stop button and your music appears on the staff.

Ballade is not as successful as most pro-level programs at producing legible notation from an imperfect performance. The staff often displays more rests, ties, and short note values than are strictly necessary. The program does let you quantize the music—there's a simple Quantize command—but this changes both the appearance and the music playback. There's no provision to clean up the score while leaving the performance untouched. When the notation looks the way you want it to you can print any track or the entire score.

For step-entering notes Ballade offers three options. You can select a note value from the Note palette and then insert it on the staff by clicking with the mouse. Or you can select a note value from the palette and enter the pitches from your MIDI keyboard.

As an interesting third option, you can use the on-screen virtual keyboard (Figure 6-73) to enter pitches by clicking on the keys with the mouse. You can even use the virtual keyboard for real-time recording, but it's hard to get good results that way.

Ballade also provides an excellent option with its Chord palette. It contains a series of letters and chord types that you can choose to insert entire chords onto the staff. There are even two arrows that let you cycle the chords through several inversions. This is a great tool for entering background accompaniment parts.

Once you have notes on the staff you can drag them (one at a time) to the left or right and up or down. To modify a note's characteristics you choose the magnifying glass icon in the Tools palette and click on a note. This pops open a small display that lets you set parameters like pitch, duration, velocity, and location. You can also select groups of notes and edit them with commands from the Edit menu.

FIGURE 6-73

Ballade's Keyboard

palette

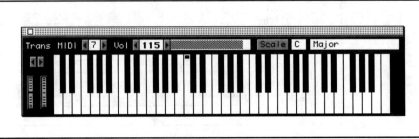

Graphic Editing

In the Windows version of Ballade there's an extra editing window that is currently lacking in the Mac version. The Piano Roll Editor (Figure 6-74) provides a conventional graphic display of note data. This display works very much like the Score Editor but offers a different way to view your music. You can record directly into the Piano Roll Editor (it uses the same Transport palette) and move notes around the way you can in the Score Editor. You can also enter notes individually onto the piano-roll grid and stretch or shrink them (to change duration) by dragging with the mouse.

Clicking the Velocity View button above the vertical keyboard lets you see Velocity values as thin vertical stems—much like the Velocity features in Master Tracks Pro and Metro. You can adjust the Velocity values by dragging up or down with the mouse or by clicking on one of the buttons in the Velocity palette.

For extra versatility, Ballade also lets you trigger WAVE files from the Piano Roll Editor. A special track at the top of the window lets you position markers to play digital audio files along with your music—a handy feature for adding sound effects and narration to a score.

Other Windows

Ballade's Mixer window (Figure 6-75) is actually the first window you see when you open the program. It's a good-looking, colorful mixing panel with a fader and a set of buttons and knobs for each of the 16 possible tracks.

FIGURE 6-74

Ballade's Piano Roll

Editor

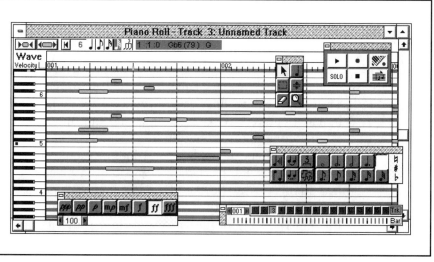

FIGURE 6-75

Ballade's Mixer

window

■

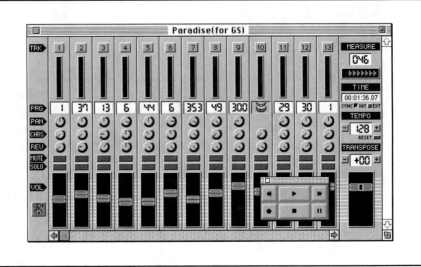

Above each Volume fader there are separate Mute and Solo buttons. And above the buttons there are knobs for controlling Reverb, Chorus, and Pan position on each track.

The Reverb and Chorus controls are specifically for Roland GS instruments. Ballade provides special palettes for setting the Reverb and Chorus characteristics—very handy if you're using a Roland sound module. The Pan control will work with any instrument that supports MIDI Pan messages. In keeping with the requirements of General MIDI (and the GS Standard) track 10 defaults to being the rhythm track.

The buttons at the top of the window let you record-enable each track. Below these buttons a set of VU-style meters show the loudness of each track (based on Velocity values).

Because the Mixer window is designed to function like a multitrack tape recorder, you can only do real-time recording with it. The right side of the window provides a counter that shows the current measure. This is for display only—you can't enter new numbers to relocate to a new position. The arrows below the Measure counter light up in sequence to show each beat as it's played. To re-create fader and knob movements, Ballade provides a Mixer Action Record button.

Ballade offers an additional window for creating drum tracks. The Rhythm Track Editor (Figure 6-76) looks a bit like a piano-roll display. Instead of a vertical keyboard, however, a list of percussion names appears along the left side of the window. You use the mouse to enter notes in the Rhythm Track Editor the way you do in the Score Editor. A Rhythm palette lets you select one of seven diamond shapes that represent Velocity values.

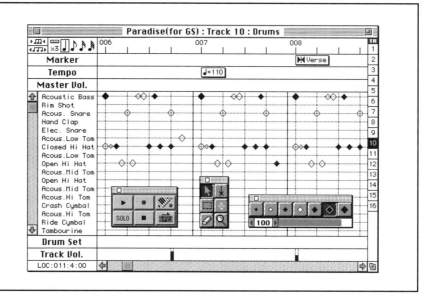

You simply insert the chosen diamond shape on the grid where you want a particular drum sound to occur. Ballade comes preconfigured with a number of General MIDI and Roland GS percussion key maps.

More Editing

Most of Ballade's editing functions are rather basic. Options for quantizing, transposing, and looping are minimal and the program doesn't even support many types of continuous controller data. Beginners will not likely find these limitations too troublesome, but more advanced users might. The non-note data that is supported by Ballade is edited through pop-up palettes. They let you change settings with adjustable selection buttons or sliders.

For users of Roland instruments, Dynaware makes **GS/SC7 Controller**. It lets you operate GS synths and sound modules from your computer. And you can use your monitor as a virtual front panel for editing sounds and playback parameters.

Musicator Win

PC

CD-ROM

Musicator Win (from Musicator A/S) shares a number of characteristics with Ballade. It provides a readily accessible user interface, a minimum of editing options, and support for General MIDI and Roland GS instruments. And its notation-based design lets you print out your music. But Musicator Win is a more advanced program than Ballade. Its music manuscript capabilities are more substantial and its transcription capabilities are more sophisticated.

While neither Ballade nor Musicator provide an event list editor, Musicator does include a track-overview display and separate windows for editing continuous controller data. Although Musicator doesn't quite qualify as a true pro-level sequencer, its strong notation and page layout features make it an attractive choice for those who work with printed music.

Controls

Musicator's transport controls are nestled in the midst of its Toolbar—a narrow strip of 19 buttons that always appear at the top of the screen (Figure 6-77). To the left of the buttons a small display shows the current measure and elapsed SMPTE time (Musicator can sync to external timecode).

Musicator operates with a resolution of 480 ppqn. It offers all of the standard record modes including Replace, Overdub, and Punch In/Out, but not Loop recording (or playback). In addition to real-time recording you can enter notes with the mouse or with the usual step-entry method.

Tracks

Musicator's OverView window (Figure 6-78) combines a standard-style track list with a measure-by-measure view showing the presence of MIDI data. You can have up to 32 tracks assigned to 32 MIDI channels and Musicator lets you have as many as 6 different OverViews.

The right side of the window shows the measures in each track. Measures containing MIDI data appear as black rectangles. Measures without data are indicated with small dots. You can select any measure by clicking on it or you can select a group of measures in one or more tracks by dragging across them. You can't, however, select nonadjacent tracks or measures. The OverView lets you drag and drop chunks of music to make large-scale changes to your arrangement.

FIGURE 6-77

Musicator's Toolbar

FIGURE 6-78

Musicator's

OverView window

	Inst	Mute	Vol	Pan	Eff 1	Eff 2	Trans		40	50
Trumpet	Instr. 62	-	108	64	64	6	-2	ⅼ·······ⅼ·ⅼ·ⅼⅼ ⅼⅼ·		
Alto	Instr. 66	-	100	52	60	0	-9	ⅼ··ⅼⅼ·ⅼⅼ···ⅼⅼⅼ·ⅼ		
Tenor	Instr. 67	-	100	64	67	0	-14	ⅼ··ⅼⅼ·ⅼⅼ···ⅼⅼⅼ·ⅼ		
Baritone	Instr. 68	-	100	77	71	0	-2	ⅼ··ⅼⅼ·ⅼⅼ···ⅼⅼⅼ·ⅼ		
Trombone	Instr. 58	-	100	64	40	0	0	ⅼ······ⅼⅼⅼ·ⅼⅼⅼⅼ·ⅼ		
Piano	Instr. 1	-	100	64	40	0	0	ⅼⅼⅼⅼⅼⅼⅼⅼⅼ·····ⅼⅼ		
Bass	Instr. 33	-	94	64	40	0	-12	ⅼⅼⅼⅼⅼⅼⅼⅼⅼⅼⅼⅼⅼⅼⅼ		
Drums	Instr. 33	-	90	64	40	0	0	ⅼⅼⅼⅼⅼⅼⅼⅼⅼⅼⅼⅼⅼⅼⅼ		

OverView - Setup 2

Graphical Editing

In Musicator the piano-roll display is called the Roll View (Figure 6-79). It shows note events in the traditional piano-roll format with black bars on a grid. Changes made in the Roll View will not be reflected in the Notation window unless the Transcribe box is checked. This lets you keep the performance separate from the notated music.

If you click on a note with the left mouse button, a display at the top of the window shows the note's pitch and position. Dragging up or down changes the pitch and dragging left or right changes the attack time (you can change both simultaneously). If you click on a note with the right mouse

FIGURE 6-79

Musicator's Roll

View

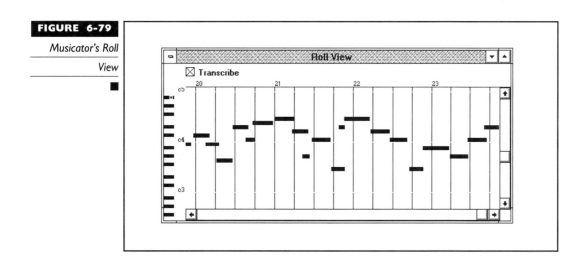

Roll View

☒ Transcribe

button the display shows the note's Velocity and duration. Dragging up or down changes the Velocity value and dragging left or right changes the duration. You can't select non-adjacent notes.

For creating and editing drum tracks, you can change the Roll View to Drum mode. In this mode, the names of the different drum sounds appear along the left side next to a vertical keyboard. Clicking on a drum name pops open a Drum Settings module that lets you adjust the Volume, Pan, Reverb, and Tuning of the sound—very nice.

Notation

Musicator's notation and page-layout capabilities are its strongest features. The Notation View (Figure 6-80) lets you display and edit up to 32 staffs at once. You can record directly into the Notation View in real time. Or you can enter notes by step recording. You can also enter notes directly onto the staff with the mouse.

As a guide to note placement, a thin horizontal bar called the Ruler hovers over the cursor at the current measure. The Ruler indicates where the beats are and also shows the subdivisions of each beat.

To enter notes you simply choose the Note Entry pointer. Then, using the Ruler as a guide, click where you want the note to start and drag to where

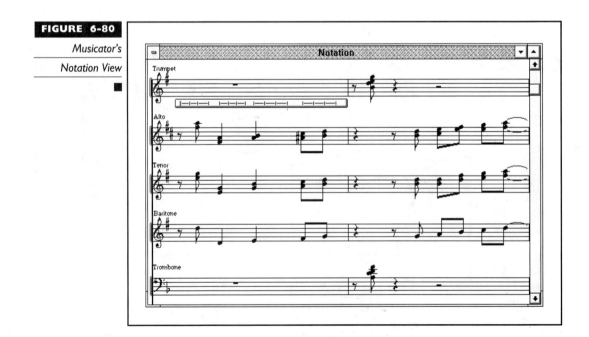

FIGURE 6-80

Musicator's

Notation View

you want it to end. To make changes you can select a single note or several adjacent notes and drag them anywhere on the staff. This also works for symbols and text.

Musicator provides a number of useful features that let you improve and modify the appearance of your notated music. You can quantize the notation without affecting the performance data. And you can change the horizontal and vertical spacing to optimize viewing.

The Minimize Rests command removes unwanted rests and changes the associated note values to produce a more readable manuscript. The One Voice command removes the slight overlaps that often occur from one note to the next in a performance. This reduces the rests and tied notes that make the notation hard to read.

Clicking the right mouse button in the staff area opens the Note Attributes palette. It lets you modify selected notes in a number of ways. For instance, you can flip stems, split or join beamed groups, and change accidentals. The Part Processing function lets you divide music into separate subparts by simply drawing a line where you want to split the parts. This is a powerful tool for dividing chordal progressions into separate voices. Musicator also lets you enter a variety of musical symbols, repeat signs, titles, lyrics, and transposable chord symbols. The program even provides tools for creating drum notation with a number of specialized symbols. Several page-layout features, including score- and part-printing options, ensure quality output.

Other Windows

To view and edit continuous controller data and other types of non-note messages, Musicator provides its Controller window (Figure 6-81). It uses the familiar bar-graph–style display, which lets you add new data or edit existing values. By clicking the right mouse button you can draw in new data for things like tempo, Volume, Program Change, Pan, and Pitch Bend.

You can also edit selected areas in a number of ways. You can shift data forward or backward in time with the Clock Shift command. Or you can change values by a specific amount with the Level Shift command. The Compression command compresses data by a factor of from 1 to 10 based on the average value in the selected range. Expansion does the opposite. Interpolate generates new controller events between existing ones to create smoother transitions.

Musicator also provides a well-designed Mixer window (Figure 6-82). The 32-track mixer lets you mix your music in real time and record the fader movements. Although the faders and pan controls will work with most MIDI instruments, the Mixer window is specifically designed for use with General MIDI and, especially, Roland GS instruments.

FIGURE 6-81

Musicator's

Controller window

■

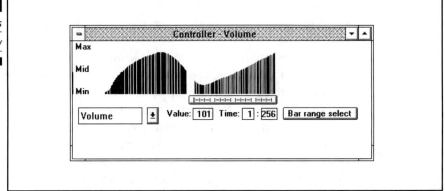

If you have a GS sound module, the knobs above the faders let you adjust the amounts of reverb and chorus effects in each track. At the top of the window there are more knobs for adjusting vibrato and filter parameters. And you can edit a sound's envelope characteristics with three scroll bars.

If you own a Roland GS instrument, the Mixer window is a valuable plus. It provides a handy front-end control panel that's conveniently integrated with the rest of the sequencer/notation package. There's even a separate GS Reverb and Chorus window that lets you modify all of the onboard GS effects (e.g., reverb, chorus, flanger, and delay).

FIGURE 6-82

Musicator's Mixer

window

■

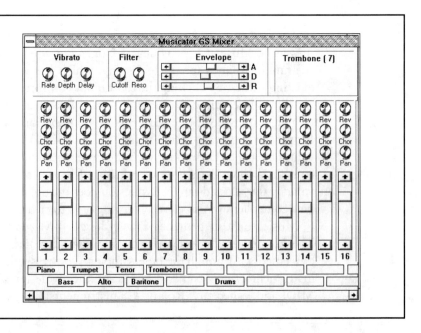

More Editing

Musicator's Quantize and Transpose commands are rather minimal. The Quantize options include a setting for strength and two offset adjustments that you can use to create a swing feel. The Transpose command is even more basic. It lets you transpose up or down by a specified number of semitones.

Overall, Musicator Win strikes a good balance between sequencing power and notation capabilities. For a mid-level program it packs a good number of important features. If working with notation is important to you, and if page layout and output quality are important as well, Musicator Win is worth a look. And this is doubly true if you own a General MIDI or Roland GS sound module.

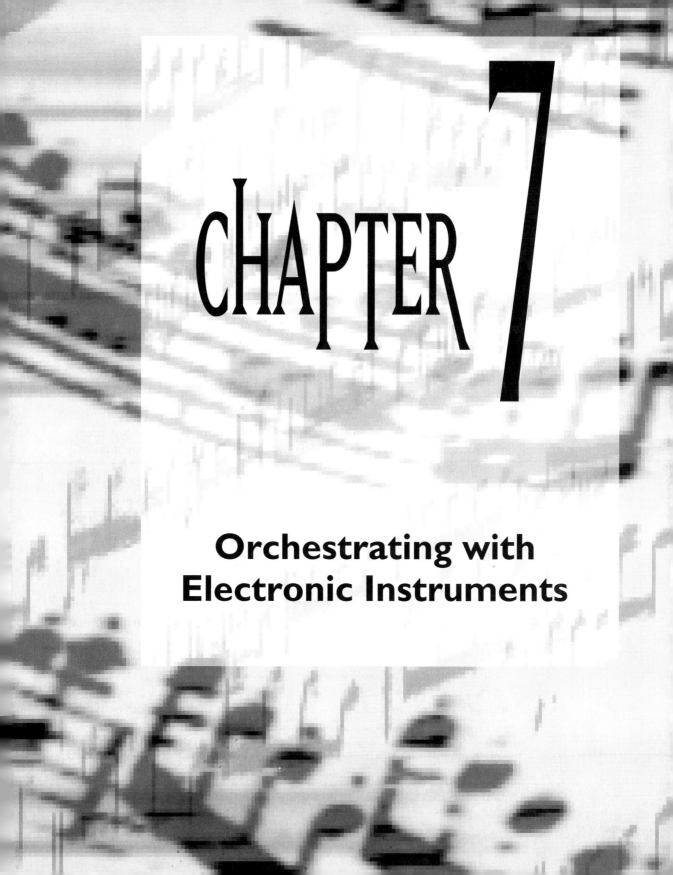

CHAPTER 7

Orchestrating with Electronic Instruments

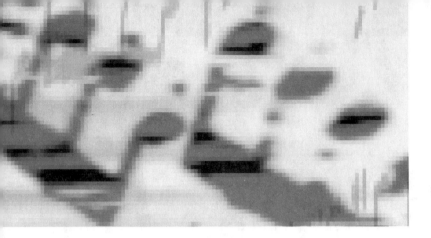

W OW! A whole symphony orchestra right at my fingertips! What power! What potential! What do I do now? Is this what you thought the first time you hooked up a synthesizer or sound module? If so, you're not alone. Most people are amazed at the musical horizons that open before them as they enter the world of MIDI. But translating musical potential into a finished piece is another story.

Actually, composing for MIDI instruments is really no different than composing for any musical medium. You must start with good material to achieve a satisfactory result. Composition is composition. You must have strong themes, well-crafted melodies, appropriate harmonies, and rhythms that propel the piece forward.

The best pieces strike a balance between familiarity and surprise. They vary the texture, yet strive for stylistic consistency. They offer new ideas, but remain accessible to the listener. It's a lot to juggle at once. That's why people spend years studying the art of composition. And that's why just plugging in a sound module won't turn you into Stravinsky overnight.

But that doesn't mean you should get discouraged. MIDI offers unprecedented opportunities for studying music and developing compositional techniques. MIDI's interactive nature lets you try things out and change things all around any time you want. And listening to the fruits of your labor is always just a mouse click away. So whether you're writing for an orchestra, a jazz ensemble, a rock group, or a polka band, MIDI can help you hone your skills.

Many people, however, have perfectly good musical ideas that simply don't survive the translation into sound. And that brings us to the focus of this chapter: orchestration—the art of transforming musical notes into musical colors. Of course, orchestration need not be limited to symphonic instruments. We can now create musical sounds and textures that Bach and Mozart could not have dreamed of. So if your interests lie in producing electronic scores with a distinctly "synthesized" sound, the sky's the limit.

But a great many people want to use their desktop systems to re-create the sounds of traditional acoustic instruments. And in the process they invariably step into one or more of the many pitfalls that await them. That's because the "virtual" instruments in a MIDI system are just not the same as their real-world counterparts. So let's take a look at some of the things to consider when orchestrating with MIDI.

Loudness, Pitch, and Timbre

As I described in Chapter 2, the three characteristics that distinguish one musical tone from another are loudness (amplitude), pitch (frequency), and timbre (harmonic content). In a good orchestration, all of the musical sounds cooperate to produce an effective result. If you find that your sounds are competing rather than cooperating you can often solve the problem by changing one or more of these variables.

Pitch Versus Loudness

As an example, let's say you have a trumpet and a flute, both playing loudly on the C above middle C. The odds are pretty good that you won't hear the flute at all. In that register, the trumpet is much stronger than the flute and it will simply overwhelm it. This phenomenon is known as *masking*. When two tones occur at or near the same pitch, the louder sound obscures the softer sound.

Masking occurs when a stronger instrument overpowers a weaker one. If the passage is a loud one it would not make sense to have the trumpet play softly. Simply boosting the flute's volume setting, on the other hand, would create an artificial blend that most listeners would perceive right away. In fact, having the flute louder than the trumpet would imply to the listener that the flute was much closer than the trumpet. This can destroy the natural sense of placement in the ensemble.

A better solution would be to change the flute's pitch. By placing the flute an octave higher you can have it play in a stronger register. And separating it from the trumpet gives it some space to stand out. Furthermore, if you really want to balance the trumpet you can add a piccolo to the flute and have the piccolo play two octaves higher than the trumpet.

The basic goal is always to create clear orchestrations. The orchestral textures should be sufficiently transparent that each instrument's contribution to the whole is important. Of course there are times when you may want a massive blended sound, but be careful not to overdo it. Just because you have an orchestra at your fingertips doesn't mean that everybody has to play all the time. The most effective orchestrations combine instruments in ever-changing combinations that explore the potential of the orchestra. And that's when the issue of timbre comes into play.

Choosing Timbres

Each of the instruments has its own unique timbre and that's how we tell them apart. In an orchestral setting, however, these timbres are often combined with other timbres. Whether the music consists of chords (any combination of notes sounding together) or polyphony (two or more independent melodies playing together), the juxtaposition of timbres can change the character of the music.

For example, if you have three different melody lines occurring at once you can treat them in several ways. You might assign a distinctly different instrument to each line such as violin, trumpet, and piano. This will certainly make each line stand out. But it also creates problems in attaining the right balance among the different lines. Such divergent sounds may also be more of a distraction than a help in some cases.

A better solution might be to use instruments from the same family. If you choose flute, oboe, and clarinet, for example, you will still have a distinct sound for each line, but the sounds will blend better. There are also times when the music itself supplies plenty of contrast. Or you simply might not want such distinct timbres. Then you can choose closely related sounds such as violins, violas, and cellos. This gives the most textural consistency and allows the sounds to blend smoothly.

Doubling Up

One common reason for combining timbres is to reinforce a melody line. This is called *doubling* (synthesists call it layering). The flute and piccolo example that I used earlier illustrates the point. To strengthen the flute line we needed something extra. I could have added a second flute in unison with the first, but the results would have been disappointing. In spite of what common sense would seem to dictate, two flutes are not twice as loud as one flute.

A doubling is produced when two instruments play the same part. Doubling is used to add strength or to provide a new timbre.

Raising the flute an octave was a partial solution, but the most dramatic results came from doubling the flute with a piccolo. The piccolo playing an octave higher adds lots of upper harmonics to the sound. This gives the line a brighter quality that can hold its own against a trumpet. In fact, a piccolo is so bright you can hear it through an entire orchestra.

Melody lines are often doubled to make them stand out against a chordal background. Although octaves and unisons are the most common doublings, any consonant interval (i.e., 3rds, 5ths, 6ths) can work in the right context.

Bass lines are also good candidates for doubling. Adding a second instrument an octave below the bass line gives greater weight and a stronger foundation to the music. If your trombone section needs a little help you might add a tuba an octave lower. The cello section is routinely doubled an octave lower by the double basses.

tip   *Doubling the melody an octave higher and the bass an octave lower works well to expand the orchestral range without causing problems. Doubling the inner parts, however, is trickier. If your doublings start to overlap each other your transparent texture may quickly turn to mud. Be careful not to get too carried away with interior octave doublings.*

Mixing Timbres

Reinforcing musical lines is not the only reason that orchestrators employ doubling. Sometimes you may need a hybrid sound to give the right quality to a line. Let's say you have a beautiful melody that you've assigned to the oboe. But the oboe sounds a little edgy for your taste. Try adding a flute in unison. The reedy quality of the oboe blends well with the breathy quality of the flute to give you a new softer sound—the best of both worlds. Try experimenting with other combinations like muted trumpet and clarinet, or bassoon and French horn.

On the Attack

The attack part of a sound is extremely important. It's filled with transient overtones that give the sound much of its character. It also provides another opportunity to apply doubling. Let's say you like the silky sound of the flute in the middle register, and you also need its ability to sustain notes. But the flute line isn't standing out enough in the ensemble. Its relatively slow, breathy attack lacks the necessary definition. Try bolstering the attack part of the sound by doubling it with a more percussive instrument.

You might, for example, double the flute with orchestral bells. That will give you a metallic, percussive attack combined with the flute's nice sustaining quality. This flute/bell combination will cut more easily through the ensemble and impart a twinkling, magical quality to the music. There are many combinations that work well. For example, try doubling piano with strings, harp with bassoon, marimba with clarinet, and snare drum with trumpets.

In My Experience

As a professional composer, I'm called upon to write in a variety of styles. In previous centuries composers wrote primarily in one style, but today's composers are often expected to be musical chameleons. You not only need to know how to compose in all the basic styles, but you also need to know how to orchestrate your composition accordingly. It's not uncommon for one project to call for music in the style of Mozart, for example, and another to need a pop ballad or "outer space" music. Therefore, my musical orientation changes from one project to next.

Even though the styles and demands of each project change from week to week, the one constant that remains is the instruments (or their electronic equivalents). For example, the range of a flute is always the same whether it's used in Mozart's "The Magic Flute" or Jethro Tull's "Thick as a Brick." And the same violin that plays "Orange Blossom Special" in a bluegrass band can also play the Brahms violin concerto. The point is that the instruments, themselves, don't determine the style, but rather how they are used.

Sometimes you'll find that orchestration involves the process of trial and error. If one particular instrument doesn't sound right or achieve the desired effect, then experiment, trying several different instruments if necessary. In one of my pieces, for example, I was using a full string section to provide the harmony with woodwinds for the melody line. However, in one section, no matter what woodwind I tried—clarinet, oboe, bassoon, etc.—I could not produce precisely the sound I was looking for. Even though I had initially thought that any brass instrument would be inappropriate, I decided to try several as an experiment. I was pleased to find that muted trumpet worked quite well and blended smoothly with the other instruments.

Although experimentation is a good way to explore new or unique orchestrations, the key to successful desktop orchestrating is to know your instruments, their sounds, their capabilities, their limitations, and their peculiarities. Professional composers have typically studied most of the traditional instruments in significant detail. While you may not have had that luxury, listen widely to the way instruments are used in the style in which you are working. If you apply your "electronic instruments" in the same way, you'll achieve more professional results.

Variety

As the old saying goes, familiarity breeds contempt. In the case of orchestration this is certainly true, even if "contempt" is a little harsh. Perhaps "boredom" is more accurate. In any case, keep in mind that "variety is the spice of life." Listeners quickly tune out repetition and sameness. Sometimes composers use this fact to good effect, but usually too much sameness is a sign of poor orchestration.

Remember, just because you have an orchestra in a box sitting on your desk doesn't mean that all of the instruments have to play all of the time. Your music will be much more effective if the different instruments and groups of instruments come and go in an ever-changing kaleidoscope of orchestral color. This is true even when you're working with limited resources. Listen to the string quartets of Mozart and Beethoven. Even though the composers had only four very similar instruments to work with you still hear many creative changes in texture, density, and performance techniques.

tip   *As you're orchestrating be aware of how many "virtual" people are playing. And try to avoid the trap of writing too much of your music in the middle orchestral range. Passages in the lower range also work well to capture the listener's interest, especially if they're balanced by other passages in the upper range.*

Polyphonic Colors

Polyphonic music offers many great opportunities for trying out various orchestral colors. You can assign the different melodic lines to solo instruments, groups of similar instruments in unison (saxes, trumpets, trombones, horns, and strings all work well), or mixed instruments with doublings (as described above).

When two or more instruments play exactly the same part, they are playing in unison.

An important point to remember is that any instrument or group of instruments that has been playing for many measures will no longer be a focal point to the listener. In other words, the sound has become a part of the orchestral *status quo* and, therefore, doesn't draw attention to itself.

If a significant entrance is about to occur it's important that the instrument that enters has not been sounding for quite awhile beforehand. For example, if the melody is about to enter in the cellos, it's a good idea to drop out the cellos for several measures before their entrance. When the cellos do enter with their melody, the sound will seem fresh to the listener and the impact of the entrance will be much stronger. But what if you can't afford to drop the cellos for several measures? Then try adding an interesting doubling at the entrance. It may not be quite as effective, but it will draw attention to the new sonority.

Adjusting the Volume

And finally, don't forget to vary the loudness. This is true of the individual sections of instruments as well as the orchestra as a whole. Continuous loud music is very fatiguing. Continuous quiet music might just put your audience to sleep. And music that never varies from the middle ground quickly becomes boring and lifeless.

Of course, loudness is not just a matter of playing louder. Loudness is also affected by the numbers and types of instruments that are playing. And it's affected by the ranges in which they're playing. Higher frequencies (around the top two octaves of a piano) are perceived by the listener as being louder than much lower frequencies. So they may not need to be played as loudly to cut through the ensemble.

Voicing Your Thoughts

One of the most important tasks that face an orchestrator is deciding where to place the notes that form the changing harmonies in a piece. The notes that make up a chord can be arranged in a number of ways. And each different arrangement of chord tones produces a different effect, even though the harmony itself is the same. The trick is to achieve clarity and balance at the same time.

As I described in Chapter 2, the individual harmonics that form a single musical tone fall into a pattern called the natural harmonic series (Figure 7-1). If you study the example for a moment you'll see that the lower harmonics have more space between them than the upper harmonics. (Actually, as you

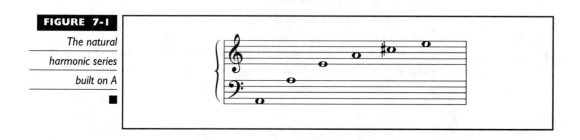

FIGURE 7-1

The natural harmonic series built on A

move from bottom to top, the spaces get progressively smaller.) This acoustic phenomenon carries over when you combine the different pitches in a chord.

If you follow Mother Nature's lead and allow plenty of space between the low notes in a chord (Figure 7-2), you'll be rewarded with clear-sounding harmonies. That's because the upper harmonics in the bass notes will blend nicely with the lower harmonics in the treble notes. If you bunch together notes in the low range (Figure 7-3) the clashing harmonics will turn your chord to mud.

Aside from knowing that bass notes need some acoustic space, orchestrators must also know how to position the other chord tones across the orchestral spectrum. The notes in chords are often referred to as *voices* (a carry-over from early choir music). So the way a chord's notes are arranged is referred to as its *voicing*.

Chord voicings fall into two categories. In *close voicing* the chord tones are arranged close together so they take up a minimal amount of space on the staff (Figure 7-4). If you can play a chord with one hand on the piano, then it's probably using close voicing. With *open voicing* you can have the same note names, but this time they're rearranged so they spread out more (Figure 7-5).

Close voicing produces a tighter, denser harmonic quality. It's often used in woodwind and French horn sections, but it also works with trumpets and saxes. Open voicing covers a wider range of the audio spectrum and produces a more transparent quality. It's often used with strings, brass, and saxes. Under the right circumstances either type of voicing can work, so consider the type of music and the context. And think about each player's part as it moves from note to note. Keeping the instruments within a comfortable range may affect your voicing decision.

In close voicing, the notes that make up a chord are as close together as possible. In open voicing, the notes that make up a chord are spread apart.

FIGURE 7-2

Allow plenty of space between the low notes in a chord

FIGURE 7-3

This chord will sound muddy because of the closely spaced notes in the bass

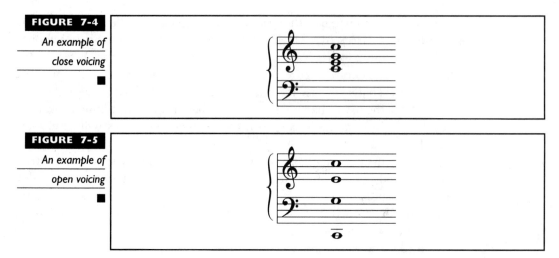

FIGURE 7-4

An example of

close voicing

FIGURE 7-5

An example of

open voicing

Home on the Range

And speaking of ranges, how high and low an instrument can play is one of the characteristics that defines that instrument's sound. So if you want your virtual orchestra to sound realistic it's a good idea to keep your electronic instruments within the normal ranges for their acoustic counterparts. A real violin, for instance, simply can't play lower than the first G below the treble clef (MIDI note #55). Nor can an oboe play lower than the B-flat below middle C (MIDI note #58). And if you hear trumpets blithely playing along two octaves above the treble clef, it's a sure bet that they're not real trumpets being played by real trumpet players.

To help keep you in the ballpark, I've put together a chart (Figure 7-6) showing the common ranges of several orchestral instruments. Keep in mind that these are *not* the extreme possible note ranges for these instruments. A good player can always expand an instrument's range beyond the "normal" range. The ranges in the chart are simply those most commonly associated with the instruments under *most* circumstances. If you stick to these conservative ranges, your virtual instruments will not sound strained and your performances will sound more natural and more characteristic.

Think Like a Player

Most desktop musicians use some kind of keyboard to input their performances into a sequencer. Although there are lots of other kinds of input devices (see Chapter 4), keyboards are by far the most versatile and remain the most popular type of controller.

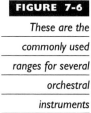

FIGURE 7-6

These are the commonly used ranges for several orchestral instruments

Characteristic Instrument Ranges

A keyboard is a good universal input device and provides a consistent interface between you and your sequencer. But keyboards do have disadvantages. And the main disadvantage is that they encourage you to play like a pianist rather than an orchestral player. This is perhaps the biggest pitfall that faces a beginning synthesist. And it's the most common reason (aside from poor patch quality) that synthesized scores don't sound convincing.

So the first thing you need to do is to start thinking like the players. Put yourself in the shoes of each member of the orchestra and try to imagine how their parts should sound. This is a tall order, but it's not insurmountable. After all, you don't have to know every little bit of information about an instrument to produce a credible performance. It's not really important, for instance, which notes on a clarinet are awkward to trill, or which slide position you're in when you play middle C on a trombone. You don't need to know where on a cello's fingerboard the A-flats occur and you don't have to worry about your reed drying out just before that important oboe entrance. You just have to capture the *style* of the performance. So here are a few things to keep in mind as you perform orchestral parts.

Strings

Strings are commonly available both as solo instruments and as sections. Of course you can take a solo string sound and perform it over and over again to create the sound of a string section. But that would consume lots of MIDI notes and you'd soon run out of available polyphony on your synth. That's why nearly all MIDI instruments provide at least one string section sound.

Here's another thing to consider. A string section is simply not the same as a single instrument overdubbed dozens of times. When a room full of violinists all play *simultaneously*, the sounds from the different instruments interact to create a unique acoustical blend. It's the interaction of the instruments that's largely responsible for that lush string sound that synthesists strive so hard to capture. Reproducing the sounds of large ensembles is one area where samplers (and sample playback modules) excel.

Pizzicato indicates that the strings of a violin (or other stringed instrument) are to be plucked rather than bowed.

String players are capable of many interesting techniques that add color to their parts. Aside from the usual bowing, they can pluck the strings (pizzicato), mute the strings, and employ an assortment of exotic bowing techniques that use different attacks, note lengths, and bow positions.

When you write for real players you simply indicate in the music which technique to use and the player does the rest. MIDI musicians, on the other hand, must have a separate patch for each technique used. If you're changing from bowed notes to pizzicato, for example, your sound module must accommodate both sounds. This requires a little planning.

The best method is to assign the bowed sounds to one track on one channel and the pizzicato sound to a second track on another channel. Then you can edit each section separately and adjust the volume accordingly. If you can't spare the tracks or you have limited multitimbral capabilities, you can include a Program Change message in a single String Ensemble track. (Of course then you couldn't have both bowed and plucked strings at the same time.)

Violinists can play very rapid passages when they're bowing the strings. When they pluck the strings, however, it's a little different. String players only use one finger to pluck the strings (unlike guitarists and harpists). So there's a limit to how fast they can play a series of plucked notes. If you suddenly insert a three-measure burst of sixty-fourth notes in a pizzicato passage it will be obvious that a keyboard player was playing the part and not a violinist.

Because of their long, fat strings, the double basses have similar limitations on speed—for both plucked and bowed passages. Rapid playing in the low registers sounds muddy and it's completely uncharacteristic.

Legato is a style of playing in which notes connect smoothly from one to the next.

To create a *legato* style of playing (smoothly connecting notes) you have to slightly change the usual note durations. Simply entering a series of notes with exact note values onto the staff (or through step recording) will not produce the desired effect. Even when each note ends precisely where the next one begins, the music will lack the legato quality. To solve the problem, overlap the notes very slightly by extending each note's duration by a small amount (5 to 10 percent). The listeners won't perceive the overlap, but the notes will blend smoothly from one to the next (Figure 7-7).

Sometimes violinists play a series of notes by changing the bow direction for each note. This gives a more detached sound to the passage. With this technique the down bows tend to sound slightly heavier than the up bows. You can approximate this feel by shortening the duration on every other note by a tiny bit (Figure 7-8). The differences should not be too obvious so try experimenting to achieve an appropriately subtle quality. Also, try adding or subtracting Velocity amounts to every other note. See how this changes the feel of the piece.

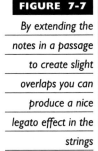

FIGURE 7-7

By extending the notes in a passage to create slight overlaps you can produce a nice legato effect in the strings

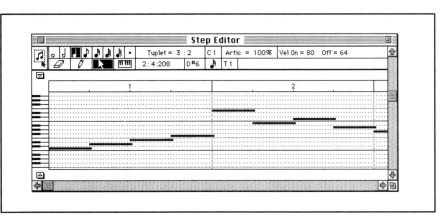

In this example every other note has been shortened slightly to simulate alternating bowing ■

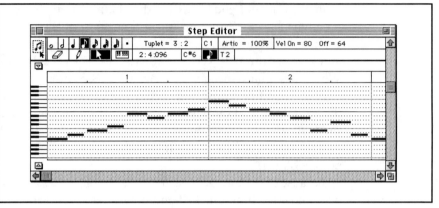

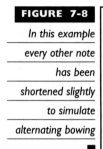

tip   *For solo parts, don't forget vibrato. String players always add vibrato to sustained notes. Many people use the Modulation wheel to add vibrato to a note. If your keyboard supports it, try using Aftertouch to introduce vibrato to the notes. You may find that it gives you more control and you can keep both hands on the keyboard.*

Wind Instruments

The biggest mistake that keyboard players make when they write for wind instruments is that they don't leave places to breathe. It's an understandable oversight, but to wind players breathing is essential. Even though your virtual players never have to take a breath, your wind parts will sound more convincing (and musical) if you think like a wind player. Writing 20 continuous measures without a rest for your oboe part is simply not characteristic of the instrument. Nor is a 17-measure sustained chord in the trombone section.

Melodic writing for winds is typically organized into phrases. This lets the players take a quick breath in the transition from one phrase to the next. And it gives a musical shape and structure to the melodies. It's a good idea, therefore, to look over your wind parts and find logical places to insert a brief silence. It will make the parts more realistic and more interesting.

The different woodwind instruments each have a distinctive timbre. That's why they're so often used to add color to an orchestration. One good way to work out ideas for a woodwind section is to create a setup with several of the woodwind sounds spread across the keyboard. You can set up your keyboard with splits so that different instruments are heard as you play from left to right. This works well with strings because they blend so nicely from one to another. Woodwinds, however, are trickier. It will be obvious when you cross a split point that the sound has suddenly changed from a bassoon to a clarinet or from a clarinet to an oboe. So if you plan to map your woodwind instruments across the keyboard try to anticipate the essential ranges that you'll need for each instrument and write accordingly. You can always go back later and assign each woodwind to a separate MIDI channel and sequencer track. This is the best option if you have the necessary multitimbral capabilities.

Although the woodwinds have distinctive timbres, they still blend quite well when used to score harmonies. You can achieve many subtle shadings of orchestral color depending on which notes are assigned to which chord tones (Figure 7-9). Try experimenting with different voicings and different combinations of instruments. But be aware that the different woodwind registers have their own unique qualities (aside from the overall timbres) and some registers are notably stronger than others. (The flute, for example, is rather weak in its low register, but much stronger when it plays above the staff.) Therefore, not all combinations will work equally well.

Brass instruments are more alike than the woodwinds, so they often blend more smoothly. Brass instruments can provide great strength to an orchestration and they also make excellent solo instruments. Just don't forget about phrasing.

Brass instruments can also be played with mutes to provide an additional palette of colors. There are actually several types of mutes (e.g., Harmon, cup, and straight), each with its own distinctive sound. The General MIDI instrument list includes a muted trumpet sound (#60) and some sound modules and samplers provide more. When a brass instrument is using a mute its range is significantly reduced. So you can't play very high notes and the lowest notes sound funny and unmusical. Try combining muted trumpets with woodwinds or strings to see what orchestral colors you can produce.

tip *As with strings, vibrato is an important part of a wind instrument's sound. Wind instruments, however, don't initiate vibrato right from the attack. Usually following the attack there's a slight delay as the tone stabilizes. Then the vibrato evolves as the note sustains. For the most musical effect always pause very briefly before introducing vibrato and then allow it to build smoothly.*

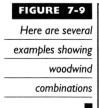

FIGURE 7-9
Here are several
examples showing
woodwind
combinations

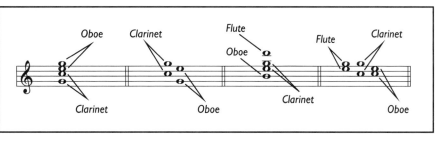

Panning for Gold

The instruments in your MIDI system are all probably coming out of a couple of boxes sitting on the desktop in front you. Or they might even be coming from a single sound card buried somewhere in the bowels of your CPU. In either case it's easy to forget that we're creating a virtual orchestra. And to be convincing, your desktop orchestra must create the illusion of taking up space. To accomplish this, we have two tools at our disposal: panning and reverberation (reverb).

Panning establishes where in the stereo soundfield (from left to right) an instrument appears to be. The first rule here is to strive for consistency (unless you're experimenting with special effects). If your ensemble only has one bassoon and the first time it plays you hear it on the left, that's where it

Of Interest (continued)

solos in the higher ranges. These two instruments work well together because they have similar string-based sounds. And they function as a team to supply the notes that form the harmonic accompaniment.

The trumpet typically plays in the high range. Its distinct timbre works in this setting because it's used as a solo instrument and it must cut through the harmonic background. The drum set provides a rhythmic foundation and also adds to the overall texture of the music. From the low thud of the kick drum to the high frequencies of the cymbals, the drum set, itself, covers a wide audio range while adding contrast and variety to the music.

A rock band is another example. It typically consists of a bass guitar, a lead guitar, a rhythm guitar, and a drum set. Because the three tonal instruments are guitars, their sounds are naturally compatible. As expected, the bass guitar provides the low range, the rhythm guitar plays in the mid-range, and the lead guitar generally solos in the high range. As is the case for the jazz ensemble, the drum set provides the rhythm and fills out the overall texture.

As you can see, the most effective ensembles often contain instruments that cover a wide frequency range and that complement each other appropriately. Each instrument must carry its own weight within the group while not overshadowing the other instruments. Strive for a balance between consistency and variety. If your compositions don't sound quite right to you, perhaps you're not working with a good ensemble.

should be the second time as well. If the second entrance occurs on the right it gives the impression to the listener that the player has picked up the bassoon and carried it across the stage before playing again. The best way to arrive at a consistent result is to imagine where the players are seated and pan accordingly.

In a typical orchestra the strings are arranged more or less in a semicircle at the front of the stage. The woodwinds are in the center. And behind the woodwinds are the brass (Figure 7-10).

In this example you would pan the first violins hard left and the second violins hard right. The cellos and violas would be similar, perhaps with a bit less separation. The woodwinds would be in the center with just a little separation between the oboes and clarinets. The horns and bassoons would also be slightly panned to the left and right, respectively. And the trombones and double basses would get a moderate amount of panning.

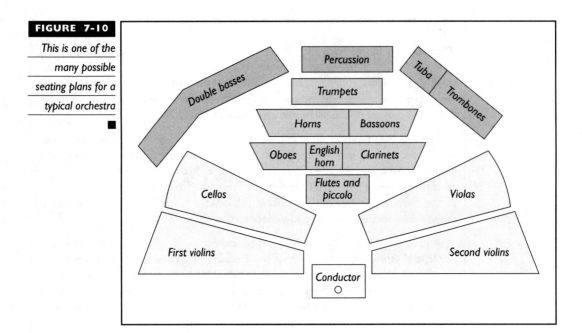

This is only one possible arrangement for an orchestra. You can set things up in a number of ways. For example, some orchestras place the first and second violins on the left and the cellos and violas on the right. Sometimes the double basses are on the right and the percussion is on the left. The type of music that you write will play a role in determining the placement of the instruments. The same general principles apply for ensembles of any size.

Lost in Space

Aside from its location left and right, each instrument also has a position within the acoustic environment. A clarinet sounds a lot different in a phone booth than it does in a cathedral. And if the clarinet is in a cathedral it will sound much different right in front of you than at the back of the room. Creating the illusion of an acoustic space is what reverb is all about. It simulates the acoustics in different types of rooms and brings dry electronic sounds to life.

When working with reverb there are two variables to consider: the type of reverb (e.g., small room, medium room, or large room) and the amount of reverb added to the sound. The type of reverb will be based on the size of your virtual ensemble and the effect you're trying to create. The amount of reverb is based, in part, on how far away you want the sound to seem.

Some sound modules have a built-in reverb function, other don't. If you have one or more sound modules that don't include reverb, an inexpensive external reverb unit makes a good investment. Perfectly acceptable units are available for well under $200.

If you're working with more than one MIDI device, you may find that some of your sounds already include reverb while others don't. Your clarinet, for example, may sound like it's coming from the back of a concert hall, while the oboe, right next to it, may sound like its right in front of the listener. Try to balance out the type and amount of reverb to give a consistent

---

Guidelines for Better Orchestration

1. Always start with a good composition. Imaginative orchestration cannot overcome poor writing.

2. The orchestra consists of four families of instruments: strings, woodwinds, brass, and percussion.

3. Within families the players are often grouped into sections (e.g., 1st violins, 2nd violins, trumpets, and trombones).

4. These sections are often subdivided into smaller groups and soloists.

5. Use doublings within sections or between sections to enhance melodies, bass lines, and harmonies.

6. Create variety by combining timbres in interesting ways.

7. Vary the loudness in the individual lines and throughout the piece as a whole. Avoid creating a static volume level.

8. Use the full orchestral range from treble to bass. Avoid orchestrating everything in the middle range.

9. Use voicings that provide clarity. Avoid closely spaced groups of notes in the bass range.

10. Use phrasing and performance techniques that are characteristic of the instruments.

11. Use your MIDI controllers (e.g., Modulation wheel, Aftertouch, and Pitch Bend) to add expressiveness to the instrumental parts.

12. Stay within reasonable instrumental ranges.

13. Use panning and reverb to create the illusion of an acoustic space.

14. Always strive for a transparent orchestration with well-balanced textures.

impression of the performance environment. And be careful not to use so much reverb that the sounds begin to blend together too much. Always strive for consistency and clarity.

Last Word

In this chapter we've focused on orchestral writing because it affords a good level of complexity with lots of problems to solve. But the basic principles apply to ensembles of any kind. Those who write big band jazz and arrangements of popular music must also deal with performance techniques, doublings, voicings, ranges, and sound placement. Creating the illusion of "real" instruments from a desktop system is as much a state of mind as it is a matter of technique. Remember, think like the players and listen like the audience.

CHAPTER 8

Spontaneous MIDI

I T might well be argued that MIDI's most important quality is the real-time, interactive environment that it offers musicians. It's true that setting up and configuring a MIDI system takes a bit of planning. But once you have your music system ready to go, and you're familiar with its workings, many exciting things are possible. Unfortunately, as MIDI musicians, we often get bogged down with the minutia of music making and fail to enjoy the scenery along the road to the perfect composition.

It doesn't always have to be that way, though. Computers can be much more than tools for recording, editing, and storing music. They can also act like partners that guide us in new directions. And fortunately, there are now a number of applications designed specifically to do just that. Some of these programs encourage improvisation by supplying an easy-to-configure musical context. Others simply take a new approach to the process of writing music. Still others employ interactive composition functions to generate new music from your mouse or keyboard input. Whatever approach is taken, however, the goal is always the same—to help you explore new musical places and to recapture the spontaneity that's so much a part of MIDI.

In this chapter we'll explore several programs that can help you turn your desktop studio into an interactive musical environment. If you want to make music as quickly as possible, with the least amount of effort, you may find these products especially appealing.

Music Mouse

MAC

PC

Laurie Spiegel's **Music Mouse**—introduced for the Mac in 1986—was the first commercially available "intelligent instrument" software. As its name suggests, it uses the computer's mouse as its primary source of input for generating interactive performances. The output goes to a MIDI device and the Mac can also use its internal sounds. The program's main window (Figure 8-1) consists of two halves. On the left there are several user-definable parameters that affect the musical outcome. On the right there's a large grid surrounded by keyboards.

Music Mouse is a program that's easier to use than to explain. On the surface it's simply a program that generates music in response to movements of your computer mouse. But such a simple explanation doesn't give a true sense of the creative potential that the program offers.

With Music Mouse you actually perform using both hands. One hand generates mostly step-wise melodies and harmonies by moving the mouse. The other hand changes a number of parameters (that affect the musical interpretation) by pressing the keys on your computer keyboard.

FIGURE 8-1

The Music Mouse

main screen

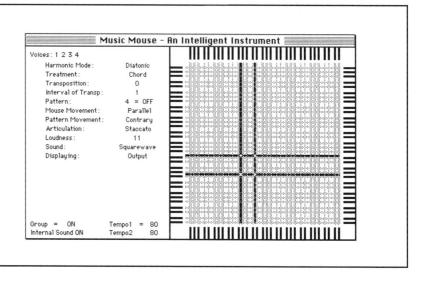

The x-axis and y-axis movements of the mouse produce two independent melody lines while the software generates two more melody lines for a total of four voices. The two lines supplied by the software move in various ways that relate to the two lines produced by the mouse. The final results depend on which keyboard options are currently in effect.

As you move the mouse around, four dark lines point to the currently playing notes on the keyboards that border the grid. The lowest notes are at the bottom-left corner. The highest notes are at the top-right.

Although the mouse is the primary source of input, the computer keyboard is more than just an appendage. In fact, you can create a lot of interesting music simply by pressing various keys without moving the mouse. The keyboard's main purpose, however, is to modify the musical output from the mouse in several important ways. With the appropriate keystrokes, for example, you can change the scale that Music Mouse uses in creating its melodies and harmonies. (The choices include Chromatic, Diatonic, Middle Eastern, Pentatonic, and others.)

You can also transpose the music up or down by semitones, increase or decrease the volume, and make the tempo faster or slower. Other keystrokes let you change MIDI parameters such as Velocity, Aftertouch, Modulation, Program Number, and others. The key assignments are all logically laid out and easy to use. They make it simple to introduce a variety of changes in real time as you create your music.

Things get even more interesting when you use keystrokes to change the way Music Mouse structures its music. For instance, you can choose how to group the four voices. The program lets you have a solo voice (on the y-axis) with three-note chords (on the x-axis). Or you can have two pairs of voices—one pair on each axis. And for even more variety, you can specify whether the voices move in parallel or contrary motion.

The number keys let you select one of ten different "melodic contours." These abstract patterns of intervals include an assortment of arpeggios and note cycles of varying lengths. They affect the final melodic outcome. The accompanying chords can be played with the notes sounding together, arpeggiated, or in combinations decided by the program.

Music Mouse's user interface is so readily accessible that a child of virtually any age can start improvising immediately. But the program also offers sufficient complexity that adults will find it challenging as well. In fact, most people will find it quite addictive as they explore the musical cause-and-effect relationships that spring forth from their computers. Although the music always has a certain pleasant-sounding, rambling quality, you can introduce a good level of variety into your performance.

The x-axis and y-axis mouse movements are completely independent of one another, so you can play separate melody lines by moving the mouse vertically or horizontally. For example, if you move the mouse on either a vertical or horizontal axis while holding it still on the other axis, you can produce a moving melody against a constant drone. Or you can generate an interesting melody/harmony interplay by repeating a pattern of motions on one axis and then on the other. Furthermore, the same pattern will produce quite different feelings depending on where in the grid it's played. Resourceful players will find an array of intriguing musical effects to experiment with.

Unfortunately, Music Mouse doesn't provide any way to record your performances and save them as Standard MIDI Files. If you have an external sequencer you can record the MIDI output in real time and import it later into your computer. And you can always record your performances on tape. But Music Mouse (from Dr. T's Music Software) should be thought of primarily as a real-time interactive instrument that lets you explore the music-making process in some unique and fascinating ways.

Jam Factory

MAC

Jam Factory (from Dr. T's) is a more complicated program than Music Mouse and it demands more from the user. The results, however, are well worth the effort. In Jam Factory you create a combo of up to four virtual players who each take a different bit of music that you supply and "improvise" on the material in various ways. The resulting music is affected by a bunch of sometimes arcane yet always fascinating "intelligent" functions that generate new music from your original input.

The program's main screen is divided into seven windows (Figure 8-2). Four of these are the Player windows labeled P1 through P4. Across the middle of the screen, the Control Strip contains transport-like buttons and a small track list called the Assignment Matrix. It lets you assign MIDI channels and set up each player for recording and playing. The ten boxes between P1 and P2 let you store and recall (in real time) different setups. The area between P3 and P4 lets you record and play back macros for controlling the program.

Jam Factory offers a substantial level of complexity to those users who are willing to explore its inner workings. But you don't have to delve too deeply into the program to start having fun.

Here's the basic procedure. You begin by recording a few measures of music (notes and/or chords) into one of the Players. Let's say you're starting out with a bass part. Simply record-enable the first Player, click the Go button, and perform your bass line. Jam Factory records with a resolution of 96 ppqn and quantizes on input. You don't have to record much. For a

FIGURE 8-2

Jam Factory's main

screen showing the

four Player windows

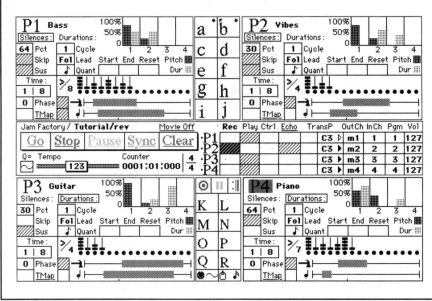

simple bass line two or three measures is enough. For more complex melodies several measures will produce better results.

To edit your performance, Jam Factory provides a rudimentary piano-roll-style editor (Figure 8-3). It lets you add new notes, change wrong pitches, set durations, and delete unwanted notes. When you're happy with the performance you return to the Player window where you specify how the Player will treat your music.

In the lower-right corner of Player 1's window there are a couple of horizontal bar graphs. The upper one indicates the range of accents (Velocity values) that the player can choose from. You can change the accent range instantly by dragging with the mouse. Directly above the accent range bar, what appears to be several small stacks of bricks is actually another kind of bar graph. It indicates the accent patterns that the player will use. The other horizontal bar graph—at the bottom of the window—lets you specify an articulation range (staccato to legato).

Keep in mind that these controls all work in real time. So as you listen to your bass line repeat over and over, you can change these parameters and hear the effects immediately. You can also transpose the music as it plays.

It's fun to fiddle around with the accent and articulation controls. But the really exciting action revolves around a set of small, unobtrusive bar graphs in the upper-right corner of the Player window. These are the Pitch and Rhythm Variation graphs. They determine which notes and rhythms the Player will choose as it improvises on your original music.

FIGURE 8-3

Jam Factory

provides a simple

piano-roll-style

editor

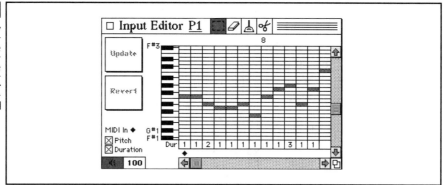

Here's how they work: Jam Factory analyzes your original music and records the transitions between pitches in a structure called a Transition Table. It does the same thing for note durations. Then using a process known as a Markov chain, it independently rearranges the notes and rhythms based on a set of probabilities. Because the likelihood of any pitch or duration occurring is derived from the original music the improvised versions will always sound related to the original. And Jam Factory lets you influence this relationship by providing control over four "orders" of transitions. These are represented by the four sets of bar graphs that you see in the window.

With a first-order Transition Table Jam Factory decides which note to play next by looking at the previous note and basing its decision on a set of probabilities. With a second-order Transition Table the program examines the previous two notes. A third-order Transition Table uses three notes and so on. The higher the order, the more like the original the new music will sound. As the program examines the pitches, the same process is also occurring independently for note durations. By adjusting the bar graphs, you can determine the odds of any particular Transition Table being used in the selection process (the values always total 100 percent).

Fooling around with these Transition Tables is truly fascinating as you change the nature of the improvisations. And since everything is happening in real time the feedback is immediate. Any time you want you can return to your original ordering of pitches and durations by clicking on the words Pitch and Dur below the bar graph.

For a different type of improvisation you can click on the word Silences at the left side of the window. The music then plays back with all of the durations the same, but with varying amounts of silence (skipped notes) between groups of notes. Jam Factory lets you control several parameters that affect the Silences algorithm. For instance, you can set how often (by percentage) notes are skipped and whether or not the note that precedes the missing note will sustain through the "silence."

Once you have a great bass part going you can move on to Player 2 and add a guitar or piano part or whatever you like. After you've set up all four players (you don't have to use all four) you can sit back and enjoy your combo of improvisers. As the music plays you can continue to interact with the parts by tweaking parameters. Or you can simply play along with your own part.

There's actually much more to Jam Factory than I've described here. For example, you can make real-time performance changes from your MIDI controller by assigning actions to various MIDI keys. And you can arbitrarily remap notes into other notes to make players change scales during a performance. You can even modify a Player's rhythmic nuances by using the graphical Time Distortion window.

Jam Factory has plenty to keep you busy, but if you're looking for an even bigger ensemble you can connect two copies of Jam Factory and have them run at the same time. And to capture any performances that you like you can save the music as a Format 0 Standard MIDI File. You can also import the same kind of MIDI files to use as input data for the Players. And for some real variety try having different people provide the music for each of the Players. You might say the possibilities are "virtually" endless.

UpBeat

MAC

Writing good rhythm section parts is an art form unto itself. And because drum parts have their own unique requirements they deserve a special program. If you're looking for a way to turn your computer into a sophisticated, interactive drum machine then **UpBeat** is the answer. It lets you input MIDI events from your keyboard (or from the pads on a drum machine) and outputs drum sounds from your sound module (or drum machine). When you're through you can save your rhythm part as a Standard MIDI File and import it into your regular sequencer.

UpBeat (from Dr. T's) has been around for several years now. And some of its features have even been incorporated—to a greater or lesser degree—into a number of sequencers. But UpBeat still remains viable today because it does so much so well. At the simplest level, UpBeat works like most drum machines. You create short Patterns of one or more measures and store them in a list called a Library. To create a rhythm track you chain together different combinations of Patterns into a playlist called a Song. Since you can also have Songs in a Library you can include Songs inside of other Songs.

To create a Pattern, you first create a Device. This is simply a list containing the names of your drum (or other) sounds and the MIDI notes that trigger them. These names then appear along the left side of the main display (Figure 8-4).

Opposite each name there's a separate track that shows where in the Pattern that sound is triggered. You record your sounds in real time by playing them in from your MIDI controller as a metronome and a bouncing ball provide references. UpBeat loops a specified number of measures as you record and lets you overdub new notes with each pass. As the notes are triggered, little symbols appear indicating where the different sounds occur.

If you don't have a MIDI controller or you prefer a more graphical approach you can paint notes (called strikes) directly into the Pattern window. The Strike Tools palette provides several tools for entering and editing notes. The top five drumstick-like tools represent different Velocity values (from highest to lowest). The tool with the question mark enters strikes with Velocities that are randomly selected from the other values.

To enter notes you just select a Strike tool and click in the appropriate track at the appropriate beat. For immediate feedback you can do this while the Pattern is playing. If you want to enter a string of notes (such as sixteenth notes on the hi-hat) you can click and simply drag through several beats. If you use the Random Strike tool your string of notes will appear with an assortment of different Velocities.

The remaining tools let you edit your Patterns in a number of ways. You can select one or more strikes and drag them forward or backward in time

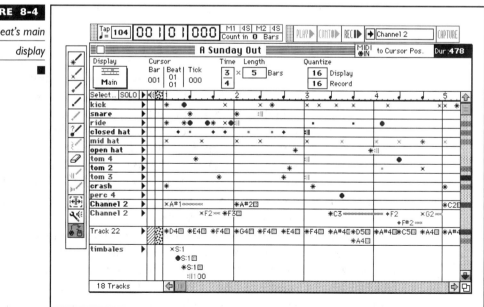

FIGURE 8-4

UpBeat's main

display

by a few ticks (UpBeat records with a resolution of 192 ppqn). You can also change a note's Pitch, Velocity, or Duration by dragging with the mouse.

If you click the Fill button in any track, UpBeat adds a fill to that track. Fills consist of extra notes—played at unpredictable times—that UpBeat adds between the notes in the track. They add an improvised quality to the rhythm section and keep things from getting too mechanical.

Fills are only one of several randomness processes that UpBeat provides for adding a certain "human" feel to the music. And, as with the other processes, you can influence the final outcome. For example, you can specify a track other than the original to play the fill. That way you can have a snare drum fill for the kick drum track or a hi-hat fill for the snare drum.

You can also decide how many subdivisions between notes there will be for fill notes. And you can insert Rest events to ensure that fill notes won't occur on certain beats. But that's not all. You can also specify a Fill Density—how often a fill note will occur given an empty space between events. And you can apply the Limit Filter to restrict where and how the fills occur.

Whenever a Fill note or Random Strike is added to a Pattern, its Velocity is selected from the track's five user-defined Velocity values (each track can have its own set of values). With the Random Velocity display you can control how often, by percentage, any particular Velocity will be chosen. The display shows the probability that each value will be selected for a random strike or fill.

A similar type of control exists for articulation (amount of staccato/legato). In the Random Articulation display you can determine the probability that any of five values will be selected for a note when it's played with random articulation or as part of a fill.

The Time Settings display lets you create variations in the feel of a track. There are two variables: Note Density and Time Deviation. Note Density lets you specify a certain percentage of notes to randomly skip in a track. For example, a setting of 50 percent means that only half the notes in the track will be played (although which notes are played is not predictable).

Time Deviation lets you determine whether notes will be played early or late and by how much. This is an important factor in creating that illusive "human feel." With the Time Deviation display you can cause all notes to be early by a set amount or randomly within a range. Or you can have all notes play late by a set amount or randomly within a range. You can even have the notes play randomly before and after the beat.

UpBeat provides lots of ways to create interesting drum parts, but it's a mistake to think of this program only as a glorified drum machine. That's because you can use UpBeat to record other instrumental parts as well. In fact you can put together a whole rhythm section including bass parts, piano chords, guitar lines, brass parts—whatever you want. And you can use the

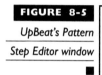

FIGURE 8-5

UpBeat's Pattern
Step Editor window

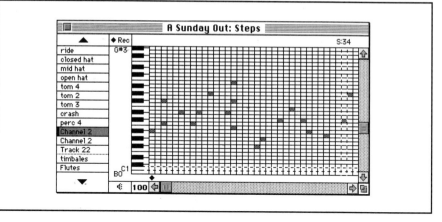

same kinds of randomness processes to enliven these parts too. The Pattern Step Editor window (Figure 8-5) lets you step-record and edit melodies (and drum tracks) in a piano-roll–style environment.

Aside from Timing, Velocity, and Articulation functions there's also a feature called Fill Following. It examines the previous notes in a melody and adds fill notes in a melodically useful way. You specify how far back UpBeat should look (up to eight events) and the program selects from those notes to create its fill.

If you enjoy working with rhythm section parts you'll love UpBeat. It provides lots of interesting ways to keep your rhythms from getting dull. And its graphic approach to editing encourages experimentation.

Band-in-a-Box

PC

MAC

CD-ROM

The name of this program pretty much says it all. **Band-in-a-Box** (from PG Music) turns your computer and MIDI sound module into a full-blown back-up band consisting of bass, piano, drums, guitar, horns, and strings. And this band is versatile. It can play in a wide variety of styles, in any key, and at any tempo. If you're looking for a program that will let you start making music fast without getting mired in too many details, Band-in-a-Box won't disappoint you. With this program you don't have to worry about which notes each of the instruments play. Editing is minimal. And the software comes with hundreds of pieces (including many standards) that are set up and ready to go. Creating your own accompaniments is easy.

Here's the procedure: the main window in Band-in-a-Box (Figure 8-6) includes a large area with numbered measures. You simply type in the chord symbols for each measure. The program lets you have up to four chords per measure and Band-in-a-Box has a very large vocabulary of chords. Next you indicate the structure of the song (intro/verse/chorus/verse, for example) by placing markers at the beginning of each new part. Band-in-a-Box uses these markers to add drum fills at the ends of sections to set up the next section. This adds momentum to the piece the way a live drummer would.

Once you've entered your chords and marked the sections you can select the style in which you'd like to have the music played. Band-in-a-Box comes with 24 built-in styles that you can't change (Figure 8-7). But the software lets you create your own styles and save them as User-Defined styles. The program includes over 100 of these already. After you select a style, all you have to do is set the tempo and you're ready to go. The whole process only takes a few minutes.

When you click the Play button, Band-in-a-Box "constructs" the accompaniment and immediately begins playback. At the same time, the original set of buttons is replaced with a new panel that includes two keyboards (Figure 8-8). The keyboards show which notes are playing in the piano and bass parts. The instrument buttons let you select individual players in the ensemble and mute them or change their patches. If you're using a Roland GS instrument there are also buttons that let you adjust the Reverb and Chorus effects and set the pan position.

FIGURE 8-6

The main window in Band-in-a-Box includes a large area with numbered measures

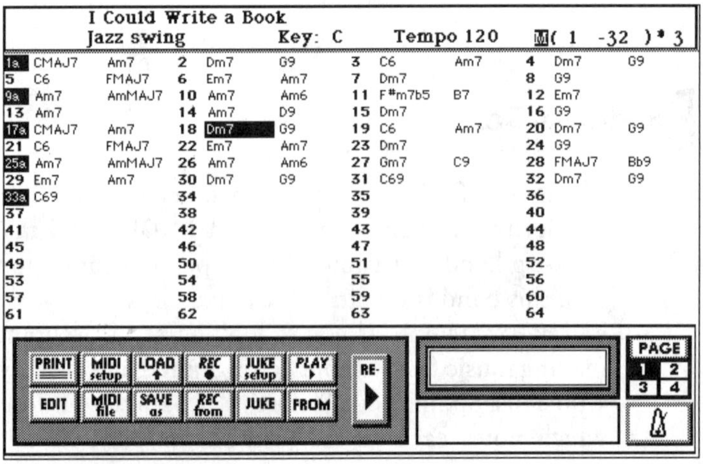

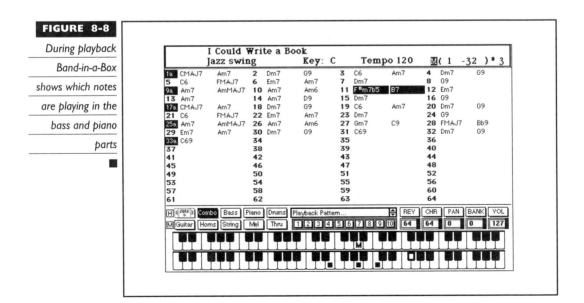

FIGURE 8-7

Band-in-a-Box comes with an assortment of built-in styles

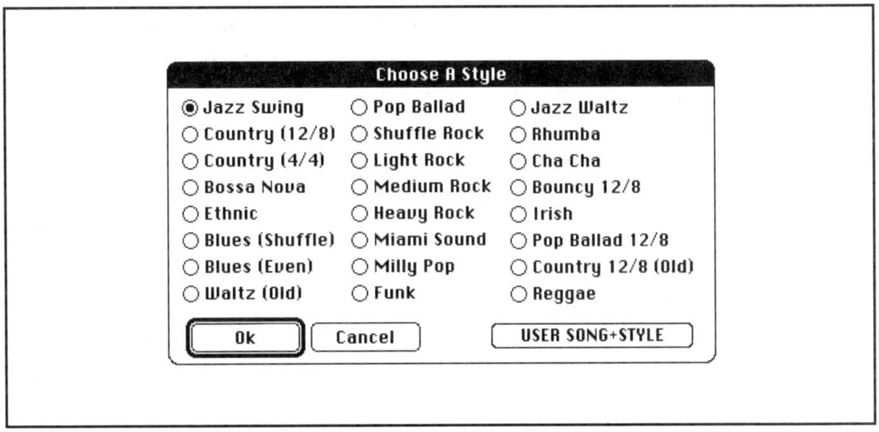

The amazing thing about Band-in-a-Box accompaniments is how musical they are. They don't just sound like those cheesy rhythm boxes that budget-priced organs and toy synthesizers use. This band is good. And there are several reasons why. Adding markers at the ends of sections helps give the drum part a human feel. And for more variety you can add fills anywhere you want by just clicking on a measure number to add an extra marker.

Another important feature is the program's use of *substyles*. Each of Band-in-a-Box's musical styles has two substyles labeled "a" and "b." In the

FIGURE 8-8

During playback Band-in-a-Box shows which notes are playing in the bass and piano parts

Jazz Swing style, for example, the "a" substyle is in a 2-beat feel and the "b" substyle is in swing feel. These substyle labels are easily added with the click of the mouse when you insert a marker at the end of a section. When the music hits one of these markers the drummer plays a lead-in fill and the entire ensemble changes to a new feel—just the way real bands do.

In some musical styles (mainly jazz, swing, and some Latin) it's common for the pianist to enhance chords to provide a richer harmonic texture. This is done by introducing additional related notes (called extensions) to the chords. To provide the right harmonic feel, Band-in-a-Box includes a Piano Chord Embellishment feature that "intelligently" adds extensions where they're needed (you can turn this off if clashes develop between your melody and the accompaniment).

And finally, to give your piece a more complete structure, Band-in-a-Box can add a stylistically appropriate introduction and ending.

When Band-in-a-Box first came out it was designed primarily as a simple accompaniment program. The newer versions, however, let you record (in real time) your own melody along with the other parts. This means you can create full arrangements complete with a soloist and back-up band. What's more, the program can automatically change your melody from "straight" to "swing" or vice versa if you switch to a style that demands it. When you're through, you can save your arrangement as a Format 1 Standard MIDI File and import it into your sequencer program for further editing and development.

Band-in-a-Box is a lot of fun to play around with. And it offers some exciting possibilities. For soloists, here's a great way to practice. And you can assemble a virtually unlimited number of your favorite songs to work with. Furthermore, you can try them out in different keys, at different tempos, with different chord changes, and in different styles. This raises the concept of "music-minus-one" to a much higher plane. And singers can get in on the act as well. (Band-in-a-Box even lets you type in lyrics to your songs.)

And if you're not a soloist, Band-in-a-Box offers the same opportunities. By muting any of the rhythm-section parts you can "sit in" with the ensemble. This can provide valuable experience playing in different keys and in different styles.

For nonkeyboard players, Band-in-a-Box lets you throw together a musical arrangement without having to enter every single note for each instrument. And if you're a composer and your rhythm-section writing skills are weak, here's a great way to create and study rhythm parts.

Finally, live performers can use Band-in-a-Box as a reliable back-up band in a number of situations. And the program is adaptable to an endless variety of musical styles through its StyleMaker feature. It lets you create and save your own styles to add to those that already come with the program.

MiBAC Jazz

MAC

CD-ROM

MiBAC Jazz is a lot like Band-in-a-Box. You type chord symbols onto the screen and the program generates an "intelligent" back-up band for you to play along with. MiBAC, however, takes a somewhat different approach to creating its accompaniments. And as its name suggests, the program focuses on jazz styles.

The back-up group consists of only three players: piano, bass, and drums and you can't record a melody part along with the ensemble. But MiBAC Jazz is no scaled-down version of Band-in-a-Box. It has its own assortment of sophisticated features that make it ideal for jazz players and others interested in working with jazz styles.

The MiBAC Jazz main window (Figure 8-9) provides a large area for entering chords. Unlike Band-in-a-Box, MiBAC's chords appear above a musical staff that includes slashes to indicate the number of beats in each

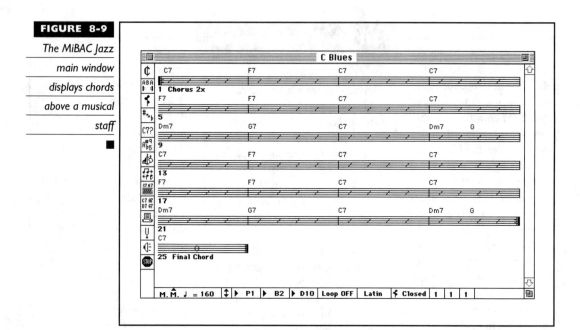

measure. This is a nicer layout if you're playing along while reading the chord changes from the computer monitor.

The left side of the window provides a Tool palette with 14 tools that give you easy access to most of MiBAC's common functions. At the bottom of the window, the Control palette lets you change the tempo, select a style, and turn on the looping function. You can also mute any of the three instruments and change their MIDI channels.

One of MiBAC's most unique features is its Piano Voicings function, which you can access directly from the Control palette. It lets you specify whether the piano part will use open or closed voicings. This is a great feature that changes the quality of the accompaniment part from a tight, closed sound to a lighter, more open sound.

MiBAC Jazz offers a selection of four main styles: Jazz 4/4, Latin, Slow 4, and Jazz 3/4. Each of these has three substyles: Ballad, Normal, and Up Tempo. The substyles incorporate different textures and rhythms that add variety within the main styles. For example, the substyles for Jazz 4/4 include a slow swing ballad, a medium jazz swing, and a sparse bebop style. The Latin substyles include a rock shuffle, a bossa nova, and a samba. Unlike Band-in-a-Box, MiBAC's substyles are tempo dependent. In other words, you trigger a new substyle by setting or changing the tempo within the piece.

Entering chords is easy. You just type the chord symbols above the staff. The program lets you have two chords per measure except in Jazz 3/4 style, which only accepts one chord per measure. MiBAC's large harmonic

Even though sequencers are the backbone of the desktop studio, they can present a rather heavily structured environment. Also, the sheer number and variety of their features can be intimidating to the newcomer and inhibiting in their complexity. Even for professional composers, the sequencer is not always the right tool.

For example, sometimes I just want to brainstorm ideas, sketch out concepts, or rough in a harmony part. Other times I just want to make some music and I want to do it quickly, before I lose the core of an idea. For these activities, other music software (like those described in this chapter) better meet my needs than does a sequencer.

For example, one day I decided to work on a pop tune. I had a general idea for the piece, but I couldn't nail down the exact melody. While I had in my mind the basis for the piece, I didn't want to get distracted with the specifics yet. (Actually, I was afraid I would lose my focus if I got bogged down with details too early.)

To develop my melody, I needed a musical background to work against, but I didn't want to take time to create it from scratch. So I used one of my background rhythm programs to supply the context for my musical thoughts. Using this backdrop I was able to experiment with ideas until I finally found the melody I was looking for.

There are many different angles to the art of composing. The desktop studio, with its interactive nature and its automated tools, is one. It lets you compose in real time without having to fully define all the details in advance. Later, once your ideas are fully formed, you can replace the automated music tracks with your own parts. In my case, once I had developed my melody, I went back and replaced the generic accompaniment, filling in the other parts at my leisure. Using an interactive desktop environment let me spontaneously compose the melody without diluting my creative thoughts at that moment. It's one of the marvels of MIDI.

MiBAC Jazz

MAC

CD-ROM

MiBAC Jazz is a lot like Band-in-a-Box. You type chord symbols onto the screen and the program generates an "intelligent" back-up band for you to play along with. MiBAC, however, takes a somewhat different approach to creating its accompaniments. And as its name suggests, the program focuses on jazz styles.

The back-up group consists of only three players: piano, bass, and drums and you can't record a melody part along with the ensemble. But MiBAC Jazz is no scaled-down version of Band-in-a-Box. It has its own assortment of sophisticated features that make it ideal for jazz players and others interested in working with jazz styles.

The MiBAC Jazz main window (Figure 8-9) provides a large area for entering chords. Unlike Band-in-a-Box, MiBAC's chords appear above a musical staff that includes slashes to indicate the number of beats in each

FIGURE 8-9

*The MiBAC Jazz
main window
displays chords
above a musical
staff*

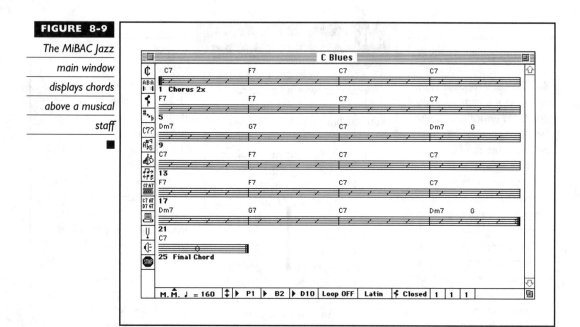

measure. This is a nicer layout if you're playing along while reading the chord changes from the computer monitor.

The left side of the window provides a Tool palette with 14 tools that give you easy access to most of MiBAC's common functions. At the bottom of the window, the Control palette lets you change the tempo, select a style, and turn on the looping function. You can also mute any of the three instruments and change their MIDI channels.

One of MiBAC's most unique features is its Piano Voicings function, which you can access directly from the Control palette. It lets you specify whether the piano part will use open or closed voicings. This is a great feature that changes the quality of the accompaniment part from a tight, closed sound to a lighter, more open sound.

MiBAC Jazz offers a selection of four main styles: Jazz 4/4, Latin, Slow 4, and Jazz 3/4. Each of these has three substyles: Ballad, Normal, and Up Tempo. The substyles incorporate different textures and rhythms that add variety within the main styles. For example, the substyles for Jazz 4/4 include a slow swing ballad, a medium jazz swing, and a sparse bebop style. The Latin substyles include a rock shuffle, a bossa nova, and a samba. Unlike Band-in-a-Box, MiBAC's substyles are tempo dependent. In other words, you trigger a new substyle by setting or changing the tempo within the piece.

Entering chords is easy. You just type the chord symbols above the staff. The program lets you have two chords per measure except in Jazz 3/4 style, which only accepts one chord per measure. MiBAC's large harmonic vocabulary includes 28 chord "qualities." And if you don't like the way the program names chords you can substitute your own names.

Once you've entered your chords, MiBAC analyzes the progression and applies sophisticated algorithms to produce a highly musical sounding accompaniment. The piano voices move logically from measure to measure, the bass lines step smoothly through the changes, and the drum parts swing.

Creating a basic accompaniment, however, is not all this program can do. MiBAC lets you customize the performance in a number of ways. For example, you can vary the rhythmic placement of the bass part to provide a laid-back feel. Or you can have it right on the beat or slightly ahead of the beat. And you can have these changes throughout the piece or only in sections that you specify.

You can also save custom drum setups and have them available for special rhythmic and textural effects. And you can apply the Piano Voicing feature wherever you want to change the quality of the piano parts from a closed voicing sound to an open voicing sound.

Furthermore, MiBAC Jazz includes a powerful Random Chord Alterations function. It lets you specify any of several chord substitutions within the piano part. The program then randomly substitutes these chords to impart an improvisatory quality to the piano accompaniment (Figure 8-10).

And that's not all. You can change the dynamics (independently for each instrument) and tempo anywhere you want in a piece. If you'd like to play a solo you can use the Write Rests command to insert one or more measures of silence for any combination of instruments. And you can transpose into any key, send Program Change messages, and "humanize" the rhythms by varying amounts.

Each song can have up to 96 measures with a 16-measure introduction and coda. You can repeat the song as many times as your computer memory

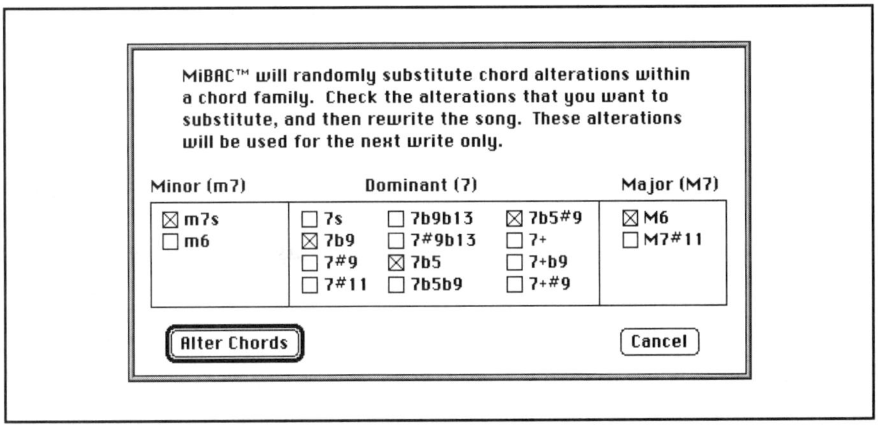

FIGURE 8-10

MiBAC Jazz lets you randomly substitute chords to provide an improvisatory feel to the piano part

MiBAC™ will randomly substitute chord alterations within a chord family. Check the alterations that you want to substitute, and then rewrite the song. These alterations will be used for the next write only.

Minor (m7)	Dominant (7)		Major (M7)
☒ m7s	☐ 7s ☐ 7b9b13	☒ 7b5#9	☒ M6
☐ m6	☒ 7b9 ☐ 7#9b13	☐ 7+	☐ M7#11
	☐ 7#9 ☒ 7b5	☐ 7+b9	
	☐ 7#11 ☐ 7b5b9	☐ 7+#9	

[**Alter Chords**]   [Cancel]

will allow and each repeat will be unique. That's because the program draws from a large assortment of piano voicings, accompaniment rhythms, bass lines, and drum phrases. And these variations combined with the different styles create a back-up band that's exciting and occasionally surprising—just like a real band.

When you're finished with your arrangement you can print out your chord changes or save the accompaniment as a Standard MIDI File. This is a great program for learning more about jazz and for developing your playing skills.

The Jammer

PC

CD-ROM

Both Band-in-a-Box and MiBAC Jazz do a great job of creating accompaniment parts. But they both assume that you have a pre-existing chord progression or that you have some chord changes of your own in mind. Soundtrek's **The Jammer** goes one step further. It supplies everything for a composition—the chord progression, the musicians, the styles, the melody, the whole shebang!

The Jammer is the brainchild of a songwriter who wanted to capture that spontaneous quality that often gets lost in the music-making process. The program is actually a combination sequencer and algorithmic composer that generates music on command, yet provides plenty of control over the end result.

The Jammer's opening screen includes two main windows—the Tracks window and the Measures window (Figure 8-11). The Tracks window lists The Jammer's 256 available tracks. Each track is followed by several fields that show related parameters. The program is set up with specific instruments assigned to tracks 1-27 and specific drum sounds on tracks 28-55. You can use the rest of the tracks for adding your own music to the arrangements.

In the Measures window, you can enter your own chord progression (and lyrics) or simply view the chords that The Jammer comes up with. You can also add drum fills—both long and short—by inserting a thin blue line in the top space of the staff. Creating music with The Jammer is relatively simple.

Here's what you do: first you open a dialog box where you specify the number of measures that your piece—or section of a piece—will have. The same dialog box also lets you select a time signature. If you check the Insert Drum Fills box, The Jammer will automatically insert drum fills every fourth measure (a long fill every eight measures, shorter fills in between).

Next you select the style that you want from the program's list of 125 choices. These include variations on such diverse styles as Bluegrass, Classical, Blues, Country, Funk, Hard Rock, Ballad, Jazz, Latin, Reggae, and others. Each style contains a preset group of selected "virtual musicians" on

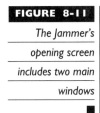

FIGURE 8-11

The Jammer's

opening screen

includes two main

windows

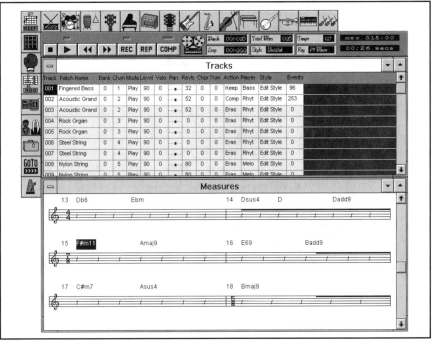

specific tracks. These musicians are set up to provide a complete band with the proper sound for the chosen style. In other words, the different styles use different instruments and different numbers of players.

Once you've established the length, time signature, and style for your piece, the next step is to choose a key for the musicians to jam in. When you're ready you just click the Compose button in the control panel. The Jammer—using randomization and algorithmic composition functions—then creates a chord progression, displays the chords in the Measures window, writes track parts to fit the chords, and plays back the results.

If you don't like what you hear, just click the Compose button again. The Jammer will create a completely new chord progression with all new tracks. You can do this over and over again as long as you want and The Jammer will obligingly keep spitting out new compositions. When you hear something you like you can save it. But with The Jammer this is never an all-or-nothing proposition. That's because the program lets you keep only the parts that you like and regenerate the rest.

For example, let's say that you like a chord progression that The Jammer comes up with, but you don't like the instrumental parts that go with it. You can keep the chords and continue to regenerate new instrumental parts to go with them. And let's say that after a few more tries you come up with a bass part that you like. You can keep the chords and the bass part while continuing to recompose the piano, drums, and guitar parts.

In fact The Jammer lets you keep, erase, or recompose any combination of parts any time you want. And that's not all. You can also apply these changes to any measure or group of measures with The Jammer's Punch-In feature. This means that you can, for instance, regenerate only the piano part in measures 6 through 8. You can also insert and remove drum fills where necessary. And for the adventurous types out there The Jammer even lets you combine styles. That way you can have a Funk drummer playing with a Country piano, or a Bluegrass guitarist sitting in with a Rhythm and Blues band. It may not always work, but it'll always be interesting. And finally, The Jammer also lets you chain together different sections even if they're in different styles.

Soundtrek has recently released a new professional version of The Jammer. It provides some advanced editing features along with additional windows for controlling and changing the performance styles of the different musicians. This allows you to control the basic styles, note ranges, velocity ranges, durations, repeat and transition probabilities, transition timing, scale choices, and more.

The Jammer is lots of fun to play with and you don't have to know too much about music to make it work. If you're looking for some new musical ideas The Jammer might be just what you need.

Power Chords Pro

PC

CD-ROM

Power Chords Pro (from Howling Dog Systems) is not a style-oriented program like Band-in-a-Box or the Jammer. Nor does it generate music on its own. It's more like a pattern-based sequencer, but with a decidedly different take on the process of creating music. In fact, Power Chords Pro carries the concept of patterns to a new level. It views music as being composed of small segments called *objects*. The pattern-like objects consist of various types of music-related data including bass parts, chords, chord rhythms, drum parts, and controls.

Although objects can be just about any length, the program works best with mostly small musical phrases—about one to four measures in length. After you record each object (in real time or by step recording) it's stored in one of several dedicated windows called palettes. Each object—represented graphically—is then available as a building block for your musical arrangement. To create a song, you just drag various objects from their palettes and place them in a special Song window where they're assembled into a finished piece (Figure 8-12).

FIGURE 8-12

To create an

arrangement in

Power Chords Pro

you drag "objects"

from their palettes

and place them in

the Song window

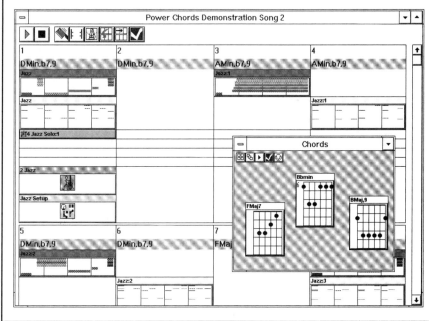

You can audition the objects by clicking on them and you can experiment with different arrangements by simply dragging objects from one place to another. Many songwriters will find this a more spontaneous approach to music making than that offered by more traditional track-based sequencers. For instance, you can assemble a palette of chords and try them out in different ways before adding the drum and bass parts. Or you can start with the drums and work the other way. It's easy to throw together a basic framework and develop it as you go. That's because drum parts and chord rhythms repeat automatically once they're placed in the Song window. And they continue until a different part of the same type comes along. Furthermore, a single pattern can appear more than once in a song so you don't have to enter the same data twice or make copies of objects.

By far the most intriguing (and entertaining) part of Power Chords Pro is its Stringed Instrument window (Figure 8-13). It contains a graphic representation of a guitar-like fingerboard. You use this on-screen instrument to create, play, and experiment with chords, chord rhythms, melodies, and other things. Although the default instrument looks a lot like a 6-string guitar, you can configure it to have anywhere from 2 to 12 strings and from 4 to 24 frets. And since you can tune the strings however you want, you can have anything from a balalaika to a bass guitar to fool around with.

Creating chords is easy. You just click with the mouse wherever you want a finger marker to appear. If the program recognizes your chord it displays the name at the bottom of the fingerboard. Otherwise, you can choose a

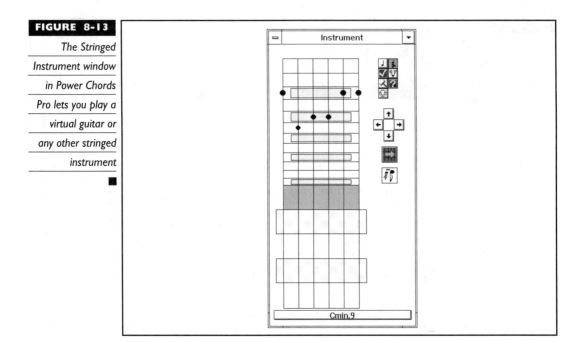

name of your own. Once you've created a chord the real fun begins—you get to play the instrument.

In Melody mode you can play notes individually. And by moving the cursor into the String Bend area (the shaded rectangle) you can grab any string and pull it to the left or right to change its pitch—very cool. The String Pluck area lets you play strings one at a time for arpeggios. And the Chord Strum area lets you strum the strings with each click. The program even generates hammer-on (grace note) effects. You can record any of these actions as a performance and save them as a melody, chord, or chord-strum object for later use in your song.

The Stringed Instrument window was clearly designed with guitar players in mind. But Power Chords Pro doesn't abandon the keyboard players out there. The Keyboard window provides an on-screen keyboard that also lets you play and record melodies and chords. And this keyboard is Velocity-sensitive. With the Variable Volume function active the keys will send different Velocity values depending on where you click them (front to back).

Power Chords Pro's Rhythm Editor window (Figure 8-14) is where most of the composing and editing activities take place. It mainly resembles a piano-roll display, but its appearance changes according to the kind of object being created or edited. Four buttons let you select among Chord, Melody, Drum, and Bass editing modes. You can step-enter notes onto the grid by clicking with the mouse or you can record notes and/or chords in real time (Power Chords provides a resolution of 96 ppqn).

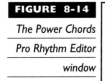

FIGURE 8-14

The Power Chords
Pro Rhythm Editor
window

■

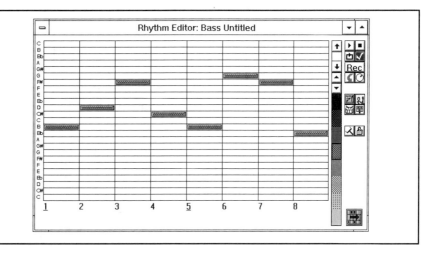

Once you have your data in the Rhythm Editor you can apply a number of "intelligent" effects to create new rhythm data. These affects—using randomization and probability—work on melodies as well as drum parts and chords.

Three Strum commands let you create up, down, and alternating strums. The Roll/Pick effect lets you create drum rolls and alternating picking. Other effects let you add random notes to a part or randomly affect the Velocity values of chords. The Arpeggiate effect lets you create plucking-style chord rhythms and also creates some interesting drum solos. And of course there's a Quantize effect.

If you're a guitarist you'll enjoy working with Power Chords Pro. And even non-guitarists may find that this chord-and-rhythm–oriented approach to composing unleashes some new ideas. Songwriters and pop composers will especially benefit from the graphical, pattern-based style of arranging that encourages experimentation. And when you're through you can save everything as a Standard MIDI File.

FreeStyle

PC

As we saw in Chapter 6, there are currently lots of powerful sequencers on the market. But sheer power alone is not necessarily what everybody needs. Long lists of advanced editing functions are great for some composers. But many desktop musicians just want a tool that lets them get their ideas into the computer as quickly and easily as possible. In response to these needs, Mark of the Unicorn has recently released a new sequencer called **FreeStyle**. As with Power Chords, FreeStyle is primarily a pattern-based sequencer (although you can use it linearly if you want) and it lets you construct songs by dragging graphically represented sections of music into a window. (In that regard it closely resembles Performer and its use of Chunks for constructing Songs.)

But FreeStyle is a more sophisticated program than Power Chords and with its 960 ppqn resolution and ample editing capabilities, you can use it as a full-function sequencer in a variety of situations. In spite of its power, however, FreeStyle tackles the problem of lost spontaneity by approaching MIDI composition from a slightly different angle.

To record a track with a traditional-style sequencer, you must first select a track, name it, assign it a patch and a MIDI channel, and record-enable it. After a while you can end up with lots of tracks. And keeping them organized can be a problem. Although this method of sequencing provides a great deal of flexibility, many people find that it slows them down when they're trying to sketch out their ideas.

FreeStyle solves this dilemma by taking a different approach to the sequencing process. In FreeStyle you begin by creating an ensemble of "players." Each player is assigned its own instrument (and MIDI channel). You then work with your ensemble of virtual musicians by recording (in real or step time) their different parts and listening to them play back.

Each time you record a performance, FreeStyle saves it as a "take" and identifies it with a number. You can recall any take for playback and editing any time you want by selecting it from a pop-up menu next to the corresponding player. The Ensemble palette (Figure 8-15) shows a list of the players in the current ensemble, along with the take that each is playing or recording into, the current patch, and other related information.

Although the Ensemble window looks more or less the same as you make new recordings, FreeStyle keeps track of everything behind the scenes (and

FIGURE 8-15

FreeStyle's

Ensemble palette

shows a list of the

players in the

current ensemble

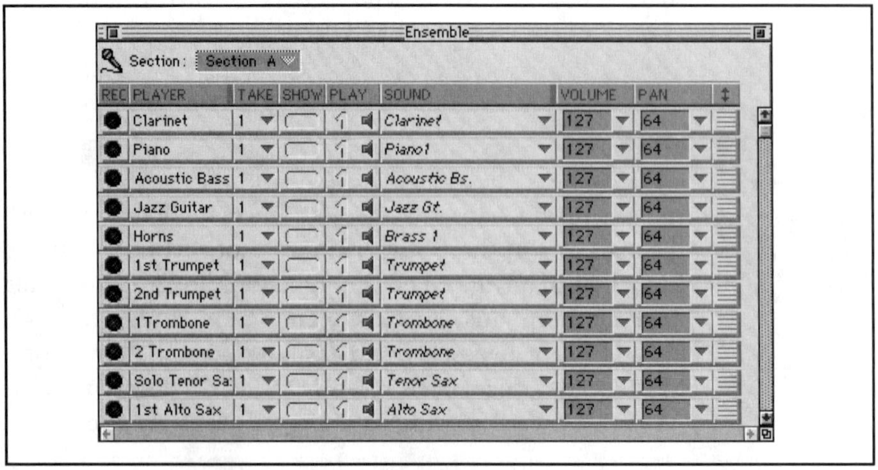

never throws away a take unless you want it to). This means that all of your alto sax solos are kept together. And you can make A/B comparisons in a jiffy. You can also try out different combinations of takes from different instruments by making a few quick selections from the pop-up menus.

For real-time recording you'll need a metronome. And FreeStyle offers the usual options for sound output: the computer speaker or a MIDI note. But in keeping with its goal of encouraging creativity, FreeStyle also offers a clever new option called the "Riff" metronome. Unlike the uninspiring tick, tick, tick, of most metronomes, the Riff metronome provides you with a list of over 30 drum loops to put you in the mood for composing.

The built-in riffs range from gospel to jazz and they're a big help in getting you in the proper frame of mind for composing songs and other kinds of popular music. Furthermore you can make up your own riffs and add them to the list. And riffs aren't limited to just drum patterns either. You can create riffs that include bass parts, piano parts, or anything else. Once you work out your musical ideas, if you want to keep the Riff metronome part, you can turn it into one of the players in the ensemble. The Riff metronome is a terrific idea that more sequencers should include.

To view and edit your music FreeStyle provides two displays. You toggle between them with a set of buttons at the top of the window. The Graphic Editing view (Figure 8-16) is a standard piano-roll display. The current takes for any players selected in the Ensemble palette appear in the note grid. If several instruments are selected their notes appear in different colors. Beneath the note grid there's another area that shows controller data in colors that correspond to the notes.

FIGURE 8-16

FreeStyle's Graphic Editing view shows notes and controller data in a piano-roll display

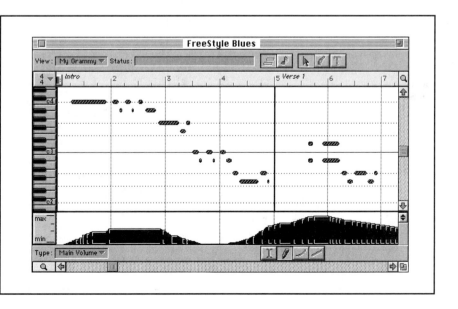

The other display provides a look at your music in standard notation. In the Notation view the parts for any selected players appear on separate staves. Several sophisticated features ensure proper transcription and legible page layout. In both the piano-roll and the notation displays you can drag notes up and down to change pitch and location. You can also change a note's duration by dragging with the mouse. And you can insert notes wherever you want. Both displays also have a scrolling wiper that you can drag to "scrub" notes.

In FreeStyle a Song is created in the Arrangement window by dragging sections from a list onto a timeline (Figure 8-17). You can add the same section as many times as you want and you can freely drag sections around to rearrange your music. Each section shares the same set of players and has its own set of takes for each player. If you often work with structures like intro/verse/chorus/verse you'll appreciate this approach to composing.

FreeStyle provides a number of features that can help keep your creative momentum going. For example, you can use your MIDI keyboard to control most of FreeStyle's functions. Without leaving your MIDI controller you can add players, change sounds, record new takes, and play back your music.

If you're using a single sound module and you need more players than your sound module can handle, FreeStyle can "steal" a MIDI channel from an idle player and temporarily reassign it to another player. This can be very handy if you're working with a small setup and you need just one or two extra players for a short time.

The creators of FreeStyle took a fresh look at the art of sequencing and came up with some interesting solutions to some age-old problems. If you prefer working with an ensemble of players rather than staring at an empty track list, then FreeStyle's the program for you.

FIGURE 8-17

In FreeStyle's Arrangement window you drag sections from a list onto a timeline

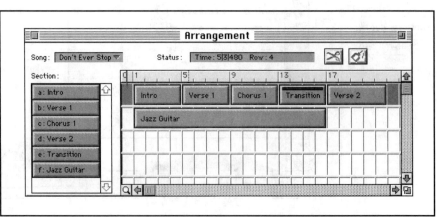

Final Thought

The programs that I've covered in this chapter represent a cross section of products that can help you create new music in new ways. Some programs use algorithmic composition formulas, while others use various probability and randomization schemes. Still others simply provide you with a new kind of working environment or a new methodology for producing music. In all cases, however, the goal is always to provide some new insight into the creative process and to offer a new slant on some familiar tasks. After all, one of MIDI's great gifts to the world of music is its spontaneous nature and the surprises that it brings. Let's hope that it flourishes in the future.

CHAPTER 9

The Paper Connection:
From Music to Manuscript

S

INCE the earliest days of electronic instruments musicians have
dreamed of being able to perform music into a computer and have it print
out perfectly in standard notation. It seems like an obvious thing. Computers
are so adept at handling text and graphics. Why not do the same with music?
In fact, it is now becoming *de rigueur* for dedicated notation programs to
transcribe real-time performances and display the music in standard notation. But bridging the gap between a performance and a printed score is a
formidable assignment. That's because music notation—in spite of hundreds
of years of evolution—is still not a precise method for indicating how a piece
should sound.

A trill is the very quick, repeated alternation of two adjacent notes.

During the Baroque period, for example, trills and other ornaments were
often omitted from manuscripts because it was assumed that the players
would know what to do and how to do it when the time came. And in popular
music today there are similar notational shortcuts that allow some latitude
on the part of the performers.

Even when music appears to be carefully notated, things are not always
as they seem. In jazz swing style, for instance, a passage written in "straight"
eighth notes will actually be played more like long-short, long-short, long-
short (Figure 9-1). The players know this because they understand the style
and they interpret the notation accordingly. From the software's perspective,
however, the whole process becomes one giant guessing game.

As an analogy, suppose you had a word processor that could catch and
correct misspellings in real time. That would be a pretty cool piece of
software because the spell checker would have to not only identify the wrong
words but also figure out what you meant to type in the first place. And let's
carry the analogy one step further and say that your intelligent spell checker

FIGURE 9-1

In jazz swing style, eighth notes written as in the top staff are actually played more like the notes in the bottom staff

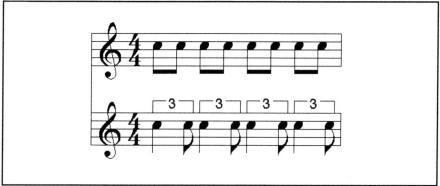

could also catch a word like "board" and replace it with "bored" when appropriate. That's just the kind of thing that notation programs are routinely expected to do as they transform your performance into printed music.

If you lift your finger off of the key a fraction of a second too soon should the program insert a 32nd rest? Or not? If you play a note a tad early should the program tie a 64th note to the front of the main beat? Or not? And is that a G-sharp or an A-flat in measure three? A literal transcription of most music would fill the page with so many dotted notes, ties, rests, and accidentals that it would be virtually unreadable. That's why the best programs use an assortment of algorithms for interpreting a performance and rendering it into legible notation. In essence, they quantize and organize the notation without necessarily affecting the actual performance. Even so, you can expect to do some fixing and reorganizing of your own to make things look right (Figure 9-2). And that brings up the second major function of a notation program—page layout and editing.

The music software market has recently been inundated with products that include music printing capabilities—including most of the sequencers discussed in Chapter 6. But if you're serious about working with printed music you'll want to turn your attention to the many programs that specialize in producing publisher-quality scores in a variety of page layouts.

Cranking out professional-looking manuscripts, however, is no easy task. Unlike simple text, music involves a complex set of interrelationships that exist on a truly two-dimensional plane. The software must deal not only with the notes themselves, but with their positions relative to one another. And it must understand how and when the notes connect to each other and how to position the notes for the proper spacing. Aside from the notes, there are also myriad performance markings, different types of text, and a raft of

FIGURE 9-2

If you play your quarter notes with less than full durations, how should they be notated? Here are a few possibilities

symbols to contend with. And the software must handle all of these variables for a range of different instrumental setups from a single percussion staff to a multi-staff orchestral ensemble.

It should therefore come as no surprise that the best and most advanced notation programs are both expensive and complex. These are not just fancy music typewriters, they're sophisticated page-layout programs that offer power and flexibility for those willing to expend the energy to learn them. Fortunately, you don't always have to tackle a steep learning curve just to print out some nice-looking music. Many of the pro-level programs come in less expensive, scaled-down versions that may work fine for your particular projects. And some of these programs come with upgrade paths to the high-end versions if your needs change.

Because people use notation software in so many ways, it's important to assess your requirements before going shopping. If you're a band teacher who just wants to throw together a marching band score for the next football game, your needs will be quite different from an avant garde composer who's preparing a score for publication. And a singer who just wants a good-looking piano-vocal score won't need the same features as an arranger writing for a 30-piece orchestra. Following are a few things to think about when you're comparing programs.

Input

Converting a performance directly into notation is often not the best way to produce printed music (unless your music is metrically simple and your playing is very accurate). Even though most notation programs can record and play back MIDI music, they're not ideally suited to fine tuning and editing performances. If you're trying to capture a musical performance on paper you're much better off recording your performance into a sequencer first and carefully editing it. Then you can save your music as a Standard MIDI File and import it into a notation program.

Most of the current notation programs let you import and export MIDI data in Standard MIDI File format—an important feature. Typically each track in the sequence is assigned its own staff. And once again the software must guess at your intentions. So the cleaner and more accurate the sequence the better the results. Most notation programs let you set a quantization level for the music display. That way you can avoid having millions of unnecessary sixty-fourth notes and rests. And you can also apply a key signature to the piece to eliminate unnecessary accidentals.

Many people, however, are less interested in transcribing performances than in producing clean-looking detailed manuscripts. If you're working from a sketch or composing directly on-screen you typically have two options for entering notes. Nearly all programs let you use your mouse—either alone or in conjunction with the computer keyboard—to enter notes directly into the score. With the most common approach you select a note value (or rest, accidental, articulation, expression, etc.) and simply click where you want it to appear on the staff. This is a little slow, but it's intuitive and very easy to learn. If the program provides key equivalents for some of the selections you can use one hand to make selections and the other to deposit the notes on-screen. Once you get used to it this can speed things up alot. Some programs let you do just about all of your note entry from the computer keyboard alone. This may appeal to those with good typing abilities.

The other option involves step-time entry using a MIDI keyboard. With this approach you choose note values from an on-screen palette (or with the computer keyboard) and enter the pitches by playing them from your MIDI keyboard. This is a handy alternative even if your keyboard skills are somewhat limited.

Output

Once you've entered your music into the score, nearly all notation programs let you play back your piece using MIDI. The different staves are treated like the tracks in a sequence—you can assign a different MIDI channel and patch to each. The best programs even let you have several parts (referred to as *voices*) on a single staff.

Of course the main benefit of MIDI playback is that it gives you an idea of how your piece will sound with live players. But it's also extremely useful as an aural proofreading aid. Sometimes it's easier to hear a mistake than to see it. If you're not set up with MIDI some programs, like ConcertWare, let you use the onboard sounds from the Macintosh to play back the score.

Although most programs provide some MIDI playback capability, the level of MIDI implementation varies widely. Low-end programs just recognize Note On and Note Off messages. Many pro-level programs are more "intelligent." Aside from the notes themselves, they respond to a range of other markings, including such things as accents, crescendos, pedal indications, staccato marks, dynamics, and tempo changes. A few programs even let you add Program Changes and other nonstandard markings.

A crescendo indicates increasing loudness.

As far as printed output goes, all of the best programs support PostScript and/or TrueType music fonts (for notes, rests, clefs, and other symbols). That means you can expect excellent results with high-resolution printing. Many programs, like Mosaic, come with Adobe's popular Sonata font, but some programs use their own proprietary fonts. Encore, for example, uses a font called Anastasia. And Finale uses its own Petrucci font. There are subtle differences among the various fonts. So if you're concerned about fine details, it's a good idea to get a sample printout from a program before making a purchase. Also, some programs will let you substitute different fonts for the one they come with.

A staccato mark indicates that a note should be played in a shortened and detached manner.

There's one other feature worth considering. Some programs will let you save your score as a graphics file such as EPS, TIFF, or PICT. This can come in handy if you need to print examples for a worksheet or as illustrations.

∫taves

Among the first things you have to consider when comparing notation programs is how many staves you'll need. Are you only writing for small ensembles or are you also working with big band arrangements and orchestral scores? Low-end programs may offer as few as 8 staves, while professional-level programs offer more than 30. Some programs even let you have an unlimited number of staves—restricted only by your available RAM.

The maximum number of allowable staves is important because it limits the kinds of music that you can work with. Right now you might only be writing four-part choir music, or woodwind trios, or piano music, but things

Different voices on a single staff are distinguished by stems that point in different directions. These are often assigned to different MIDI channels

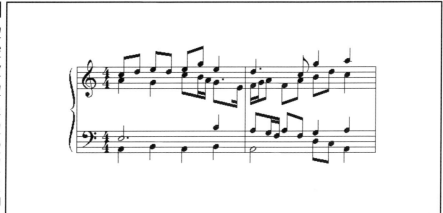

may change in the future. Since MIDI supports 16 channels, it's a good idea to look for programs that provide at least that many staves. Then you can assign a different MIDI channel to each staff for playback. More staves, of course, provide even greater flexibility. And for full orchestral scores you'll want to have at least 30 staves at your disposal.

Many programs also let you have more than one part per staff. This is indicated in print with stems that point in different directions (Figure 9-3). In the better programs you can assign a different MIDI channel to each of these parts, so you can have a distinct timbre for each line.

Some notation programs also let you work with staves other than the standard five-line variety. At the very least, a good program should include a traditional one-line percussion staff. And some programs now include guitar tablature—a six-line system of notation that indicates guitar strings and finger positions instead of notes (Figure 9-4). The most flexible programs let you work with several kinds of staves or even no staves at all (for rhythm examples in a text book, perhaps).

Tablature indicates strings and finger positions instead of notes

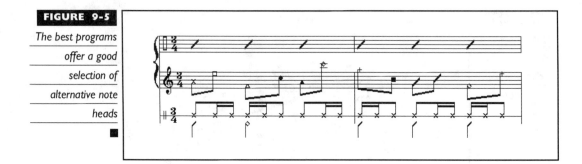

Notes and Rests

In addition to non-standard staves, a good notation program also provides different types of specialized note heads. String harmonics, for example, are often notated with small diamonds instead of the usual oval-shaped note heads. Percussionists often use small x's to indicate notes on an unpitched instrument. And jazz scores typically use slashes instead of notes to show the beats in a rhythm section part (Figure 9-5). Some programs let you select several notes and change all of the note heads at once—a nice convenience. While most notation programs will let you place a small grace note on the staff, the better programs also let you add cues—in small notes—to the staff. This ability to mix note sizes is especially important for certain kinds of parts.

In band and orchestra scores, individual players often sit through several measures without playing. In the full score this is notated with a separate whole rest for each measure. When the individual parts are printed out separately, however, multiple whole rests are often consolidated into a single measure with a number to indicate how many rests are represented (Figure 9-6). This saves space on the page, reduces page turning, and makes it easier

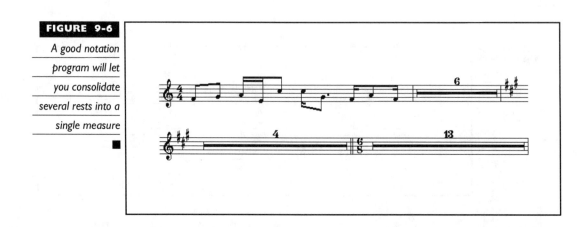

for the players to count. The ability to combine rests is therefore an essential feature for any pro-level notation program and something you should seriously consider. Also consider whether the program will automatically combine rests when you extract the parts or whether you must do it manually.

Rhythms and Beams

The available range of rhythmic values is another point to consider. Although you probably won't use 128th notes very often, it's nice to have them

In My Experience

The best way to understand the benefits of a good notation program is to consider the traditional method of writing music. Over the years, I have written scores for a variety of different ensembles, from full orchestras and big band jazz to woodwind trios and other small groups. Until recently, however, I had to prepare my scores by hand. Here are some of the problems involved in the process.

The first problem anyone faces when scoring music by hand is maintaining a stock of specialized manuscript paper. Finding the proper paper for each complement of instruments is often difficult. There are different design layouts for orchestral scores, piano solos, piano-vocal duets, string quartets, and the like.

For example, if you want to write a piece for flute, piano, voice, and percussion, the exact combination of staves will be difficult (if not impossible) to find. More often than not, I've had to use pre-existing score paper, modifying it to work for my ensemble. By contrast, using a notation program, you can create any type and combination of staves that you want.

Once you've acquired the manuscript paper, you can begin handwriting the score. To create a finished score involves painstaking entry of notes using black ink, special pens, rulers, and lots of erasers and correction strips. This is often a frustrating and tedious process. You can even ruin an entire page with a simple mistake.

After the score is completed, duplication of a handwritten score offers its own challenges. For example, many orchestral scores are too large for a standard photocopier. In fact, many scores have to be written on special onionskin paper and reproduced like blueprints.

Fortunately, with today's notation programs, you can reduce scores and print multiple copies as needed.

One other problem with handwritten scores is that someone has to manually extract the individual parts for the different instruments. In a symphonic score, for instance, the flutes, the violins, the trumpets, etc. all need to have their own parts—and only their parts—on separate pages. Using a notation program, part extraction can be completely automated.

While handwritten scores may have some romantic appeal, the publisher-quality, computer-generated scores are easier to produce, easier to read, and more consistent from page to page. Once you use a notation program, it's hard to imagine going back to handwritten scores.

FIGURE 9-7

High-end programs let you notate "tuplets" in a variety of ways

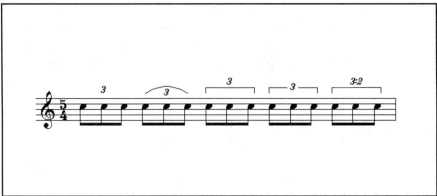

if the need arises. As with most other features, you get what you pay for. You can expect a good low-end program to provide 32nd notes as an option. Mid-level programs typically offer down to 64th notes. And the best programs provide down to 128th notes (and in a few cases even smaller).

All notation programs let you notate triplets, and some also allow quintuplets. But the best programs provide enough flexibility to create any kind of "tuplet" that you want. If you want to place a 7 or a 9 or a 15 over a group of notes you should be able to do it. And the program should provide some flexibility in how the tuplets are notated—with or without brackets, with or without slurs, with different number positions, etc. (Figure 9-7).

Another important feature to consider is how the program handles beaming. Cross-staff beaming is so common in keyboard music that serious manuscript work demands it as an option (Figure 9-8). Also consider how easy it is to adjust the positions and angles of beams. Some programs let you grab a beam and change its angle or position just by dragging with the mouse. Inexpensive programs often place beams automatically without providing a way to optimize the position of the beams. This can affect the legibility of

FIGURE 9-8

Cross-staff beaming is an important feature for keyboard notation

FIGURE 9-9

The better

programs let you

place notes above

and below a single

beam

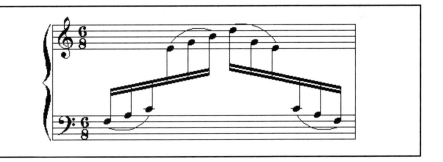

beamed notes in some cases. Better programs let you control a variety of beam parameters and they also let you place notes above and below a single beam (Figure 9-9).

Clefs, Keys, and Meters

All notation programs include the familiar treble clef (G clef) and bass clef (F clef). But the better programs also include an alto clef (C clef) for viola parts and a tenor clef (C clef) for instruments—such as bassoons and trombones—that occasionally use it. A special percussion clef is also a nice feature (Figure 9-10). And a good notation program will let you place any clef anywhere within a measure.

Aside from the standard clefs, you can also expect to have all of the standard key signatures available in all notation programs. But suppose you

FIGURE 9-10

For serious

notation work,

you'll need a

variety of clefs. As

a minimum, you

should have treble,

bass, alto, tenor,

and percussion clefs

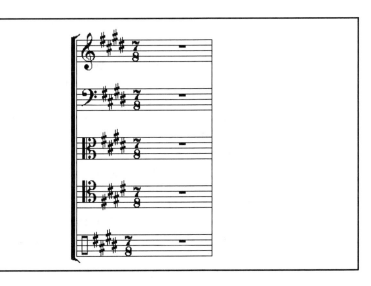

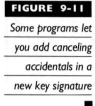

want to use a non-standard key signature such as one that mixes sharps and flats or one that places sharps or flats in an untraditional order? Not all programs allow such flexibility. And if you change key signatures in the middle of a piece, not all programs let you include natural signs in the new key signature to indicate which sharps or flats are no longer in effect (Figure 9-11). Depending on the kind of writing that you do, these can be important considerations.

Many programs are similarly lacking in options for handling time signatures. All programs let you insert any of the common meters at the beginning of a piece. And most let you place new meters in any measure throughout the music. But only the best programs let you create time signatures like 3+2+3 over 4 or 2.5 over 8, or even 6/8 + 3/4 (as Leonard Bernstein used in "America" from *West Side Story*). If you're working with contemporary compositions this level of flexibility can be very important.

Chord Symbols

Most notation programs now provide a means for adding chord symbols above a staff. In some cases you just type in the letters and numbers, such as Am7 or D9. Other programs let you choose the chord symbols from a large menu. With some programs you can even play a chord on your MIDI keyboard and the software will read the notes and insert the corresponding symbol in the score. Aside from the alphanumeric types of symbols, some programs also let you add guitar fretboard diagrams showing typical fingerings for chords (Figure 9-12).

The best programs treat either type of chord symbol as more than just simple text or graphics. If you transpose a passage of music, the chords in that passage should automatically transpose as well.

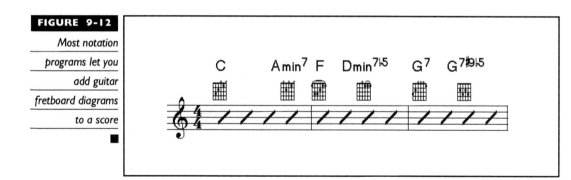

FIGURE 9-12

Most notation programs let you add guitar fretboard diagrams to a score

Text

Most of the text in a musical score falls roughly into two categories: lyrics and other text. Lyrics are a unique kind of text because they relate directly to the notation. In lyric writing each syllable in a word is separated by a hyphen and corresponds to a note. If more than one note applies to a syllable (this is called a melisma) you use an extended line to indicate the duration of the syllable. In the best programs the lyrics are truly tied to the notes so if you move a note, the corresponding syllable moves with it.

How you input lyrics varies from program to program. In some cases you simply type the words directly into the score beneath the appropriate notes. Sometimes the words are just independent lines of text. This makes editing and reformatting the score difficult because you have to go back and reposition the lyrics with each change. In other cases the lyrics are linked to the notes as they're typed in—a much better arrangement. Some programs let you type the lyrics into a special window or import the text from your favorite word processor. The software then applies the syllables (which you've separated by hyphens or spaces) to the notes in the score.

A melisma is a section of music where several notes are sung to a single syllable.

The other type of text includes such things as titles, composer names, credits, page numbers, copyright notices, performance directions, extra lyrics, and other comments. Ideally, you should have a good selection of fonts to choose from and the flexibility to reposition and size the text as needed.

To help you decide which notation software will best suit your needs, let's take a close look at several popular manuscript programs in the remainder of this chapter.

Finale

PC

MAC

Coda Software's **Finale** has long held an esteemed position in the world of notation programs. It is unquestionably one of the most powerful programs of its type, offering the user unparalleled control over the details of notation and page layout. And its level of MIDI implementation further adds to its impressive list of features. As you might expect, this is a big, complex program with a learning curve to match.

When Finale was first introduced several years ago, its user interface was so unfriendly and difficult to navigate that many people found it too frustrating to use on a regular basis. Since then, the program has undergone a number of changes and the newest version is much improved. It's helped even more by its well-written documentation consisting of three volumes totaling more than 850 pages! The result is a package that's hard to beat—power and flexibility, excellent documentation, and extensive MIDI input and output capabilities.

Finale lets you enter notes into a score in a number of ways. Most activities begin with a single movable, resizable palette providing 35 tools for entering or editing notes, markings, or layout-related elements (Figure 9-13).

When you click on a tool icon you're presented with a specialized palette for entering markings or a dialog box that lets you set various parameters. Sometimes a new menu item appears that provides additional options or a window might open to let you modify the elements on the page. The Articulation tool, for example, opens a window providing a generous assortment of markings to add to your score (Figure 9-14).

FIGURE 9-13

Finale's main

window with its

tool palette

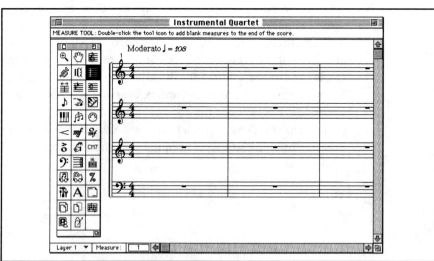

FIGURE 9-14

*Finale's Articulation
window offers a
wide variety of
markings*
■

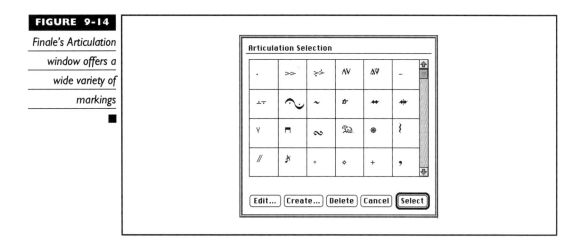

In Simple Entry mode you use your mouse to select note values from a palette and click where you want them to appear in the score. Click a second time on a note head to turn it into a rest. The Mass Mover tool lets you select entire sections of music to drag and drop copies onto other staves or onto the same staff in another location.

For a better overview of your work you can open additional windows showing different views of the same piece. Each window can have its own zoom level and it can show different measures and/or different staves in the same score.

If you're working with a MIDI keyboard, Finale lets you step-enter notes (and chords) with its Speedy Entry tool. You just select note values from your computer's numeric keypad and enter pitches with MIDI. You can also enter notes entirely from the computer keyboard by specifying pitches with letter keys and rhythms with numeric keys.

Finale also offers two methods of real-time note entry. The first of these is called HyperScribe. With HyperScribe you can perform at any tempo and Finale transcribes it directly into notation. Unlike most other programs, however, you don't rely on a metronome to provide the reference beat. Instead you provide the beat yourself by tapping on a designated MIDI key or any type of MIDI controller such as a Sustain pedal (for two-handed playing) or Modulation wheel. HyperScribe lets you speed up or slow down as you play and the notation will still appear with the notes placed correctly. This is great for pieces that involve tempo changes and it lets you play your music without the mechanical restrictions of a perfectly regular beat.

Finale's other real-time entry method is accomplished with its Transcription tool. It works much like a sequencer to capture your performance exactly as played. Unlike HyperScribe, the Transcription tool lets you put in the key taps *after* you've recorded your performance. In this way the performance is preserved at high resolution (1,024 ppqn) and the notation is aligned after the fact. The Transcription window even includes a miniature piano-roll display that lets you see how your key taps align with the notes (Figure 9-15). When you're satisfied with the note alignment you can have Finale transcribe the performance into notation.

For both the HyperScribe and Transcription tools you need to specify a quantization level so the notation can avoid unnecessary tied notes and rests. But quantization often forces note values into rhythms that aren't what you intended. To solve this problem Finale provides its unique Floating Quantization feature. This "intelligent" version of quantization senses the number of notes in each beat and adjusts the resolution accordingly. Floating Quantization means that Finale can more accurately handle music that mixes 8th and 16th notes with triplets. And it can also correctly transcribe swing rhythms.

Finale has a more thorough implementation of MIDI than most dedicated notation programs. With its standard-looking track list you can assign MIDI channels and instrument patches to any staff. Each staff can have as many as eight independent voices and Finale can play music over 32 MIDI channels at the same time.

Once you've captured a performance, Finale lets you edit the performance data in a number of ways. The MIDI Tool window (Figure 9-16), for instance, provides a graphic display of Pitch Bend, Velocity, patch changes, note durations, and other kinds of data. And it even lets you alter the rhythmic feel of the music. Although you can't edit performance data as easily in Finale as you can in a good pro-level sequencer, Finale does provide plenty of options for serious editing.

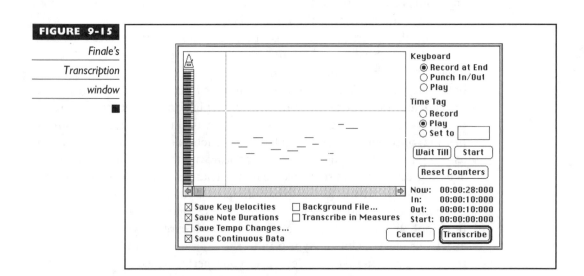

FIGURE 9-15

Finale's Transcription window

Finale's MIDI Tool window lets you edit many kinds of MIDI data with its graphic display

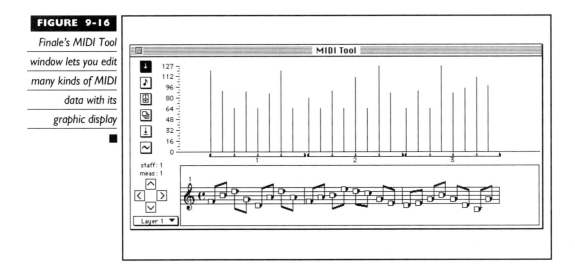

One area where Finale really shines is in its ability to respond intelligently to notational markings during playback. Aside from such common items as notes and repeat signs, Finale responds to a wide range of other symbols (and text indications) such as dynamic markings, crescendos, ritardandos, rallentandos, pedal indications, trills, staccato marks, accents, and many others. You can even create your own symbols in the Shape Designer window and assign them to affect a variety of MIDI parameters.

Lyric entry is similarly flexible. You can type the words directly into the score or you can use the Lyric window to type out the words and have Finale apply them to the notes. Or if you prefer, you can type the lyrics into your word processor and import them into Finale. And of course, Finale lets you add transposable chord symbols and guitar fretboard diagrams.

Overall, Finale's great power lies in the fact that the program lets you alter just about every element in a score. You can position accidentals and expression marks exactly where you want them. You can adjust note stems, move measures around, change note and staff spacings, and customize pretty much every aspect of your score's appearance.

The list of Finale's features goes on and on, but here are a few examples to give you more of a flavor for the program: Finale supports non-standard key signatures, time signatures, and cross-staff beaming. It lets you have up to 32,768 staves and any staff can have from 1 to 100 lines. Note values go down to 128th notes. And to view the notes you can zoom from 5 to 1,000 percent. Finale also provides a choice of 8 clefs and the program even includes a clef designer so you can create user-definable clefs. As you can see this is one powerful program!

Finale Allegro

PC

MAC

Many people may find the cost, complexity, and power of Finale to be more than they're ready for. If you're one of these people you might consider **Finale Allegro**. It's a considerably scaled-down version of Finale that costs about half as much. Finale Allegro uses the same basic tools and commands as its bigger brother, but the number of options are reduced (for instance, there's a HyperScribe tool, but no Transcription tool).

Nonetheless, this is a full-featured notation program that can handle a great many tasks. You can have up to 32 staves with eight voices per staff. And its note values go down to 32nd notes. Staves can have either one or five lines and clef choices include treble, bass, alto, tenor, and percussion. If you don't need Finale's myriad customization options, Finale Allegro makes an excellent compromise.

Mosaic

MAC

Mark of the Unicorn's **Mosaic** is a pro-level notation program that strives to balance power and flexibility with ease of use. Although it shares a number of features with its predecessor, Professional Composer, it's significantly redesigned, offering a new look and feel with a long list of advanced features.

To keep you from having to dig too deeply for tools and commands, Mosaic provides 11 tool palettes that you can open, close, and reposition as

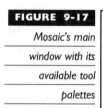

FIGURE 9-17

Mosaic's main window with its available tool palettes

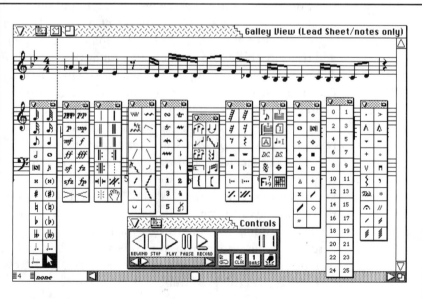

needed (Figure 9-17). Adding notes and markings to a score is easy—just click on the appropriate symbol and place it where you want.

There are separate palettes for notes, rests, expression marks, ornaments, and just about anything else you'd need. When you click on some icons a dialog box opens that lets you set parameters or choose options. Clicking the tuplet icon, for example, lets you select one of several ways to indicate the tuplet grouping (Figure 9-18).

Inserting slurs is a breeze. You just choose the Slur tool and drag from the first to the last note of the slurred section. To adjust the shape of the slur you simply click on it to make its grab handles appear. You can then drag these handles to change the arch of the slur. Ties and tuplets are similarly adjustable.

Entering text is also easy. You just select the Text tool and drag diagonally to form a text box (the way you do in many graphics programs). Then you can enter text in any available font and size. You can even link the text to a note or staff so it moves with it if the layout changes.

Of course, Mosaic also lets you enter music with your MIDI keyboard. You can step-enter notes by selecting values (with mouse or key equivalents) from the Note palette and entering pitches from your MIDI controller. Or you can play your music in real time (with a metronome) and have Mosaic transcribe it.

For working with lyrics, Mosaic provides a Lyric window that works like a mini word processor. You can cut, copy, and paste words and change fonts. Or if you prefer, you can import files from your regular word processor. When it's time to apply the lyrics Mosaic automatically "flows" the syllables so they align underneath the notes in the score. As with Finale, Mosaic lets you add transposable chord symbols and guitar fretboard diagrams. And it provides a complete set of tools for creating tablatures for a variety of different stringed instruments.

FIGURE 9-18

Mosaic offers several ways to indicate tuplets

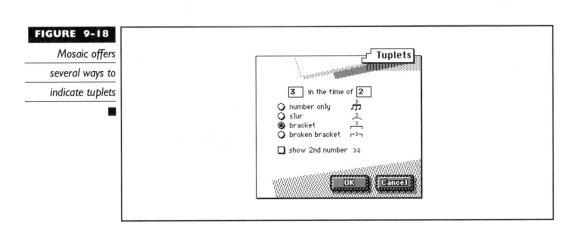

Mosaics Staff Configuration window (Figure 9-19) typifies the program's intuitive design. You can select any combination of staff lines (from 0 to 63) by clicking the small arrow heads to the right of the staff display. The left side of the window shows the different voices assigned to that staff and it lets you specify the stem directions for each voice.

As you might expect of a pro-level notation program, Mosaic provides full support for such things as cross-staff beaming, complex time signatures, non-standard key signatures, and complete flexibility in placing and shaping graphic elements.

During playback, Mosaic recognizes and responds—in a limited way—to a few musical symbols. But its MIDI playback capabilities are nowhere as complete as Finale's. Mosaic responds to such basic things as metronome settings, repeat endings, staccato marks, dynamic marks, and accents. But these are not as fully implemented as they are in Finale.

Mosaic does, however, offer an impressive list of other important features. Most notable is its unlimited Undo/Redo commands that let you retrace your steps no matter how far back you go. This is really an important asset. Mosaic also provides an unlimited number of staves (depending on how much RAM you have) and an unlimited number of voices per staff. And you can view your music with zoom levels that range from 20 to 800 percent. The excellent documentation comes in two volumes totaling more than 700 pages.

FIGURE 9-19

Mosaic's Staff Configuration window lets you easily create staves with as many lines as you want

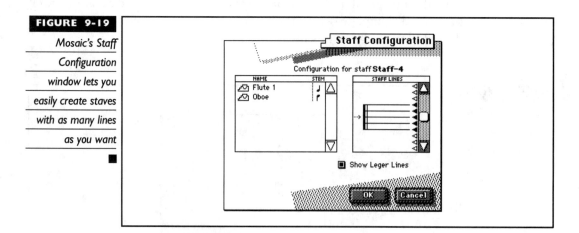

Encore

PC

MAC

CD-ROM

Encore, from Passport Designs, has long enjoyed a reputation for being one of the most intuitive of the notation programs. Although not quite at the level of Finale or Mosaic, Encore is nonetheless a full-featured program roughly comparable to Finale Allegro. If you don't need every conceivable bell and whistle Encore will likely fit your needs. And Encore has several strengths that will appeal to a number of users.

As with Mosaic, Encore's notes, rests, expression marks, articulations, graphic symbols, and other notation elements appear on a number of palettes (there are ten altogether). They provide a very complete selection of tools and you can open, close, and move them as necessary while you work (Figure 9-20). Entering a note, rest, accidental, or whatever is simply a matter of making a selection with the mouse and clicking where you want it to appear in the score. You can even change the clef at the beginning of a staff by picking a new clef from the Clef palette and clicking on top of the old one.

If you have a MIDI keyboard, you can also enter notes with the usual step-entry method. And Encore does a good job of transcribing real-time performances when played along with the internal or MIDI metronome click. If you're using Passport's Master Tracks Pro as your sequencer, Encore can open those files. It transcribes the music and assigns a staff to each track.

FIGURE 9-20

Encore's main window with its available palettes

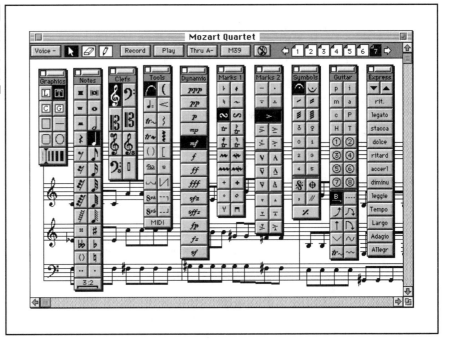

Once you have your notes entered you can add lyrics by typing them directly into the score. Other kinds of text are entered as they are in Mosaic: drag to define a text box and then enter the text. Adding chord symbols is also easy. When you click on a note with the Chord tool a dialog box opens offering a large selection of chord types from which to choose (Figure 9-21). You can also insert guitar fretboard diagrams in your music. And chord symbols and diagrams are both transposable.

One of Encore's strengths is its ability to recognize various kinds of notation symbols during MIDI playback. It may not be quite as sophisticated as Finale in this regard, but it does offer a more complete MIDI implementation than Mosaic. Encore recognizes the usual things like notes and tempo indications. But it also responds to crescendo and decrescendo markings (often called hairpins or wedges). And it lets you assign specific offset values to dynamic markings (Figure 9-22). Encore also recognizes pedal indications, octave indications (ottava signs), multiple endings, articulation marks (staccato, legato), accents, and more. The MIDI tools feature even lets you enter Program Change messages and continuous controller data to your score.

Encore is also strong in the area of guitar notation. Aside from the usual chord symbols and fret diagrams, Encore includes a generous assortment of specialized marks and symbols. The Guitar palette supplies string marks for tablature as well as indications for bending, slurring, trilling, and adding tremolo to notes. There's also a Barre tool (to indicate chords in higher positions) and a complete set of marks for right hand fingerings (*p,i,m,a*).

Additionally, Encore provides a full set of tools for creating tablature for instruments with as many as eight strings. The Make Tab command will actually create a tablature staff and convert standard notation into tablature (Figure 9-23).

FIGURE 9-21

Encore's Chord Tool dialog box offers a large selection of chord symbols

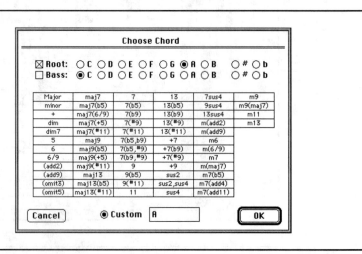

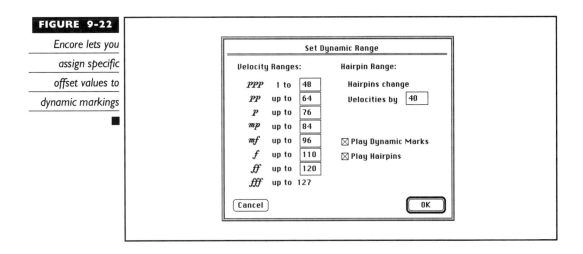

FIGURE 9-22

Encore lets you assign specific offset values to dynamic markings

Another nice feature in Encore is its Expressions palette. It lets you create custom text items (like "ad lib" or "a tempo") and store them for later use. Expressions that you use often are then just a mouse click away. The Expressions palette can hold up to 48 expressions that you can modify (e.g., font, size, and style) any time you want.

Encore can handle most of the notation tasks that you'll likely encounter. You can move bar lines by dragging with the mouse, insert slurs by clicking and dragging, enter notes with cross-staff beaming, and export files in EPS format. You can have scores with as many as 64 staves and each staff can have up to eight voices. Avant garde composers will no doubt miss the ability to add nontraditional key signatures and unusual, complex meters, but most people will not likely feel too restricted by Encore's limitations. Furthermore,

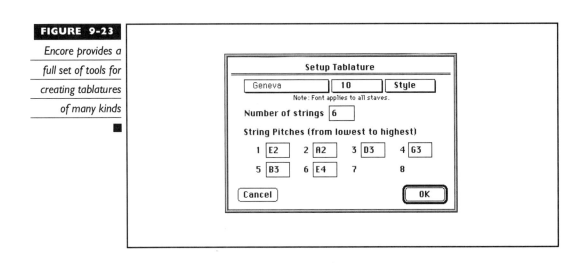

FIGURE 9-23

Encore provides a full set of tools for creating tablatures of many kinds

the Mac and Windows versions of Encore share the same file format so you can transfer files across platforms.

MusicTime

PC

MAC

CD-ROM

If you like the look and feel of Encore, but your notation requirements are minimal, consider Passport's entry-level **MusicTime**. It provides Encore's basic tools (including chord symbol and lyric entry) in a greatly scaled-down program (Figure 9-24). In MusicTime you can have up to eight staves with as many as four voices per staff.

Many of Encore's tool palettes are available in MusicTime and the program adds a few interesting features of its own. The coolest of these is its ability to display and print your music in color. The Color palette lets you assign a different color to each staff and you can even have different colors for the different voices on a single staff. In fact, you can have a staff one color and the notes on it another. I'm not sure what this is good for but it's lots of fun. MusicTime also provides an on-screen keyboard so you can step-enter notes with your mouse instead of with a MIDI instrument.

MusicTime is clearly aimed at amateurs and hobbyists whose notation needs are limited. The documentation is a little thin, but the program is easy to use and makes a nice introduction to notation software.

FIGURE 9-24

MusicTime's main

window

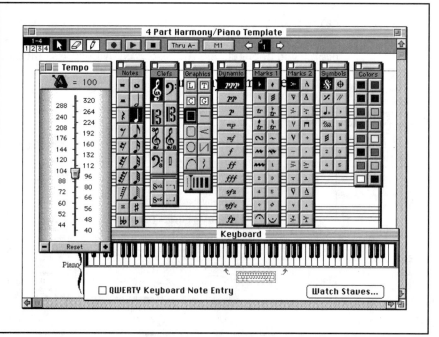

ConcertWare

PC

MAC

ConcertWare from Jump! Software combines a number of unique features in an inexpensive entry-level program that divides its resources between music production and notation. The main screen (Figure 9-25) includes a row of boxes that indicate note values (down to a 32nd note). To the left the Pitch Palette lets you select pitches from a stack of whole notes. Or as an option you can make selections from an on-screen keyboard.

To enter notes onto a staff you first click where you want the notes to appear. This establishes the insertion point. Then you click on a note value from the row of boxes. Finally, you click on one of the notes on the Pitch palette or the on-screen keyboard and the appropriate note appears (after a pause) at the insertion point. I found this to be a more cumbersome and less intuitive approach to note entry than the usual method of clicking directly on the staff where you want the notes to go.

Of course you can use your MIDI keyboard to step-enter notes. And ConcertWare will competently transcribe real-time performances and imported MIDI files. It does this through its use of "intelligent" transcription algorithms that analyze the music in each measure and make plausible decisions about note durations.

One of the things that you notice right away when you start working with ConcertWare is the number of options that you're presented with for each

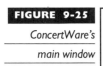

FIGURE 9-25

ConcertWare's

main window

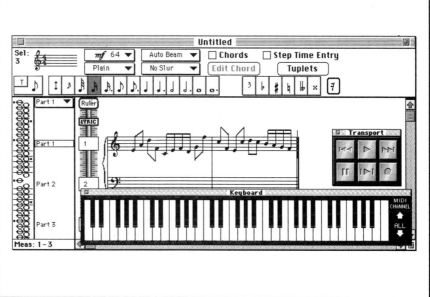

operation. This can be a double-edged sword. It gives you control over a great many details when working with your music. But sometimes setting lots of little parameters just gets in the way. To record in real time, for instance, you select Record from the Sound menu (or transport palette), which then opens a densely packed dialog box offering an array of choices (Figure 9-26).

ConcertWare is an interesting mix of advanced and entry-level features. You can have up to 32 staves in a score with as many as four voices per staff. The staff options are limited to a one-line percussion staff or a standard five-line staff (there's no provision for tablature). Chord symbols and guitar fretboard diagrams are treated as text objects and are not transposable. Tuplet brackets generated by the program cannot be repositioned. And there is no zoom feature for the main window.

The program is much stronger in the area of MIDI playback. Although the program doesn't respond to articulation marks (like staccato dots and accents), it does recognize dynamic indications. A pop-up menu lets you assign a Velocity value to different dynamic marks and you can insert these as you enter notes with the mouse. You can also insert Program Change markers in the score and ConcertWare will recognize repeat signs and tempo changes. There's also a mixer window that lets you send Continuous Controller data to any MIDI channel during playback. Other windows let you scale Velocities and tempos and there's even a dialog box that lets you add harmony lines to a melody (Figure 9-27).

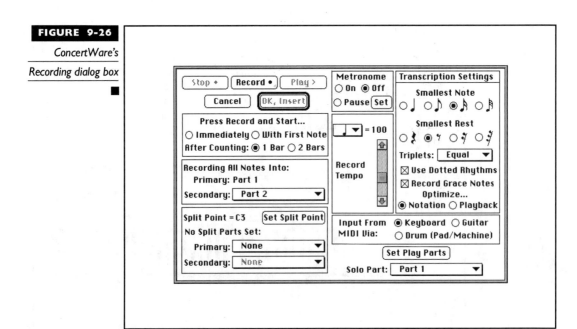

FIGURE 9-26

ConcertWare's

Recording dialog box

FIGURE 9-27

ConcertWare lets you add harmony lines to a melody

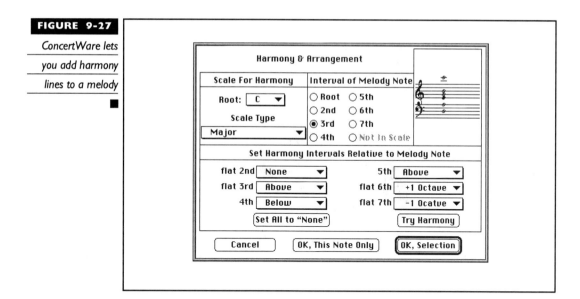

In ConcertWare you enter lyrics by typing them directly into the score. After you type each word or syllable you must hit the TAB key to advance to the next note. The program also supplies a palette of symbols that you can add where needed.

The Macintosh version of ConcertWare includes a unique application called InstrumentMaker. You can use it to create and edit instrument sounds for playback through the Macintosh's built-in sound generator. The program comes with a collection of over 40 instruments, but you can create as many as 256 instruments of your own.

With the InstrumentMaker window (Figure 9-28) you create new timbres by adding together different harmonics and changing their relative volume settings. Or you can draw a new waveform directly into the Waveform display. You can also draw an envelope for the sound and add vibrato. If you don't have a MIDI setup for listening to your scores, the Instrument-Maker provides a terrific alternative for small ensembles—even though the instruments don't sound nearly as good as a typical MIDI synthesizer. ConcertWare comes with a large complement of standard instrument sounds. And you can create new instruments at any time.

As an entry-level program, ConcertWare is clearly not in the same league as Finale, Mosaic, or Encore. But, then again, it costs hundreds of dollars less. Even so, many people will appreciate the level of control that it offers for MIDI configuration and playback. Others will enjoy some of its more quirky features like its ability to display note heads in different colors. To help you get acquainted with the program, Jump! Software is offering an

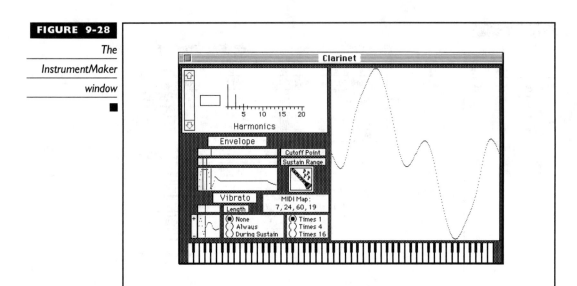

interactive guided tour on CD-ROM or floppy disk. If you're on a tight budget and you don't need high-end notation and page-layout tools, ConcertWare is worth a look.

Other Options

The products described in this chapter are really only a small sample of the growing market for notation software. There are many other programs that range from minimal entry-level software for kids and hobbyists to top-notch professional manuscript programs for serious musicians. For example, Temporal Acuity Products offers two full-featured notation programs: **Nightingale** for the Mac and **MusicPrinter Plus** for the PC. Personal Composer offers its high-end **Personal Composer for Windows**. And Opcode offers its new **Overture** program. At the other end of the spectrum check out the newly improved **QuickScore Professional for Windows** from Dr. T's Music Software.

If your main goal is to transcribe music I suggest first recording and editing your performance with a good sequencer and then importing the file into a notation program. Of course this involves two pieces of software. You might, therefore, consider one of the integrated sequencer/notation packages if your page-layout and notation requirements are modest. **Cubase Score** (Windows and Mac), for example, combines an excellent pro-level sequencer with a nice general-purpose notation program. The mid-level **Musicator Win** is an example of a notation-based sequencer with a good set of tools for printing scores.

If possible, try to get a demo of the programs you're considering to see how they feel when you work with them. Remember, the feature list is only half the story. The more important consideration is how easy it is to access the features.

CHAPTER 10

Working with Digital Audio

U NTIL now I've focused mainly on MIDI as the primary means for creating and editing music with your computer. But as powerful and amazing as MIDI is, it does have its limitations. For one thing, you might want to use your computer to record acoustic instruments and singers—something that MIDI can't do. Or you might just want your music in a form that doesn't require a MIDI system for playback. And finally, you may need to deliver your music in a format that other computer programs can easily incorporate.

Fortunately, desktop musicians have another powerful resource at their disposal—digital audio. In essence, digital audio simply refers to music and other sounds that have been converted, during recording, into digital data and then converted back into sounds again for listening.

Whether you realize it or not, digital audio is just about everywhere. High-end recording studios have been using large multitrack digital tape recorders for several years now. And stereo DAT (digital audio tape) recorders are becoming more commonplace in smaller studios. Every time you listen to your favorite compact disc or interact with the sound effects and narration from a CD-ROM, you're using digital audio. The sounds that come from your keyboard sampler or sample playback module are also digital audio. And don't forget the sound effects and snippets of music that many people use instead of system beeps. They're also digital audio.

It seems like digital audio is taking over the universe—and for several good reasons. First of all, with the right equipment, digital audio can produce recordings of crystalline clarity with little of the background noise that has long plagued earlier recording methods. And you can make multiple copies of digital audio recordings without any degradation of sound quality.

But for the average desktop musician the great advantage of digital audio can be summarized in one word—control. Once a sound has been turned into numbers, computers can get in on the action, and that means you can do things to your music that you couldn't otherwise do. You can take sections of recordings and cut, copy, paste, and delete them. You can slice and dice to your heart's content, play sections backward, combine pieces in different ways, and add reverb and other effects. And finally, you can export your music to a variety of computer applications for playback in such things as games, multimedia presentations, and even business software.

There are now a number of excellent sound cards for both the Mac and the PC that let you turn your computer into a powerful digital audio recorder. Since the introduction of Microsoft Windows, the market for PC sound cards has absolutely skyrocketed. There are now literally dozens upon dozens of sound cards ranging from less than $200 to over $1,000. And they all provide a means for recording sounds and saving them on your hard disk as *soundfiles*. In fact, for a sound card to qualify as an MPC (Multimedia PC) compatible card it must have (in addition to MIDI) digital audio recording and playback capability.

note   *The MPC specification is defined by the Multimedia PC Marketing Council—an organization formed to establish PC multimedia hardware standards. The Level 1 standard, published in 1990, established a base-level system for multimedia computing. Because the Level 1 standard quickly became obsolete, an enhanced specification—Level 2—was established in 1993. Among other things, it guaranteed a higher level of digital audio quality for MPC-certified computer systems. Most PC sound card manufacturers are moving in the direction of providing the enhanced features of the Level 2 specification.*

Because the Macintosh has always had built-in digital audio playback capability, the sound card market is more limited. The sound cards that are available for the Mac are mainly targeted toward those seeking pro-level, CD-quality sound. Prices start in the neighborhood of about $1,000 (Digidesign's popular Audiomedia II is a good example) and go up considerably for professional recording-studio–level equipment.

Once you've installed your sound card, recording is relatively straightforward. Most sound cards come with audio recording and editing software, and the software always includes a set of transport controls that work just like the ones on a mechanical tape deck (Figure 10-1). Most programs also include a set of on-screen meters so you can set your record levels before you start recording.

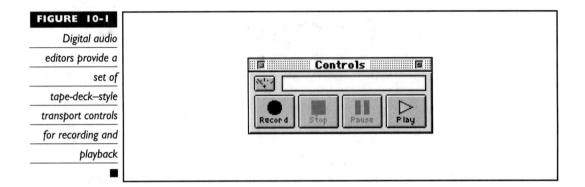

FIGURE 10-1

Digital audio

editors provide a

set of

tape-deck–style

transport controls

for recording and

playback
■

By clicking the Record button, you can record from a microphone or a line-level source—such as a tape recorder, CD player, or MIDI sound module. When you're through recording, just click the Stop button and your recording appears on your hard drive as a *soundfile*. Click the Play button to hear your recording play back. Most programs also let you view your recording in a waveform display where you can edit the sound in a number of ways. That's when things get really exciting.

But before we go any further, let's take a look at the digital audio process—how it works, and the basic concepts that you'll need to understand for making professional-sounding recordings.

An Introduction to Digital Audio

As you may remember from Chapter 2, sound occurs when a vibrating object sets up pressure patterns in the air called sound waves. To capture these sound waves in a recording you can use one of two methods—*analog* or *digital*. These terms are used so often in describing recording and playback equipment that it's important to understand the distinction. Both methods are currently in widespread use and both methods have their staunch advocates. Let's look first at how analog recording works.

Analog Recording

The explosive popularity of personal computers has focused a lot of attention on digital recording. But long before the invention of digital recording, all recording devices were analog. In fact, most of the tape recorders in current use—by amateurs and pros alike—use analog technology. So let's briefly explore the topic.

The analog recording process works like this: Sound waves impinging on a microphone cause a small diaphragm within the microphone to vibrate (the same way your ear drums vibrate in response to a sound). The vibrating diaphragm produces an electrical signal with continuously varying voltages. These fluctuations in voltage correspond to the vibrations of the diaphragm, which in turn correspond to the vibrations of the sound wave.

High frequencies cause rapid fluctuations, low frequencies cause slower fluctuations. Loud sounds cause the voltage to increase a lot while softer sounds cause less of an increase. In other words, the electrical signal is directly analogous to the original sound. When the tape deck's recording head receives these fluctuating voltages, it creates magnetic patterns on the tape that correspond to the original electrical signal. By doing this it stores an analog version of the sound wave that started the whole process.

Playback is essentially the reverse of the recording process. The playback head reads the magnetic patterns on the tape and reconstructs the audio signal. The speaker at the end of the line responds to the fluctuating voltages by vibrating in a way that re-creates the original sound wave. The important point to remember is that throughout the entire recording and playback process each component of the system responds in a way that mimics the original sound. You might say that the analog relationship between the sound and the recording is always preserved.

Digital Recording

Digital recording starts out just like analog recording. Sound waves are captured by a microphone that converts the vibrations in the air into an electrical signal. At this point the process is still analog. Things change quickly however, as the digital recorder transforms the fluctuating voltages into a series of binary numbers (1's and 0's). It does this with an electronic circuit called an *analog-to-digital* converter (A/D converter or ADC for short).

An analog-to-digital converter translates analog signals into digital values.

Here's how it works: When the electrical signal leaves the microphone, it first encounters something called a *sample-and-hold circuit*. The sample-and-hold circuit grabs the incoming signal and freezes it momentarily. This "snapshot" of the signal captures the current voltage level at a specific point in time. The A/D converter then comes along and assigns a series of numbers that represent that instantaneous voltage reading. Once the A/D converter does its job, the sample-and-hold circuit can let go and the whole process repeats over and over again—many thousands of times per second (Figure 10-2).

The process of grabbing and reading an incoming signal is often referred to as *sampling*, and the number of times per second that the process occurs is therefore referred to as the *sampling rate*. The higher the sampling rate, the more accurately the recording device can capture the tiny variations

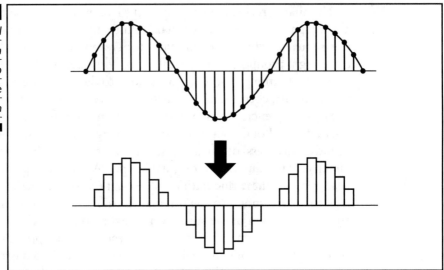

in the sound wave. This produces higher fidelity recordings with less distortion. Inexpensive sound cards typically record and play with approximately 11kHz or 22kHz sampling rates. Compact discs use a 44.1kHz sampling rate while DAT recorders can go as high as 48kHz. I'll come back to this topic in a minute, but first let's look at another aspect of digital audio—resolution.

Resolution

The process of converting an electrical signal (which represents a sound wave) into a series of numbers is called *quantization* or *digitization*. Each time the A/D converter receives a voltage reading from the sample-and-hold circuit, it spits out a series of binary numbers (bits) that represent the signal's amplitude at that moment. The more bits that are available to describe the amplitude reading, the more precisely the ADC can match that reading. If it can't match the reading exactly, it just comes as close as it can and moves along.

The resolution of an A/D converter determines how closely the digital translation corresponds to the actual analog signal.

How closely the circuit can match the signal is referred to as its *resolution*. The situation is similar to the way that resolution affects image quality on computer monitors. Inexpensive low-resolution monitors provide fewer pixels per square inch, so the image quality tends to be coarse and blurry. High-end monitors provide more pixels per square inch, so they can offer greater clarity by capturing fine details.

Digital audio aficionados refer to the disparity between the original analog signal and its digital version as *quantization noise*. This is a type of distortion unique to digital media.

In the world of digital audio, resolution is expressed in terms of the number of bits available during the quantization process. Some common resolutions include 8-bit, 12-bit, and 16-bit. The internal sounds on all of the early Macintosh models used 8-bit resolution, as do most of the inexpensive PC sound cards currently on the market. Compact discs, DAT recorders, high-end sound cards, and the internal sounds in some of the newer Macintosh models use 16-bit resolution.

Quantization noise is due to the imprecise translation of a sound from analog to digital.

16 bits is not just twice as good as 8 bits, it's a whole lot better. That's because for every additional bit that's used, the number of numerical combinations that can represent a signal's amplitude is increased by a factor of 2. In other words, an eight-bit number has 2 to the 8th power or 256 possible values. A 16-bit number has 2 to the 16th power, or a whopping 65,536 possible values! This means that sounds captured with 16-bit resolution will much more accurately match the original signal. Aside from reducing quantization noise, a higher resolution results in a higher *signal-to-noise ratio*. That's the difference between the loudest sound that a device can handle without distortion and the inherent noise level of the device itself.

n o t e *The signal-to-noise ratio of a device is expressed in decibels such as 84dB or 92dB. The higher the number, the better.*

Sampling Rate

As we've seen, the resolution of a digital audio recording is very important in determining its sound quality, but resolution is only half of the story. The sampling rate is equally important.

As I mentioned earlier, the sampling rate tells us how often the incoming signal is examined, or "sampled," during the recording process. Even if you had 100-bit resolution, it wouldn't do you any good if you only sampled your audio signal 3 or 4 times a second. That's because different sounds are filled with subtle irregularities and fine details that give them their distinct characteristics. And unless your sampling rate is high enough, you'll miss most of these details. This, in turn, results in a muddy-sounding approximation of the original sound—the audio equivalent of a blurry computer monitor.

To illustrate this point, try sitting on the front steps of your house looking out at the street. Open your eyes for one second and then close them for a second, open them for a second and close them for a second. Continue to do this as you observe the scene in front of you.

Our sampling rate of 30 blinks per minute makes it easy to see some things and harder to see others. For example that old man strolling along the sidewalk is easy to see. Each time you open your eyes he's a little farther along the sidewalk. But overall you can get a pretty good idea of what he's doing as he enters and leaves the scene. But what about that bird over there? You see it as it enters on the left, but the next time you open your eyes the bird has already landed in the neighbor's tree. You saw it arrive. You saw it land. But what happened in between is uncertain. Did it swoop? Did it flap its wings? Did it do a barrel roll? It's hard to know because our visual sampling rate is too slow to fill us in on those details.

And what about the small things going on around you? A bee zips by. A lizard darts out from a rock. A leaf falls from a tree. You might miss these events completely if they happen when your eyes are closed. One solution is to increase your sampling rate to 60 blinks a minute. Then you'd pick up more of the details that are happening around you.

The same is true in the world of digital audio. The old man on the sidewalk is a lot like the low frequencies in a sound wave. They're easier to capture because they don't change as quickly from one instant to the next. The bird is like the mid-range frequencies. If the sampling rate is too slow you'll start to lose some important details, even if you do get the general picture. And the bee and the lizard are like the high frequency elements in a sound wave. Unless you have a sufficiently high sampling rate, many of these little events will be overlooked entirely.

In audio terms, the range of frequencies that a recording device can accurately capture and reproduce is called its *frequency response*. And as you can see, the sampling rate is largely responsible for determining the frequency response.

Frequency response refers to the range of frequencies that a device can reproduce accurately.

But how high of a sampling rate do you need to properly record music? Well, in theory, each audio cycle in a waveform must be sampled at least twice in order to represent both the positive and negative parts of the wave's cycle (Figure 10-3).

If your digital recorder can't grab at least two samples per cycle, you'll get an annoying form of distortion called *aliasing*. That's because without enough samples to show the basic shape of the waveform, the resulting numbers from the ADC appear to represent a frequency that is much lower than the actual waveform being recorded (Figure 10-4). This undesirable variant of the original tone is called an *alias frequency*.

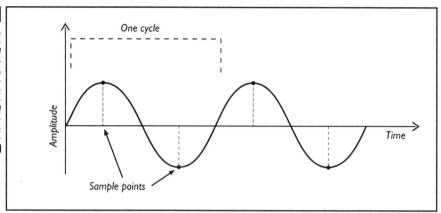

FIGURE 10-3

Each audio cycle must be sampled at least twice to represent its positive and negative parts ∎

At the Movies

Whether you realize it or not, you've probably seen an excellent example of aliasing—at the movies. Movie cameras work, in principle, a lot like digital audio recorders. They "sample" the visual world (in a series of photos) at the rate of 24 frames per second. That's a lot slower than the thousands of samples per second needed for audio recording. But fooling your eyes into perceiving fluid motion from a series of still "snapshots" is much easier than fooling your ears with the audio equivalent of the same thing.

Nonetheless, once in a while something happens on screen that reminds us that our eyes are indeed being fooled. I'm talking about what is often referred to as the "wagon wheel" effect. How many times have you seen a stage coach racing across the plains and noticed that the spokes on the wheels seem to be standing still? Sometimes they even seem to be going backward. (You may also notice this effect with helicopter blades and airplane propellers.) This is an example of aliasing.

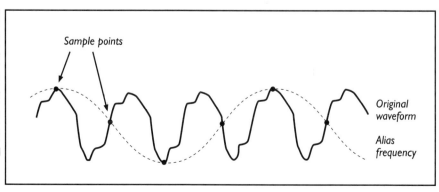

FIGURE 10-4

Aliasing occurs when too few samples are taken to adequately represent the waveform ∎

In My Experience

As a composer, noise is something that I must always take into account because it is, for better or worse, an integral part of music. Over the years, I have found noise to be one of the more intriguing aspects of music for several reasons. As this chapter discusses, noise was always a problem with analog recording and can also be one with digital recording when sampling rates or resolutions are too low. However, not all noise is bad. That is, in music there is good noise and there is bad noise.

Consider the flute. When the flute generates a tone, it does so by creating a disturbance in a column of air. Specifically, the player produces a burst of air that is directed into the flute's mouthpiece. This causes the column of air within the flute to vibrate. However, not all of the sound generated by this process is the note. Part of the "wind" produced by the flutist becomes turbulence instead of the note.

This turbulence causes noise. However, in the case of the flute, this noise is also an important component of the flute sound. In fact, the burst of noise preceding the initial note is a defining characteristic of the flute.

The sound of a violin is another example of noise being an important part of an instrument's acoustic texture. When the violinist bows a string, the string is set into motion because the bow drags across the string. However, the motion of the bow is not smooth. Rather, it consists of a series of tiny jumps and lurches that are caused by the bow hairs repeatedly grabbing and releasing the string. (If the bow hairs were completely smooth, no sound would be produced!) Each time the bow grabs and releases, tiny bits of noise are added to the actual pitch.

Another example of musical noise is generated by the guitar. As players move from note to note on the wire-wound strings, the movement of the fingers creates tiny squeaking sounds. Although guitarists usually try to minimize these noises as much as possible, their presence is an important part of what we expect to hear when the guitar is played. In fact, some synthesizers even include special "finger-noise" patches so you can add realism to the guitar sounds.

Even though many of the innovations in recording and audio technology have been driven by the desire to reduce noise, it is ironic that the inherent noise of acoustic instruments must still be accurately reproduced. Since noise is an essential part of most acoustic instruments, any technique used to record (or synthesize) those instruments must also faithfully reproduce their noise components. It has been my experience that the noise associated with an instrument is often the element of its sound that adds character and "defines" the instrument.

Aliasing is distortion caused by too low a sampling rate.

If the spokes on the wheel keep arriving at the same position every time the movie camera's shutter opens, the camera will be tricked into seeing the spokes as stationary. If the spokes arrive slightly behind the same position each time, they'll appear to rotate backward. The problem is that the "sampling rate" of the camera is simply too slow to accurately capture the rapid rotation of the spokes. So along with all of the on-screen images of forward motion—and in spite of the fact that we know that the wheels are turning—we also get the false image of stationary wagon spokes.

The same kind of thing happens when alias frequencies appear in an audio recording. Along with all of the musical tones that belong in a piece, you'll also get some frequencies that simply don't belong. That's why the sampling rate must be high enough to accurately capture all of the different frequencies in a waveform.

This business about adequate sampling rates is clearly summarized in the *Nyquist Theorem,* which states that the sampling rate must be twice as high as the highest frequency recorded. Or expressed another way: the highest frequency that you can record without aliasing will be one-half of the sampling rate. This frequency is often referred to as the *Nyquist Limit.*

To tackle the problem of aliasing, sound cards and other digital audio devices include a type of filter called a *low-pass filter.* This is also known as an *anti-aliasing filter* because, in this case, its job is to eliminate the high frequencies that could cause trouble for the A/D converter (Figure 10-5). Ideally, the filter should cut out everything above the Nyquist Limit. But in real life the filter's cutoff point is not so precise. So the filter is set to a frequency a little below the Nyquist Limit just to be on the safe side.

But why is this important to know? Well, it's important because if you're recording with a sampling rate of 22kHz, for example, you can't really expect to capture frequencies up to 11kHz. Your actual upper limit will probably be something closer to 10kHz.

The Nyquist limit is the highest frequency that can be recorded for a given sampling rate.

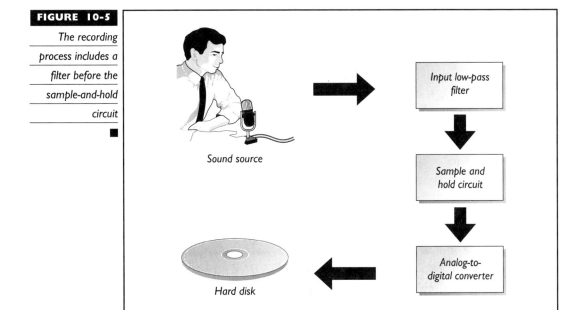

FIGURE 10-5

The recording process includes a filter before the sample-and-hold circuit

Sound source

Input low-pass filter

Sample and hold circuit

Analog-to-digital converter

Hard disk

remember *The upper range of frequencies that a digital recorder can accurately record will be slightly less than one-half its sample rate.*

At first glance, 10kHz seems like a pretty generous upper limit. After all, that's more than twice as high as the highest note on a piano. But remember, we're not just recording the fundamental of each musical note. We're also recording all of the harmonics that go with it. And these upper partials can go quite high indeed. In fact, as we learned in Chapter 2, it's these upper harmonics that give musical sounds their unique timbres. That's why sound cards that only sample at rates of 11kHz or 22kHz produce music that sounds kind of muffled.

Since people can hear as high as about 20kHz, you need a sampling rate of over 40kHz to adequately capture the full range of musical sounds complete with the interplay of upper harmonics. Compact discs with their 44.1kHz sampling rate and DAT recorders with their 48kHz sampling rate provide plenty of leeway for capturing the full musical spectrum.

A low-pass filter only allows sounds below a certain frequency to pass. It blocks sounds higher than the specified frequency.

All of this talk about resolution and sampling rates simply begs the question: why not always use 16-bit, 44.1kHz digital audio for your recordings? The answer is that—if you're serious about the quality of your music—you should! But reality has a way of poking its nose into our creative efforts and there are times when you just have to compromise your standards.

First of all, sound cards that offer CD-quality audio cost more than low-end cards aimed primarily at game players and casual users. And second, there's the issue of compatibility. If you're writing music for games or multimedia, the producer will probably request that you submit your music as 8-bit, 22kHz soundfiles. That's because the built-in audio capability of most Macintosh computers only supports that level. The same is true for most of the sound cards that PC owners use. So to ensure maximum compatibility, you have to address the lowest common denominator.

But there's another even more important consideration when you use your computer as a digital recorder: storage space. If you're planning to record CD-quality sound on your computer, you're in for a rude awakening. A single minute of 16-bit, 44.1kHz, stereo audio requires more than 10MB of disk space! That's right, a 10-minute piece of music in CD-quality stereo will use up more than 100MB of space on your hard drive.

So once again, the topic of compromise comes up. You can cut that 100MB file in half if you record in mono rather than stereo, and you can cut it in half again if you record at 22kHz instead of 44kHz. You can cut it in half yet again if you choose 8-bit rather than 16-bit resolution. So now your original soundfile is down around 13MB, which is a lot less daunting than 100MB. But in the process you've lost quite a bit of audio quality, and the difference will be obvious.

That's why professional recording studios that do direct-to-disk recording always have several gargantuan hard drives around. You'll just have to assess the requirements of each project as it comes along and decide on the best compromise. Table 10-1 shows some of the more common options that you can choose from.

Numbers into Sound

To play back your digital audio soundfiles, your sound card (or other recording device) simply reverses the recording process—more or less. First the music, which is stored as a bunch of numbers, is sent to a circuit called a *digital-to-analog converter* (D/A converter or DAC for short). It transforms the numbers back into a series of voltages. The reconstructed analog signal is then sent to an *output sample-and-hold circuit* that helps to stabilize the output. Finally, the signal is sent through an *output low-pass filter,* which smoothes out the irregularities caused by the digital recording process. By now the analog signal with its fluctuating voltages should closely resemble

Resolution	Sample Rate (kHz)	Stereo/Mono	File Size for 1 Minute	Quality
16-bit	44.1	Stereo	10.5MB	CD-quality, also known as Red Book Audio
16-bit	44.1	Mono	5.25MB	A good compromise; fine for dialog and most sound effects
16-bit	22.05	Stereo	5.25MB	Cleaner sounding than 8-bit, but lacking in highest frequencies
16-bit	22.05	Mono	2.6MB	Useful for dialog
8-bit	44.1	Stereo	5.25MB	Best quality for 8-bit sound cards; not as clean sounding as 16-bit
8-bit	44.1	Mono	2.6MB	Useful compromise
8-bit	22.05	Stereo	2.6MB	Moderate sound quality, very often used in multimedia
8-bit	22.05	Mono	1.3MB	Maximum compatibility for all computers; reasonable compromise for sound effects and dialog
8-bit	11	Mono	650K	Not suitable for music; may work for some dialog
8-bit	5.5	Mono	325K	Unacceptable for music and just about everything else

TABLE 10-1 *Some Common Recording Options* ■

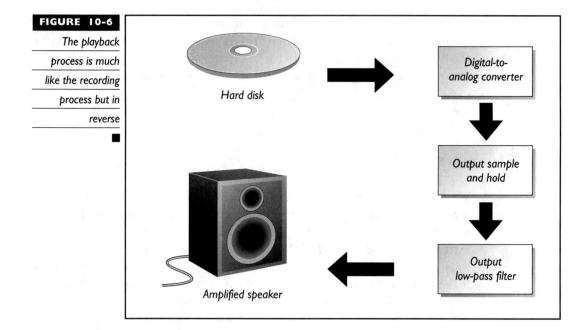

FIGURE 10-6

The playback process is much like the recording process but in reverse ■

Hard disk

Digital-to-analog converter

Output sample and hold

Output low-pass filter

Amplified speaker

the original signal that started the whole process. When you send it to an amplifier and speakers the electrical current is once again transformed into sound and you can then listen to your music (Figure 10-6).

Getting Started

The great thing about using your computer to record music is that once you've made your recording, you can intervene in a number of ways before playback. It's this ability to alter recordings in myriad ways that sets computer-based recording devices apart from earlier analog equipment. And it's one of the main reasons why so many professional recording studios are turning to direct-to-disk recording systems. But you don't need $100,000 to enter the realm of digital recording. A half-way decent sound card and some audio editing software will get you started.

Here are a few things that you should know about sound cards and files.

■ There are a number of different formats for soundfiles. The most common formats for the Macintosh are Sound Designer II (SDII), AIFF (Audio Interchange File Format), and SND. AIFF is currently the most universal of the three. For Windows-based PCs, the WAVE (.WAV) format is by far the most common. Some programs can translate between AIFF and WAVE files.

■ Most MPC sound cards won't let you do multi-track recording. You can record a single channel or two channels at once, but the end result is always a single mono or stereo soundfile. You can't, for instance, record one soundfile on one channel and then record another soundfile on the other channel. Pro-level digital audio cards are a different story, but they're much more expensive.

■ For work with music, always use a 16-bit sound card, but don't be fooled by advertising hype. Manufacturers are fond of declaring that their 16-bit sound cards deliver "CD-quality" sound. However, there's more to true CD-quality sound than uncompressed, 16-bit resolution and a 44.1kHz sampling rate. The quality of the A/D and D/A converters, the design and layout of the circuit board, the amount of shielding, and the quality of the filters all play an important role in determining the final audio quality. To some extent you get what you pay for. It's unlikely that you'll get true CD-quality audio from a $200 sound card—even with 16-bit resolution.

note   *The MPC Level 1 standard only requires 8-bit digital audio capability. Level 2 calls for 16-bit digital audio. (Both levels also require MIDI capability.)*

■ To solve the problem of storing large soundfiles, many sound cards let you compress your recordings in various ways. Although this does save storage space, it also invariably causes some deterioration in sound quality. As a general rule, it's best to avoid using compression on your digital audio recordings unless it's absolutely necessary.

note   *Compression rates are often expressed as ratios such as 3:1 or 4:1 or 8:1. In general, the greater the ratio the poorer the sound quality. When working with music, it's best to avoid file compression altogether.*

- As a guide to sound quality, check a sound card's signal-to-noise ratio. It tells you how much background noise to expect in your recordings. Professional-level sound cards typically rate above 90dB. Semi-pro cards rate in the mid- to high-80dB range. Anything below 80dB may be fine for many kinds of projects, but it's definitely not true CD-quality.

- Keep in mind that the computer itself can add noise to your recordings. Power supplies, disk drives, video cards, and other components generate a lot of electrical noise. IBM-compatible PCs, in particular, are highly variable in this regard because they're made by so many different manufacturers. A sound card that's relatively quiet in one machine may be quite noisy in another. The best sound cards are designed to minimize this problem through advanced shielding techniques and the use of high-quality electronic components. Expect to pay around $500 or more for one of these better PC cards.

Built-in Recording

In many cases, you don't actually need any extra software to make recordings with your computer. Several models of Macintosh computer boast onboard recording capabilities. You just plug a microphone (or line-level source) directly into the microphone input jack on the back of the computer. Then you open the Record dialog box, which provides you with a simple set of transport controls.

PC users have an even better set of tools. The Sound Recorder applet (Figure 10-7) lets you make recordings from a microphone or line-level source that's plugged into your sound card. Aside from a set of transport controls, Sound Recorder includes a small waveform display and some basic editing commands.

These basic tools are fine for adding a few sound effects to a presentation or providing voice annotation for a business document. But they're not really suitable for serious work with music. Most sound cards come with some kind of recording and editing software, but their usefulness and performance vary widely.

If you're dedicated to making high-quality recordings, it's important that you acquire a good audio editing program. Some excellent examples for the PC include Sound Forge from Sonic Foundry and Wave for Windows from Turtle Beach Systems. For the Mac there's Sound Designer II from Digidesign and SoundEdit 16 from Macromedia. Of course, there are other good

FIGURE 10-7

The Windows

Sound Recorder

applet

■

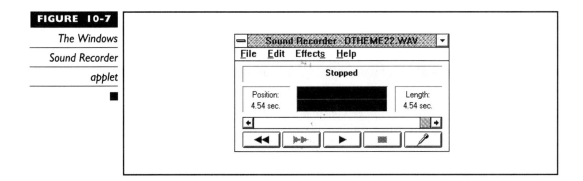

programs for both platforms, but these represent a good cross section. We'll look at them more closely later on, but for now let's take an overview of the common features offered by audio editing software.

Setting Recording Levels

The first step in making a good recording is to properly set the recording levels. To aid you in this process, almost all editing programs provide a set of digital meters that show the volume of the incoming sounds (Figure 10-8).

Watch these meters carefully as you play your music into the microphone (or into the line inputs). The meters on analog recorders typically have a "0" setting that's used as a reference for optimizing levels. When using these kinds of meters, it's common for the indicators to splash over into the +3 or +5 range (or higher).

Digital meters are different. They usually indicate a peak level beyond which you shouldn't go. To get the best recordings, you must keep the levels just below the peak level during the loudest part of the music. The trick is to set the record levels as high ("hot") as possible without crossing the threshold of the peak level. The importance of this should not be underestimated.

FIGURE 10-8

Most editing

programs provide a

set of digital

meters for setting

the recording levels

■

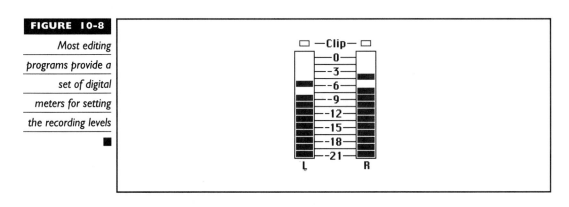

What you want is to keep the amplitude of the music as high as possible, compared to the inherent background noise of the recording process. If you decide to play it safe and record at too low a level, your recording will have an unnecessary amount of quantization noise in it (Figure 10-9).

remember *Keep the music signal as high as possible when recording to optimize the signal-to-noise ratio.*

If the input levels are too high, an obnoxious form of distortion called *clipping* will occur. It's called clipping because the tops and bottoms of the waveform appear to be chopped off (Figure 10-10). So the goal is to minimize quantization noise while avoiding clipping.

Clipping occurs when input levels are greater than the device can handle.

This should be relatively easy if you pay close attention to the on-screen input meters. Unfortunately, many low-end, entry-level editing programs provide meters that are unstable and less than reliable.

If you're using one of these programs, you'll have to do some experimenting to get consistent results with your recordings. This should be possible once you learn the idiosyncrasies of your sound card/software combination. The better programs, like Sound Designer and Wave for Windows, provide more reliable metering so they're easier to work with.

Working with Silence

Once you've made your recording, the next step is to trim away the blank spaces from the beginning and end of the recording. The digital recording process does not care whether you're recording dead air or a 70-piece orchestra at full volume. Either way it still takes up the same amount of storage space per second for the soundfile. So by trimming away the silence before and after a recording, you can reclaim valuable disk space, and you

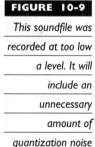

FIGURE 10-9

This soundfile was recorded at too low a level. It will include an unnecessary amount of quantization noise

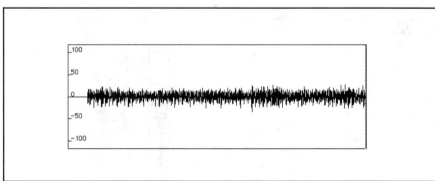

FIGURE 10-10

This soundfile was recorded at too high a level. Notice how some of the peaks have been cut off ■

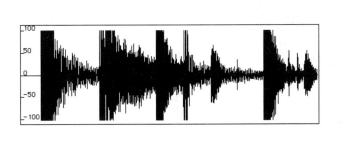

can reduce the amount of processing time when applying other editing commands. Furthermore, if you're adding your music to games or multimedia, it's important that the music start precisely when it's triggered. Cutting away the unnecessary silence at the beginning of a piece gets rid of annoying time lags when applying music to visuals.

Cutting Silence

Eliminating silence is easy. You just select the area in front of (or behind) where the waveform takes shape by dragging through the area with the mouse. Then you simply choose one of several commands such as Cut, Clear, or Erase (Figure 10-11).

Trim

Some programs also provide a Trim command. To use it you select the part of the waveform that you want to keep, and the software trims away everything outside of the selected area.

Mute

Many times there's a place in the music that's supposed to be silent, but isn't (like the pause in the music where somebody trips over a microphone stand). A good editing program lets you select that area and turn it into silence with a Mute or Silence command. It doesn't remove the selected area—it just turns all of the amplitude values to zero (Figure 10-12). This is also handy when working with drum tracks if you want to isolate certain beats without changing the timings.

The top display
shows a recording
with silence before
the music; the
bottom display
shows the same
recording without
the unnecessary
silence

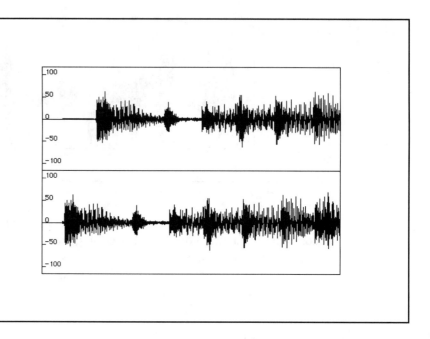

Changing the Volume

Most audio editors provide commands that let you modify the amplitude of a recording in various ways. You can apply these modifications to the waveform as a whole, or to selected areas within the waveform.

In the top display,
an unwanted noise
is selected; in the
lower display, the
same recording is
shown with the
noise replaced by
silence

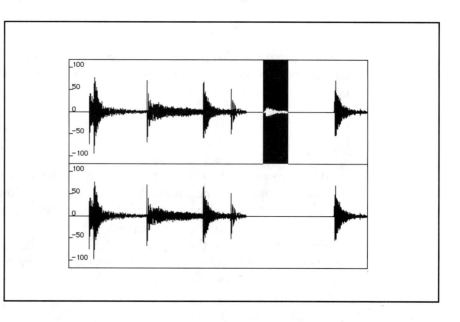

Normalize

The Normalize command scales the loudness of a selected area for recordings that were made at too low a level. The software scans the selected area to find the loudest point in the waveform. It then raises the amplitude of the entire area so that the highest point is now at full allowable amplitude without clipping. Normalize is a very useful tool because it ensures maximum output levels from your soundfiles and helps keep them consistent from one to the next.

tip *Normalizing a waveform is no substitute for setting the recording levels correctly in the first place. That's because, when the amplitude of the waveform is increased, everything gets increased—music and background noise together.*

Change Gain

Another important tool is often called Change Gain or Gain Adjust. It lets you increase or decrease the overall amplitude of a selected area by an amount that you specify. This is a very handy tool for smoothing out a recording with sections that are too loud or too soft.

Let's say you're recording a vocal part and during one phrase the singer steps back from the mic a little bit. With your editing software you can identify and select that section and increase the loudness for just that musical phrase. Or you can tone down a drum fill that seems a little loud, or perhaps adjust sections of a trumpet solo.

Fade In/Out

There are many times when it doesn't seem appropriate to have music start and/or stop abruptly. That's when the Fade In and Fade Out commands come in handy. To use them you select the part of the waveform in which you want the fade to occur. The software then decreases the level (for a fade out) from 100 percent of the original amplitude to zero. Fade In works in the opposite direction (Figure 10-13).

If you select a large area, the fade will be more gradual because the effect is spread over a longer area. For a quick fade, simply select a short region.

FIGURE 10-13

The top display shows the original recording. In the lower display the music has been faded in and faded out ∎

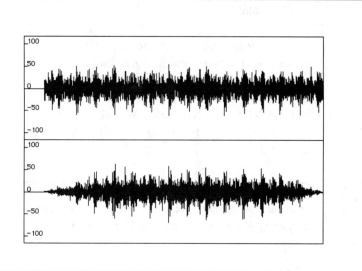

tip *Fades are useful in places other than the beginning and end of a recording. For example, let's say you have a recording that consists of several short pieces, one after another. With your editing software you can cut the silence between each piece. Then you can fade out the tail of one piece and fade in the beginning of the next. This can provide a smooth transition from one section to the next.*

You can also use the Fade command to create some interesting effects. For example, by fading out one channel of a stereo recording while simultaneously fading in the other channel you can create the impression of a sound moving from left to right (Figure 10-14).

Some programs also include a Crossfade command. It lets you overlap two soundfiles in such a way that the first file fades out as the second one fades in. This provides the smoothest kind of transition from one section of music to another.

Changing Direction

Many audio editors let you play a soundfile backward by using a Reverse command. It literally flips the waveform around so the front is the rear and the rear is the front (Figure 10-15). You can reverse an entire recording or you can select a section within a recording for reversal. The Reverse

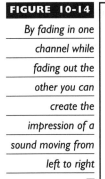

FIGURE 10-14

By fading in one channel while fading out the other you can create the impression of a sound moving from left to right

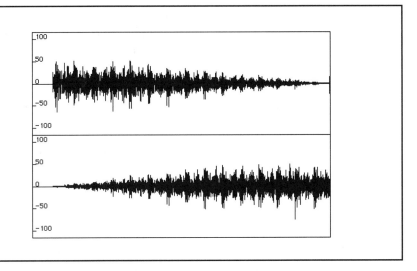

command is mainly for use with sound effects, but occasionally you might find a use for it musically. For example, you might use it to create an interesting reverse cymbal sound. And it could work well in producing an effective reverse snare hit. Also, try using it with ambient sounds to see how it works.

Some programs also include an Invert command. It flips the waveform around the zero crossing line. In other words, it changes all of the positive

FIGURE 10-15

The top display shows the original recording; the bottom display shows the same recording in reverse

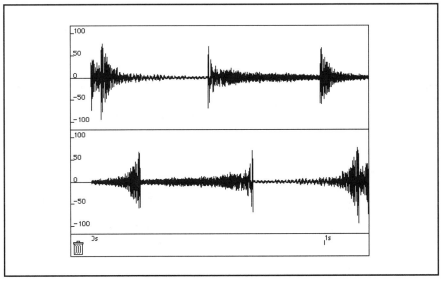

waveform values to negative values, and vice versa. This might be useful in a few cases where there are phase problems between the channels. And it may also be useful for enhancing the stereo effect in some recordings.

Changing the Specs

Many audio editors let you change the format of a soundfile to maximize compatibility. For example, you can import a soundfile as an AIFF file and save it as an SND file. Or in some cases you can import a Macintosh AIFF file into a Windows editor and save it as a WAVE file. If you do a lot of work with multimedia, it's worth checking out which file formats an audio editor can open and convert. Sonic Foundry's Sound Forge is especially versatile in this area.

Down-sampling allows you to record at a high sample rate but produce a version at a lower sample rate.

Aside from changing file formats, a good editor will also let you change the sampling rate of a soundfile—a process known as *downsampling* (Figure 10-16). This lets you record your material at a high sampling rate, such as 44.1kHz, for maximum fidelity. Then you can make a copy of the file and reduce the sampling rate to 22kHz for exporting to a multimedia application. Some programs also let you change a 16-bit recording to an 8-bit recording, again for compatibility with applications and hardware that demand it.

tip *Whenever possible, it's best to keep a master copy of each of your recordings at a high resolution and sampling rate. That way you can make high-quality copies if you need to in the future, and you can always downsample to accommodate another format. Remember, it's a safe bet that future applications will call for higher rather than lower audio standards.*

FIGURE 10-16

A good editor will let you change the sampling rate of a soundfile

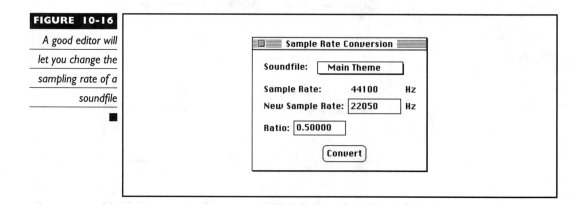

note *Increasing the sampling rate of a soundfile after it's recorded will increase its size, but it won't improve the sound quality.*

Equalization

Most audio editors let you apply some form of equalization (EQ) to your music. With analog recorders this is always done with an external piece of equipment called an equalizer (it's often built into the mixing board). An equalizer is a special kind of filter that divides sounds into different frequency bands so you can increase or decrease the amplitudes of different frequencies. The tone control (bass/treble) on your home stereo is an example of a simple equalizer.

With a digital audio editor, however, you don't need an external equalizer. Since the soundfile exists as numbers in your computer, the software can apply various algorithms to the digital data to produce the same EQ effect without leaving the digital domain. This effect can be applied to the recording as a whole or only to a selected region.

The two most common types of equalizers are called graphic and parametric.

There are several different types of equalizers, but the two most common are called *graphic* and *parametric*. Graphic equalizers typically provide a set of sliders, each of which controls a specific range of frequencies. The more sliders there are, the smaller each frequency band is, and the more precisely you can adjust the frequency content of the recording.

With a parametric equalizer, on the other hand, you control the center frequency and width of several bands. Each of these is fully variable, as is the amount of boost or cut that's applied. Parametric equalizers provide more precise control over the frequencies being affected, but they're less intuitive. Some audio editors combine the two types into a hybrid equalizer (Figure 10-17). With these you typically have a set of sliders, as with graphic EQ, but you can adjust the width of each band, as with a parametric equalizer. This gives you the best of both worlds—flexibility and ease of use.

Reverb

Many audio editing programs let you add reverb (reverberation) to your recordings. *Reverb* refers to the effect on a sound from the multiple reflections (from walls, floor, and ceiling) that are added to a sound when it occurs within a particular environment. These reflections, which decay over time, give recorded sound a sense of presence. Some programs (like Wave for Windows) provide elaborate reverb options allowing you to adjust a number of parameters. Other programs (like SoundEdit 16) simply include a few preset algorithms (Figure 10-18).

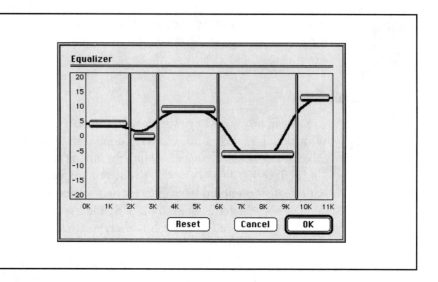

 tip *Keep in mind that reverb quality varies from program to program. Some reverb effects are quite complex, offering subtleties that add to their realism. Other reverb effects are less sophisticated. Also keep in mind that your results will depend on the quality of the recording itself. Reverb will be most effective with 16-bit recordings because they are inherently less noisy. Reverb is less satisfactory with 8-bit soundfiles, although it may help in some situations where subtlety is not essential.*

Some programs also offer other related effects. These include Echo, Flanging, and Chorus. With *Echo* (also known as *Digital Delay*) the sound

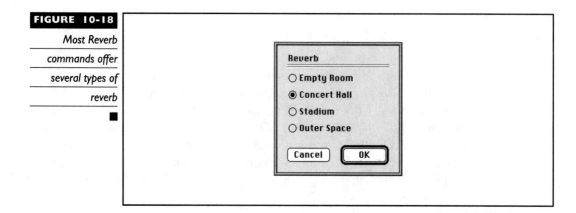

repeats several times as it slowly decays. *Flanging* imparts a whooshing sound to a recording by adding a slightly delayed version of a sound to the original sound. It's used to impart a sweeping quality to music and sound effects. *Chorus* adds slightly delayed copies of a sound to the original to create the illusion of multiple instrument sounds playing at once. It's often used to "fatten" ensemble sounds or to animate individual instruments.

Cleaning Up

One of the most powerful aspects of digital audio editing is the ability that it provides for making microscopic edits to a waveform. This can come in very handy if you've got an otherwise good recording with an annoying click or pop in it.

To do this kind of editing, you need a program that lets you zoom in on the waveform and perform the equivalent of audio brain surgery. This requires a zoom level that lets you view individual cycles in the waveform. When you locate the click, you can then select it and erase it. (When shopping for an audio editor be sure to ask about this feature.) Some programs even let you reconstruct the waveform by drawing a new shape with the mouse (Figure 10-19).

Most programs also provide a simple command called Smooth. It helps to reduce clicks, ticks, hiss, and static from a recording by passing the music through a low-pass filter. Unfortunately, this also tends to dull the sound a bit.

FIGURE 10-19

The best audio editors let you zoom in on a waveform and let you select and cut a single click or pop

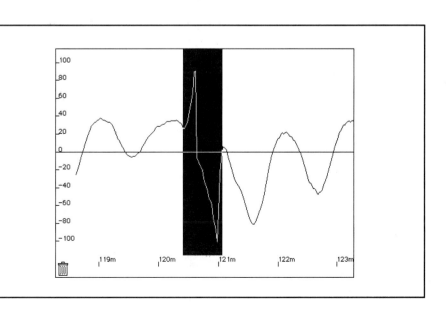

Other Views

All audio editors provide some way to view a soundfile. The most common display shows the waveform in a two-dimensional window with amplitude along the y (vertical) axis and elapsed time along the x (horizontal) axis. This is the most intuitive way to work with waveforms and the easiest to edit. But it's not the only way to conceptualize sound.

To give you a more complete sense about the changing harmonic content in a soundfile as it evolves, many programs offer alternative types of displays. One of the most popular of these is the *FFT* (Fast Fourier Transform) display. For an FFT display, the software analyzes the soundfile (or selected part of a soundfile) and produces a three-dimensional graph that shows time along one axis, frequency along another axis, and amplitude along a third axis (Figure 10-20).

The result is a series of time slices showing the frequency content of the music and how it changes over time. FFT displays do not permit editing. They're mainly offered to provide a more detailed look at the nature of a given waveform and to help you make decisions about later edits. And more importantly, they're really cool to look at. I'll show you more examples of FFT displays a little later.

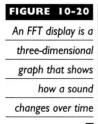

FIGURE 10-20

An FFT display is a three-dimensional graph that shows how a sound changes over time

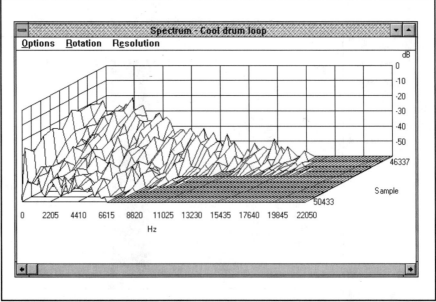

Destructive/Non-Destructive Edits

Most of the editing functions that I've described so far fall into the category of destructive editing. This is not a critique of your ability to handle soundfiles—it merely means that when you perform the editing operation, it permanently changes the waveform. Operations such as cutting, pasting, normalizing, mixing, reversing, and click removal actually rearrange or change in some way the sample values that make up the soundfile.

Playlist editing marks the beginning and end times of various waveform regions and specifies the order in which to play them.

There are other kinds of editing procedures, however, that do not alter the waveform itself. These are called non-destructive edits. The most common type of non-destructive editing is referred to as *playlist editing*. With playlist editing you can make as many changes as you want and the original recording remains intact.

Here's how it works: first you select different parts of the original waveform (usually by dragging across the desired areas). Each region is then identified and the names are kept in a list. You can rearrange these regions any way you want, and even play the same region more than once. The completed playlist does not actually produce a new soundfile, nor does it rearrange the original. Instead, it's a set of markers that indicate the start and stop times of the different regions and the order in which they are to be played back. The software simply *refers* to the original waveform—it doesn't *change* it.

If you record a song, for example, you can select the different parts of the song—e.g., verse 1, verse 2, chorus, or bridge—and play them back in any order you want. You can even repeat any of the parts as often as necessary. Playlist editing is also effective in creating new drum tracks from a basic pattern. In fact, by selecting the different beats in each measure, you can generate a whole rhythm track from just a couple of measures.

tip   *Not all audio editors provide playlist editing. It's usually reserved for more advanced programs that also support SMPTE timecode. If you think you might be doing professional work, however, it's a feature worth looking for.*

A Closer Look at Several Audio Editors

Mac and PC users have dozens of digital audio editors to choose from, ranging in price from well below $100 to as high as about $500. Many of the low-end programs are little more than novelties offering only limited editing capabilities. These entry-level programs are fine for having fun with digital audio (especially for sound effects and dialogue), but most are not suitable for more demanding work with music. If you're serious about recording and editing your music you should look to programs that offer pro-level features. These are not necessarily unaffordable. There are some very good audio editors for less than $200.

Let's take a look at several of the more popular programs (in different price brackets) to see how they're put together.

Sound Designer II

MAC

No discussion of audio editors would be complete without mentioning Sound Designer II from Digidesign. This program has been around for many years and has now established itself as a kind of industry standard for the Macintosh. Unfortunately, you can't buy the software as a stand-alone product. It only comes with Digidesign's various pro-level digital-audio cards, which include Audiomedia II, Sound Tools II, Pro Tools, and SampleCell II.

Sound Designer lets you do detailed editing of waveforms, as well as non-destructive playlist editing. It will open multiple files in SDII, AIFF, and SND formats in 8- or 16-bit mono or stereo. It also supports 2:1 and 4:1 compression ratios, and it fully supports SMPTE timecode.

The main window (Figure 10-21) includes a large waveform display showing the left and right channels (for stereo). At the top of the window,

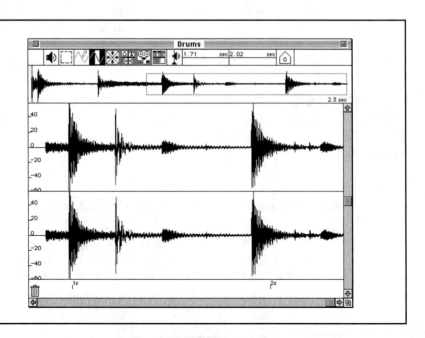

FIGURE 10-21

The main window in Sound Designer II

a number of small icons provide access to editing, viewing, and recording functions. There's also a scrubbing tool that lets you drag the mouse across the waveform and hear it in slow motion in forward or reverse.

Between the main display area and the row of icons, there's a small overview display that shows the entire soundfile for reference. If you're using a color monitor you can set the different elements of the main display (e.g., waveforms, overview, scales and markers) to appear in different colors.

To make a recording, you open the Tape Deck dialog box (Figure 10-22). It provides a complete set of transport controls and an effective set of tri-color level meters with clipping indicators. When your recording is done you can return to the waveform display to view your soundfile.

As you might expect of a professional editor, Sound Designer provides nearly all of the editing commands that I mentioned earlier. Although there's no reverb feature, Sound Designer does provide two kinds of EQ. The first of these is a graphic equalizer with adjustable bandwidth settings. The second is a kind parametric equalizer that lets you alter the frequency curve with great accuracy by selecting and adjusting one of five types of filters (Figure 10-23).

For a better view of the harmonic content of your music, Sound Designer provides a user-definable FFT display (Figure 10-24). With the Frequency Plot dialog box you can specify the number of time slices, the time interval between each, the type of amplitude scale used, and other parameters that affect the appearance of the display.

Other important features include a well-designed Time Compression/ Expansion tool, a Compressor/Limiter (to restrict the dynamic range of a

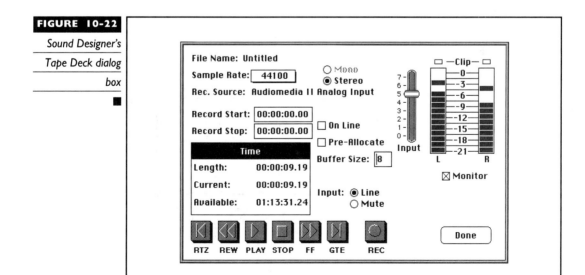

FIGURE 10-22

Sound Designer's

Tape Deck dialog

box

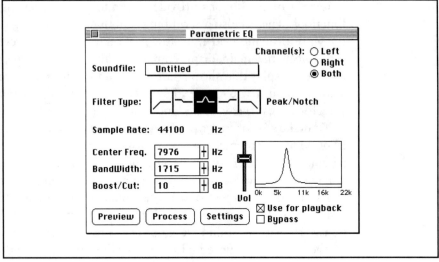

soundfile), a Merge function (that lets you crossfade between soundfiles), a Looping feature (for working with instrumental sounds), a Pencil tool for drawing out clicks, and the ability to mix up to four soundfiles into a single soundfile.

Finally, Sound Designer's Playlist window (Figure 10-25) lets you assemble a piece of music by specifying and arranging segments of your soundfile

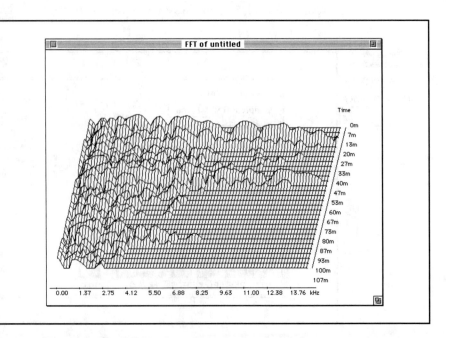

FIGURE 10-25

Sound Designer's

Playlist window

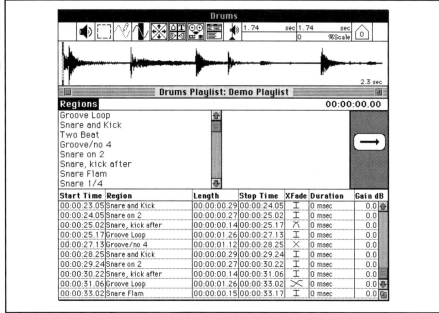

in any order. You simply drag a predefined segment from the Regions area of the window into the Playlist area. You can audition the playlist at any time and make changes. And you can also specify one of several types of crossfades or transitions to occur between segments.

Wave for Windows

PC

In spite of its modest price tag, Wave for Windows from Turtle Beach is one of the best of the audio editors for Windows users. Although the program offers a full list of editing functions, the colorful interface makes the program relatively easy to use.

The main window (Figure 10-26) includes a large waveform display in the center. The Toolbar at the top of the window provides numeric displays and several buttons to access commonly used functions. In the upper-left corner, two scroll bars let you zoom in or out vertically or horizontally.

Between the waveform display and the Toolbar, there's a thin black bar that serves as a timeline to indicate the length of the entire recording. This Soundfile Overview is where you select the section of the soundfile that will appear in the waveform display.

Wave for Windows lets you open up to four different soundfiles at once and view them together in separate windows. You can then cut, copy, and paste between soundfiles.

FIGURE 10-26

The main window

in Wave for

Windows

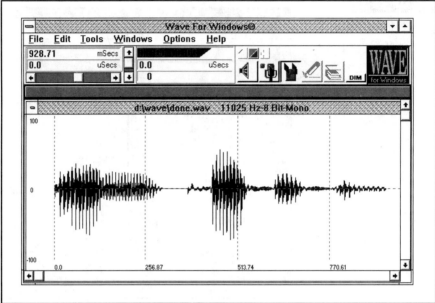

The recording process is straightforward. When you open the Record dialog box (Figure 10-27), you're presented with a complete set of transport controls and a set of level meters with clipping indicators. Depending on your sound card's capabilities, you can record with 8- or 16-bit resolution at 11.025, 22.05, or 44.1kHz. Wave for Windows can also import a number

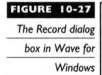

FIGURE 10-27

The Record dialog

box in Wave for

Windows

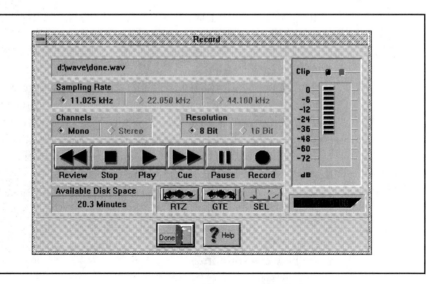

of file formats. Aside from .WAV files, the program imports Turtle Beach's own file formats, .SFI and .SMP, as well as .VOC (Sound Blaster) files and several others.

Wave offers an extensive list of editing options, including virtually all of those mentioned earlier. Although it doesn't provide playlist editing, the program does boast an impressive array of high-quality effects. These include Flange/Chorus, Digital Delay, Reverb, and Distortion.

For each effect, the program offers a long list of types for you to choose from. The Distortion effect, for example, lists 9 options ranging from Total Grunge to Soft Fuzz Guitar. The Flange effect lists 24 flange/chorus options, Delay lists 27 options, and the Reverb effect includes an impressive 28 options. Furthermore, each of these effects comes with a dialog box for advanced users. It lets you adjust on-screen knobs to create your own effects and add them to the list (Figure 10-28). If you need an audio editor with a built-in multi-effects processor, this is the program for you.

For a more complete view of your soundfile, Wave provides a nicely designed FFT display (Figure 10-29). It lets you specify the range, number, and scaling of the time slices. There's even a Browser display that lets you view each time slice individually.

Other features include a Pencil tool that lets you draw out clicks, the ability to mix three soundfiles into a fourth, and an unusual four-band, graphic, parametric equalizer.

FIGURE 10-28

On-screen knobs let you create and save custom effects ■

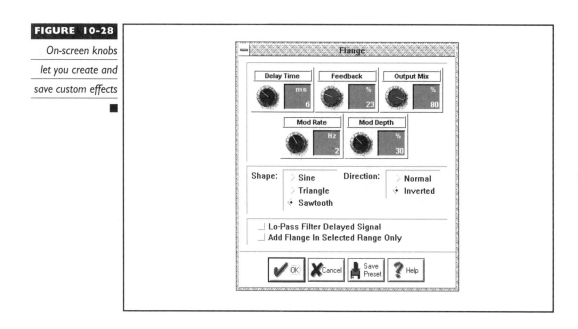

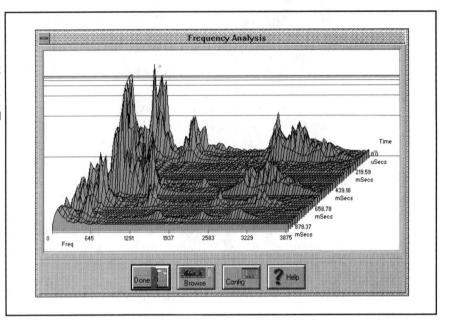

FIGURE 10-29

Wave for Windows provides a nicely designed FFT display ■

SoundEdit 16

MAC

SoundEdit 16, from Macromedia, is the latest incarnation of the ever-popular SoundEdit program that dates back to the early days of the Macintosh. As its new name implies, SoundEdit 16 offers full support for 16-bit sounds, as well as sampling rates up to 64kHz. It works with any hardware that's compatible with the Apple Sound Manager extension and System 7.

SoundEdit's main window (Figure 10-30) is simplicity itself. In fact, there's little to look at besides a waveform display and a horizontal time scale. At the bottom of the window a small indicator lets you select one of several horizontal zoom levels. In the upper-right corner, a similar indicator lets you adjust the vertical zoom level. The lower zoom control includes a small diamond shape. Clicking on it changes the display to Fat Samples view. Here each sample is represented on-screen by a diamond that you can drag up or down to change the sound.

Recording takes place with a small bare-bones set of transport controls. Above the controls, a single input-level meter lets you monitor recording levels, although there are no sliders for making adjustments. Once you've created or imported a soundfile, you can apply any of a long list of editing commands to your music. The list includes most of the commands mentioned earlier along with several that are not so common.

The Bender effect, for example, superimposes a "pitch adjustment" line over the waveform display. You can click anywhere along this line to create

SoundEdit 16's

main window

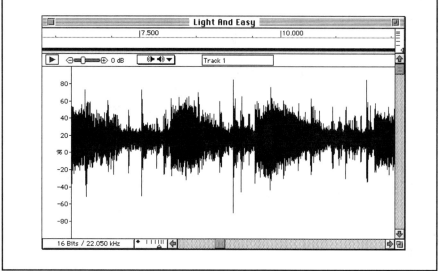

a grab handle, which you can then drag up or down (Figure 10-31). Dragging the line up causes the pitch to rise during playback; dragging it down lowers the pitch. You can create some interesting pitch bend effects with this tool, and it's fun to experiment with.

The Fade In and Fade Out commands work in a similar manner. You create as many handles as you want along an "amplitude adjustment" line. Then you drag the handles to shape the fade in or out curve. This provides

FIGURE 10-31

SoundEdit's Bender

effect lets you

apply pitch bend

effects to your

soundfile

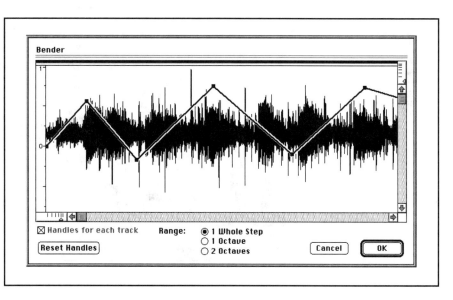

you with an infinite variety of fade shapes from a simple straight (linear) fade to any shape you can think of. It's very intuitive and easy to control.

SoundEdit 16 also provides three ways to generate sounds. The FM Synthesis effect lets you create simple sounds using a single carrier frequency and a single modulation frequency. The Tone Generator effect will produce a tone of a definable frequency and amplitude with one of three waveform shapes. And the Noise command generates random noise for a specified length of time.

Aside from the standard waveform display, SoundEdit offers several other types of displays for viewing and analyzing your recordings. The Spectrum or spectral view shows time along the horizontal axis just as the usual waveform does. But instead of amplitude, it shows frequency along the vertical axis. The power of each frequency is represented by different colors—higher powers are shown in reds, lower powers in shades down through the rainbow. Grayscale monitors show shades ranging from dark to light. This display is fascinating to look at but difficult to make sense of. There's also a 3-D version of the same display. The most useful tool for analyzing sounds is the standard FFT display showing a series of time slices (Figure 10-32).

SoundEdit lets you import, edit, and save soundfiles in 11 different formats, including SoundEdit, AIFF, Sound Designer II, System 7 Sound, and QuickTime. For cross-platform compatibility it also supports uncompressed WAVE and QuickTime for Windows files. It works equally well with 8-bit and 16-bit sounds and offers four different compression options.

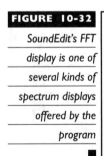

FIGURE 10-32

SoundEdit's FFT display is one of several kinds of spectrum displays offered by the program ■

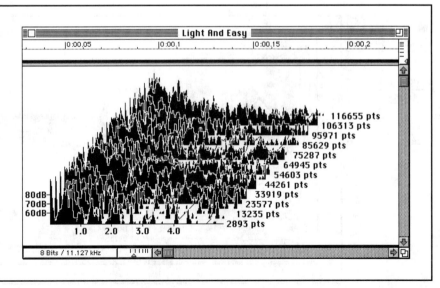

SoundEdit lets you include as many tracks in a file as your computer memory and disk space allow (Figure 10-33). You can play any combination of tracks simultaneously and you can edit each track separately. When you've decided which tracks to include, and you've set the start time for each, you can use the Mix command to combine them into a single mono or stereo soundfile.

One of SoundEdit's most appealing features is its full support for Quick-Time. You can do virtually all of your QuickTime sound recording, editing, and synchronization from within the program. You can even convert audio CD tracks into sound-only QuickTime movies. From there you can export them to other applications—very handy.

Sound Forge

PC

Sound Forge from Sonic Foundry is a relative newcomer to the field of digital audio editors. In the past couple of years, however, it has evolved into a full-featured pro-level program for Windows users. It combines a well-designed user interface and an excellent help system with an impressive set of editing tools. If you're looking for a high-end program that does just about everything, check out Sound Forge.

The main window in Sound Forge (Figure 10-34) is deceptively simple when it first opens. Waveform displays appear in the large center area. At the top of the window, a row of buttons provides ready access to most of

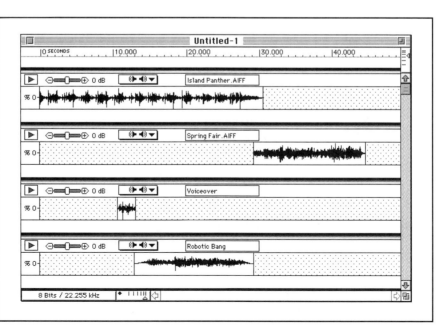

FIGURE 10-33

SoundEdit 16 lets you include multiple tracks in a file

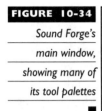

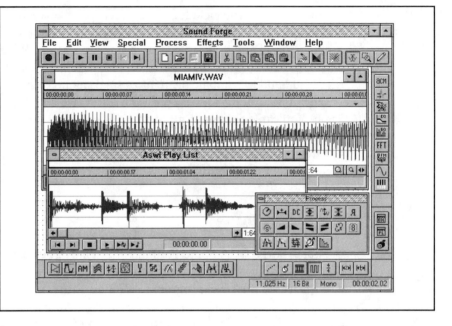

the primary editing tools. There's also a small set of transport controls for recording, rewinding, and playing back soundfiles.

Actually these sets of buttons are just two out of a total of ten user-configurable tool palettes that let you perform a wide variety of operations. You can have any combination of palettes on-screen at one time. To reduce screen clutter, you can drag any of the palettes to the edge of the main window, where they snap into a narrow band surrounding the main display—very cool.

Working with waveforms is fast and intuitive. You can select any area in a waveform and simply drag it from the waveform's window into the main window. The selected area instantly appears in its own window, where you can then edit it independently of the original. You can even drag the newly edited waveform back into the first window and add it to the original.

Creating non-destructive playlists is a breeze. You just select an area in the waveform and drag it directly into the EDL (Edit Decision List) window. A dialog box lets you name the selection and fine-tune the beginning and end points. The selected region then appears by name in the list (Figure 10-35). To create a playlist file you simply drag entries from the EDL window into the Playlist window where you can arrange the selections to play any number of times in any order.

Sound Forge's drag and drop approach to editing makes it easy to use, and the well-designed dialog boxes provide the requisite power for customizing editing operations. For example, choosing Reverb from the effects

FIGURE 10-35

Sound Forge's EDL
and Playlist
windows, shown
here beneath the
waveform that they
refer to

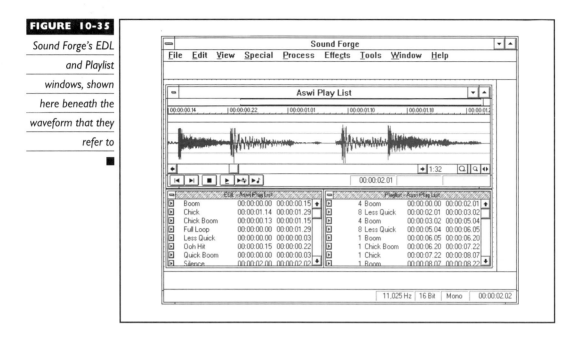

menu opens a dialog box that offers at least two dozen different kinds of reverb. And if you're not satisfied with any of these, Sound Forge provides an extensive set of controls that let you modify the effect in every way imaginable (Figure 10-36). If you create a reverb effect that you like, you

FIGURE 10-36

Sound Forge's
Reverb dialog box

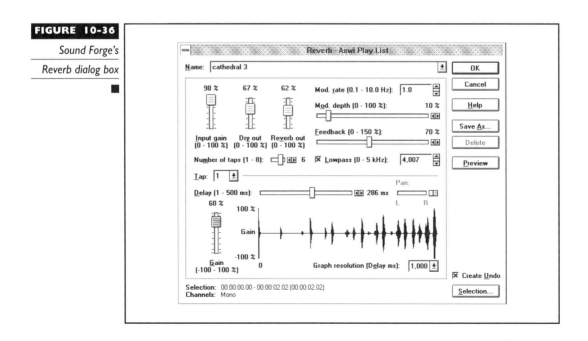

can name it, save it, and add it to the list for future use. Other effects, such as Chorus, Echo, Flange, and Distortion, have their own specialized dialog boxes that also let you create and save your custom effects.

The dialog boxes in some effects, such as Pitch Bend, Envelope, and Fade, include a graph with drag handles. They let you change a waveform's pitch or amplitude by dragging the handles to change the shape of the graph. This is easy and intuitive.

To tailor the harmonic content of your recordings, Sound Forge includes two well-designed equalizers. The Graphic EQ tool provides a standard 10-band equalizer with three selectable bandwidth options. The Parametric EQ includes four different filter options. Both equalizers let you name and save your settings and add them to a list for later retrieval.

Sound Forge also includes two options for generating sounds from scratch. The Simple Synthesis tool lets you generate a tone based on one of several wave shapes. And the FM Synthesis tool provides a genuine four-operator FM synthesizer to play around with (Figure 10-37). Both synthesizers include a graphic envelope display with grab handles.

The list of features offered by Sound Forge is impressive and long. Here are just a few more features worth noting: full support for SMPTE timecode, support for file transfer between most brands of samplers, a Pencil tool for drawing out clicks, advanced looping functions, and an FFT spectrum

FIGURE 10-37

Sound Forge's FM

Synthesis tool

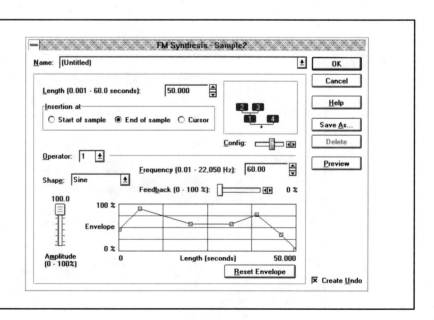

display. You can also have any number of files open at once and cut, copy, and paste between them. And finally, Sound Forge lets you work with an extensive array of file formats, including many for the PC, Macintosh, Amiga, and NeXT/Sun platforms.

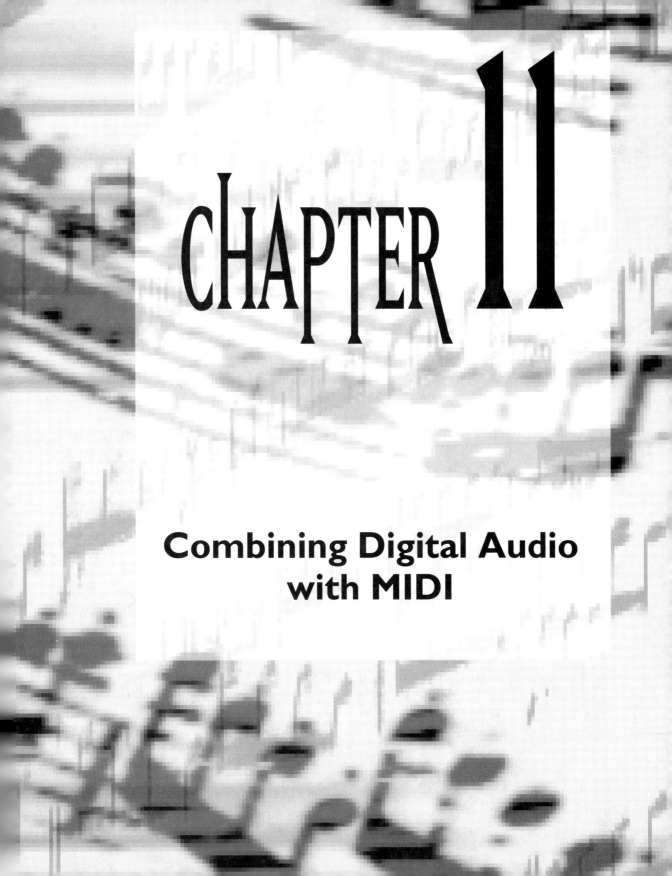

CHAPTER 11

Combining Digital Audio
with MIDI

M IDI is a fantastic tool for composing music because it lets you have a gaggle of virtual instruments all playing at once from your desktop. Furthermore, you can take any one of these instrument parts and edit it to within an inch of its life. But in spite of MIDI's power and flexibility, it still can't be all things to all people. And it's more successful at doing some tasks than others.

Adding a vocal part to an arrangement, for example, is clearly not the kind of thing that MIDI was intended to do. And it's difficult to capture the expressiveness and subtle nuances of some instruments even with a high-quality sampler and a good keyboard controller. Solo violin, solo saxophone, and guitar rhythm patterns, for instance, are notoriously difficult sounds to re-create using electronic instruments.

Digital audio, on the other hand, lets you capture any kind of instrument that you want. And as we saw in Chapter 10, you can edit digital audio soundfiles in many ways that MIDI can't. Unfortunately, digital audio won't let you change the *performance* of the music. You can't change the tempo or the meter of a piece. Or fix sloppy rhythms. Or boost the volume on the hi-hats without changing the rest of the drum track. Or substitute a trumpet for the alto sax part in an ensemble. In other words, digital audio is another great tool for musicians, but it isn't perfect.

It was therefore inevitable that software companies would combine these two powerful technologies to bring the best of both worlds to the desktop.

The Three Approaches

There are actually several ways to combine MIDI with digital audio and they range from simple to sophisticated. All of the approaches, however, fall roughly into three categories: adding audio to MIDI, adding MIDI to audio, and combining audio and MIDI within a third environment. In all cases, the object is to maintain synchronization between the audio tracks and the MIDI tracks so you get consistent results during playback.

To combine audio with MIDI you'll have to assemble all of the required components for both recording methods including a MIDI interface, a sound module or synthesizer, and a large-capacity hard drive. Macintosh users will need a digital audio card—such as Digidesign's Audiomedia II, Sound Tools II, or Spectral Innovations' NuMedia card. Or you can use one of the Macintosh models with built-in 16-bit recording capability.

Unfortunately, there are few options for PC users when it comes to integrated audio/MIDI combinations. Most of the available software is targeted toward pro and semi-pro applications and that field is still heavily dominated by the Macintosh.

There are lots of multimedia programs that can trigger both MIDI and audio tracks, but the two sound sources play out independently of one another so it's difficult to achieve a predictable level of synchronization. Furthermore, music editing capabilities in most of these multimedia programs are minimal or nonexistent. This makes them unsuitable for serious music production work.

A few sequencers for the PC—such as Cakewalk Pro for Windows—let you trigger audio (.WAV) files from within a sequence. This approach provides a full set of MIDI recording and editing tools plus the ability to incorporate audio playback. But once again, the audio files are treated simply as events. You cannot view and edit the waveforms along with the MIDI data. And the two types of data can easily lose synchronization with one another.

To truly gain the advantages of a MIDI/audio combination you need a program that provides a fully integrated working environment—one that lets you record, view, edit, and play back both kinds of tracks. As I pointed out, there are several ways to achieve this goal. So let's take a closer look at some of the options.

Adding Audio to MIDI

This is by far the most popular approach, and there are several excellent programs to choose from. All but one (Cubase Audio) are available only for the Mac. These programs start with a professional-level sequencer and add digital audio capabilities to it. As a result, they all deliver great editing power and flexibility—but at some expense. Retail prices range from around $600 up to nearly $1,000. As professional tools in a studio setting, however, they're well worth the price.

These programs are all based on sequencers that I've discussed in detail in Chapter 6. Since the MIDI aspects of the programs are nearly identical in the audio and non-audio versions, I'll focus mainly on the audio-handling features. Here's a quick look at several of the leading programs.

Studio Vision Pro

MAC

Opcode's famous Vision sequencer was the first pro-level sequencer to appear in a digital-audio version. The latest incarnation—**Studio Vision Pro**—includes all of Vision's recent improvements, along with greater flexibility in viewing and handling audio files. As much as possible, Studio Vision handles audio tracks the way it handles MIDI tracks.

Adding audio to a sequence is relatively straightforward. Once you record-enable a track, you open the Record Monitor window, name the new file, and check the recording levels. Then you just click the same Record button that you use for MIDI.

Although your recording can be of any length, the program initially treats it as a single entity called an "audio event." The audio event is treated much like a MIDI event. It appears in the Event List window with a start time, a duration, and even a Velocity value. (In this case, Velocity refers to an initial volume setting for the recording.) You can also view your recording as a miniature waveform display in the Track Overview window, along with the miniature piano-roll MIDI displays (Figure 11-1).

In the Track Overview you can select any of the little waveform displays and drag them left or right to change their start times. You can also drag them from one track to another and you can cut, copy, and paste the same way you can with MIDI data.

For more serious editing, Studio Vision's Graphic window displays the audio tracks in an area between the piano-roll and the Strip Chart. This area—called the Audio Pane—lets you view several audio tracks at once, each in a different color. You can even have data in the Strip Chart—such as Volume or Pan—apply to any of the audio tracks. And you can select areas for editing that include MIDI notes, audio events, and Strip Chart data at the same time (Figure 11-2).

When viewed as a waveform display, each of the audio events appears in a rectangular box. As in the Overview display, you can drag audio events

FIGURE 11-1

Studio Vision Pro's

Track Overview

window

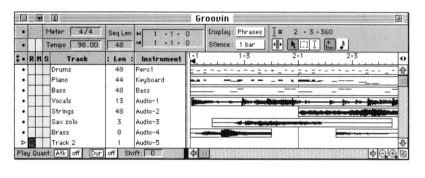

left or right and up or down. You can also drag the right side of the rectangle inward to shorten the audio part.

Actually, when you trim the waveform this way you aren't really altering the waveform itself. You're just causing it to stop playing before the end of the file. Conversely, you can also stretch an audio event up to its full length.

This is one example of Studio Vision's many non-destructive editing functions. In fact, most of Studio Vision's editing commands are non-destructive. Changes that you make to audio events simply manipulate pointers that refer to the original waveform. The original recording stays unchanged. This means you can make copies of selected areas in audio tracks and arrange audio events in any order you want without increasing the size of the actual soundfile.

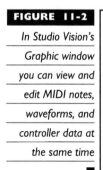

FIGURE 11-2

In Studio Vision's

Graphic window

you can view and

edit MIDI notes,

waveforms, and

controller data at

the same time

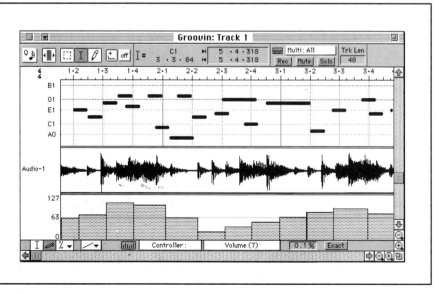

To offer maximum control over your audio recordings, Studio Vision provides a number of ways to break up a single audio track into several separate audio events. The Retain command lets you select a region of audio to keep. It then clears everything on either side of the selected area. You can even select an area through several audio tracks at once.

The Separate command provides two options for splitting an audio event. You can drag across a section of an audio event and separate it from the rest of the waveform. Or you can simply split the waveform at the current cursor position. In either case, if you play the audio event right after you split it, you won't hear any difference. But on screen the separate sections will appear in their own boxes that you can then edit and move independently of one another.

Studio Vision's Strip Silence command removes all audio in a selected area that falls below a specified amplitude threshold. It then creates separate audio events for the remaining parts of the audio track (Figure 11-3). This is a powerful tool for cleaning up recordings with dead air space. And it makes it easy to view and manipulate the important parts of a recording.

The ability to separate audio tracks into segments opens up all kinds of postproduction possibilities. For example, you can record several takes of a solo part and select your favorite sections from each. You can then select the best sections and assemble them into a "perfect" performance (Figure 11-4). Or you can separate the different hits in a drum part into discrete audio events and use the Quantize command to tighten up the rhythm section. (Each event will snap to a specified beat or subdivision—just like with MIDI notes.)

Studio Vision Pro imports Sound Designer II and AIFF files. And the program's File Management window lets you delete unused parts of recordings to free up disk space. Other features include excellent documentation, support for SMPTE timecode, and the ability to mix tracks together.

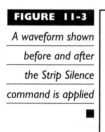

FIGURE 11-3

A waveform shown before and after the Strip Silence command is applied

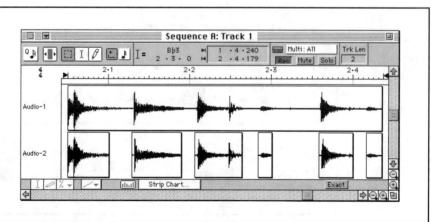

FIGURE 11-4

With Studio Vision, you can select and audition different audio events from different recordings. Then you can assemble the best parts into a "perfect" take ■

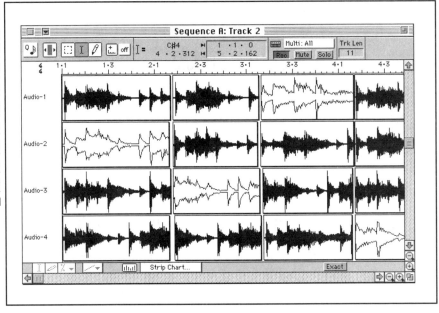

In My Experience

The value of combining MIDI with digital audio was driven home to me a while back. At that time, I was collaborating on a song that was to be used in a film. The director needed a quick, preliminary copy of the arrangement, so I produced the song using my home studio.

First I created the orchestral accompaniment with my MIDI system. Then I brought the singer into my studio to add the vocal part. I routed the output from the microphone into the mixing board along with the MIDI tracks generated in real time by the sequencer. To add the vocal part, the singer listened to the MIDI playback through headphones and sang along. The output was then mixed directly to a stereo master tape.

Although this approach seemed simple enough, it was actually rather frustrating. The problem was that every time the singer made a mistake, we had to go back to the beginning and record the song again from the top. For example, it was not uncommon to have a mistake occur on the third verse after the first two were done perfectly. Other times the song started out a bit rocky but sounded great by the end. After numerous takes, we still didn't have a "perfect" performance even though each performance contained perfect parts.

During this process of repeated takes I remember wishing that I had a means of combining my MIDI tracks with a digital audio recording of the vocal part. The reason for this is simple: By using the digital-audio sequencers currently available, I could have saved a great deal of time and effort by cutting and pasting parts from the different takes into a "perfect" vocal performance. With only three or four takes I would have had enough material to put together the recording that I wanted.

If mixing MIDI with audio tracks is in your future, you should definitely consider a sequencer that supports digital audio. It has made my life much easier.

Cubase Audio

PC

MAC

First Steinberg created Cubase—the powerful MIDI composing and editing application. Then it added advanced notation features and introduced it as Cubase Score. The most recent version of the program adds digital-audio capabilities to Cubase Score. The resulting program—**Cubase Audio**—has all the power and versatility of the MIDI-only versions—along with their inherent complexity.

(The Windows version of Cubase Audio only supports the Yamaha CBX-D5. It's an external four-track, hard-disk recording system. The Mac version supports all of the usual audio cards, such as those from Digidesign.)

Although Cubase Audio's additional terminology can get a bit confusing at times, the overall structure of the program is consistent. So if you've used Cubase in the past, you'll adapt easily to this digital-audio version.

Cubase Audio handles audio data in more or less the same way that it handles MIDI data. All operations center on the Arrange window (Figure 11-5), which gives a graphic overview of your sequence. Recorded sections called Parts appear as rectangles opposite their related track names. If you choose the Show Events option, the presence of MIDI data appears as black bands inside the rectangles. Audio Parts are shown with a miniature representation of each waveform.

The Arrange window lets you select Parts (both MIDI and audio) and drag them left or right. You can cut, copy, and paste among the MIDI Parts, and you can do the same with the audio Parts. The Class column in the left half of the Arrange window identifies which type of data is in each track.

To adjust and monitor recording and playback levels, Cubase Audio provides a nice set of meters in its Record Monitor window (Figure 11-6).

FIGURE 11-5

Cubase Audio's

Arrange window

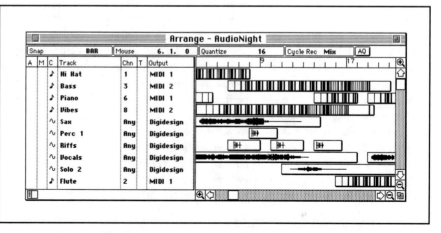

FIGURE 11-6

Cubase Audio's

Record Monitor

window

■

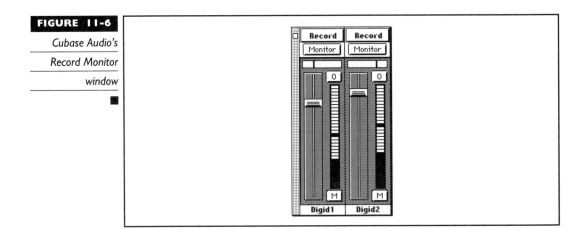

Each meter is accompanied by a fader, a Mute button, and a control for setting the pan position. The meters also include handy clipping indicators that show how many times the recording passes the clipping threshold.

As soon as your recording is finished, a new audio Part with its tiny waveform appears in the Arrange window. You can then move the Part around as you can with the other Parts. Or you can double-click on the Part to open the Audio Editor window with its full-size waveform display (Figure 11-7).

In the Audio Editor each waveform appears in a rectangular box with a label in the upper-left corner. If you slice the original recording into segments (using the Scissors tool), each one will have its own label.

Each segment also has a set of arrows—in the upper-left and lower-right corners. They let you drag the borders of the rectangle to change the place within the waveform where the audio segment starts and stops. As with

FIGURE 11-7

Cubase Audio's

Audio Editor

window showing a

waveform divided

into several

segments

■

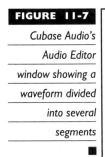

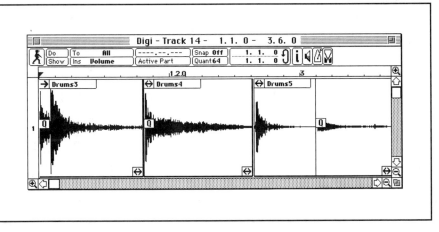

Studio Vision, these and most other edits are non-destructive. In other words, they don't alter the original recording—they just affect playback.

Each audio event also has a "Q-point" that is indicated by a small box on the left side of the waveform. The Q-point lets you set a marker in the audio segment that is taken as its "musically significant" position. For example, you might choose the first downbeat in the segment. Or you might choose a particular word in a vocal part.

You can drag the "Q" handle anywhere you want—up to about a minute into the audio segment. Then, using Cubase Audio's Quantize command, you can align the Q-point to the beginning of a measure or to any subdivision of a beat. You can also use the Snap function to "kick" the segment forward or backward in increments.

To help you manage all of your recordings and related segments, Cubase Audio provides an overview of your soundfiles in its Audio Pool window (Figure 11-8). There you can see information about the current soundfiles, as well as all of the audio segments that are derived from them.

The Audio Pool lets you do standard housekeeping tasks, such as deleting unused segments and importing new soundfiles. It also lets you access several editing commands. Furthermore, you can drag a segment from the Audio Pool into the Arrange window to create a new Part. Or you can drag a segment into the Audio Editor window to add it to a Part being edited.

Cubase Audio provides several powerful tools for editing your recordings. The Banish Silence command works much like Studio Vision's Strip Silence command. It masks out silence (or sounds below an adjustable threshold) and leaves the remaining sounds in separate segments. Other commands let you normalize, mix, and repeat segments. And Cubase Audio's unique Match Tempo command lets you adjust a given number of measures and

---

FIGURE 11-8

The Audio Pool window in Cubase Audio helps you manage your audio files

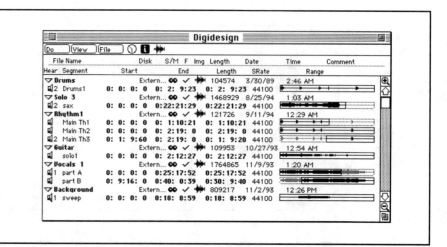

beats in a sequence to match the length of a section of audio. There's also full support for SMPTE timecode.

CD-ROM

Cubase Audio also provides menu items that let you directly access **TimeBandit**—another Steinberg product. TimeBandit is a time correction, pitch-shifting, harmonizing application that works with mono and stereo Sound Designer files (the same format used by Cubase Audio).

With TimeBandit, you can stretch or shorten a soundfile's playback time without affecting its pitch. Or you can change the pitch of a recording without changing its length (Figure 11-9). You can also transpose the pitch to several different levels at once to create chords.

Digital Performer

MAC

Mark of the Unicorn's venerable Performer has long been among the most favored of the pro-level sequencers. Over the years it has continued to attract new recruits with its stylish graphics, long feature list, excellent documentation, and intuitive interface. The audio version—**Digital Performer**—continues that tradition by adding hard-disk recording and playback capabilities without significantly altering the rest of the program.

Digital Performer lets you manipulate both audio and MIDI data by using many of the same commands in many of the same kinds of windows (Figure 11-10). The overview section of the Tracks window, for example, shows

FIGURE 11-9

TimeBandit's Pitch

Shift window

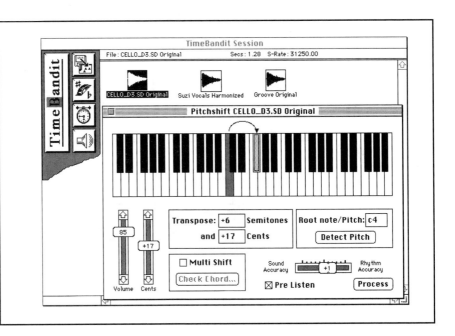

FIGURE 11-10

Digital Performer

lets you view and

edit audio data

with a set of

windows that are

much like those in

the MIDI-only

version of the

program

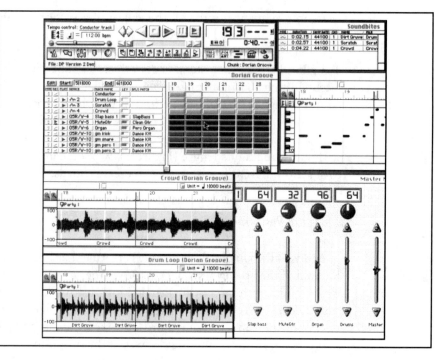

little rectangles to indicate the presence of MIDI data. The same rectangles are used to indicate audio data. (The small waveform icon in the device column identifies a track as an audio track.)

Digital Performer also lets you import Sound Designer II soundfiles, regions, and playlists, as well as AIFF files. And the Tracks window lets you select audio and/or MIDI data and apply the ubiquitous cut, copy, and paste commands.

Recording new material is very straightforward. First, you add an audio track to the Tracks window, and then record-enable it. Next, you open the Audio Monitor window (Figure 11-11). It provides a set of input/output

FIGURE 11-11

Digital Performer's

Audio Monitor

window as it

appears with a

four-channel system

CH	-36	-24	-12	0 dB	TAKE FILE	REC TIME	MON	TAKE FOLDER
1					Takefile Ch1-1	1.1 MB	in	PowerPC::Audio Files:
2					Takefile Ch2-1	0:13	out	PowerPC::Audio Files:
3					Takefile Ch3-1	1.1 MB	out	PowerPC::Audio Files:
4					Takefile Ch4-1	0:13	out	PowerPC::Audio Files:

Audio Monitor

level meters with clipping indicators. Recording starts when you click the Record button in the Controls panel.

When you're finished, your recording appears in the Tracks window as a new box—ready for editing. Performer automatically names each new recording as you make it so each take is saved and you won't have a problem with duplicate names. To help you organize, locate, delete, and rename your audio files, the program includes a Soundbites window.

A "soundbite" is essentially the same as an audio event in Studio Vision or a region in Sound Designer II. In other words, it doesn't consist of actual audio data. Instead, each soundbite consists of start- and end-time pointers that refer to the data in a soundfile stored on your hard disk.

Soundbites also appear in the Audio Event List window for each track. In the Event List, each soundbite is shown with an adjustable velocity (initial volume) setting, name, attack time, and duration—just like with MIDI data.

For close viewing and editing of waveforms, Digital Performer provides a separate Audio Graphic Editing window for each track. It includes a Continuous Controller Grid (similar to the Strip Chart in Studio Vision) where you can graphically insert and edit Volume and Pan position data that applies to the waveform.

Performer's list of audio-editing commands is not extensive, but it does supply several essential tools. The Trim command lets you select an area in a waveform and remove the portions that are outside the selected area. The Split command lets you break up a waveform into separate soundbites. The Compact command removes unused parts of soundfiles to reclaim disk space.

The Strip Silence command removes the parts of a selected area that fall below a specified amplitude. The remaining parts then appear as separate soundbites that you can move around and edit individually.

To further edit soundbites, Digital Performer provides a direct link to Sound Designer II (assuming that you have the program installed). In Sound Designer you can apply destructive edits and create playlists that are export-able back to Performer.

Digital Performer also provides a quantize command that's similar to its counterpart in Cubase Audio (although without the Q-point). You can change the start and stop times of a soundbite by dragging its borders inward or outward. Then the front edge of the visible part of the waveform will snap to the nearest selected quantize division.

The program's other important features include full support for SMPTE timecode (with high-quality continuous sync) and the ability to mix sound-bites. There's also a separate version of Digital Performer that is specifically for the Yamaha CBX-D5. It offers four-channel recording and playback from an external unit with built-in digital effects and EQ.

Of Interest

Synchronizing Tracks

To keep your MIDI and digital-audio tracks synchronized you have to understand the inherent differences between these two types of files. MIDI is extremely flexible. You can select a MIDI track (or section of a track) and change the tempo as much as you want without changing the pitch. That's because MIDI data deals with performance activities and not the actual sounds. When you change the tempo in a MIDI track you're actually moving events closer together or farther apart (temporally speaking).

Digital audio files on the other hand contain data for the actual sounds. If you change the playback speed of a digital-audio recording, the pitch will change as well. Therefore, when it comes to audio files (audio events), you can only change their start and stop times and not their tempos. Here's what this means in practical terms:

To accommodate both types of music, it's best to start with several MIDI tracks. Do some preliminary editing and then settle on the exact tempo that you want for your piece. With the tempo set, you can use the MIDI tracks for a reference as you record your audio tracks. You can always go back and add more MIDI tracks later—as long as you don't change the tempo. If you change the tempo, you'll immediately lose synchronization between the MIDI and audio tracks. That's because eight measures in the audio track will still take the same amount of time as before. But the same eight measures in the MIDI tracks will now take more or less time depending on the new tempo.

If you must add MIDI to an existing audio track, some sequencers provide a Tap Tempo feature that lets you tap-out a tempo as you listen to a track. This may work in some cases, but you'll probably get the best results by establishing your tempos ahead of time.

Adding MIDI to Audio

The products that I just described are all designed in a similar manner. They start with a sequencer and add to it audio recording and playback features. This is a logical approach if the main part of your work includes sequencing and you're most comfortable working with a sequencer as your primary composing tool. For many musicians, however, recording to disk is the more common activity. So they prefer a user interface that more closely resembles a multi-track tape recorder. But that doesn't mean you have to give up the benefits of MIDI. Here's one program that handles this approach quite well.

Deck II

MAC

With OSC's **Deck II** your hard disk becomes a multichannel tape deck and your computer screen becomes a mixing board/editor. The program's Mixer window (Figure 11-12) is based on a multi-track, portable-cassette-recorder metaphor. Each track in the Mixer includes a volume fader and a 10-segment, tricolor meter with a clipping indicator. You also get Record-enable, Mute, and Solo buttons and a Pan position slider.

The Transport window (Figure 11-13) provides a full set of "tape-deck" controls and a large digital readout for showing elapsed time. Deck II lets you record and keep as many tracks as you want, but only four to eight of those tracks (depending on your hardware configuration) can play back at one time.

Recording a new track is easy. After selecting an input, you click the Record-enable button for the track that you want to record on. The meter for that track registers the input levels, and the fader lets you adjust the volume level for monitoring (it doesn't affect the record level). Finally, you activate the Record button in the Transport window, record your music, and click Stop when you're done. You can then listen to the first track while recording new material on a second track, and then listen to the first two tracks while adding a third, and so on.

If you have an existing MIDI sequence to which you're adding audio tracks, you first load your MIDI file into Deck's MIDI window (Figure

FIGURE 11-12

Deck II's Mixer window

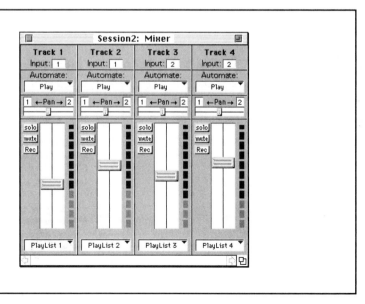

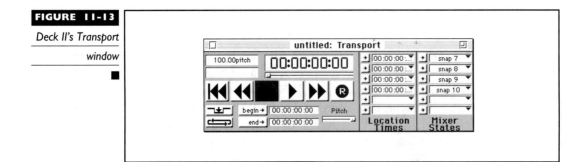

11-14) before recording. Then you can use the MIDI playback as a reference while you record your audio.

If you prefer to record audio first and then add MIDI tracks, you can create a metronome track with your sequencer. That way you'll have a reference click during recording and later when building your sequence.

Deck II's built-in MIDI-handling capabilities are rather minimal. They mainly provide for playback of Standard MIDI Files so you can combine MIDI tracks with audio. This arrangement lets you develop your MIDI compositions with your favorite sequencer and then import them into Deck for adding audio tracks. But this doesn't provide the level of integration that you get with a digital-audio sequencer.

So to solve this problem, Deck II includes the ability to synchronize to **Metro**—OSC's full-featured sequencer (see Chapter 6). With these two programs running simultaneously you can have the best of both worlds. For

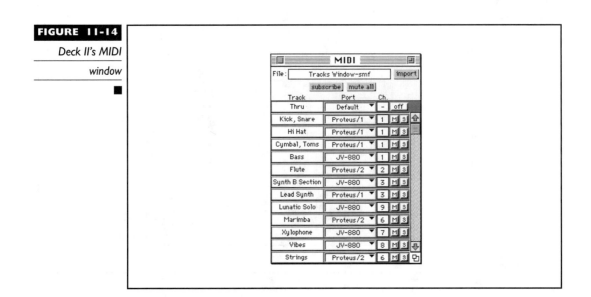

example, you can perform keyboard parts into the sequencer while you record the vocal parts onto your hard disk. You can even switch between the two programs (without stopping) while you're listening to and editing parts. Also, Metro can run in the background to generate a MIDI metronome click while you record your audio tracks.

To view and edit your recordings, Deck provides its Track window (Figure 11-15). In the Track window, the 4-8 "play" tracks (the ones you'll hear during playback) appear in separate waveform displays. These waveforms let you cut, copy, delete, and paste as usual. And you can also apply several other useful editing operations.

You can drag through one or more waveforms to select regions. And Deck allows you to select discontiguous regions for "checkerboard" style editing. Furthermore, you can drag through a waveform range to select it and then simply "tear off" the selected region and drop it on any track at any location.

The Slice command lets you create new regions from a selected range. And you can drag regions from track to track and from one place in a track to another. Each region appears in its own rectangle with grab handles in the corners. The grab handles let you shrink and expand the visible part of the waveform by dragging the left and right borders in or out. This changes the part of the waveform that plays back.

Deck also provides a versatile Crossfade feature that lets you overlap two audio regions on the same track. The Fade Selection command offers seven different types of fade curves for fading out the first region and seven more for fading in the second region.

FIGURE 11-15

Deck II's Track

window

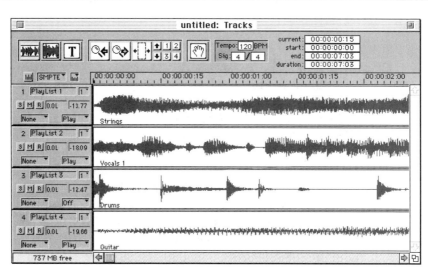

In addition to the non-destructive editing commands mentioned so far, Deck also offers a few destructive editing commands including Normalize, Reverse, Invert, Duplicate, and Strip Silence. If you don't want to permanently alter your original soundfile, the program gives you the option of applying these commands to a copy of the original.

As an added bonus, Deck has the ability to import, play, and synchronize to QuickTime movies. In fact, Deck can simultaneously play back several tracks of 16-bit audio and a QuickTime movie from the same hard disk. And if you're using Metro along with Deck, you can even synchronize your MIDI tracks to the same movie at the same time.

Deck II is a relatively easy program to work with and it lets you get started with pro-level multi-track recording without the usual expense. Other features include good documentation, support for SMPTE timecode, the ability to mix together tracks, and the ability to record and save fader movements.

MIDI, Audio, and Multimedia

So far I've described products that emphasize either MIDI or Audio recording and then add the missing element. But multimedia authoring applications offer a third alternative: treating MIDI and digital audio simply as two of several building blocks in a project. Once again, though, the issue of synchronization rears its ugly head. If a multimedia program just triggers MIDI and audio files you won't get consistent results, especially if you move from one model of computer to another. Furthermore, to be useful as a music production tool you need some way to edit your recordings. Few multimedia programs address these needs. Here's one that does.

Producer Pro

MAC

Producer Pro from Passport Designs is a multimedia authoring program that lets you assemble graphics, animation, digitized video, and sound. The sound options include MIDI music, digital audio, and playback of CD-audio tracks. Producer Pro is of special interest to desktop musicians because of its emphasis on synchronizing the different elements in a multimedia production (through SMPTE timecode) including MIDI and digital audio tracks.

The outwardly simple structure of Producer belies its powerful capabilities. Most of your work with the program takes place on a single screen called the Cue Sheet (Figure 11-16). The Cue Sheet consists of several (you can have as many as you want) vertical tracks that contain the various multimedia elements.

FIGURE 11-16

Passport Producer

Pro's Cue Sheet

window

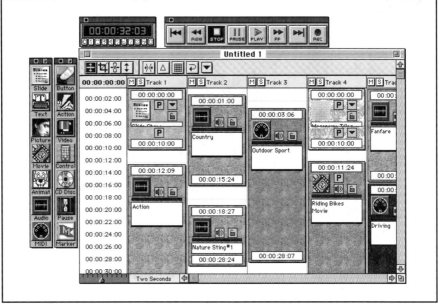

Along the left border there's a vertical timeline that shows elapsed time in standard SMPTE format. Elements such as graphics, animation, and music that appear in different tracks, but at the same place along the timeline, will play back together. This is very much like the overview window in many sequencers, but with a vertical orientation.

Adding a new element to the Cue Sheet is easy. First, you click on one of the icons in the Cue palette (the group of icons next to the timeline) and drag it onto the Cue Sheet. Each icon represents one type of media element and you can place the icon anywhere along the timeline and in any track you want.

Next, a dialog box opens so you can select the specific file to import. When you've imported the file it appears as a colored rectangle with a picture that indicates the type of file. The rectangle also shows the start and end times for the "cue," and the length of the box graphically represents the length of the file.

For assembling a project you can drag cues from track to track and from one place along the timeline to another. You can also drag the ends of the boxes to change their durations. Producer lets you place different kinds of files in the same track, but you may want to keep your digital audio files on separate tracks from your MIDI files. That way you can use the Mute and Solo buttons on each track to selectively monitor the parts of your composition.

Producer provides a basic set of editing tools for each type of cue so you can make a few changes without leaving the program. The Audio Editor lets you view a soundfile in a simple waveform display (Figure 11-17). You can

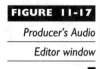

FIGURE 11-17

Producer's Audio

Editor window

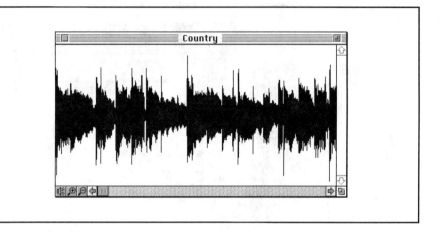

select areas within the waveform and cut, copy, paste, and delete. And there's also a Silence command that eliminates background noise by setting all of the amplitude values to zero in the selected area.

The MIDI Editor is a bit more advanced. It provides a multi-track mixing console with a volume fader for each track of MIDI data (Figure 11-18). You also get level meters, Mute and Solo buttons, Pan controls, and a Master volume fader. With the mixer you can change playback channels, transpose the sequence, assign different instruments to the tracks, and adjust each track's Pitch Bend range.

For both MIDI and digital audio cues you can fade the overall volume in and out with Producer's Envelope tool. It superimposes a gray envelope line

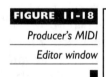

FIGURE 11-18

Producer's MIDI

Editor window

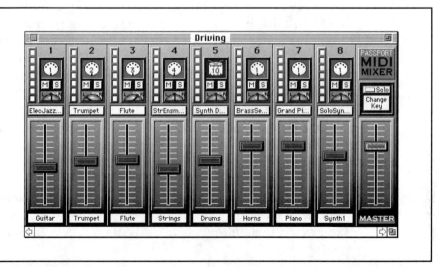

over the selected cue. By dragging points along the line you can cause the playback volume to increase or decrease at the designated places.

To do more extensive editing of your music, Producer lets you create links to other programs. That way you can open a file in your favorite sequencer or audio editor, make the necessary changes, and return the file to Producer. For this, however, you'll need lots of RAM. And speaking of RAM, Producer requires a minimum of 12MB just to run the program. You'll also need at least a 68040 model Mac.

Producer supports 8- and 16-bit AIFF, Sound Designer I and II, SND, Standard MIDI Files, and QuickTime (in addition to various non-musical formats). To distribute your finished product (to both Mac and Windows users), Passport includes a free run-time player called Media player. It improves playback performance and provides broader compatibility for more consistent results.

Last Thought

The marriage between digital audio and MIDI was destined to happen. Each music-production tool brings its own strengths to the union, and the result is a more versatile composition and music-production environment. If you're interested in adding high-end, music-workstation capabilities to your desktop, this is one way to do it. And the good news is that each of these products approaches the audio/MIDI connection in a different way. So there's bound to be a solution that works for your particular studio setup.

CHAPTER 12

Using Your Computer to Learn About Music

T HERE'S no doubt about it, the computer has had an enormous impact on the entire music industry—from creating and editing sounds to producing and playing back complete compositions. The personal computer has become so impressive in its ability to handle information that many musicians consider it to be an indispensable tool for delivering the right product at the right time.

But there's more to music than just the finished product. It's easy to forget that making music is also a process—an ongoing process that changes and evolves over time. A very big part of that process involves learning and using new skills. It doesn't matter whether you're an accomplished musician or a total amateur. There's always more to learn. There's always another level of insight to acquire, and you can always gain more understanding and a greater appreciation of music and its many styles.

These experiences, however, are not always easy to come by. For some people, private lessons are too costly or too difficult to schedule. Taking classes may also be impractical. There are many excellent books on music, but reading about music is sort of like reading about food—you're never really getting the total experience. Just listening to music without guidance, on the other hand, is also not the solution. Once you get past the pretty melody, it's hard to know what to listen for or what the historical context of the piece is, or how to analyze the piece in terms of harmony, form, and structure.

In fact, music education has always been a tricky subject to teach. Music encompasses such a broad range of styles—from Monteverdi to Madonna—that it's hard to know where to begin.

Fortunately, computers have once again come to the rescue. Actually, it might be more accurate to say that *multimedia* has come to the rescue. With its ability to combine text, graphics, animation, narration, and music, multimedia is exactly what the field of music education has been waiting for all these years. Now the floodgates have opened, and the music software marketplace has been inundated with products that can teach you everything you always wanted to know about music—and much more.

There are programs that can teach you to read music, and others that help you develop your musicianship abilities. Some programs teach you to play a specific instrument—like piano—while others are more general, helping you improve the instrument that you already play.

One place where computers really shine is in the area of music appreciation. There are currently a number of superb CD-ROM titles that help you analyze and understand famous musical pieces while providing historical background at the same time. Other titles start out with an historical perspective and add a little theory along the way. Moreover, music education software is not limited to just classical music. There are lots of good programs that teach about various aspects of folk music, rock, jazz, and other genres.

If you're interested in further pursuing your musical education, I strongly advise getting a CD-ROM drive. Although there are a few good programs that still come on floppies, the trend is toward publishing music education programs on compact discs. It's easy to see why. At 10MB per stereo minute, high-quality music takes up a lot of storage space (see Chapter 10), and many programs add graphics and animation to that. PC users should also have an MPC-compatible computer to make the most of many of the educational titles.

There are so many ways to approach the study of music that arranging programs into pigeonholes is difficult if not impossible. The three main categories might be described as music fundamentals and theory, developing musical skills, and music analysis and appreciation. However, these categories are often mixed together to provide a broader educational experience.

In many ways, the computer is the perfect teacher. It never gets upset, it never has "bad days," and it's always patient and forgiving. However, like most readers of this book, I learned music from real teachers. As you might expect, I had teachers I liked and teachers I didn't like. The problem is that a bad teacher can have a negative impact on your ability to learn. Consider the following examples.

As a college student I didn't get along with my first clarinet teacher. As a result, I did quite poorly in his class. Eventually, I had a new teacher and I did much better. One of my piano teachers was so exasperated with my playing that she would hit my hands when I made mistakes. (I even had one piano teacher who tried to convince me to get out of music altogether!) For many years I studied classical guitar and some of my teachers were traditional and unoriginal in their teaching approach. With these teachers my interest in guitar waned. Other teachers were more innovative and exciting. Under their instruction I advanced rapidly.

The point is this: The kind of teacher that you have has a great effect on how you learn music and what your future direction will be. The great thing about computers is that they allow you to learn at your own rate, focusing on those elements that most interest you.

Even though I studied music for many years before I got my first computer, I've found that composing music with my desktop system has led me down new avenues of musical thought. Computers are powerful tools for many things, and this is especially true for music. Your desktop studio offers you an exciting, open-ended passage through which you can explore the world of music in your own unique way.

Let's take a look at several noteworthy programs to give you a taste of what you and/or your children can learn about music with your computer.

Learn the Basics

The logical place to begin talking about the study of music is to study some programs for beginners. Many of these programs are targeted toward school-age children and serve simply as an introduction to music fundamentals. But some programs extend the learning process into more advanced territory. And these are well suited to adults.

One such program—**MiBAC Music Lessons**—is a collection of 11 drills in different skill levels that start with basics, such as the names of notes, and take you into advanced topics. The program doesn't offer fancy graphics or color, just a series of no-nonsense exercises that focus on music theory and basic listening skills.

The program's interface is clear and easy to use, and it encourages you to move ahead at your own pace. You can quickly switch from one topic to the next, so if you get tired of working on scales, for example, you can try a little ear training as a change of pace.

PC

MAC

MiBAC Music

Lessons

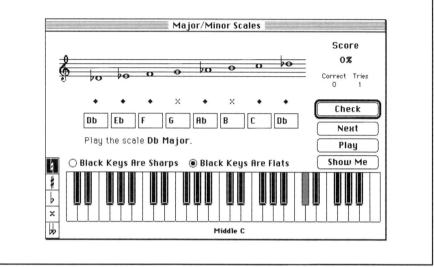

Figure 12-1

The windows for the various drills are similar in design. Most displays include a staff where notes, scales, and intervals appear. Below the staff there are one or more boxes where you enter the required information (Figure 12-1). If you have a MIDI keyboard you can use it to enter notes. Otherwise, you can use the on-screen keyboard. Mac users without a MIDI setup can play back notes from the Mac's internal sound source.

Aside from naming notes, other drills cover key signatures, major and minor scales, and note durations. As you get a little more advanced you can practice naming intervals and identifying scale degrees. And finally you can test your knowledge of jazz scales and modes and tackle more challenging ear training exercises.

Overall, MiBAC Music Lessons is a great tool for honing your musical skills. And the program is suitable for a wide range of users—from grade-school students up through teenagers and adults.

Just for Kids

PC

Howling Dog Systems has made a name for itself with its rather unconventional approach to music-making software. If you were intrigued by Power Chords Pro (see Chapter 8) and you want your kids (ages 3 to 9) to get in on the act, check out **Mr. Drumstix' Music Studio**. It's a kind of musical Romper Room where young children can explore the music-making process and express their creativity in a variety of ways.

The program is conceptually divided into two parts—Activities and Games. These are easily accessed from rows of colorful buttons. One of the best parts of the program—the Song window—provides a graphic display that scrolls along as the music plays (Figure 12-2). Each measure in the song (the program comes with 20 children's songs) is represented by a wide column containing pictures of the instruments that you hear as that measure plays. You can change any instrument sound by clicking on it and selecting from an assortment of other pictures.

There's also a Lyrics window that provides the words—karaoke-style—to each song and the Mr. Drumstix window that shows the eponymous cartoon character surrounded by a set of drums. Mr. Drumstix plays along as the songs are played. And when you're not playing songs, you can play his drums by clicking on them. As you click each drum, its name appears in the window. And if you click the Rhythm button, Mr. Drumstix plays a solo. You can even create your own solos with the Rhythm Editor.

The music studio also includes an on-screen keyboard—Ms. Florida Keys—that you can play by clicking with the mouse. As you play the keys they light up in different colors. And you can have them say their names if you want.

For budding guitarists there's Guitar George—an on-screen guitar fretboard much like the one in Power Chords Pro. Guitar George will show you how to finger different chords and let you create your own. Then you can strum the strings by dragging across them with the mouse. Also, you can bend strings like on a real guitar.

FIGURE 12-2

Mr. Drumstix'

Music Studio

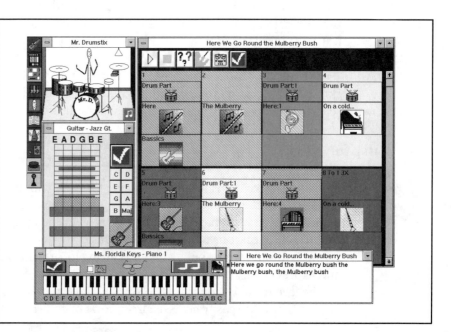

The Games section of the program includes a good assortment of activities designed to develop beginning musical skills. Follow the Leader, for example, helps develop memory for musical phrases. Hi/Lo develops pitch discrimination. Other games challenge you to identify instrument sounds, determine how many notes are played, match musical patterns, or recognize chord types.

There's lots to do in Mr. Drumstix' Music Studio, so your little ones should stay busy for some time. And as they have fun exploring the program they'll begin to develop some useful musical skills.

∫ing a Song of Sixpence

PC

If you've got young kids running around your house, there's no better way to introduce them to the joys of music-making than through our rich legacy of children's songs. Children love to sing, and CD-ROMs can make the experience even more delightful by adding colorful graphics and animation to the music.

And that's just what Dr. T's Music Software does with its award-winning **Sing-A-Long Kids' Classics**. This CD includes over 25 traditional children's songs, such as "I'm a Little Teapot," "I've Been Working on the Railroad," "O My Darling Clementine," "Red River Valley," "Oh Susanna," and other great tunes. Each song appears on-screen with animated characters, lyrics, and music notation. The interface has been designed so that even young children can run the program and everyone can have fun singing as the lyrics and notes scroll by.

Following on the heels of its first Sing-A-Long disc, Dr. T's has now released a second CD entitled **Sing-A-Long Around the World**. This new title—designed for kids ages three to ten—includes 22 popular children's songs, each from a different country. In addition to English-language songs from Ireland, Canada, and England, you also get songs from France, Germany, Holland, Ghana, Japan, Brazil, and other far-away places. When you play the CD you can listen to the songs in English or in the native language. There's even a nicely printed songbook that provides the foreign-language lyrics.

As a little introduction to geography, children can select songs by pointing to the native country on a world map. Once a song is selected, an animated scene appears with a cast of characters and an animated story (with sound effects) that plays along as the song unfolds (Figure 12-3).

Beneath the scene, the music and lyrics scroll by as a moving icon helps children keep their place in the song. You can also have the guitar chords

FIGURE 12-3

Dr. T's Sing-A-Long

Around the World

appear on-screen and you can hide the lyrics and/or notation if you just want to sing and watch the animation.

For very young children, Sing-A-Long includes a Little Kids Mode that lets them operate the program without accessing their parent's files. Large, colorful, 3-D buttons with icons let them select and play songs. And when they click a button they hear the name of the selection.

Once your children have learned a song, they can play just the accompaniment without the vocals and perform karaoke-style. In fact, if you plug a microphone into your sound card your kids can hear their own voices, along with the accompaniment, coming through your speakers. And by connecting a cassette recorder to your sound card you can record the whole performance.

Finally, you can print out the lyrics, notation, and guitar chords if you want to bring the songs to a party or to school for classroom use.

If your kids are showing an interest in singing, Dr. T's Sing-A-Long is a great way to get them started with music, while teaching them about other cultures at the same time.

Improve Your Singing

Young kids aren't the only ones who like to sing. Adults do too. But unless you're a diva from the Metropolitan Opera, the chances are good that you can use some improvement. Unfortunately, for most of us non-professional

MAC

CD-ROM

singers, hiring a private voice coach is not very practical. There is an alternative, however, that's almost as good, and in some ways even better than a private teacher. Opcode's **Claire** software turns your Macintosh into a personal music coach that's available any time of the day or night and never gets cranky if you're having an off day.

Claire is a fully interactive program that listens to your voice, gives verbal instructions, and uses animation and graphics to help you develop your singing skills. To use Claire you need a Macintosh with a built-in microphone; or you can use an inexpensive audio digitizer such as Macromedia's MacRecorder. The software uses proprietary pitch recognition technology that's as sensitive as the human ear, tolerates background noise, and works with all voice ranges and many musical instruments.

To use Claire you first take a brief tour that shows how the program works. During the tour you establish your *tessitura* (voice range) and find a comfortable key for singing in. When you're ready to go, you open the Practice window (Figure 12-4) where you're presented with three or more notes on a large staff.

Claire explains the exercise and then sings the notes for you. Then it's your turn. Following Claire's lead you sing each note as the program evaluates your intonation (pitch accuracy). If you sing a note a bit too sharp or flat a little arrow appears over the note showing how you were off. At the end of the exercise your performance is immediately evaluated and you get to try again with a new exercise.

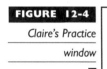

FIGURE 12-4

Claire's Practice window

Claire listens patiently and praises you when you do well. As you progress, the program alters the lessons according to your strengths and weaknesses. The software includes over 500 exercises that cover major and minor scales, intervals, and arpeggios. You can even view and print a detailed Intonation Profile that shows—in bar-graph form—which pitches you need the most work on. And you can track your progress by reviewing a complete history of each exercise.

This program is an excellent tool for developing sight-reading skills and improving the accuracy of your singing. Adults at all levels will find it challenging and even professional singers can get a lot out of the lessons. Furthermore, the simple interface, the friendly voice prompts, and the easy-to-read notes make Claire a perfect tool for kids as well.

Learn to Play Piano

PC

MAC

The piano keyboard is the most universal of musical interfaces and an essential tool for desktop music production. As we've already seen, computers make excellent music teachers. So why not have your computer teach you to play the piano? If taking piano lessons has always seemed too intimidating, too inconvenient, or too much work, then think again. **The Miracle Piano Teaching System** from Software Toolworks makes learning the piano fun and convenient.

The complete system includes a 49-key, velocity-sensitive synthesizer with 128 presets and built-in speakers. It attaches to your computer with a special serial cable. The software is nicely designed with wonderful 3-D graphics and animation.

Based on the metaphor of a private music school, the program opens to an overhead view of The Miracle Conservatory (Figure 12-5). There you see the six "rooms" that form the structure of the program.

The Classroom is where you spend most of your time as you learn your way around the keyboard. The curriculum consists of 40 progressive chapters, each of which covers a specific concept. One chapter, for example, covers the basics of notation, another introduces rhythm. The chapters are divided into a number of small lessons, each of which focuses on a particular piece of music. The lessons (there are hundreds) involve reading instructions from the "chalkboard," watching demonstrations, and practicing keyboard skills (Figure 12-6).

But The Miracle is not just an on-screen piano-instruction book. It teaches by interacting with you the way a human teacher does. It listens to and evaluates your playing and then gives you special exercises to help you

FIGURE 12-5

The Miracle

Conservatory

FIGURE 12-6

One of the lessons

from The Miracle

Piano Teaching

System

overcome your particular problems. That's what makes The Miracle system so remarkable. It doesn't just point out wrong notes, it works in a more intelligent manner to try to figure out the nature of your mistakes.

The software actually classifies errors as one of 200 types. These are further sorted into 41 categories. Some categories include ignoring an

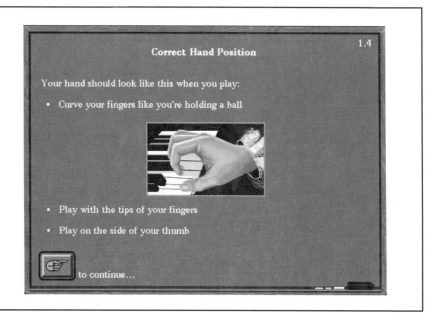

accidental, playing a note too fast, holding a note too long, ignoring a rest, hitting the crack between keys, and so on.

The program weighs the importance of the mistakes based on the nature of the current lesson. It then points out your problem area and assigns exercises that are appropriate to your needs. The exercises are evaluated just like the lessons. And once you've overcome your difficulty you're returned to the lesson where you left off. Aside from the Classroom, the other five rooms provide support in a number of entertaining ways.

For a change of pace and to develop certain skills, some lessons send you to the Arcade where you play keyboard-oriented games. Ducks, for example, is a shooting gallery game that helps you develop sight-reading skills. Little ducks swim across the lines and spaces of the staff and you "shoot" them by playing the appropriate notes on the keyboard. It's lots of fun. Ripchord is for practicing chords and Aliens works on fingering and note sequences. Children in particular will love these games.

The Practice Room is where you go to review the piece you're working on and to sharpen your skills. Once you make it through a set of lessons and you can play a new tune, it's time to go to the Performance Hall. Here you get to perform your piece accompanied by The Miracle Orchestra. This gives a good sense of what it's like to play with other musicians and it reinforces the lessons well.

If you want to record and play back a performance, you can go to the Studio and use a realistic-looking seven-track tape deck. And finally, the Administration office is where you "enroll" students, set features, and check on your progress.

The Miracle Piano Teaching System is a thoughtfully designed, well-structured product that can definitely teach just about anyone to play the piano. It may not turn you into a concert performer, but it will certainly get both children and adults past the beginner stage. It's a great introduction to music. If you already own a synthesizer there are also versions of the program that include just the software.

Learn from the Pros

PC

MAC

One of the best ways to improve your playing technique and to acquire new material is to study the performances of other musicians. And what better way to do this than through the interactive nature of MIDI and a personal computer. PG Music (the company that produces Band-in-a-Box) offers three programs that let you listen to and study performances by professional artists. All performances are recorded with a sequencer in real time (without quantization) by the performers themselves.

The Jazz Guitarist features a large assortment of jazz standards and popular songs performed on a MIDI guitar by studio guitarist Oliver Gannon. The main screen (Figure 12-7) provides a piano keyboard along the top and a large guitar fretboard just beneath it.

When you select a song from the list at the bottom of the window a short description with background information appears just above it. Clicking the Play button starts the selected song, and the notes appear on the piano keyboard and the guitar fretboard simultaneously.

For many guitarists, watching the notes appear on the fretboard is preferable to seeing the music as written notation. And you can slow the tempo way down if you're trying to learn a piece. In fact, the program provides a set of buttons that lets you step (forward or backward) through the piece one chord at a time. And another set of buttons lets you step one note at a time. These are great tools for scrutinizing a performance. If you need a little rest and relaxation you can also play the music jukebox-style in the background, or you can play one of two guessing games that come with the program.

For keyboard players, PG Music offers **The Jazz Pianist**. Its main window (Figure 12-8) is much like its guitar counterpart, but without the fretboard. This program also lets you change the tempo and step through chords and notes one at a time. And it has the same games. It also includes several "lessons" that offer insight into jazz harmonies and styles.

If your interests run more toward classical music, PG offers **The Pianist**. It includes a collection of over 200 popular classical piano pieces performed by a

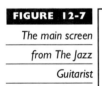

FIGURE 12-7

The main screen from The Jazz Guitarist

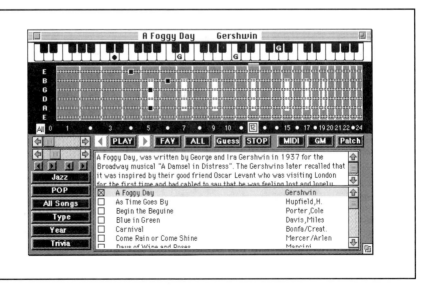

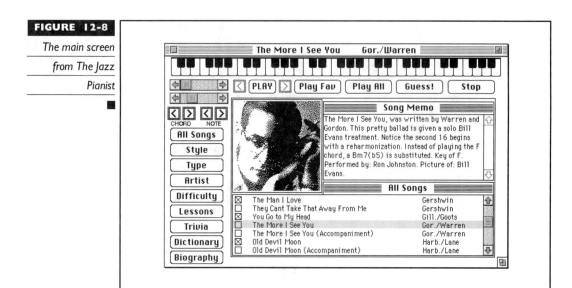

FIGURE 12-8

*The main screen
from The Jazz
Pianist*
■

concert pianist on an 88-note weighted MIDI keyboard. The main screen resembles The Jazz Pianist screen, but without the step buttons. As with the other programs you also get biographical information and a dictionary.

The Jazz Guitarist, The Pianist, and The Jazz Pianist illustrate once again that MIDI is more than just a performance tool. It's also a valuable educational tool.

A Well-Rounded Introduction

PC

MAC

Opcode Interactive's **The Musical World of Professor Piccolo** is an excellent example of how multimedia can open new dimensions into the study of music. The many colorful drawings and photos will certainly appeal to young students, but it's the teenagers and young adults out there who will gain the most from this program. And just because it has a name like Professor Piccolo doesn't mean it's not also for grown-ups. In fact, if you're looking for a well-rounded introduction to the study of music this program is hard to beat.

The Musical World of Professor Piccolo opens with an aerial view of Music Town (Figure 12-9). Around the center of this quaint village you'll find seven buildings, each of which offers insight into some aspect of music theory and/or musical styles. To enter a building you just click on it. As the screen dissolves you're greeted with ambient sounds characteristic of the

FIGURE 12-9

The main screen

from The Musical

World of Professor

Piccolo

■

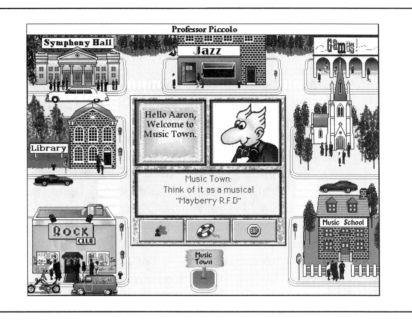

establishment: an orchestra tuning up in Symphony Hall, for example, or people talking and applauding in the Jazz club.

Entering Symphony Hall you find yourself in the audience looking out over the Boston Symphony Orchestra (Figure 12-10). By clicking buttons

FIGURE 12-10

Inside Symphony

Hall

■

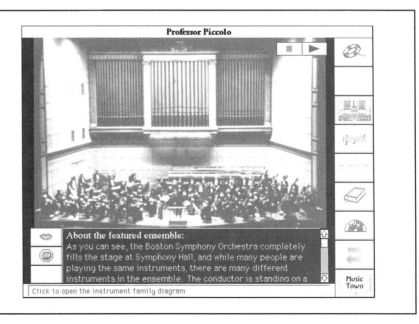

along the right side of the screen you can study the makeup, layout, and history of orchestras.

In another window a large chart lets you see (and hear) the ranges of the instruments. And for further study, you can open a separate window for each instrument showing the names of its parts and giving some background information. By clicking a button you can even hear a short piece of music featuring that instrument.

After you're familiar with the parts of the orchestra, things really get interesting. You can listen to a recording of Haydn's Symphony No. 88 as a colorful graph points out the different structural elements of the piece as it plays. Meanwhile a running commentary below the graph explains what's going on. You'll learn (and hear) how the first theme differs from the second theme in the first movement. And how the first movement's structure compares to that in the second and third movements. If you don't know what a development section or a recapitulation is, you will by the time you're through. And you can click on any structural element to hear it play.

This same thorough approach is also used in the Jazz and Rock clubs. You can study each of the instruments in a typical group just as you can with the classical instruments. Learn how they sound, what their ranges are, and how they're played. In the Jazz club you get a nice summary of jazz history. The Rock club provides the equivalent for rock music.

As each combo plays a piece typical of the style, you can view an analysis of the piece as it progresses. You'll learn what a verse, a chorus, and a bridge is and how each is used in a pop song. You'll learn what "trading fours" means as you listen to how the melody is treated in a jazz piece. In the church you can listen to an excerpt from Bach's Mass in B Minor as you study the score and learn about the history of church music.

The music analysis and history parts of Professor Piccolo are actually just the beginning. The program also offers an extensive self-paced music theory course. If you've read my summaries in Chapter 2 on sound and musical concepts, and you feel that you need more study, this is a great place to get it.

Using animation and sound clips you can explore concepts in ways that ordinary books simply can't. Learn how waveforms combine to produce new waveforms or what the different harmonics of a vibrating string sound like. Learn about (and hear) meters, intervals, scales, rhythms, chords, and lots of other things. If you need more information, take a trip over to the Library where you can look up musical terms and learn more about musical instruments. Finally, for a little fun, test your knowledge at the Game Parlor where you can try your hand at any of four musical games.

Professor Piccolo is a captivating program that makes learning about music fun. Its broad scope and thoughtfully designed lessons make it a terrific way to study the basics of music.

Learn About Composers

PC

If Professor Piccolo whets your appetite for more knowledge about classical music, you might turn to another CD-ROM from Opcode Interactive. **Composer Quest** is an interactive music history guide combined with an educational, time-travel game.

Your tour of music history begins with a timeline that spans the years from 1600 to the early 20th century. Along the timeline there are buttons that represent the different musical periods. If you click on the Romantic button, for example, a window opens showing seven of the most prominent composers from that period (Figure 12-11).

Along the right side of the window, three buttons provide an historical context for that period in music. The bottom button opens a window that describes world events during that time; the middle button focuses on developments in the visual arts; and the top button lets you type in any year to see an important newsworthy incident.

After you have a better historical sense of a particular musical era, you can explore the lives and works of individual composers from that time. Clicking on a composer's name opens a window that shows his picture along with a brief biographical sketch. In many cases, there are samples of his music. (The program comes with over 60 musical excerpts, although some

FIGURE 12-11

Composer Quest's

Romantic Period

menu

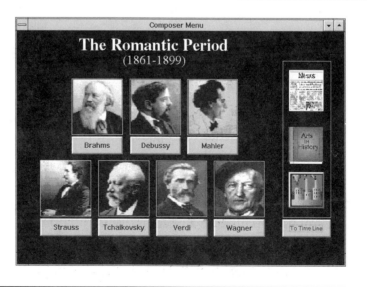

composers—especially 20th century composers—are not represented.) Clicking on a title plays a short excerpt from a famous composition.

After you've studied most of the great composers throughout history and listened to samples of their work, you're ready to play Composer Quest's time-travel guessing game. The program plays a "mystery" excerpt that you must identify by first landing in the correct musical period with your time machine. If you need help, the composers will give you hints along the way. This is a fun way to test your memory for musical styles. If you want a different kind of challenge, there's also a trivia game that tests your knowledge of music history.

Aside from its coverage of classical music, Composer Quest also delves lightly into the area of jazz. This is clearly the weakest part of the program covering only Ragtime, New Orleans, and Early Swing periods. Aside from a Scott Joplin excerpt, there are no musical examples in this section. Nonetheless, a little background in jazz does help broaden your sense of music history.

Composer Quest is a great introduction to the different styles of classical music, and it helps you understand what was happening in the world when many of the most noteworthy composers were creating their works. If you're curious about music history, it serves as a nice introductory reference work. Other features in the program include a Quick Index to search for composers, definitions of musical terms, and French and German versions of the text.

Learn About Classical Styles

PC

The best way to understand musical styles is to examine how the elements of music are used within each style. You may be able to tell the difference between the music of Bach and Mozart, for instance, but what is it that makes them sound the way they do? Why does music from the Renaissance sound so much different than music from the Romantic period? Midisoft sets out to answer these and other questions with its interactive MIDI-based program called **Music Mentor**.

The concept behind Music Mentor is actually very simple. The program is organized around six fundamental aspects of music: melody, rhythm, harmony, timbre, texture, and form. You access these topics through a row of buttons on the main screen (Figure 12-12).

If you want some introductory information on harmony, for example, just click the Basics button and then click the Harmony button. Music Mentor then presents you with a series of interactive windows. Aside from graphics and explanatory text, many windows include one or more buttons

Music Mentor's

main screen

that provide musical examples (played from your sound card via MIDI) that illustrate an important point.

This makes it easy to understand binary form, for instance, because you can listen to a Bach minuet as the program highlights the different sections on a diagram. Also, you can listen to how different scales sound or how rhythms affects a melody. If you're a real beginner, there's even a special section called the Basics of Reading Music. It introduces you to music notation to help you understand the examples in the other sections.

Once you've studied the basic concepts of music, the Program gets really interesting. You can take any of the six fundamental topics and explore them in terms of five historical periods: Early, Baroque, Classical, Romantic, and Modern (Figure 12-13). And Music Mentor lets you proceed in any direction you want. For example, you can study all six topics as they relate to a single period, such as the Baroque period. Or you can study a single topic, such as Harmony, and see how it's used throughout the different periods. In fact, you can jump from any topic and period to any other. So you might study Melody in the Classical period and then jump directly to Texture in the Romantic period.

Music Mentor does not provide an in-depth exploration of music theory, but it does offer a great way to get started studying musical concepts. Its use of simple animations, concise descriptions, and musical examples keeps the program interesting as it encourages you along. Furthermore, Music Mentor comes bundled with Midisoft's **Recording Session** sequencer—an entry-level

FIGURE 12-13

Music Mentor lets you study musical concepts within an historical context

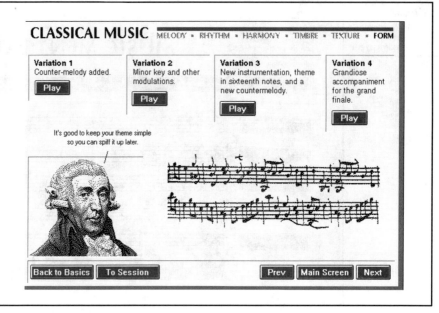

version of Studio for Windows (see Chapter 6). So if you decide—after studying about the concepts of music—to try your hand at composing, you can dive right in. Recording Session is a notation-based sequencer/mixer combination that's easy to use, and the software includes an assortment of MIDI files to play back and edit as you like.

Learn About the Orchestra

MAC

Ever wonder about all the myriad elements that go into the performance of an orchestral work? First there's the composition itself with its many interrelated parts. Then you have a stage full of instruments played in various combinations and in different ways. And finally, you have a conductor standing in front of all the musicians and waving his hands in the air. How do these elements work together to produce great music? If you've been looking for the answer you'll be glad to know that there's an excellent CD-ROM from Time Warner Interactive, called **The Orchestra**, and it tackles that very question.

The Orchestra is a multifaceted interactive exploration of music and how it's created. The heart of the program is based on an extensive analysis of Benjamin Britten's wonderful *Variations and Fugue on a Theme of Purcell*— better known as *The Young Person's Guide to the Orchestra*. Because of its creative use of the theme and variation technique of composition and its skillful use of instruments, this piece is a natural for studying orchestral music—and you get to listen to the entire piece performed by the London Symphony Orchestra, conducted by the composer himself.

When you first open the program, you're presented with the Program Map (Figure 12-14) showing the many areas that you can explore. The best way to start is to listen to Britten's music while the program provides a running commentary describing how the instruments are being used. Then you can go back and listen to the piece again using the Theme and Variation section. It offers a full annotation, in sync with the music, describing how the piece is put together.

Finally, you can use the Music Guide to navigate through the music, section by section. As the music plays, you'll see a block analysis of the different sections—each highlighting in turn as you listen. In this part of the program you can jump from one section to another just by clicking a button.

As interesting as the musical analysis is, it's really only one part of the program. The rest of the CD is filled with entertaining activities and explorations of how instruments and orchestras work. For example, in the Sounds of the Orchestra section there are audio clips from famous compositions that illustrate how the instruments in the orchestra are used to create different musical effects. Examples include works by Bartok, Stravinsky, Debussy, Ives, and others.

In the Orchestra Lab you can try your hand at orchestrating a two-part rendition of "Greensleeves." This is great stuff. But that's not all. In the Instrument Catalog you can learn more about the instruments of the

FIGURE 12-14

The Orchestra's

Program Map

screen

orchestra, how they're constructed, how they're played, and how they sound. And in the Conducting section you learn about the history of conducting. You can even take a conducting lesson and try a little conducting yourself.

There's a lot more to The Orchestra than what I've described, including an Arcade section with several games. This program has something for everyone. Adults will enjoy the analysis of the music and the other explanatory text. Children will learn to identify and better understand the instruments in the orchestra. And people of all ages will have fun with the many interesting musical side trips.

Learn About Musical Instruments

PC

MAC

There are a number of CD-ROMs, such as Professor Piccolo and The Orchestra, that teach you about common musical instruments as part of a larger program. But Microsoft's **Musical Instruments** CD focuses all of its attention specifically on music-making devices and how they're used. In fact, when it comes to exploring the world of musical instruments, this CD covers a wider range—and in more detail—than any other program.

In Musical Instruments you'll not only learn about violins, trumpets, and clarinets, but also about ukuleles, accordions, and conga drums. And that's not all. The program also takes you on a trip around the world, exposing you to instruments that you've probably never even heard of—like the darabukka, the zurna, or the kendang. And there's more. You'll also find out about historical instruments—such as the lute, the viol, the sackbut, and the hurdy-gurdy.

And to make your study of instruments more meaningful, the CD includes 500 color photographs and more than 1500 audio clips from more than 200 instruments. You get to see exactly how the instruments look (with the parts clearly labeled) and hear how they sound. The program will even pronounce the names of instruments for you in case you run into a "didjeridu" and don't know how to say it correctly.

The organization of Musical Instruments is quite simple. The CD is divided into four main sections that you can access in any order. The Families of Instruments section groups the instruments into five basic categories: brass, strings, woodwinds, keyboards, and percussion. After you select a group you can choose an individual instrument for a close-up look and further study (Figure 12-15).

The sound icon at the top of the window pronounces the instrument's name. The icon next to the instrument lets you hear how it sounds. If you want to learn more you can click an icon (available for some instruments)

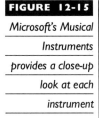

FIGURE 12-15

Microsoft's Musical
Instruments
provides a close-up
look at each
instrument

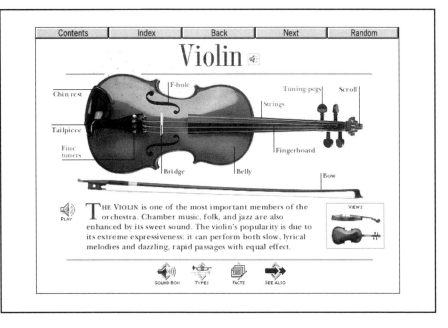

to open the Sound Box window (Figure 12-16). There you can play single notes on the instrument, hear its complete range, or listen to examples of how it sounds when it plays different styles of music.

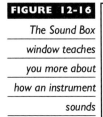

FIGURE 12-16

The Sound Box
window teaches
you more about
how an instrument
sounds

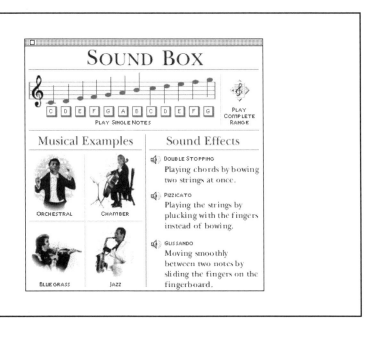

The A–Z of Instruments section lets you view an illustrated list—organized alphabetically—of all the instruments on the disc. If you already know the name of an instrument, this is where you go to find it.

In the Instruments of the World section, you're shown a map of the world that you can use to select instruments by geographical region. If you're studying Chinese music, for example, you can use this section to find a suona and listen to how it sounds, or to see what a yueqin looks like. Or you might just want to compare a Hungarian duda to an Italian zampogna. It's easy in this section.

Finally, the Musical Ensembles section teaches you about the make-up and styles associated with a variety of instrumental groups. The Orchestra entry points out the differences between Baroque, Classical, Romantic, and Twentieth Century orchestras. And each example includes a recording that illustrates how that particular orchestra sounds. The same approach is also used with several other groups. The section on jazz bands compares and contrasts jazz combo, Dixieland, jazz-rock fusion, and big band ensembles. The rock section covers rock & roll, heavy metal, soft rock, and pop. And you can also learn about chamber ensembles, marching bands, gamelan orchestras, and others if you're so inclined.

Microsoft Musical Instruments is as entertaining as it is educational. You're certain to run across some instruments that you never knew existed, and it's exciting to learn about them and hear how they sound. And the wide scope of the program makes it even more fun to explore. One minute you're learning about banjos, bagpipes, dulcimers, and nose flutes, and the next minute you're studying electric guitars, synthesizers, and digital samplers. If you've ever wondered what a zilli masa looks like or how a kalangu sounds, this is the place to find out.

A Close Analysis

PC

MAC

When the Voyager Company introduced its **Beethoven: Symphony No. 9** CD-ROM several years ago, it established a new benchmark for music education software. Impressed with the results, Microsoft adapted the HyperCard-based Macintosh program to run with Windows and called it **Multimedia Beethoven.**

Voyager then released other titles based on the same concept, including **Stravinsky: The Rite of Spring** and **Mozart: The "Dissonant" Quartet.** These have been ported over to Windows by Microsoft and released as **Multimedia Stravinsky** and **Multimedia Mozart.** Although the look and feel varies considerably between the black-and-white Macintosh and the more colorful Windows versions, the structure and content are essentially the same.

The Stravinsky and Mozart CDs share a number of characteristics, the most important being that they are authored by Robert Winter who guides the listener with text and speech throughout the programs. Winter has a natural ability to explain musical concepts in ways that open doors to neophytes without insulting the intelligence of more experienced listeners. This accessibility paves the way to a potentially rich learning experience for anyone who explores each disc's myriad nooks and crannies.

Both titles provide insight into their music through a two-pronged approach—detailed analysis of the music itself and a study of the historical contexts within which the composers worked. Teaching music analysis is often frustrating because of music's inherently transient nature. The Voyager/Microsoft CDs, however, meet this challenge by allowing the user to move freely among the different parts of the compositions.

Each disc provides a Pocket Audio Guide that lets you listen to, repeat, and compare any sections of the composition. By clicking the names in an outline, you can compare the "Sacrificial Dance" to the "Dance of the Earth" in *The Rite of Spring*. Or you can contrast the Exposition with the Development section in the fourth movement of the Mozart Quartet. You might just want to repeat a section several times or branch off into a related topic for further study.

Explaining *The Rite of Spring* to someone with limited musical background is an especially formidable challenge. With its evocative sonorities, dense textures, wild rhythms, and dissonant clashes the Rite is often difficult to fathom even for many seasoned listeners. With his Rite Listening chapter, however, Winter wades right in and guides your attention to the important elements that form the composition. Stravinsky's use of motifs, rhythms and accents, transitions, and other elements are lucidly explained with text and reinforced with audio clips.

The chapter entitled "Stravinsky's Orchestral World" takes you on a tour of the orchestra describing in detail each of the instrument groups. Audio clips let you hear the instruments and the unique ways in which Stravinsky uses them to create his orchestral colors.

Once you've explored the orchestra and the compositional elements in *The Rite of Spring*, you're ready for A Close Reading. This section plays the entire piece (performed by the Orchestre Symphonique de Montreal), accompanied by a continuous, real-time, descriptive commentary (Figure 12-17).

Finally, to provide you with a greater sense of context, Stravinsky's World provides details of the composer's life and times. The "Rite as Dance" chapter examines the original 1913 production, which—with Diaghilev's innovative choreography and Nijinsky's provocative performance—stunned Parisian society and sparked a riot.

FIGURE 12-17

*Stravinsky: The
Rite of Spring
provides real-time
commentary as the
music plays*

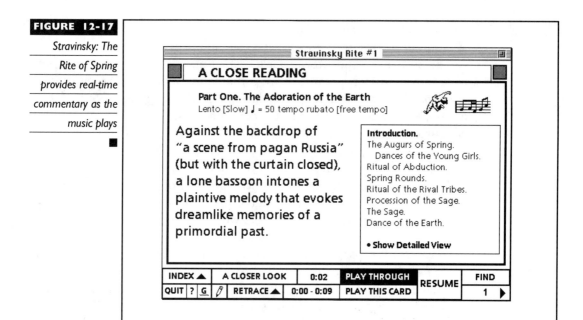

Stravinsky: The Rite of Spring has something for everyone. You don't have to read music or understand musical terminology to put this disc to good use. Throughout the program, words within the text provide links to clearly written explanations complete with audio examples where appropriate. If you don't know what *cadence* means or you'd like more information about *meter, counterpoint,* or *rhythm,* just click on the words.

Compared to *The Rite of Spring*, Mozart's Quartet in C Major K.465 (the "Dissonant" Quartet) seems rather tame. This CD, however, successfully uses the same teaching approach (including links to definitions) as its Stravinsky counterpart (Figure 12-18).

The Instruments chapter examines in great detail the instruments that make up Mozart's orchestra. Quartet Listening teaches about string quartet composition and what to listen for. Mozart's World helps you better appreciate Mozart's music by exploring the people and events that shaped the composer's life. A Close Reading takes you by the hand and leads you—with its running commentary—through all four movements of the work as it's performed by the Angeles Quartet.

To round things out, both the Stravinsky and Mozart CDs include excellent bibliographies and games to test your newfound knowledge. These CD-ROMs from Voyager and Microsoft illustrate clearly how interactive multimedia can infuse the study of music with greater depth while making it exciting to learn about great works of art.

FIGURE 12-18

Mozart: The

"Dissonant" Quartet

■

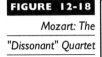

More Analysis

MAC

Voyager and Microsoft are not the only companies that offer in-depth musical analysis on CD-ROM. Time Warner Interactive has entered the field with some excellent titles, including **Beethoven String Quartet No. 14** and **Johannes Brahms A German Requiem**. These show the same comprehensive approach and attention to detail as Warner's The Orchestra, which I mentioned earlier. In fact, it's hard to imagine a more complete dissection of great music as you'll find on these discs.

The HyperCard-based programs let you switch from one type of analysis to another while you listen to the music. And there are numerous branches that lead into a variety of side trips (complete with text, graphics, music notation, and audio clips) to enhance your understanding of the music. The effect is much like filming a scene in a movie from four or five different camera angles, each revealing some new perspective.

The Beethoven CD, for example, provides four different "channels" that supply a running commentary in sync with the music as it plays. And you can switch from one channel to another without interrupting the performance.

The first channel—Exploring the Music—offers a descriptive introduction to the quartet in general terms. Structural Analysis provides a running annotation describing the music's form. Harmonic Analysis offers a continuous guide to the tonal and harmonic elements in the piece. And Blueprint supplies graphic descriptions of the music showing compositional elements, the use of themes and motives, and how the four instruments interrelate musically (Figure 12-19). There's even a fifth channel—Notes—where you can add your own comments.

By the time you've analyzed Beethoven's quartet from all of these different angles, you'll know more about the piece than you ever imagined possible. But there's actually much more to the disc.

The Quartet Map, for instance, shows all seven movements of the piece with a breakdown of each movement's parts. In this section you can switch from one part to another to focus your study in specific areas or to make comparisons.

Other sections provide information on music fundamentals, the elements of musical architecture, and the composer's life and times. There's also a Timeline section that includes pictures, text, and musical examples from the medieval period to the present, and a Final Exam that tests your knowledge.

This disc has so many areas to explore that it's hard to cover in a short space. There are more than 60 side journeys and more than 250 examples of sound and music. And you also get a complete digital recording of Beethoven's masterpiece performed by the Vermeer Quartet. If you're a Beethoven fan, and especially if you like to analyze music, you'll love this disc.

The Brahms title follows much the same formula as its Beethoven companion, but in an ambitious two-CD set. You get the entire *Requiem* (nearly

FIGURE 12-19

The Blueprint window from Beethoven String Quartet No. 14

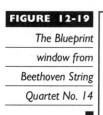
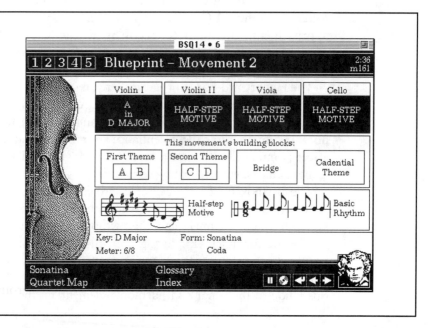

FIGURE 12-20

The German Requiem CD-ROM includes an interesting biography of Brahms

■

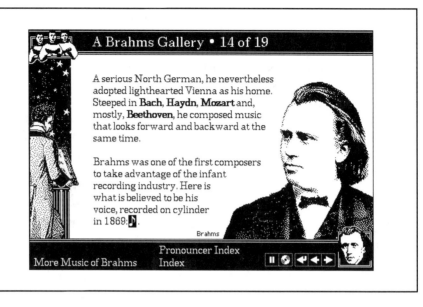

A Brahms Gallery • 14 of 19

A serious North German, he nevertheless adopted lighthearted Vienna as his home. Steeped in **Bach, Haydn, Mozart** and, mostly, **Beethoven**, he composed music that looks forward and backward at the same time.

Brahms was one of the first composers to take advantage of the infant recording industry. Here is what is believed to be his voice, recorded on cylinder in 1869: ▶.

Brahms

More Music of Brahms

Pronouncer Index
Index

70 minutes long) performed by Robert Shaw and the Atlanta Symphony Orchestra and Chorus. The four channels that run in sync with the music provide a complete guide to the music, an English translation of the text, the original German text, and a running narrative about the music from the conductor's perspective.

Other parts of the program include the Requiem Map, which supplies a theme-by-theme guide to the music. There are also sections exploring music theory, Brahms' use of harmony, choral basics, the music of Romanticism, and the composer's life (Figure 12-20).

All together there are dozens of side trips and more than 400 audio clips. This is another impressive examination of a great masterpiece. If you're an opera lover you might also be interested in Time Warner Interactive's three-CD examination of Mozart's *The Magic Flute*.

Music History

MAC

If you're interested in history, Voyager offers a great way to learn about the evolution of music in Western civilization. **So I've Heard** is a five-volume series of CD-ROMs that provides an entertaining overview of history from ancient Greek rituals to modern electronic music. These HyperCard-based programs include photographs, drawings, and numerous musical examples to make the study of music history come alive.

Each volume is an essay consisting of several chapters by the noted music critic Alan Rich. He presents the material in a breezy, often witty style that keeps you entertained as you learn about great music. I especially like the way he compares earlier works with more modern pieces to show how one influences the other. And there are other comparisons that help you view compositions in a new light.

The first volume in the series is called **Bach and Before**. It covers music history from early examples of Greek chant up through the masterpieces of Bach and Handel (Figure 12-21). In addition to a generous assortment of musical examples, there's a glossary that defines musical, cultural, and historical terms. As you work your way through the essay, you can enter your own notes and mark cards for later reference.

Furthermore, the chapters in Bach and Beyond are linked to a handy collector's guide, called the Catalog, that lists the musical examples in the essay. The Catalog provides complete information on the recordings along with suggestions for further listening. If you're trying to assemble a collection of noteworthy recordings, this is a valuable resource.

The second volume in the series is called **The Classical Ideal**. It's a six-chapter essay that picks up where the first volume leaves off and continues through the works of Haydn and Mozart. The other titles are **Beethoven and Beyond, Romantic Heights**, and **Here and Now**.

FIGURE 12-21

Bach and Before

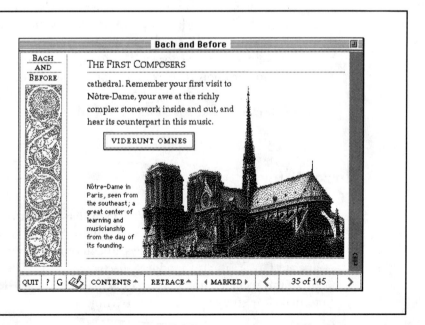

Modern Music

MAC

If you've ever wondered what impact electronic music technology has had on 20th century composition, Voyager offers an excellent way to find out. **All My Hummingbirds Have Alibis** is a CD-ROM featuring the music of Morton Subotnick, one of this country's foremost composers. The work—which premiered in 1992—is inspired by the collage novels of surrealist artist Max Ernst and explores in musical terms the love and tensions between men and women.

The music is written for MIDI keyboard, MIDI mallets, flute, cello, and computer (it also includes some vocal sounds). As the music plays you view images and text from Ernst's novel *A Little Girl Dreams of Taking the Veil* (Figure 12-22). You can also include the composer's comments as the images appear. Or optionally, you can view Subotnick's modern-looking score in its entirety.

If you want to learn more about how the composition was created, the program offers several options. The section called About The Music provides brief explanations describing how Subotnick structured the 17-part work and how he treated text, harmony, melody, and rhythm. You can also learn about interactive logic and the role that the computer played in the piece. And finally, you can learn how Subotnick used digital signal processing, synthetic sounds (FM and sampled), and other sounds.

FIGURE 12-22

Morton Subotnick's

All My

Hummingbirds

Have Alibis is

based on the

surrealist works of

Max Ernst

Elsewhere on the disc you can listen to audio clips of the composer sharing his thoughts on the creative process and his use of technology in composing music. You can even read comments from the programmer and the recording engineer.

The Voyager disc also includes a second work called *5 Scenes from an Imaginary Ballet*. This piece, derived from Hummingbirds, was composed by Subotnick especially for the CD-ROM medium. It uses images and text from the Ernst novel to create multimedia "chamber music" for CD-ROM.

All That Jazz

PC

MAC

If you've always wanted to learn more about jazz but you didn't know where to start, Compton's NewMedia has the answer. Its CD-ROM entitled **Jazz: A Multimedia History** teaches you about the evolution of jazz from 1923 to 1991. Based on the Prentice-Hall book *Jazz: From Its Origins to the Present,* this CD is itself a kind of textbook on jazz, but with a big difference.

Aside from the text, there are more than 120 musical examples totaling over 60 minutes of audio. You get to hear recordings from such legendary greats as Duke Ellington, Ella Fitzgerald, Charlie Parker, and Miles Davis.

And that's not all. There are also several video clips (totaling about 30 minutes), including some memorable fragments from jazz history—like Louis Armstrong's first European tour in 1933 or Billie Holiday singing "Fine and Mellow." In addition to the music and video clips, the CD also provides numerous still photographs.

The structure of Jazz: A Multimedia History is quite simple. From the Table of Contents you can choose to read the text, view the pictures (photos or videos), or listen to the music.

Most people will want to begin by reading the text, which does an excellent job of covering jazz history. Some chapters explore various styles, such as early jazz, swing, bebop, cool, and fusion. Other chapters focus on prominent artists like Charlie Parker, Miles Davis, and John Coltrane (Figure 12-23).

Throughout the 24 chapters of text, you'll also find lots of small icons that you can click to play sections of music. The musical examples include numerous MIDI files that re-create famous solos and improvisations to illustrate important points in the text. These are often accompanied by the written notation so you can analyze the music in detail. You can export the same MIDI files to your sequencer to experiment with them and to study them further. Or you might even try playing along. There are also 16 CD audio recordings that you can play with a standard CD player.

If you choose to play the musical examples without the text you can arrange the pieces by artist's name, song title, date, or by order in the text.

FIGURE 12-23

A page from Jazz:

A Multimedia

History

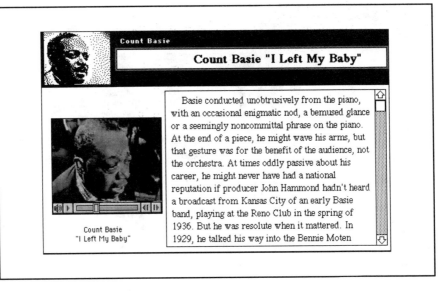

Figure 12-23 A page from Jazz: A Multimedia History

Other features include a guide for listening to jazz, a glossary of jazz terms, a bibliography, a discography, and a list of special musical symbols used in notating jazz.

6 0s Rock

Fans of 60s rock music can now use their computers to learn more about the music and the performers from that pivotal era in rock history. By combining images and text with high-quality recordings, CD-ROMs capture the nostalgia while providing new insight into the music of that period.

One such disc comes from a collaborative effort between Opcode Interactive and Time Warner Interactive. Entitled **Woodstock: 25th Anniversary CD-ROM**, it's based on "Woodstock," the award-winning film from Michael Wadleigh. The interactive CD includes text, photos, colorful graphics, and video clips from the film to recapture the mood of the three-day festival (Figure 12-24). The musical offerings consist of eight songs from such notables as The Who; Jefferson Airplane; Crosby, Stills & Nash; Country Joe & the Fish; and Janis Joplin.

You can listen to the music while photos appear randomly on-screen, or you can display the lyrics if you want to sing along. You can also find out more about the artists, view their album covers, and learn about the backstage activities.

Want to know more about the Beatles? Well here's your chance. **A Hard Day's Night** from Voyager includes the entire 90-minute black-and-white Beatles film directed by Richard Lester. This QuickTime version of the 1964

PC

MAC

MAC

FIGURE 12-24

Woodstock: 25th

Anniversary

CD-ROM

■

movie shows the group at the peak of its popularity after its first visit to the United States. Aside from the film, you also get the complete script, an essay about the Beatles and their music by film historian Bruce Eder, the theatrical trailer, and clips from Richard Lester's other films (Figure 12-25).

FIGURE 12-25

A Hard Day's

Night provides lots

of information

about the film and

its music

■

The music consists of 12 classic Beatles songs, including "Can't Buy Me Love," "All My Loving," "I Should Have Known Better," and other memorable hits. The commentaries that accompany the songs offer fascinating insight into the music industry and the performers of the time. If you enjoy early Beatles music, you'll love this CD-ROM.

Conclusion

As you can see, the concept of music education encompasses a wide range of knowledge, and perhaps an equally wide range of skills. The great thing about computers is that they're always there waiting to impart some new understanding. And they'll teach you new skills at whatever pace you require—even if you have to go over the same material 12 times in a row. Computers never get bored, they're never judgmental, and they don't get impatient. In other words, they make terrific teachers. Furthermore, with the advent of multimedia we can all study music in ways that have never before been possible. All it takes is the right software, some time to study, and a little motivation.

APPENDIX A

Glossary

accidental   In music notation, a sharp, flat, or natural that appears in front of a note.

ADSR   Abbreviation for *attack, decay, sustain, release*; a typical envelope configuration.

Aftertouch   A MIDI continuous-controller message that indicates how hard a synthesizer key is pressed after it is played but before it is released.

AIFF   Abbreviation for *Audio Interchange File Format*, a standard audio file format supported by Macintosh and Windows applications.

algorithm   A set of digital instructions used by a computer to perform a specific task or operation. In FM synthesis, algorithms define the relationships between carrier waveforms and modulator waveforms.

aliasing   A type of digital distortion caused when the sampling rate is too low to adequately capture all of the frequencies in a sound.

amplitude   The strength or intensity of a sound or audio signal.

analog-to-digital converter   A circuit that changes the continuously-fluctuating voltages of an analog audio signal into a series of numbers. Abbreviated as *A/D converter* or *ADC*.

analog   In audio terms, a type of electrical signal whose frequency and amplitude vary continuously in direct relation to the original acoustic sound wave that it represents.

arpeggio   A chord whose notes are played in succession rather than simultaneously.

attack   The initial part of a sound.

bit   A binary digit, represented by a value of either 0 or 1.

bar line   A vertical line drawn through a staff or staves to mark off measures.

beam   A thick line joining the stems on a group of notes to replace their individual flags.

beat   A regularly occurring pulse or unit of rhythm.

CD-ROM   Abbreviation for *compact disc, read-only memory*. A laser-encoded disc that stores large amounts of data for personal computers.

channel   One of the 16 discrete data paths that MIDI uses to send and receive messages.

chord   Three or more notes that sound together.

clef   A symbol that indicates the names of the lines and spaces on a staff.

clipping   A type of digital audio distortion caused by recording at too high a level.

continuous controller   A type of MIDI message—usually generated by a wheel, lever, or slider—that represents a continually changing aspect of a performance. Continuous controller messages are mainly used to add expressiveness to MIDI music. Also, a device—such as a wheel or lever—that is used to generate continually varying MIDI data.

crescendo   A section of music that gradually grows louder.

cycle   A single complete vibration or oscillation of an object.

daisy chain   A network in which data flows from one device to another in succession.

DAT   Acronym for *digital audio tape*; a recording medium that uses a small cassette—much like a miniature video cassette—to store sounds in a digital format.

dB   Abbreviation for *decibel*—a unit for measuring sound level differences.

decay   A decrease in a sound's loudness; also the part of a typical amplitude envelope immediately following the attack.

digital   In audio terms, using numerical values in discreet steps to represent the continuously varying voltages of an audio signal.

digital-to-analog converter   A circuit that changes digital data into a continuously fluctuating voltage. Commonly abbreviated as *D/A converter* or *DAC*.

digitize   To convert an audio signal from analog to digital format.

dynamics   Changes of loudness within a musical context.

dynamic range   The difference between the loudest and softest sounds that a device can accurately record and/or reproduce.

enharmonic   A term used in describing notes having different names, but producing the same pitch (e.g., C-sharp and D-flat).

envelope   A shape that represents the changes in a sound's amplitude (or other parameter) over time.

EQ   Abbreviation for *equalization.*

equalization   The selective alteration of an audio signal's frequency spectrum.

FFT   Abbreviation for *Fast Fourier Transform,* a type of 3-D audio spectrum display that shows how the amplitudes of a sound's different frequencies change over time.

filter   A device or circuit that removes or reduces certain frequencies in an audio signal.

flat   A symbol that lowers a pitch by a half step. Also: sounding lower than the desired pitch.

FM synthesis   Abbreviation for *frequency modulation synthesis*—a method of generating complex sounds wherein simple waveforms, called carriers, are affected by other simple waveforms, called modulators.

frequency   The number of times that an object vibrates (or oscillates) per second; expressed in hertz (Hz).

fundamental   The first and lowest harmonic of a sound.

General MIDI   A subset of the MIDI Specification that defines a set of standards for "consumer-level" MIDI instruments. Among other things, General MIDI compatibility requires the presence of 128 instrument sounds in a particular arrangement. It also requires a set of drum sounds assigned to specific MIDI notes.

grand staff   Two staves—one with a treble clef and one with a bass clef—linked together in parallel to form a single continuous staff.

harmonic   One of the simple sine-wave components of a complex waveform. A harmonic's frequency is a whole-number multiple of the fundamental frequency.

hertz   The unit of measurement for frequency, abbreviated Hz. 1Hz equals 1 cycle per second.

Hz   Abbreviation for *hertz*.

interval   The distance between two pitches.

key   The main tonal center (and corresponding scale) to which a composition's notes are related.

kHz   Abbreviation for *kilohertz*. 1kHz equals 1,000 cycles per second.

layering   Playing two or more sounds simultaneously. Also, triggering two or more different sounds from a single synthesizer key.

ledger lines   Small horizontal lines that appear above or below a staff to extend its range.

loop   To repeat a passage of recorded music two or more times. Also, to repeat a section of a recorded sound several times to extend its duration.

measure   The area on a staff between two bar lines.

meter   The grouping of beats into measures based on the underlying pulses in a piece of music.

metronome   An adjustable device that supplies a steady ticking sound as a reference when practicing or recording music.

MIDI   (Pronounced "middy") an acronym for *Musical Instrument Digital Interface*; a digital communications protocol and set of hardware standards that allow electronic instruments and computers to communicate with one another.

MIDI interface   A hardware device that converts MIDI messages into and out of a data format that a computer can understand.

mixer   An electronic circuit or device that combines two or more audio signals.

monophonic   Capable of playing only one note at a time.

multitimbral   (Pronounced "multy-tambrul") capable of producing several different instrument sounds at once.

natural   A symbol that appears in front of a note indicating that it is to be played neither sharp nor flat.

note   The symbol for, or the sound of, a particular musical pitch.

Nyquist limit   A frequency—equal to one half of the sampling rate— representing the highest frequency that you can record digitally without causing aliasing.

octave   An interval between two pitches where one is twice the frequency of the other. In music notation, both notes will have the same letter name.

oscillator   An electronic circuit, or the software equivalent, that produces audio signals.

overdub   A recording mode wherein new material is added to a pre-existing recording without erasing the original material.

overtone   Another term for a harmonic above the fundamental.

partial   Another term for harmonic.

patch   A group of parameter settings that produces a specific synthesized sound. Also known as a *program, timbre,* or *voice.*

pitch   How low or high a sound is within a musical context; related to frequency.

Pitch Bend   A type of MIDI continuous-controller message—typically sent from a wheel or lever—that momentarily raises or lowers the frequency of a sound.

polyphonic   Capable of playing more than one note at a time.

PPQN   Abbreviation for *pulses (or parts) per quarter note.* The unit of measurement that describes a sequencer's resolution. Also known as *ticks* or *clocks per quarter note.*

Program Change   A MIDI message that tells a synthesizer to change from one instrument sound to another.

punch-in   A recording mode wherein a section of music (between two specified points) is replaced by new material without erasing the music before or after the designated section.

quantization noise   A form of distortion that occurs when the digital translation of a sound doesn't closely match the original analog signal.

quantize   To correct the rhythmic irregularities in a passage of sequenced music by moving notes to the nearest division of a beat.

release   The final part of a sound's envelope, during which time the amplitude typically returns to zero.

rest   A period of silence within a piece of music.

reverb   Short for *reverberation*; an audio effect that re-creates the multiple sound reflections that occur within various acoustic environments.

rhythm   The patterns formed by the combination of note durations within a metrical context.

sample   A digitally recorded sound.

sampler   An electronic instrument that digitally records sounds and lets you play them back from a keyboard.

sampling rate   In a digital audio device, the rate at which the incoming audio signal is examined to produce numbers representing its instantaneous amplitude levels. The higher the sampling rate, the higher the sound quality.

sequencer   A software application or hardware device that records performance data in the form of MIDI messages.

scale A series of notes, and the intervals between them, that form the basis of a musical piece.

score Music notation that shows all of the parts in an ensemble at once. Also, to write music for a film, video, or similar project.

sharp A symbol that raises a note by a half step. Also, sounding higher than the desired pitch.

sine wave A simple periodic waveform that results from a single frequency with no overtones.

slave A device that responds to incoming data.

SMPTE (Pronounced "simpty") acronym for Society of Motion Picture and Television Engineers.

SMPTE timecode A timing reference—based on hours, minutes, seconds, and frames—used in film, video, and audio applications.

sound module A synthesizer or sampler without an attached keyboard. It requires input from an external MIDI device to produce its sounds.

split To divide the range of a MIDI keyboard (or other controller) into different sections each of which controls a different instrument or sound. Also, the point at which this division occurs.

staff The five horizontal lines, and the spaces between them, upon which music is written.

Standard MIDI File A universal MIDI file format that most sequencers can import and export.

step time   To record music into a sequencer one note (or chord) at a time.

stripe   To record timecode onto a tape.

sustain   The part of a sound's envelope (preceding the release) where the amplitude remains constant.

synthesizer   An electronic musical instrument that generates complex wave-forms using audio signal-processing circuitry.

SysEx   Abbreviation for *System Exclusive*.

System Exclusive   A special kind of MIDI data that applies only to one specific brand of instrument.

tempo   The speed at which a piece of music is performed.

timbre   (Pronounced "tambur") the characteristic that distinguishes one sound from another at the same pitch and loudness. Also called tone color, it is the result of each sound's unique combination of harmonics.

timecode   A timing reference used to synchronize music to film and video.

time signature   A symbol consisting of two numbers that indicate how many beats occur in each measure and which note duration represents one beat.

transpose   To shift the notes in a piece up or down to another pitch or key.

unison   Two notes sounding at the same pitch.

Velocity   A MIDI message that indicates how hard a note is played or released. Often used to control the volume of notes.

waveform   The graphic representation of a sound wave showing amplitude along the vertical axis and time along the horizontal axis.

WAVE   A standard soundfile format (abbreviated .WAV) for Windows applications.

watt   The unit of measurement used to indicate an amount of electrical or acoustic power.

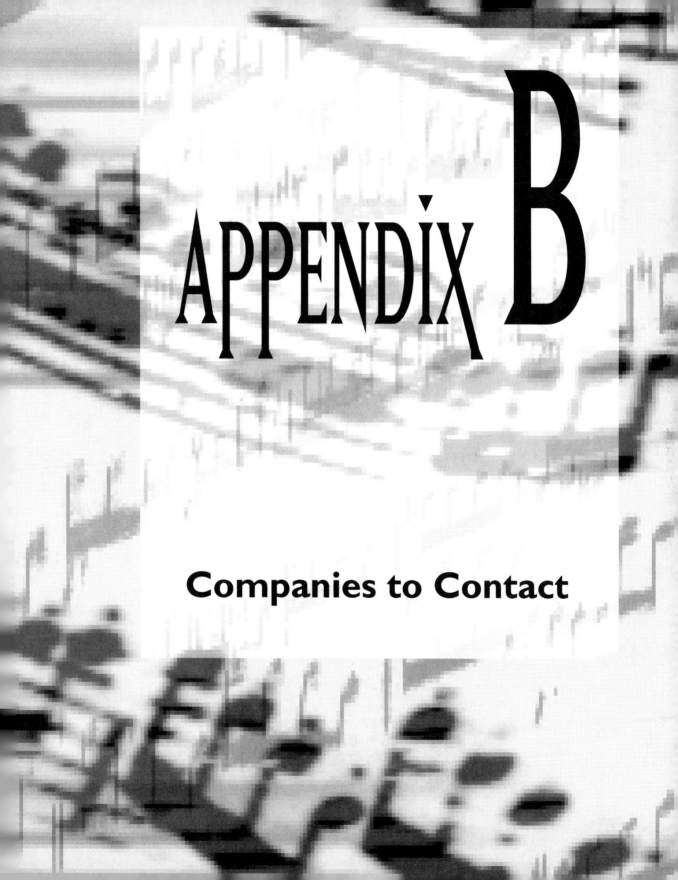

APPENDIX B

Companies to Contact

Advanced Gravis Computer Technology Ltd.
7400 MacPherson Ave., Suite 111
Burnaby, BC, Canada, V5J 5B6
(800) 663-8558
(604) 431-5020

Advent Speakers
(a division of: International Jensen Inc.)
25 Tri-State International Office Center, Suite 400
Lincolnshire, IL 60069
(708) 317-3700

Apple Computer, Inc.
20525 Mariani Ave.
Cupertino, CA 95014
(800) 776-2333
(408) 996-1010

Akai Professional
P.O. Box 2344
Fort Worth, TX 76102
(817) 336-5114

Alesis Corporation
3630 Holdrege Ave.
Los Angeles, CA 90016
(800) 5-ALESIS
(310) 558-4530

Altech Lansing Consumer Products
P.O. Box 277
Milford, PA 18337
(800) 648-6663
(717) 296-4434

Big Noise Software, Inc.
P.O. Box 23740
Jacksonville, FL 32241
(904) 730-0754

Broderbund Software, Inc.
500 Redwood Blvd.
Novato, CA 94948
(800) 521-6263
(415) 382-4400

Coda Music Technology
6210 Bury Drive
Eden Prairie, MN 55346
(800) 843-2066
(612) 937-9611

Compton's NewMedia
2320 Camino Vida Roble
Carlsbad, CA 92009
(619) 929-2500

Creative Labs, Inc.
1901 McCarthy Blvd.
Milpitas, CA 95035
(408) 428-6600

Digidesign
1360 Willow Road
Menlo Park, CA 94025
(415) 688-0600

Dr.T's Music Software
124 Crescent Road
Needham, MA 02194
(617) 455-1454

Dynaware USA, Inc.
950 Tower Lane, Suite 1150
Foster City, CA 94404
(415) 349-5700

E-mu Systems
P.O. Box 660015
Scotts Valley, CA 95067
(408) 438-1921

Fatar Srl
Distrib: Music Industries Corp.
99 Tulip Ave.
Floral Park, NY
(516) 352-4110

ForeFront Technology
Distrib: Music Industries Corp.
99 Tulip Ave.
Floral Park, NY
(516) 352-4110

Howling Dog Systems
Kanata North P.O. Box 72071
Kanata, ON, Canada K2K 2P4
(800) 267-HOWL
(613) 599-7927

International MIDI Association
23634 Emelita St.
Woodland Hills, CA 91367
(818) 598-0088

JLCooper Electronics
12500 Beatrice St.
Los Angeles, CA 90066
(310) 306-4131

Jump! Software, Inc.
201 San Antonio Circle, Suite 172
Mountain View, CA 94040
(415) 917-7460

KAT, Inc.
53 First Ave.
Chicopee, MA 01020
(413) 594-7466

Key Electronic, Inc.
7515 Chapel Ave.
Fort Worth, TX 76116
(800) 533-MIDI
(817) 560-1912

Korg USA, Inc.
89 Frost St.
Westbury, NY 11590
(800) 645-3188
(516) 333-9100

Kurzweil Music Systems
(Young Chang America, Inc.)
13336 Alondra Blvd.
Cerritos, CA 90701
(310) 926-3200

Labtec Enterprises, Inc.
11010 N.E. 37th Circle, Unit 110
Vancouver, WA 98682
(206) 896-2000

Macromedia
600 Townsend
San Francisco, CA 94103
(415) 252-2118

Mark of the Unicorn, Inc.
1280 Massachusetts Ave.
Cambridge, MA 02138
(617) 576-2760

MiBAC Music software
P.O. Box 468
Northfield, MN 55057
(507) 645-5851

Microsoft Corporation
One Microsoft Way
Redmond, WA 98052
(800) 426-9400
(206) 882-8080

Midiman
236 W. Mountain St., Suite 108
Pasadena, CA 91103
(818) 449-8838

Midisoft Corporation
P.O. Box 1000
Bellevue, WA 98009
(206) 881-7176

SynchroVoice
Distrib: MidiVox Marketing
1237 Cedar Post Ln., #A3
Houston, TX 77055
(800) 433-6434

Monster Cable Products, Inc.
274 Wattis Way
South San Francisco, CA 94080
(415) 871-6000

Multimedia PC Marketing Council
1730 M Street, NW, Suite 707
Washington, DC 20036
(202) 452-1600

Musicator A/S
P.O. Box 16026
Oakland, CA 94610
(510) 251-2500

Music Quest, Inc.
1700 Alma Drive, Suite 330
Plano, TX 75075
(214) 881-7408

Opcode Systems, Inc.
3950 Fabian Way, Suite 100
Palo Alto, CA 94303
(415) 856-3333

OSC
480 Potrero
San Francisco, CA 94110
(415) 252-0367

Passport Designs, Inc.
100 Stone Pine Road
Half Moon Bay, CA 94019
(415) 726-0280

PG Music, Inc.
266 Elmwood Ave., Suite 111
Buffalo, NY 14222
(800) 268-6272
(905) 528-2368

Roland Corporation US
7200 Dominion Circle
Los Angeles, CA 90040
(213) 685-5141

Society of Motion Picture and Television Engineers
595 W. Hartsdale Ave.
White Plains, NY 10607
(914) 761-1100

Software Toolworks
60 Leveroni Court
Novato, CA 94949
(800) 234-3088
(415) 883-3000

Sonic Foundry
1110 East Gorham St.
Madison, WI 53703
(608) 256-3133

Soundtrek
3384 Hill Drive, Suite E
Duluth, GA 30136
(404) 623-0879

Steinberg/Jones
17700 Raymer St., Suite 1001
Northridge, CA 91325
(818) 993-4091

Time Warner Interactive
2210 W. Olive Ave.
Burbank, CA 91506
(818) 295-6600

Turtle Beach Systems
52 Grumbacher Road
York, PA 17402
(717) 767-0204

Twelve Tone Systems
44 Pleasant St.
P.O. Box 760
Watertown, MA 02272
(800) 234-1171
(617) 926-2480

WaveAccess
P.O. Box 4667
Berkeley, CA 94704
(800) 697-8823
(510) 526-5881

Voyager Company
1 Bridge St.
Irvington, NY 10533
(800) 443-2001

Voyetra Technologies
5 Odell Plaza
Yonkers, NY 10701
(800) 233-9377
(914) 966-0600

Yamaha Corporation of America
P.O. Box 6600
Buena Park, CA 90620
(714) 522-9011

Zeta Music Systems, Inc.
2230 Livingston St.
Oakland, CA 94606
(800) 622-6434
(510) 261-1702

INDEX

A

Accidentals (in notation), 24, 278

Accompaniment backup band, 249-253

Acoustics, 234-236

Additive synthesis, 76

Address list (manufacturers), 414-421

ADSR envelope, 21-22

Advanced integrated synthesis, 80

Advent Powered Partners 570 speakers, 120

Aftertouch control, 44

Aftertouch-sensitive keyboards, 44

AIFF files, 311

Akai EW13000, 95

Akai MX1000, 94

Alesis ADAT, 109

Algorithms, waveform, 76

Alias frequency, 304

Aliasing, 304-309

All My Hummingbirds Have Alibis (Voyager), 393

Altech Lansing ACS 300.1, 120

Alto clef, 277

Amplitude (recording), 17-18
  ADSR envelope, 21-22
  changing, 316-318

Analog recording, 300-301

Analog synthesis, 77

Analog synthesizers, 77, 100

Analog-to-digital converter (ADC), 301

Anti-aliasing filter, 307

Atonal composition, 28

Attack (amplitude), 21, 221-222

Attack time (amplitude), 21

Audio, digital. *See* Digital audio

Audio editing
  adding reverb, 321-323
  changing soundfile formats, 320
  changing the volume, 316-318
  destructive and nondestructive, 325
  playing a sound backwards, 318-320
  sequencer capabilities, 132-141
  setting recording levels, 313-314
  smoothing a waveform, 324
  trimming silence, 314-316

Audio editors (audio editing programs), 312-339. *See also* Audio editing

Audion vacuum tube, 28

B

Bach and Before (Voyager), 392

Backup band, 249-253

Ballade (Dynaware), 203-209

Band-in-a-Box (PG Music), 249-252

Bar line, 26

Bars/measures, 26

Bass, 17

Bass clef, 24, 277

Beaming, cross-staff, 276-277

Beams (note), 26

Beethoven, 386, 389-390

Biosensor, 105

Biowaves, 107

Brahms, 389-391

Brass instruments, orchestrating, 231

Buchla Electronic Music System, 31-32

C

Cakewalk Home Studio (TwelveTone Systems), 186

Cakewalk Professional (TwelveTone Systems), 179-186

CAL (Cakewalk Application Language), 186

Carriers (waveforms), 76

CD-quality sound, 311

Change Gain command (audio editors), 317

Channel Mode messages, 50

Channel Pressure, 44

Channels, MIDI, 49-50, 63-64, 126-127

Chord symbols, 278-279

Chord tones, 224-225

Chords, 25

Chorus, 323

Chromatic scale, 25

Claire (Opcode Systems), 371-372

Clarinet registers, 78

Classical music styles, learning about, 380-382

Clefs, 23-24, 277

Clipping, 314
Clocks, MIDI, 108-109
Close voicing, 225-226
Columbia-Princeton
   Electronic Music Center, 30
Company address list, 414-421
Compatibility, 51-57
Complex waveform, 20
Composer Quest (Opcode
   Interactive), 379-380
Composers
   historical patronage of, 4
   learning about, 379-380
   music of famous, 386-391
Composing
   access to, 4-5
   atonal, 28
   opportunities for, 5-7
   with a sequencer vs. paper,
      133
Compression rates, recording,
   311
Computer-music labs, 10
Computers, choosing, 60-62
ConcertWare (Jump!
   Software), 291-294
Continuous controller, 44, 402
Controllers, 48. *See also*
   Guitar controllers;
   Keyboard controllers;
   Mind controllers; Pedal
   controllers; Percussion
   controllers; String
   controllers; Vocal
   controllers; Wind
   controllers
Counter (sequencer), 127-128
Count-off, 129-130
Crescendo, 272
Crests (sound wave), 16
Cross-staff beaming, 276-277
Cubase Audio (Steinberg),
   174-175, 348-351
Cubase Lite, 179
Cubase Score, 174-175
Cubase (Steinberg), 169-179
Cycle (waveform), 16
Cycles-per-second (cps), 16

D

Daisy chaining, 112
DAT (digital audio tape)
   recorders, 298
Decay (amplitude), 21
Decibels (dBs), 17-18
Deck II (OSC), 9, 355-358
Desktop music workstations,
   32
Desktop musician
   access, 4-5
   opportunities, 5-10
Desktop speakers, 115-120
Destructive editing, 325
Diatonic scales, 24
Digital audio, 297-339
   combining with MIDI,
      341-361
   introduction to, 300-309
   playback process, 309-310
   recording, 310-325
Digital Delay, 322
Digital meters, 313
Digital Performer (Mark of
   the Unicorn), 351-354
Digital recording, 9, 301-302
Digital-to-analog converter
   (DAC), 75, 309
Digitization, 302
DIP switches, 69
Doubling, 220-222
Downsampling, 320
Drivers, speaker, 116-117
Drop-frame, 111
Drum machines, 88-90,
   102-103, 246-249
Drum pads, 101
Drum triggers, 101-102
DrumKAT EZ, 102-103
DrumKAT 3.5, 102
Duration (note), 25-26
DX7 synthesizer (Yamaha),
   49, 76
Dynamic voice allocation, 84

E

Ear, sound capture in, 16
Echo, 322
Editing. *See* Audio editing
Educational software, 7,
   363-397
Efficiency (amplifier), 117
Electronic Age, 28
Electronic instruments. *See*
   MIDI instruments
Electronic music, development
   of, 27-32
Encore (Passport Designs), 8,
   287-290
Enharmonic equivalents, 24
Ensembles
   creating, 232-233
   writing for, 5
Envelope, sound, 21-22
Envelope generator, 21
Equal temperament system, 25
Equalization (audio editors),
   321
Equalizers, graphic and
   parametric, 321-322
Event lists, sequencer, 133-134
Expanding your system,
   112-113
EZ Vision (Opcode Systems),
   167-170

F

Fade commands (audio
   editors), 317-318
Faders, on-screen, 115
Faders windows, sequencer,
   137
Fatar MP-1 pedalboard,
   106-107
Fatar Studio 2001, 94
FFT (Fast Fourier Transform)
   display, 324
Files, sound. *See* Soundfiles
Finale Allegro (Coda
   Software), 284

Finale (Coda Software), 280-283
Finger-noise (guitar), 306
First harmonic, 18
Flags (note), 22, 25-26
Flanging, 323
Flats, 24-25
Flute, 306
FM (frequency modulation) synthesis, 49, 76
Fonts, notation, 272
Foot controller, 48
Footswitch units, 100
Fourier analysis, 20-21
FreeStyle (Mark of the Unicorn), 261-264
Frequency, sound, 16-18
Frequency response, 117-118, 304
Front-panel patch cords, 100
FSK (frequency-shift keying), 109
FT5 MIDI Thru box (ForeFront Technology), 114
Fundamental frequency, 18

G

Gain Adjust command (audio editors), 317
Galaxy Plus Editors (Opcode Systems), 168-169
Games, music in, 6-7
General MIDI,
    specification/standard, 46, 82, 404
    file format, 53-57
    Instrument Patch Map, 54-55
    Percussion Key Map, 56
    symbol for compatible instruments, 57
Glossary of terms in this book, 399-410
Grand staff, 23-24
Graphic equalizer, 321-322
Groove, 153

GS/SC7 Controller (Dynaware), 209
Guitar controllers, 97-99
Guitar finger noise, 306
Guitar fretboard diagrams, 278-279
Guitar tabulature, 273

H

Hammond organ, 30
Handwritten scores vs. notation programs, 275
Hard Day's Night, A (Voyager), 395-397
Harmonic series, 19, 224
Harmonics, 18-19
Heads, note, 274
Hearing, threshold of, 18
Hertz (Hz), 16
High pitch, 17
Hi-hats, 101
Homophonic music, 28
Hybrid synthesis, 80-81

I

IBM PC interfaces, 64-69
    entry-level, 65-66
    IRQs and I/O, 67, 69
    mid- and pro-level, 65, 67
IBM PC vs. Mac, 61
Instrument Patch Map, 54-55
Instruments, 3 (*see also* MIDI instruments)
    noises of, 306
    virtual, 6
Interactive Phrase Synthesizer (IPS), 176-177
Intervals, 23
Invert command (audio editors), 319-320
I/O, PC, 67, 69
IRQs (interrupts), 67, 69

J

Jam Factory (Dr. T's Music Software), 243-246
Jammer, The (Soundtrek), 256-258
Jazz groups, 232
Jazz Guitarist, The (PG Music), 375
Jazz: A Multimedia History (Compton's), 394-395
Jazz Pianist, The (PG Music), 375-376
Jazz swing style, 268-269
JLCooper MacNexus, 71
JLCooper SyncLink, 73
JMSC (Japan MIDI Standards Committee), 47

K

Key Electronics MS-124, 68
Key signatures, 25, 277-278
Keyboard controllers, 90-93, 98
Keyboard input, 226-227
Keyboard range, 91
Keyboard splits, 41-42
Keypress pressure data, 44
Keys, weighted vs. unweighted, 92
Korg M1 synthesizer, 80
Kurzweil K2000 sampler, 78
KX-88 (Yamaha), 94

L

Layering, 36, 220
Learning
    about classical music styles, 380-382
    about composers, 379-380
    about modern music, 393-394
    about music, 376-378
    about music history, 391-392

about music instruments, 384-386
about the orchestra, 382-384
piano, 372-374
Ledger lines (staff), 23
Legato, 229
Line mixer, 114
Linear/arithmetic (L/A) synthesis, 80
Linear-oriented sequencer, 140-141
Live musicians, working with, 7-9
Longitudinal Time Code (LTC), 111
Loop recording, 131-132
Looping (sound samples), 79
Loudness, 17-18
vs. pitch, 219-220
varying, 224
Low pitch, 17
Low-pass filter, 307-309
Lyrics in music scores, 279

M

Mac vs. PC, 61
Macintosh interfaces, 69-72
entry-level, 70-71
mid- and pro-level, 70, 72
Major scale, 24
MalletKAT PRO, 104
Manufacturers' address list, 414-421
Marimba, 104
Masking, 219
Master synth, 38
Master Tracks Pro (Passport Designs), 155-161
Maximum polyphony, 83-84
Measures/bars, 26
Media Control Interface (MCI) files, 181
Melisma, 279
Merging MIDI data, 64
Messages, MIDI, 41-48
Meta-events, 52
Meters, 26, 278

Metro (OSC), 186-193, 356
Metronome markings, 27
Metronome (sequencer), 129-130
MFS-40 footswitch unit, 100
MiBAC Jazz, 253-256
MiBAC Music Lessons, 366-367
Middle C, 23-24
MIDI (Musical Instrument Digital Interface), 35-57
birth of, 36-37
combining with digital audio, 341
In port, 38-39
orchestra, 40
Out port, 38-39
plugs, 38
ports, 38-39
serial interface, 37
spontaneous, 239-265
Thru box, 113-114
Thru port, 38-39, 112
MIDI channels, 63-64
MIDI Clocks, 108-109
MIDI devices, 41
MIDI Express (Mark of the Unicorn), 68, 73
MIDI faders, 115
MIDI files, sharing, 53. See also Soundfiles
MIDI instruments, 40, 74-81
multitimbral, 83-84
orchestrating with, 217-236
MIDI interfaces, 63-74
MIDI keyboard controllers, 90-93, 98
MIDI Kit (Midisoft), 203
MIDI lag, 112-113
MIDI MaxPak programs, 198
MIDI messages, 41-48
MIDI patchbays, 113
MIDI Specification, 37
MIDI systems, 39, 59-120
MIDI Time Piece II, 68, 73
Midiman MiniMacman and Macman, 71
Midiman MM-401, 66

Midiman Portman PC/S and PC/P, 66
MidiVox (SynchroVoice), 105
Midrange driver, 116
Mind controllers, 106-107
Minimoog, 31
Minor scale, 24
Miracle Piano Teaching System, The, 372-374
Mixers, 114-115
Mixtur Trautonium, 29
MMA (MIDI Manufacturers Association), 47
Mock ups, soundtrack, 8
Modern music, learning about, 393-394
Modes, MIDI, 50-51
Modulation controller, 48
Modulators (waveforms), 76
Monitors, choosing, 62
Monophonic music, 28, 82
Monster Cable MacSpeaker/Persona PC, 120
Moog synthesizer, 31
Morpheus (E-mu Systems), 81-82
Morphing, waveform, 81
Mosaic (Mark of the Unicorn), 284-286
Mouse input, 241-243
Movie soundtracks, 8, 29, 111
Movies, aliasing in, 305-309
Mozart, 386-389, 391
MPC standard, 61, 299, 311
MP-1 pedalboard (Fatar), 106-107
MPU-401 (MIDI Processing Unit), 64-65
Mr. Drumstix' Music Studio, 367-369
Multimedia, opportunities in, 6
Multimedia PC (MPC) standard, 61, 299, 311
Multiport capability, 63
Multiport MIDI interface, 113
Multisampling, 78
MultiSound Monterey (Turtle Beach Systems), 87-88

Multitimbral instruments, 83-84
Multitimbral sound module, 84
Multitrack tape recorder, 109-110
Music, nature of, 13-32
Music education, 363-397
Music history, learning, 391-392
Music manuscripts. *See* Notation
Music Mentor (Midisoft), 380-382
Music Mouse (Laurie Spiegel), 241-243
Musical Instruments (Microsoft), 384-386
Musical World of Professor Piccolo, The, 376-378
Musicator Win (Musicator A/S), 209-215
Musicians, working with, 7-9
Musicians (desktop), 4-10
Musicshop (Opcode Systems), 115, 169, 171
MusicTime (Passport Designs), 290
Musique concrete, 30
Mute command (audio editor), 315
Muting (MIDI data), 64
Myst (Broderbund), 7

Natural harmonic series, 19, 224
Natural minor scale, 24
Noise
    of computer components, 312
    good and bad, 306
    of instruments, 306
Noise filters, 307
Nondestructive editing, 325
Normalize command, 317
Notation
    accidentals, 278

chord symbols, 278-279
clefs, 277
combining rests, 274-275
cross-staff beaming, 276-277
fonts, 272
guitar tabulature, 273
inputting, 270-271
key signatures, 277-278
lyrics, 279
meters, 278
note heads, 274
playing back, 271-272
quarter notes, 270
staves, 272-273
text, 279
time signatures, 278
triplets, 276
tuplets, 276
Notation programs, 8-9, 268-295
Notation windows, sequencer, 136-137
Note duration, 25-26
Note heads, 274
Note names, 23
Note Off message, 43
Note On message, 41-42
Note values, common, 26
Notes, 22-26
Notes in chords (voices), 225
Nyquist Limit, 307
Nyquist Theorem, 307

Octave, 23, 25
Omni Off/Mono mode, 51
Omni Off/Poly mode, 50-51
Omni On/Mono mode, 50
Omni On/Poly mode, 50
OMS (Open Music System), 161-162
Ondes Martenot, 29
One-man band, 2
On-screen faders, 115
Open voicing, 225-226
Operators (waveforms), 76

OPL-2FM synthesizer chipset (Yamaha), 87
Orchestra, The (Time Warner Interactive), 382-384
Orchestral instruments, ranges of, 226-227
Orchestration, 217-236
    acoustics and reverb, 234-236
    creating ensembles, 232-233
    guidelines for, 235
    learning about, 382-384
    seating plans, 233-234
    thinking like a player, 226-231
    variety in, 223-224
Oscillation, sound, 14
Oscillators, 75
Output low-pass filter, 309
Output sample-and-hold circuit, 309
Overtones, 19

Panning, 232-234
Parametric equalizer, 321-322
Partial frequency, 18
Patch cords, 31, 100
Patch editors, 47, 154-155
Patchbays, MIDI, 113
Patches, 31, 46-47
Pattern-oriented sequencer, 140-141
PC interfaces, 64-69
    entry-level, 65-66
    IRQs and I/O, 67, 69
    mid- and pro-level, 65, 67
PC vs. Mac, 61
PCM (pulse code modulation) synthesis, 80
PD-7 drum pads, 102
Pedal controllers, 106
Pedalboards, 106-107
Percussion controllers, 101-104
Percussion Key Map, 56

Performer (Mark of the Unicorn), 6, 111, 146-154
Periodic waveforms, 16-17
Physical modeling synthesis, 81
Pianist, The (PG Music), 375
Piano, 43, 372-374
Piano-roll display, 134-135
Pitch, 16-17, 25, 219-220
Pitch bend control, 44-45
Pitch bend wheel, 45
Pizzicato, 228
Playback, digital audio, 309-310
Player, thinking like, 226-231
Player seating, orchestrating for, 233-234
Polyphonic colors, 223-224
Polyphonic Key Pressure, 44
Polyphonic music, 28, 82
Polyphony, 82-83
Ports, MIDI, 38-39
Power Chords Pro (Howling Dog Systems), 258-261
Preset internal sound, 46
Pressure data, 44
Pressure wave, 15
Producer Pro (Passport Designs), 358-361
Program Change messages, 46, 53
Pulses (counter), 127

Q

Quantization, 138-140, 302-303
Quantization noise, 302-303, 314
Quarter notes, 270
Quartet Series (Zeta Music Systems), 99
Quintuplets, 276

R

Range, keyboard, 91
Ranges of orchestral instruments, 226-227

RCA Electronic Music Synthesizer, 30-31
Rechannelizing, 64
Recorders, 108-111
Recording (*see also* Sampling)
   analog, 300-301
   analog vs. digital, 300
   digital, 9, 301-302, 310-325
   loop, 131-132
   sequencer, 125-126, 130-131
   step-time, 131
Recording levels, setting, 313-314
Recording options, table of common, 309
Recording Session (Midisoft), 203, 381-382
Recording studios, 10, 309
Recordings, compression of, 311
Release (amplitude), 21
Release Velocity control, 43
Release Velocity sensing, 43
Resolution, 78, 127-128, 302-303
Rests (silence), 26, 274-275
RetroPaks (Zeta Music Systems), 99
Reverb, 234-236, 321-323
Reverse command (audio editors), 318-319
Rhythm, 26
Rhythm section machines, 88-90, 246-249
Rhythmicon, 29
Rock bands, orchestrating, 233
Roland A-30 and A-80, 94
Roland AX-1 keyboard controller, 98-99
Roland Compact Drum System, 102
Roland D-50 synthesizer, 80
Roland GK-2A Synthesizer Driver, 97
Roland GR-09 Guitar Synthesizer, 97
Roland GS instruments, 204

Roland MX-5 four-channel mixer, 115
Roland PAD-80 Octapad, 103-104
Roland RAP-10, 88
Roland SCC-1 synthesizer card, 72, 74, 88
Roland SC-88, 87
Roland SC-50, 85
Roland SPD-11, 103
Roland Super MPU, 68
Roland TD-7 Percussion Sound Module, 102
Routing (MIDI data), 64
RS-PCM, 80
RY30 drum machine (Yamaha), 89

S

Sample players, 79
SampleCell Editor (Digidesign), 88
SampleCell II (Digidesign), 88
Sample-and-hold circuit, 301, 307, 309
Sampler memory, 79
Samples (short digital recordings), 77-79
Sampling, 301
Sampling frequency, 79
Sampling rate, 79, 301, 303-308
Scales, 24
Scoring. *See* Notation
Scrubbing, 182
Seating, orchestra, 233-234
SeqMax (Big Noise Software), 193-199
SeqMax Presto!, 199
Sequencers
   approach to composing, 145
   Big NoiseSoftware's SeqMax, 193-199
   Cakewalk Professional for Windows, 179-186
   comparing, 143-215
   counter, 127-128

data organization, 140-141
Dynaware's Ballade, 203-209
editing capabilities of, 132-141
event lists, 133-134
faders windows, 137
features of, 144-145
FreeStyle (Mark of the Unicorn), 261-264
look and feel of, 145
Master Tracks Pro, 155-161
metronome, 129-130
Midisoft's Recording Session, 203
Midisoft's Studio for Windows, 199-203
Musicator Win, 209-215
Musicshop, 169, 171
notation windows, 136-137
Opcode Systems' EZ Vision, 167-170
Opcode Systems' Vision, 161-169
OSC's Metro, 186-193, 356
piano-roll display, 134-135
price of, 145
program compatibility, 51-57
quantizing, 138-140
recording modes, 125-126
recording with, 130-131
resolution, 127-128
specs of, 145
Steinberg's Cubase, 169-179
test driving, 146
tracks, 126-127, 354
Tracks Editor, 128
Unicorn's Performer, 146-154
working with, 123-141
Serial music, 28
Sharing MIDI files, 53
Sharps, 24-25
Signal-to-noise ratio, 303, 312
Silence, 16, 26, 314-316

Silence command (audio editor), 315
Silver Apples of the Moon, 32
Sine wave, 18
Singing improvement, 370-372
Sing-A-Long Around the World (Dr.T's Music Software), 369-370
Sing-A-Long Kids' Classics (Dr.T's Music Software), 369-370
Slave synth, 38
Smoothing a waveform, 324
SMPTE frame rates, 111
SMPTE timecode, 64, 72, 108-111
SND files, 311
So I've Heard (Voyager), 391
Sound
    creating, 20
    elements of, 16
    nature of, 13-32
    quality of, 54
Sound Blaster (Creative Labs), 87
Sound cards, 61, 86-88, 299, 308, 311
Sound Designer II (Digidesign), 326-329
Sound envelope, 21-22
Sound Forge (Sonic Foundry), 335-339
Sound modules, 81-86
Sound sources, MIDI, 74-81
Sound waves. *See* Waveforms (sound)
SoundEdit 16 (Macromedia), 332-335
Soundfiles, 299-300, 308, 311
    changing the format of, 320
    playing backwards, 318
    viewing, 324
Soundtracks, 8, 29
Speakers, desktop, 115-120
Speed issues, computer, 62
Staccato, 272
Staff. *See* Staves
Standard MIDI File (SMF) format, 51-53

Staves, 23-24, 26, 272-273, 286
Stems (note), 22, 25-26
Step-time recording, 131
Storage space for soundfiles, 308
Stravinsky, 386-388
Stretching samples, 78
String controllers, 99-100
String instruments, orchestrating, 228-230
String quartets, 232
Striping tape with timecode, 109
Studio 4 and Studio SLX (Opcode Systems), 73
Studio 2001 (Fatar), 94
Studio Vision Pro (Opcode Systems), 344-347
Studio for Windows (Midisoft), 199-203
Studying music, 363-397
Subsequences, 163
Subtractive synthesis, 76
Subwoofers, 117
Sustain (amplitude), 21
Sustain pedal controller, 48
Switched-on-Bach, 31
Synchronizing MIDI and digital audio, 354
Synthesis methods, 80-81
Synthesizers, 75-77
    analog, 100
    history of, 27-32
    internal numbering scheme, 46
System, expanding, 112-113
System Exclusive (SysEx) messages, 46-48

T

Telharmonium, 27
Tempo, 26, 129-130
Tempo map, 108
Tempo marks, 27
Tempo slider, 130
Tenor clef, 277

Terms in this book, glossary of, 399-410
Terpsitone, 29
Tessitura, 371
Text in music scores, 279
TG300 (Yamaha), 85
TG500 (Yamaha), 87
Theremin, 29
Three-way speakers, 116
Threshold of hearing, 18
Threshold of pain, 18
Timbres (sound), 18-21, 220-221
Time signatures, 26, 278
TimeBandit (Steinberg), 351
Timecode, SMPTE, 64, 72, 108-111
TMX Drum Trigger Module (Yamaha), 102
Tracks (sequencer), 126-127, 354
Transmission media, sound, 16
Trautonium, 29
Treble, 17
Treble clef, 24, 277
Tremolo, 48
Trills, 268
Trim command (audio editor), 315
Triplets, 276
Troughs (sound wave), 16
Trumpets, orchestrating, 233
Tuning fork, 14-15
Tuplets, 276, 285
Tweeters, 116
Two-way speakers, 116

U

UART (universal asynchronous receive/transmit), 64
UltraProteus (E-mu), 87
UltraSound (Advanced Gravis), 88
Unison, 23, 223
Unisyn (Mark of the Unicorn), 47, 154-155

Universal Synthesizer Interface, 37
Unweighted keys, 92
UpBeat (Dr. T's Music Software), 246-249

V

Variety in orchestration, 223-224
VAST (variable architecture synthesis technology), 80
Velocity control, 42-43
Velocity sensing, 42
Velocity sensitivity, 42
Velocity switches, 42-43
Vibraphone, 104
Vibrations, sound, 16
Vibrato, 48, 230-231
Videotape, working with, 111
Viewing a soundfile, 324
Violin, 306
Violinists, 228-229
Virtual instruments, 6
Vision (Opcode Systems), 161-169
VL-1 (Virtual Lead) synthesizer (Yamaha), 75, 81
Vocal controllers, 104-106
Voices (notes in chords), 46, 225, 272
Voicing, 224-226
Voltage-controlled oscillators (VCOs), 31, 75, 77
Volume messages/controller, 48
Volume (recording)
  changing, 316-318
  varying, 224

W

Wagon wheel effect, 305
WAVE files, 181, 311
Wave for Windows (Turtle Beach), 329-332
WaveBlaster card, 88

Waveforms (sound), 14-16
  complex, 20
  in FM synthesis, 76
  periodic, 17
  smoothing, 324
WaveRider (WaveAccess), 107
Wavetable synthesis, 80
WaveWare (WaveAccess), 107
Weighted keys, 92
Whole note, 25
Wind controllers, 95-96
Wind instruments, orchestrating, 230-231
Window dub, 111
Windows vs. Mac, 61
Windows Sound Recorder applet, 313
Woodstock: 25th Anniversary CD-ROM, 395-396
Woodwind instruments, orchestrating, 230-231
Woofers, 116
WT11 (Yamaha), 96
WX11 (Yamaha), 95-96

Y

Yamaha
  DX7 synthesizer, 49, 76
  KX-88, 94
  OPL-2FM synthesizer chipset, 87
  RY30 drum machine, 89
  TG500, 87
  TG300, 85
  TMX Drum Trigger Module, 102
  VL-1 (Virtual Lead) synthesizer, 75, 81
  WT11, 96
  WX11, 95-96
  YST-M10, 120

Z

Zeta MIDI System, 99-100
Z-plane synthesis, 81

EXTRATERRESTRIAL CONNECTIONS

THESE DAYS, ANY CONNECTION IS POSSIBLE...
WITH THE INNOVATIVE BOOKS FROM LAN TIMES AND OSBORNE/McGRAW-HILL

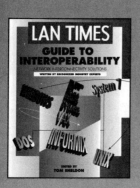

MY TOUGHEST CRITICS RIDE TRICYCLES, PLAY PATTY-CAKE, AND REFUSE TO EAT THEIR PEAS.

Hi, I'm Eric Brown. As executive editor for *NewMedia* magazine, it's my job to evaluate new multimedia technology.

As a parent, it's my job to help my kids discover the joy of learning.

The critics and their mother

That's why I've selected and reviewed the best 100 fun educational titles on the market in my new book **That's Edutainment!**

That's Edutainment! explores the new thinking behind the latest edutainment software and offers tips on building lifelong learning skills. It even includes a CD-ROM packed with try-before-you-buy software and demos.

It's not easy to get applause from media-savvy kids like Cecilia and Isabela-- not to mention their mom

ISBN: 0-07-882083-9,
400 pages, $29.95, U.S.A.
Includes one CD-ROM.

Cynthia--but **That's Edutainment!** has earned the respect from critics who really count.

That's Edutainment! A Parent's Guide to Educational Software is available now at book and computer stores. Or call toll-free 1-800-822-8158 and use your VISA, American Express, Discover, or MasterCard.

BC640SL

Draw on Our Expertise

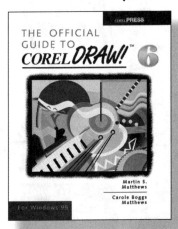

More Programming Tools on CDROM!
◆ see next page for detailed product information.

1 Please Fill Out Completely

Shipping Address
_____
Company
_____

Name
_____

Address/Mail Stop
_____

City
_____

State/Zip/Country
_____

Telephone -- with an Area and Country code.
(in case there is a question about your order)

2 Payment Method

If you are ever unsatisfied with one of our products, simply return the item with your invoice number and a short note saying what is wrong.

◆   Check enclosed. (Drawn on a United States Bank.)

◆   Please charge to my:
❑ Visa   ❑ MC   ❑ Discover   ❑ American Express

Name on Card
_____

Cardholder Signature
_____

Account #
_____

Expiration Date
_____

3 I'd Like to Order:

		Description	Price	Total
____ x	**Hobbes**	600 MB current Shareware for OS/2	$ 29.95*	Total $_____
____ x		Subscription: new every 3 months	$ 19.95*/issue	Total $_____
____ x	**CICA**	4000 new Windows™ programs	$ 29.95*	Total $_____
____ x		Subscription: you get yours first	$19.95*/issue	Total $_____
____ x	**Simtel**	Classic: 650 MB Shareware for MSDOS	$ 29.95*	Total $_____
____ x		Subscription: quarterly updates!	$19.95*/issue	Total $_____
____ x	**Space&Astronomy**	Thousands of NASA images and data files	$39.95*	Total $_____
____ x	**Giga Games**	3000 hot Games for MSDOS & Windows™	$39.95*	Total $_____
____ x	**CoC**	CDROM of CDROMs -- 4067 descriptions.	$ 39.95	Total $_____
____ x	**Libris Britannia**	DOS Scientific & Engineering with book	$ 59.95*	Total $_____
____ x	**La colección**	MSDOS/OS/2/Windows™. Spanish indexes	$ 39.95*	Total $_____
____ x	**QRZ!**	Ham Radio call sign database + files	$ 29.95*	Total $_____
____ x		Subscription: auto. new every 3 months	$ 19.95*/issue	Total $_____
____ x	**Tax Info '93**	335 IRS Tax forms & instructions	$ 39.95	Total $_____
____ x	**ClipArt**	ClipArt Cornucopia -- 5050 images	$ 39.95	Total $_____
____ x	**Fractal Frenzy**	2000 beautiful high resolution fractals	$ 39.95	Total $_____
____ x	**Travel**	202 Hi-Res US, Europe travel images	$ 39.95	Total $_____
____ x	**GIFs Galore**	5000 GIF images - all categories - no adult	$ 39.95*	Total $_____
____ x	**Gutenberg**	Project Gutenberg: classic literature, docs	$ 39.95	Total $_____
____ x		Subscription: about every 6 months	$ 24.95/issue	Total $_____
____ x	**Internet Info**	15,000 computer and Internet documents	$39.95	Total $_____
____ x	**SysV r4**	610 MB ready-to-run Unix Sys V utilities	$ 59.95*	Total $_____
____ x	**Nova**	600 MB Black Next app's, src., docs, etc.	$ 59.95*	Total $_____
____ x	**Nebula**	600 MB NeXTSTEP Intel app's, docs, etc.	$ 59.95*	Total $_____
____ x	**Aminet**	650 MB new files for the Amiga	$ 29.95*	Total $_____
____ x		Subscription: you get yours first	$ 19.95*/issue	Total $_____
____ x	**GEMini**	616 MB 3000 programs for Atari	$ 39.95*	Total $_____
____ x	**Info-Mac**	10,000 Mac files from Sumac archive	$ 49.95*	Total $_____
____ x	**X11R5 /GNU**	X Windows and GNU software for SPARC	$ 39.95	Total $_____
____ x	**Source**	600 MB Unix & MSDOS source code	$ 39.95*	Total $_____
____ x	**CUG**	C User Group C source code	$ 49.95*	Total $_____
____ x	**Ada**	Programming tools, source code and docs	$ 39.95*	Total $_____
____ x	**Sprite**	Berkeley distributed OS for SUN	$ 29.95	Total $_____
____ x	**Linux**	Yggdrasil Linux O/S. GNU & X11 src.	$ 49.95	Total $_____
____ x	**Toolkit**	For Linux - 600 MB util. + Slackware	$ 39.95*	Total $_____
____ x	**FreeBSD**	Berkeley BSD for PC, w/GNU & X11 src.	$ 39.95	Total $_____
____ x		Subscription: new about every 4 months	$ 24.95/issue	Total $_____
____ x	**FAQ**	alt.cd-rom Frequently Asked Questions	$ 1.00	Total $_____
____ x	**Jewelbox**	Clear plastic CD boxes (pack of 10)	$ 5.00	Total $_____
____ x	**Caddy**	Quality standard caddies — Best Price!	$ 4.95	Total $_____

Shareware requires payment to author if found useful.

Sub-Total $ _____
Tax 8.25%, (California residents only) $ _____
Shipping & Handling ($5 US/Canada, $10 Air Overseas per order) $ _____

Grand Total $ _____

Walnut Creek CDROM
4041 Pike Lane, Suite D-851   Phone: 510 674-0783
Concord CA 94520   Fax: 510 674-0821
USA   Email: orders@cdrom.com

Call 1 800 786-9907

ORDER BOOKS DIRECTLY FROM OSBORNE/McGRAW-HILL

For a complete catalog of Osborne's books, call 510-549-6600 or write to us at 2600 Tenth Street, Berkeley, CA 94710

☎ Call Toll-Free: 1-800-822-8158
24 hours a day, 7 days a week in U.S. and Canada

✉ Mail this order form to:
McGraw-Hill, Inc.
Customer Service Dept.
P.O. Box 547
Blacklick, OH 43004

Fax this order form to:
1-614-759-3644

EMAIL
7007.1531@COMPUSERVE.COM
COMPUSERVE GO MH

Ship to:

Name _____

Company _____

Address _____

City / State / Zip _____

Daytime Telephone: _____
(We'll contact you if there's a question about your order.)

ISBN #	BOOK TITLE	Quantity	Price	Total
0-07-88				
0-07-88				
0-07-88				
0-07-88				
0-07-88				
0-07088				
0-07-88				
0-07-88				
0-07-88				
0-07-88				
0-07-88				
0-07-88				
0-07-88				
0-07-88				
	Shipping & Handling Charge from Chart Below			
	Subtotal			
	Please Add Applicable State & Local Sales Tax			
	TOTAL			

Shipping & Handling Charges

Order Amount	U.S.	Outside U.S.
Less than $15	$3.50	$5.50
$15.00 - $24.99	$4.00	$6.00
$25.00 - $49.99	$5.00	$7.00
$50.00 - $74.99	$6.00	$8.00
$75.00 - and up	$7.00	$9.00

Occasionally we allow other selected companies to use our mailing list. If you would prefer that we not include you in these extra mailings, please check here: ☐

METHOD OF PAYMENT

☐ Check or money order enclosed (payable to Osborne/McGraw-Hill)

☐ AMERICAN EXPRESS   ☐ DISCOVER   ☐ MasterCard   ☐ VISA

Account No. [ ][ ][ ][ ][ ][ ][ ][ ][ ][ ][ ][ ][ ][ ][ ][ ]

Expiration Date _____

Signature _____

In a hurry? Call 1-800-822-8158 anytime, day or night, or visit your local bookstore.

Thank you for your order   Code BC640SL

More Programming Tools on CDROM!

CICA Shareware for Windows™ CDROM

"This disc made buying a CDROM drive worth it."
-Steve Wright, Rockville, MD.

$29.95

The CICA CDROM disc contains a copy of the Center for Innovative Computer Applications (i.e. CICA). CICA is the Internet's largest Microsoft Windows ftp site, with 600 MB of MS Windows programs. The CICA CDROM's friendly shell makes accessing all these files easy.

With the CICA disc you get hundreds of utilities, including shells, disk utilities, mouse and keyboard utilities, screen savers, backup/restore programs, performance monitors, diagnostics and data conversion programs. The CICA CDROM contains drivers for a large variety of printers and video monitors. You'll also get demos for many commercial Windows programs.

There's plenty of fun stuff on the CICA disc too. You'll find 200 games like asteroids, checkers, chess, word and card games. Liven up your writing with Postscript, ATM, and TrueType fonts. You'll get thousands of icons and dozens of bitmaps to personalize your desktop.

When programming, you'll find the programming tools on the CICA disc vital. There are programming tools for C, C++, Toolbook, Turbo Pascal, and Visual Basic. Many programs include their source code. The CICA CDROM is BBS-ready, with file indexes for opus, RBBS, PCBoard, Wildcat, Maximus, and Spitfire BBS's.

We last updated the CICA disc in December 1993. Shareware progress is rapid so we update this disc *quarterly*. You can be sure you continue to receive the freshest quality shareware with our subscription plan. Order yours today!

Other CDROMs produced by Walnut Creek CDROM include:

Cica MS Windows CDROM	Thousands of programs for MS Windows
Giga Games CDROM	Games for MSDOS and MS Windows
Space and Astronomy CDROM	Thousands of NASA images and data files
C Users Group Library CDROM	A collection of user supported C source code
Simtel MSDOS CDROM	Shareware/Freeware for MSDOS
Clipart Cornucopia CDROM	Clipart for Desktop Publishing
QRZ Ham Radio CDROM	FCC Callsign Database plus shareware
Gifs Galore CDROM	Over 6000 GIF Images
Project Gutenberg CDROM	Classic Literature and historical documents
Hobbes OS/2 CDROM	Shareware/Freeware for OS/2
Source Code CDROM	650 Megabytes of source code for programmers
Internet Info CDROM	Thousands of computer and network documents
X11/Gnu CDROM	X Windows, and Gnu software for Unix and SPARC
Aminet Amiga CDROM	Shareware/Freeware for Amiga
Ada Programming CDROM	Programming tools, Ada source code and docs
Nova for NeXT CDROM	Programs for black NeXT
Nebula for NeXTSTEP Intel CDROM	Programs for NeXTSTEP Intel
Garbo MSDOS/Mac CDROM	MSDOS and Macintosh Shareware/Freeware
Fractal Frenzy CDROM	High resolution images of fractals
FreeBSD CDROM	Complete FreeBSD Operating system, X11R5/GNU
Toolkit for Linux CDROM	Programs and Documentation for Linux OS
GEMini Atari CDROM	Programs for the Atari ST

SEE REVERSE PAGE FOR ORDER INFORMATION
OR CALL TOLL-FREE

Walnut Creek CDROM

4041 Pike Lane, Suite D-851
Concord CA 94520
Phone   510 674-0783
Fax   510 674-0821
Email   orders@cdrom.com

1 800 786-9907

Installation for Windows Programs

1. Open Windows.
2. Insert CD-ROM into drive.
3. From the File menu choose **Run.**
4. Type **E:\ibm\desktop** (If your CD-ROM drive is not labeled "E," substitute the appropriate drive letter.)
5. Hit the **Enter** key.

This will open the installation screen where you can select which programs to install. Then, simply follow the on-screen instructions.

When the installation is complete, you will see a program group icon for each installed program (some programs offer an option to not have an icon).

Additional Instructions

After installation some programs require you to restart Windows before they'll work properly.

Big Noise MaxPak: If you run the Add MIDI Ports applet type **E:\ibm\maxpak** when prompted for the last Install disk. (If your CD-ROM drive is not labeled "E," substitute the appropriate drive letter.) It might take more than one try.

Musicator Win must be installed on the default drive. Clicking the Change Drive button may cause a crash.

For **Master Tracks Pro:** you may have to press a key to exit from the final screen.

The **Mr. Drumstix** demo is a colorful slide show. To view it, open the File Manager and locate the **drumstix** folder on the CD-ROM. Double click the **cplshow.exe** file. Then select the **drumstix.cpl** file when prompted. Click **OK** to start the demo. Click each screen to proceed. Hit the **Esc** key to exit.

Installation for Macintosh Programs

To use Audioshop, Cubase, Master Tracks Pro, and Dr. T's MIDI Files, simply drag the folders from the CD-ROM window onto your hard disk to copy the folders and their contents. Then, to start a program, just open a folder and double-click its program icon.

All the other programs must be *installed* onto your hard drive. For these, click the "install" icon to start the installation process. Once installed, open a program's folder and double-click the program icon to start the program.

Be sure to check out the ReadMe files that come with each program. They include important information about setting up and running the software.

CD-ROM Contents

The CD-ROM that accompanies *The Desktop Musician* will work with Macintosh computers and IBM-compatible PCs running Microsoft Windows. The CD includes an array of music software demos so you can have some hands-on experience with a variety of well-known programs.

Following is an alphabetical list with brief descriptions of what you'll find on the disc. Have fun!

Windows Programs

Band-in-a-box (PG Music)
The popular auto-accompaniment program that creates musical arrangements from your chord progressions.

Cakewalk Pro for Windows (Twelve Tone Systems)
A full-featured sequencer that has long been a favorite of PC-based musicians. Do not install on a network.

Cubase for Windows (Steinberg)
One of the most versatile and powerful sequencers currently available for the PC.

Encore for Windows (Passport Designs)
A well-designed, intuitive notation program for creating music manuscripts.

The Jammer for Windows (Soundtrek)
This unique program combines artificial intelligence and randomness to create original compositions.

Master Tracks Pro for Windows (Passport Designs)
The powerful yet intuitive full-featured sequencer used by many professionals.

MaxPak (Big Noise)
An easy-to-use mid-level sequencer with lots of tools.

MiBAC Music Lessons (MiBAC Music)
An interactive music education program for studying music theory.

Mr. Drumstix' Music Studio (Howling Dog)
This self-running demo introduces an entertaining and educational program for young musicians.

Musicator Win (Musicator A/S)
A good-quality mid-level sequencer based on standard music notation.

Power Chords Pro (Howling Dog Systems)
A unique sequencer with some interesting features including an on-screen guitar that you can play.

Quickscore Deluxe (Dr. T's Music Software)
This is not a demo! It's a fully functional, easy-to-use, notation-based sequencer generously provided by Dr. T's. Be sure to check out the readme file that comes with the program.

SeqMax Presto! (Big Noise)
An inexpensive entry-level sequencer for musicians on a tight budget.

In addition to the programs listed above, **PG Music** and **Dr. T's Music Software** have graciously provided a number of excellent MIDI pieces in **Standard MIDI File** format. (Open the File Manager and look for the **pgmusic** and **drt_bach** folders.) You can copy these files onto your hard disk and import them into your favorite sequencer program for playback and editing.

Macintosh Programs

Audioshop (Opcode Systems)
This program lets you record, edit, and play digital audio files with its unique "CD-player" interface.

Clair (Opcode Systems)
A music education program that develops ear-training and sight-reading skills by interacting with the user.

Cubase (Steinberg)
One of the most versatile and powerful sequencers currently available for the Mac.

Encore (Passport Designs)
A well-designed, intuitive notation program for creating music manuscripts.

Master Tracks Pro 5 (Passport Designs)
The powerful yet intuitive full-featured sequencer used by many professionals.

Metro (OSC)
A well-designed, pro-level sequencer with several unique features.

MiBAC Jazz Improvisation (MiBAC Music)
This program generates excellent background accompaniments from your chord progressions.

MiBAC Music Lessons (MiBAC Music)
An interactive music education program for studying music theory.

Musicshop (Opcode Systems)
A high-quality, entry-level sequencer with basic notation capabilities.

MusicTime (Passport Designs)
An easy-to-use entry-level notation program for creating music manuscripts.

Time Bandit (Steinberg)
A powerful application for time compressing and pitch shifting of digital audio recordings.

Vision (Opcode Systems)
One of the most versatile, powerful, and popular pro-level sequencers currently available for the Mac.

In addition to the programs listed above, Dr. T's Music Software has graciously provided a number of wonderful Bach compositions in Standard MIDI File format. (Look for the **Dr.T's MIDI Files** folder.) You can copy these files onto your hard drive and import them into your favorite sequencer program for playback and editing.